THE KIDS'
ENCYCLOPEDIA OF
THINGS TO MAKE
AND DO

Annapolis and Anne Arundel
County Public Library
Annapolis, Maryland

WITHDRAWN
ANNE ARUNDEL COUN
PUBLIC LIBRAF

THE KIDS' ENCYCLOPEDIA OF THINGS TO MAKE AND DO

Compiled and Written by

Richard Michael Rasmussen and Ronda Lea Rasmussen

Illustrated by Pamela Morehouse

Toys 'n Things Press
a division of Resources for Child Caring, Inc.
St. Paul, Minnesota

To
Our Daughter
Renée Lea Rasmussen
and All the Children of the World

The Kids' Encyclopedia of Things to Make and Do copyright © 1981 by Richard Michael Rasmussen and Ronda Lea Rasmussen.

All rights reserved under International and Pan American Copyright Conventions. No part of this book may be reproduced in any manner whatsoever without written permission from the publisher, except in the case of brief quotations embodied in reviews and articles.

Second Edition
Manfactured in the United States of America

ISBN 0-934140-51-0
88-39449

Published by: Toys 'n Things Press
                   a division of Resources for Child Caring, Inc.
                   450 North Syndicate, Suite 5
                   St. Paul, Minnesota 55104

Distributed by: Gryphon House
                   P.O. Box 275
                   Mount Rainer, Maryland 20712

                   Acropolis Books Ltd.
                   2400 17th Street N.W.
                   Washington, D.C. 20009

Library of Congress Cataloging in Publication Data

Rasmussen, Richard Michael.
    The kids' encyclopedia of things to make and do / compiled and written by Richard Michael Rasmussen and Ronda Lea Rasmussen ; illustrated by Pamela Morehouse.
        p. cm.
    Includes index.
    Summary: Instructions for over 1800 art and craft projects which are listed in alphabetical order by subject.
    ISBN 0-934140-51-0
    1. Creative activities and seat work—Juvenile literature. 2. Handicraft—Juvenile literature. [1. Handicraft.]   I. Rasmussen, Ronda Lea II. Morehouse, Pam, ill.   III. Title.
GV1203.R34 1988
372.13'078—dc19
                                        88-39449
                                            CIP
                                            AC

Contents

Introduction

When a child asks, "What can I do now?", simply open your copy of *The Kids' Encyclopedia of Things to Make and Do*. In it you will find more than 1,866 fun-filled activities for one child alone, a small group, or even a classroom!

This book is for anyone who is close to children—parents, grandparents, babysitters, and teachers. You do not have to be an experienced arts and crafts expert. Most of the supplies you will need can be found around the home or classroom. By doing the activities in this book together, you and your children will discover new ideas for family fun.

For the first time, enough material to keep your children busy for years to come has been brought together in one volume. Most of the activities are for children aged four to ten. Obviously, there is quite a range of capabilities within this age group! But the large selection of material allows you to help your children choose activities suitable to their interests and abilities. Ideas can be simplified or expanded upon and adapted to various age levels. The younger children will need your help and guidance. The older children will be able to read and follow the instructions on their own.

The *Encyclopedia* is easy to use. Subjects are listed alphabetically, much like a regular encyclopedia. The Table of Contents outlines the material and topics available in the book. The Index is an added help for teachers and parents.

Following are a few tips for using the book and working with your children:

- Read instructions all the way through before starting a project.
- Gather needed supplies ahead of time so the children do not become impatient waiting to get started.
- Set newspapers over your working surface to collect splatters and spills and to make cleanup easier. Make cleanup a part of the activity.
- Encourage your children to take things a step further than the instructions, if they feel the desire to do so. These instructions are loose guidelines, intended to be starting points in the expansion of creative activity.
- Appreciate the work of your children for what it is—a step forward in their development. Do not worry if it does not look "right" to you! Be generous with your compliments.
- Set aside a special place where your children can always display their work.
- Even though this is not an "educational" book, all the activities will help your children learn more about themselves and the world around them.
- There is enough material in this book so that you need not repeat activities from year to year, unless you desire. This is particularly true in the holiday sections!
- Remember, you do not have to expose your children to every single activity in the book. Too much in too short a time may overwhelm them! Allow them to follow their interests, using the activities as "avenues of exploration."
- Keep in mind that play is a natural means of learning, of trying out new ideas, and of exercising the imagination.
- Most of all, remember to *have fun!*

Materials

Things to Save

bottle caps
bottles (bleach, plastic, etc.)
buttons
cardboard boxes
cardboard pieces
cardboard tubes
cloth and fabric scraps
coat hangers
cotton, cotton balls, and cotton swabs
egg cartons
envelopes, all kinds
jars and lids
juice cans
margarine tubs
matchboxes
milk cartons
old magazines
old socks
paper bags, all sizes
paper plates
plastic foam pieces and containers
Popsicle sticks
ribbon
spools
straws
string
tin cans
tin foil
waxed paper
yarn

Things to Buy and Have on Hand

brushes, large, medium, and small
clear tape
construction paper
crayons
felt-tip markers
food coloring
glitter
manila or newsprint paper
masking tape
paste or glue
pencils
pipe cleaners
poster board
scissors
tempera paint
water colors

Acknowledgments

Many thanks to all the parents and teachers who have supplied us with ideas. In particular we should like to thank the following: Joan Ashman, Maren Heubach, Jenny Ritchie, Marian Weir, and all the teachers and children of Learning Ladder Preschool and Day Care Center in La Mesa, California.

THE KIDS' ENCYCLOPEDIA OF
THINGS TO MAKE
AND DO

Air (Science)

Air Can Lift Things

Balloon Experiment. Place a deflated balloon on a table. Put a book on top of the flat balloon. Make sure the lips of the balloon stick over the edge of the table. Now blow into the balloon. As the balloon inflates, it will lift the book!

Paper Experiment. Fold a sheet of notebook paper in half the long way. Cut the paper in two along the crease. Match the strips together one on top of the other. Hold the matched sheets at the corners of one end. Bring this end close to your mouth and blow straight ahead across the strips. What happens to the loose end?

Tire Demonstration. Pump up a flat bike tire, using an air pump. Notice how the bike rises from the ground as air takes up the space inside the tire. Sit on the bike to see just how strong the air inside the tire is.

Air Contains Water

Jar Experiment. Did you know there is water in the air around you? Here is proof! Find a completely dry, empty jar. Fill it with ice cubes. See the water drops forming on the outer side of the jar? The cold from the ice cubes causes the surrounding air to cool. The chill makes water in the air condense and form drops along the outside of the jar!

See Your Own Breath. While indoors, blow on your hand. You can feel your breath, but you cannot see it. On a cold day, go outside and blow on your hand again. This time you can see your breath. Actually, what you see is the water vapor in your warm breath as it cools on contact with the cold air.

Air Has Weight

Weighing Air. Inflate two balloons of the same size. Tape a balloon to each end of a yardstick. Then tie a string to the exact middle of the yardstick. Hold the yardstick by the string. Notice how the yardstick is balanced evenly on both sides!

Using a pin, pop one of the balloons. Is the yardstick still balanced? The end of the yardstick with the full balloon will dip downwards. Why? Because the air inside the balloon has weight and makes that end of the yardstick heavier!

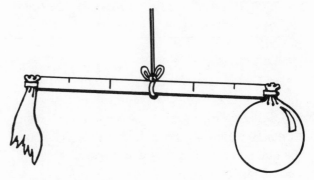

Air Movement

Book Experiment. Here is an easy experiment to prove that air moves, even though you do not actually see the air in motion. Lay a book on a table. Open the book at the middle. With one hand, hold a piece of paper close to one side of the opened book. With the other hand, slam the book closed toward the paper you are holding. What do you think made the paper move?

Box Experiment. Make a hole the size of a bottlecap in the short side of a shoe box. Glue on some crepe paper streamers so they hang over the hole. Place a lid on the box and squeeze the box with your hands. What caused the streamers to move?

Air Pressure

Jar Experiment.   Fill a glass jar with water. Poke two holes in the lid. Screw the lid on tight. Turn the jar upside down. Note how the water drips from one hole. Then place a finger over one of the holes. What happens to the water?

Pressure Change.   This is a project that needs the help of an adult. Find an old empty gallon-sized metal can with a screw cap on it. ***Do not use a gasoline can!*** Take the cap off the can. Place the can on a hot plate, and turn on the hot plate. Allow the can to get very hot.

While the can and the air inside are heating, some of the hot air is rising out of the can's pour hole. This means there is less air inside the can.

Next, using hot pads, screw the cap back onto the can very tightly. Turn off the hot plate. Watch! As the thin air inside the can cools and shrinks, the outside air pressure becomes stronger than the inner air and crushes the can inwards!

Straw Demonstration.   Put an empty glass on the table. Place a clear drinking straw upright in the glass. Add some food coloring to some water to make it colored. Pour the colored water into the glass. Notice how the water rises in the glass and also rises inside the straw.

Lift the straw from the water. See how the water falls out? Put the straw back in the water. Lift out the straw one more time, but this time keep one finger over the top of the straw while you lift. The water stays in the straw.

The first time, air pressure from the top of the straw made the water fall out. The second time, the air pressure was cut off at the top and instead pushed up from below to keep the water in the straw.

Suction Experiment.   Fill a glass almost full of water. Cover the glass with a piece of cardboard. Carefully hold the cardboard in place as you turn the glass upside down. Then remove your hand.

The water does not fall out because air pressure creates suction inside to hold the cardboard in place.

Over a dishpan, slowly remove the cardboard and watch the water fall out.

Syphon Demonstration.   Obtain a clean rubber or plastic tube that is about 18 inches long. Also get two glasses, one empty and the other filled with colored water. (Color the water with food coloring.)

Set the empty glass in a sink. Put the glass of colored water on the counter beside the sink. Dip one end of the tube in the glass of water. Place the open end of the tube in your mouth and suck the water into the tube so the water touches your tongue.

Quickly remove the tube from your mouth and place it in the empty glass in the sink. Watch as air pressure and gravity make the water flow uphill and then down.

Air Takes Up Space

Air Occupies Space.   Inflate a balloon. Notice how the balloon expands and becomes round as you blow air into it. The air has taken up the space inside the balloon.

There is another way to see how air takes up space. Wave a plastic bag through the air. Notice how full the bag becomes. Air is in the bag, taking up space, even though we cannot see it.

Air Pushing Water.   Pour some water into a wide-mouthed, gallon-sized glass jar until the jar is three quarters full. Next, stuff a wad of tissue paper into the very bottom of an ordinary drinking glass. Turn the glass upside down to make sure the tissue paper stays in place.

Push the upside-down glass all the way to the bottom of the water jar. Then, quickly remove the glass without tilting it. Take out the tissue paper. Is the paper dry?

The trapped air inside the glass took up the space inside and did not allow the water to touch the tissue paper!

Bottled Air. Place an empty bottle upside down in a pan of water. Notice that it takes a long time for the water to get inside the bottle. This is because air takes up the space inside and must escape from the bottle before any water can enter.

Warm Air Rises

Temperature Measurement. Place one thermometer on the floor. Tape another thermometer on the wall as high as you can reach. Leave both thermometers in place for awhile. Then compare the temperatures.

The upper thermometer shows a higher temperature because warm air weighs less than cold air. It rises above the cooler air. The cool air is heavier and falls toward the floor, forcing the warm air up toward the ceiling.

Airplanes

Clothespin Airplane. For this project you need three clothespins. Use one for the plane's body. Clip the other two clothespins to the body piece to make wings. *Another way to do it:* Cut a wing piece out of cardboard and glue it crossways over the clothespin body.

Paper Airplane. Fold a sheet of typing paper in half lengthwise. At one end, fold down the corners on both sides, as illustrated. Then fold each half two more times. Attach a paper clip under the wings, near the nose, for weight. Practice throwing your paper airplane outdoors.

Popsicle Stick Airplane. Glue Popsicle sticks together to form an airplane. Make many different kinds of airplanes, using photographs to guide you along. You might even try making an old-fashioned double-winged airplane!

Wooden Airplane. Use pieces of scrap lumber and nails to build a toy airplane. Make landing wheels from the lids of baby food jars, and jet engines from short cardboard tubes.

Airports

Cardboard Aircraft Hangar. Remove the lid from a deep rectangular cardboard box. Place the box upside down. On both ends cut out hangar bay entrances. Paint the box or cover it with pieces of colored construction paper cut to fit. Park toy airplanes inside the hangar.

Cardboard Control Tower. Use an empty oatmeal box or cardboard potato chip can for an aircraft control tower. Paint it or cover it with pieces of construction paper cut to fit. Draw on outside details, using a felt-tip marker.

Control Tower Play. Imagine yourself as an air traffic controller. Perhaps you can sit at a desk and use a cardboard tube for a microphone. Pretend to be a controller, giving takeoff and landing instructions to pilots.

Masking Tape Airport. On a smooth floor, use strips of masking tape to outline runways. Use

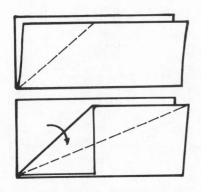

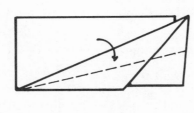

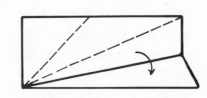

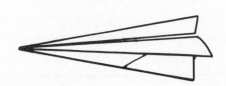

boxes and blocks for hangars and control towers. Have toy airplanes take off and land at your airport.

Animals

Alphabet Animals. Draw any letter of the alphabet on a piece of paper. Turn the letter into an animal by adding details (eyes, nose, mouth, ears, wings, tails, etc.). Try using other letters of the alphabet to make different animals.

Aluminum Foil Animals. Crumple, press, roll, and form pieces of aluminum foil into animal shapes.

For instance, you can roll a long strip of foil to form the body and head. Roll shorter strips to form legs and a tail. Fasten the legs and other parts to the body piece by making slits in the body and inserting the parts. Press the slits closed with your fingers, then stand the animal up.

Animal Charades. With your friends, act out the part of any animal. But do not make any sounds! Can your friends guess what kind of animal you are? Take turns acting and guessing.

Animal Family Cutouts. From magazines, cut out pictures of adult and baby animals. Put them together into a collage or scrapbook of animal families.

Animal Litter Bag. Open up a brown shopping bag and cut out a large mouth opening on one side. Fold down the top of the bag and staple it closed. Cut out funny eyes, ears, nose, and feet from construction paper. Glue these features to the bag. Take your animal litter bag along with you on car trips or walks. Remember, he likes to eat trash! ("Feed" him through his mouth.)

Animal Matchup. From magazines, cut out pictures of animals. Then clip off their heads, feet, and tails. Mix up all the parts. Try to match up the parts correctly.

For extra fun, create strange and funny animals by mixing and matching the wrong parts.

Box Animals. Here is how to make an animal that you can actually wear!

First, find a large box. Remove the lid flaps. Turn the box upside down. Cut a body hole in the bottom of the box large enough to fit your body.

Poke a pair of holes at each side of the body opening. To make shoulder straps tie through two lengths of cord, as illustrated. Now, when you wear the box, it will not fall down!

Decorate the outside of the box to look like an animal. Use paint, felt-tip markers, paper cutouts, pieces of cardboard, and other scrap materials to do this.

When finished, slip the box animal onto your body, around your waist. Pull the straps over your shoulders, and you are ready to play!

Cardboard Lamb. Cut out a lamb shape from a piece of cardboard. Spread glue over the surface of the lamb. Press on tufts of cotton to completely cover the lamb and give it a white coat.

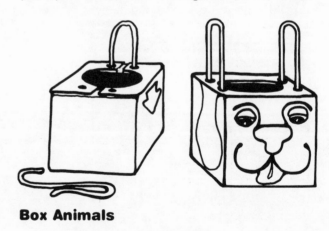

Box Animals

Cardboard Roll Sausage Dog. Glue a circle of paper, cut to fit, onto one end of a short cardboard tube. Draw a dog's face on the circle. Lay pieces of yellow yarn 3½ inches long crossways over the tube and glue them on for fur. Cut some smaller lengths of yarn to glue around the face, and some others for a tail.

Cardboard Tube Animals. Search through magazines for an animal picture. Clip out the head of the animal from the picture. Glue the head to one end of a cardboard tube. Add pipe cleaner legs and a tail. Paint the body to match.

Clay Hedgehog. Mold some modeling clay until it is roughly in the shape of a hedgehog. Form the head so the nose comes to a point. Make prickles for the hedgehog by cutting drinking straws into short pieces and sticking them all over the body.

Construction Paper Animals. Fold a sheet of construction paper in half the long way. From the open-edged side, cut away an arch. Now you have a body piece with four legs.

For a head, glue the cutout piece to one end of the body. Draw on facial features. Stand the

animal up on its four legs, or set it upright in a begging position.

Cork or Potato Animals. Use different-sized pieces of cork to form the bodies and heads of animals. Use toothpicks to join the parts together and to make legs.

Try making some animals you know. Then make some "pretend" creatures of your own.

If you cannot find any corks, use raw potatoes and potato pieces cut into different sizes and shapes to make your animals.

Crayon Rubbing Animals. Draw an outline of an animal on paper. Place a piece of sandpaper underneath the sheet with the outline. With a crayon, color within the outline, rubbing firmly against the sandpaper underneath. This will give your animal a textured look!

Drinking Straw Animals. Bend and twist paper drinking straws around each other to make flat animals. Glue them to background paper if you want to save them.

Egg Carton Camel. From a cardboard egg carton, cut away a two-cup section. This will be the camel's back. Paint this section with a brownish-yellow color. Allow to dry.

Place the section in front of you so the "humps" face up. Glue a cardboard leg to each corner of the section. To one end, glue a cardboard neck and head. Paint the leg and head pieces the same color as the body piece. For a tail, attach a piece of string with a knot tied at the end.

Eggcup Lion. Obtain a cardboard egg carton. Cut out a section two cups wide and three cups long. Then, cut away the middle two cups, making sure to leave the top rim connected. Now you have a lion body with four feet!

Make a lion face from a circle of thick cardboard. Glue the face to the front end of the lion. Glue short lengths of yellow yarn to the head to make a mane. Glue a single length of yarn to the other end for a tail.

Eggcup Pig. Cut out a two-cup section from a cardboard egg carton. Bend the cups toward each other, rim to rim. Staple them together to form a body.

Make legs from cardboard and glue them to the body. To make a tail, wrap a thick strip of paper around a pencil. Keep the paper wrapped around the pencil for awhile so the paper curls. Then remove the paper and tape it to the tail end of the pig. Glue on ears made from paper. Paint the pig pink and allow the paint to dry. Finish by painting on a face.

Envelope Animals. Cut off the flap from an envelope. Set the envelope in front of you and turn it upside down so the folded edge is on top. Draw a side view of an animal on the envelope. Make sure the animal's back touches or runs along the folded edge of the envelope.

Then cut along the animal outline. Cut through the double thickness of the envelope, but do not cut the areas where the head and back of the animal touch the folded edge of the envelope. This allows the double thickness of the animal shape to be joined at the top after it is cut out.

When finished, open the envelope partway at the bottom so the animal will stand up on four legs.

Fingertip-Printed Creatures. Press the tip of your forefinger onto an ink pad. Then make a fingerprint on a piece of paper. Make any number of fingerprints this way. Then, using a felt-tip marker or pen, turn the prints into tiny animals by drawing features (feet, beaks, wings, eyes, legs, tails, etc.). First make some real animals, then try to make some imaginary ones.

Fuzzy Animals. On a 9-by-12-inch sheet of paper, draw the outline of an animal, making it as large as you can. Next, collect some soft, fuzzy materials, such as yarn, felt, cotton, carpet pieces, and bits of fake fur.

Cut out the animal shape. With a brush, spread glue all over one side of the animal. Stick the fuzzy materials to the animal, covering it completely.

You can use yarn for the hair or tails, and cotton or fur for the body. Felt pieces make good eyes. Try different combinations of your own. You can make a silly creature by placing the pieces together in strange ways.

Hand Animals. Outline your hand on a piece of paper. Cut out the outline and paste it on another sheet of paper. Using a crayon or felt-tip marker, draw in features and details to make the handprint into an animal. See how many different kinds of animals you can make!

Hand Animals

Hinged Animals. From poster board, cut out the body, legs, tail, and other parts of an animal. Punch holes in the ends of these pieces where they will join together. With paper fasteners hook the parts together. Draw features on the animal with a felt-tip marker. See the different ways you can move the parts around!

Invented Animals. Combine the names of two different animals to form one new word to describe an imaginary animal. For example, combine *kangeroo* and *rooster* to make *kangerooster,* or *elephant* and *alligator* to make *elegator.*

Draw pictures of how you think the new animals should look, and make up stories about them.

Matchbox Sheep. For the sheep's body use an empty matchbox. Glue or tape a toothpick to each corner of the box to make legs. Cut a neck-and-head piece from cardboard. Tape this to the front end of the box. Glue cotton all over the matchbox and neck to create a woolly body.

Paper Plate Animals. Make turtles, ladybugs, and other kinds of animals from paper plates. Use the paper plate for the body of the animal.

From construction paper, cut out the head, tail, feet, and other features. Glue the pieces to the edges of the paper plate body. Add other details with a felt-tip marker; color the animal with crayons.

Paper Plate Lion Face. Turn a paper plate upside down. From paper scraps, cut out the eyes, a nose, and a mouth for the lion. Glue the parts in place on the paper plate.

Make a mane by cutting fringes in a 2-by-18-inch strip of construction or crepe paper. Glue the mane around the rim of the plate and add pipe cleaners for whiskers.

Pussy Willow Critters. Paste some real pussy willows to a sheet of paper. Using a felt-tip marker, draw features around the pussy willows to turn them into tiny animals.

Sawdust Squirrel. Outline a squirrel on a heavy piece of paper. Spread glue all over the inside of the outline. Sprinkle bits of sawdust over the picture and shake off the excess. Cut out the squirrel.

Scissor Animals. Outline an open pair of school scissors on a piece of paper. What kind of an animal does the outline suggest? Draw in features and details to turn the outline into an animal. Try again, making a different animal.

Seashell Animals. Look for some shells at the beach or buy some at a hobby store. With white glue, fasten the shells together. Form ducks, dogs, cats, birds, fish, or any other animals.

Snow Rabbit. Draw the outline of a rabbit on white construction paper. Cut it out. Glue on tufts of cotton to represent white fur.

Sponge Animals. Cut some sponges into animal shapes. Perhaps you can make your own farm or zoo animals. Cut some of them into fish and use them later when you play in the water or bathtub. Some of the animals can be used for sponging off your art table, too.

Sponge-Painted Animals. Draw animal outlines on paper. Dip small sponge pieces into paint and use them as brushes to paint the animal outlines. Use a regular paintbrush to paint in details.

Spool Animals. Use empty thread spools and index cards to make many kinds of animals. Use the spools for the bodies. From the index cards, cut out legs, wings, and heads. Join the parts together with glue. Use string or yarn to make tails.

Stocking Animals. Find an old stocking or knee-length hosiery. Stuff it full of crumpled newspaper. Close the end with a piece of string or a rubber band. Tie on another piece of string to use as a pull handle. Now pretend your animal is a snake, a worm, a caterpillar, or an alligator.

You can make him look a little different by tying other pieces of string at several points around his midsection.

Straw and Pipe Cleaner Animals. Use a drinking straw cut down to a four-inch length or smaller. Insert three pipe cleaners through the remaining length of straw. Make sure all three pipe cleaners stick out at each end of the straw.

Bend two of the pipe cleaners downward at both ends. This forms the front and back legs of the animal. Bend the tips of the legs outward to form feet.

The third pipe cleaner should be bent at one end to form a tail and at the other end to form a neck. Cut out an animal head from construction paper, draw a face on it, and glue it to the neck. Stand the animal on its feet.

Stuffed Paper Animals. Fold a very large sheet of butcher paper or brown wrapping paper in half. On one side, draw an animal outline, making it as large as you can. Now cut out the outline through the double thickness of the paper. Notice that you have two animal outlines exactly alike!

Match the outlines and staple them together along the edges of both ends and one side. Leave one side open so you can stuff the animal with crumpled newspaper. Then staple it shut. Draw features on the animal with a felt-tip marker. Paint the animal to finish it.

Wiggle-Eyed Animal. Outline an animal head on a piece of construction paper. Then cut it out. Next, cut out two holes for eyes, each a little smaller than the size of a bottle cap. Paint or color the rest of the features on the head.

Turn the head upside down. Glue two squares of clear cellophane over the eye holes. Place a small bead in the middle of each piece of cellophane. Place a bottle cap over each eye hole, rim edges down, and seal it in place with tape.

Turn the head right side up and shake it. Watch the eyes move!

Wooden Spoon Duck. Obtain two wooden ice cream spoons. The first spoon will be the head, with the handle end representing the duck's bill. The second spoon will be the body, with the handle end representing the tail. Glue the spoons together at the bowl ends, almost at right angles to each other.

Let the spoon body dry. Glue on some wings cut from colored paper. Glue on feet made from pipe cleaners. Use a felt-tip marker to draw the duck's eyes and beak.

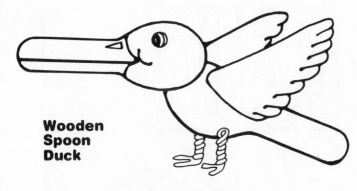

**Wooden
Spoon
Duck**

Animals (Science)

Classifying Animals

Classifying Animals Your Own Way. Scientists have developed complicated ways of classifying animals. You can make up your own, easier ways to classify animals.

Clip out as many pictures as you can of animals, birds, insects, and marine life. Then group the animals in several ways: number of legs they have; kind of body coverings (fur, feathers, skin, shells, etc.); color; size; how they move about; and so on. Paste your pictures onto a chart showing how you have classified the animals.

Observations

Amphibians. Amphibians live both in the water and on land. Frogs, toads, or salamanders are amphibians. See if you can find one to put in a terrarium. Make sure there is water in the terrarium. Observe the general features of amphibians: they have lungs and breathe air, but they also breathe through their skins, which must remain moist; they must have live food, such as flies and meal worms.

After you have observed the animal for a day or two, release it where you found it.

Animal Tracks. Go outside after it snows and look for animal tracks. Can you tell what animals made the tracks in the snow?

Caterpillars. Catch a caterpillar and keep it in an insect cage. Feed it fresh leaves every day. Since a caterpillar will eat only certain kinds of leaves, feed it the type of leaf on which you found it. If you found the caterpillar on a wall or the sidewalk, try feeding it different kinds of leaves until you find the one it likes.

Spray the caterpillar with water from time to time. Place a dry twig near it so the caterpillar can spin a cocoon.

Chicks. If you can keep a chick at home, place it in a large enough cage so it can move around. When handling the chick, remember it is a very fragile animal, and is *not* a toy. Handle the chick gently. Keep the cage bottom off the floor or ground and provide the chick with a nighttime shelter.

Feed the chick mash, which can be purchased at animal supply and feed stores, and give it plenty of water. Shine an electric light on the chick to keep it warm. Put newspapers on the bottom of the cage and change them often to keep the cage clean. Place the cage outside for a while every day, but be sure not to leave the chick in the direct hot sun.

Earthworms and Soil. Place several inches of dark soil into a large glass jar. Then add another half inch of sand, clay, or red soil. Put five or six earthworms into the jar.

Look closely at the worms. How are they shaped? What color are they? Watch a worm burrow into the soil. When it crawls through the soil, the worm mixes the dirt by passing it through his body. This helps keep the soil around plant roots loose and allows fresh air to enter the soil. All these things help plants to grow better. Pick up an earthworm and see if you can see the color of the soil in its body. Notice that the mouth is on the fat end.

Feed the worms small amounts of cornmeal. When you are not observing the worms keep a piece of black paper wrapped around the jar. The black paper keeps light from entering the soil at the sides of the jar, and encourages the worms to dig their tunnels to the edges of the jar.

Fish. Place some goldfish, guppies, or minnows in a fishbowl or an aquarium. Watch how the fish breathe by swallowing water through their mouths and passing it out their gills. The gills obtain oxygen from the water.

Observe how fish use their fins to help in swimming. But look—fish do not have ears! How do they hear? Fish feel sounds in the water through their bodies! And you might notice something else. Fish do not have eyelids! They have to sleep with their eyes open!

Frog Egg Growth. At a pond, find some frog eggs in their jelly-like mass. Scoop them into a container along with some pond water. Place some water plants from the pond in the container with the eggs. Make sure to change the water often. Eventually tadpoles will hatch from the eggs!

When the tadpoles have hatched, place some mud and algae-covered rocks from the original pond in the bottom of a large container. Add some fresh pond water. After the muddy water has settled, put the tadpoles in their new home.

Notice the tadpoles have gills for breathing. While they are young, tadpoles like to eat algae and other small plants that cling to the rocks. When the tadpoles are older, you can feed them bits of beef, liver, chopped worms, oatmeal, lettuce, or hard-boiled eggs.

As the tadpoles grow into frogs, they will need rocks to sit upon. Transfer the frogs to an aquarium with rocks and a smaller amount of water. Begin feeding them live flies and other insects.

See how the frogs have lost their tadpole tails and gills? How do the frogs breathe? Read some books about frogs and learn more about how they change from tadpoles to frogs.

Do not keep the frogs forever; return your frogs to the pond where you found them as tadpoles and let them go.

Hibernation. Some animals have found a strange way to cope with cold weather and other changes around them—they go to sleep for long periods of time! This process is called *hibernation.*

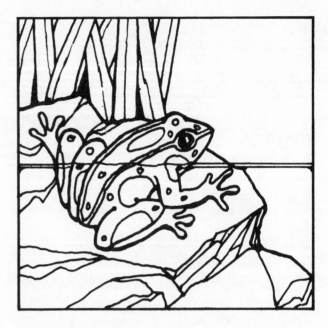

Homes for Animals. Look at some pictures to see the many different kinds of homes animals make for themselves. Some live in trees, in burrows, under eaves, in caves, on webs, under water, and so on.

Take a walk outside to see how many animal homes you can find. Look for nests, hives, burrows, webs, and anthills. Look under rocks and pieces of wood. Be sure to replace the wood and rocks after you look under them.

Likenesses and Differences. Take a walk to discover and observe living things such as ants, spiders, butterflies, birds, and squirrels. Look for any ways the animals are alike or different.

Watch for some of these things: *Likenesses*—all animals must have food and water; they are able to move about; they breathe air; they protect themselves; and they grow and produce young. *Differences*—they move in different ways; they have different numbers of legs; they have different kinds of body coverings; they grow to different sizes; and they bear their young in different ways.

What other likenesses and differences can you see?

Lizards and Horned Toads. Place lizards or horned toads into a sand terrarium with plants.

They must have sunlight part of the time, but they also need a shady spot in the terrarium. The temperature must be above 70 degrees, but you will find these creatures are much more active if the temperature is near 90 degrees. Spray them with water because they will probably not drink from a dish. They like to eat flies.

Mammals. See if you can obtain a small mammal to watch and take care of, such as a mouse, white rat, rabbit, guinea pig, or hamster. Keep it in a wire cage. Notice that, like most other mammals, it has two pairs of limbs, has a body covered with fur or hair, has teeth and a tail. Most mammals are born, not hatched from eggs, and depend upon their mothers for milk and protection. Look for a mammal care book at the pet store or library.

Snails. Find a garden snail and look at it closely. See how the snail can withdraw into its shell? It does that for protection. Also notice how the snail can withdraw its feelers when you touch them. Look at the slippery path it leaves behind. Snails like to eat plant leaves. Where do you find most snails?

Turtles. Keep a turtle in a glass bowl with a moderate amount of water and rocks. Feed it turtle food. Watch how the turtle swallows the food when it is under the water. Be sure to re-move the turtle from the water at least once a day to allow its shell to dry out a bit. Turtles like sunshine.

Ways Animals Protect Themselves

Animals protect themselves in many ways. Some hide, while others are protected by shells. Some build homes for protection, and others fly or run away from danger. Many animals have claws, horns, and sharp teeth to defend them-selves. When in danger, some even play dead!

Burrowing for Protection. Some animals burrow into the ground to protect themselves from other animals that want to catch them. Look

at pictures of gophers, groundhogs, moles, and termites. All these animals burrow into the ground. Place some earthworms in a jar of damp soil and watch them burrow into the dirt.

Escaping from Danger. Many animals can move very quickly. They use their quickness to escape danger. Wave at a fly. Leap towards a cat. Reach for a grasshopper. Jump at a pigeon. How did these animals get away from you?

Protective Coloration. Their body coloring helps some animals to hide from other animals. These animals are hard to see when their body colors blend with the colors around them.

Here are some art activities you can do to help you better understand how animals use color to protect themselves:

1. On a piece of paper, outline a number of tree branches. Color them brown. Color in clumps of green leaves. Draw a green bird with brown spots hiding in the branches.
2. Draw a desert scene, using a tan color. Draw tan-colored lizards or snakes sun-ning themselves on the sand.
3. On a sheet of paper, draw some green grass. Color in some green bugs and grasshoppers hiding in the grass.

4. Draw a snow scene, and include a polar bear or white rabbit on the snow.

Look outside for some bugs, reptiles, birds, and animals that use color for protection.

Shells for Protection. Some animals use hard shells to protect themselves. Look at a turtle. See how it draws in its head and feet when disturbed? Look at a garden snail and notice how it withdraws into the shell when touched. Examine a sow bug and watch it roll into a ball. Study some real seashells or look at pictures of them. These were used for protection, too.

Appliqué

In appliqué, figures are cut from one piece of material and used to decorate other pieces of material. Appliqués may be glued or sewn onto skirts, shirts, aprons, curtains, and bedspreads. Appliqué decorations include holiday symbols, colored alphabet letters, animals, flowers, nursery rhyme characters, or anything you want!

Leather, Felt, and Fur Appliqués. Cut appliqué shapes from pieces of leather, fur, or felt. Using fabric cement, fasten them to other materials. Be sure to work over a clean, flat surface such as a table. After the cement has dried, ask an adult to help you fasten down the appliqué better by sewing through both materials along the edges of the appliqué.

Backyard Olympics

You can have olympic games right in your own backyard! With the help of friends, plan what events you want ahead of time. If you have enough people involved, you can have three or four events going on at the same time. If you want, give prizes to first, second, and third place finishers.

Field Events

Balloon Toss. Inflate some large balloons. Each contestant must stand behind a line and balance a balloon in the palm of his hand. He then throws the balloon as far as he can.

Broad Jump. Ahead of time, dump five or six buckets of sand into an area three feet wide by six feet long. This will make a soft landing place for the jumpers. At one end, wedge a board firmly into the ground so it cannot move.

Each jumper must stand with his toes at the edge of the board. Then he must jump as far as he can from a standing position. The best jump of three tries is counted. Use a measuring tape to determine how far each contestant jumped. Measure from the starting board to the spot where the jumper's heel landed. (The jumper must land with his feet together.)

Drinking Straw Javelin Throw. Each contestant should stand behind a line for the throw. Aiming a drinking straw like a javelin, he then throws it to see how far it will go.

Frisbee Discus Throw. Pretend a Frisbee is a discus. Draw a circle on the ground about four feet in diameter. You must stay within this circle while you throw. Throw the Frisbee as far as you can. Mark the spot where it lands and measure the distance.

High Leap. Hang a small bell from a tree with some heavy twine. Make sure the bell is hanging high enough so the contestants must leap to ring it. This would be a good event to put at the end of your obstacle course. This way, contestants can ''signal'' that they have completed the course!

Jump the Puddle. With a long piece of yarn or string, outline a ''puddle'' on the ground. Take a running leap to see if you can jump over the puddle without falling into it.

Obstacle Course. For this event, you need a vacant lot, field, or other large, open area. Lay out a winding obstacle course so that it ends with the finish line close to the starting point. This way, one person will be able to time all of the contestants. Have the contestants run the course one at a time. The person with the fastest time is the winner. Here are some suggested obstacles for your course:

Barrel Crawl. Lay a barrel on its side. Contestants must crawl through the barrel and out the other end.

Blanket Bundle. Bundle several large blankets together to form a long, soft pad over which the contestants must run.

Box Tunnel. Cut the top and bottom off of a large refrigerator box and lay the box on its side to make a tunnel.

Couch Crawl. Set up an old couch along the course. Contestants must climb up one end of the couch, crawl as fast as possible to the other end, and climb off over the edge.

Course Curves. Using shoe boxes or other lightweight objects for markers, outline special curved paths, with sharp twists and turns, along the course. You can also use garden hoses or pieces of rope to outline the curves. Contestants may run or skip through the course as desired.

High-Step Boxes. Link two or three large open-top boxes. Contestants must jump or high step through the box compartments from one end to the other.

Inner Tube Walk. Line up some inflated inner tubes or bike tires. Contestants must walk on top of the inner tubes from one end of the row to the other.

Ladder Walk. Place a ladder flat on the ground. Contestants must walk along the ladder rungs from one end to the other.

Log Walk. Place a log along the course. Have contestants walk along the log from one end to the other. Or, you could require them to jump over the log.

Low Jump. Place small boxes upside down along the course at various points. Contestants must jump over the boxes.

Rope Swing. Ask an adult to help you tie a sturdy rope to a tree limb. Contestants must swing on the rope over a rug placed underneath.

Stepping Cans. Turn empty coffee cans upside down and sink them halfway into the ground. Lay them out like stepping stones so contestants can step quickly along the path of cans.

Paper Bag Hammer Throw. Blow some air into a paper bag, then twist the end closed. Tie a three-foot length of string to the bag. Stand in a circle and take hold of the end of the string. Whirl the bag in a circle above your head. Let go of the bag and see how far it goes. The longest throw wins.

Paper Plate Discus Throw. Have each contestant stand behind a line. Toss a heavy-duty paper plate like a discus. The longest throw wins.

Shoe Kick. Each contestant will need an old tennis shoe that is too big for his foot. Mark a line on the ground. A contestant must stand behind the line when kicking. Wearing the loose shoe, the contestant kicks his foot upward so the shoe flies off into the air. Measure how far it goes. Count the best of three tries for each contestant.

Slalom Course. This race requires some advance preparation. Collect 12 shoe boxes. Remove the lids and paint six of the boxes red. Paint the other six blue.

When setting up the slalom course, make sure to always have a red box paired with a blue box. Set out the pairs of boxes in a staggered pattern, outlining a course that will make the racers run

**Slalom
Course**

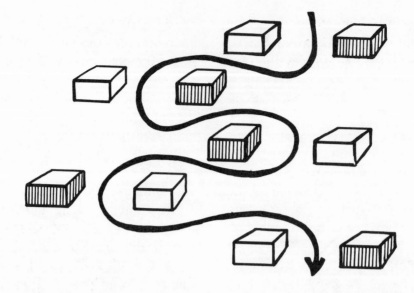

between the pairs of boxes, making sharp turns. Make the turns go first to the left, then to the right, and back the other way again. Contestants run through the course one at a time. Clock each runner, using a stopwatch. The fastest time wins.

Sock Shotput.   Ahead of time, find an old pair of socks with no holes in them. Push one sock inside the other so you have a "double sock." Fill the double sock with sand, leaving enough space at the top to tie a knot. Tuck the loose end into the knot to form the sock shotput. Draw a three-foot-wide circle in the dirt.

Stand inside the circle and shove the shotput straight out from your chest. The shot must start from your chest, not from the air. Do not step out of the circle. Count the best of three tries. The longest distance wins.

Tunnel Crawl.   Cut off the tops and bottoms of several large furniture or appliance boxes. Lay them in a row on their sides, forming a straight line of tunnels. Leave about five feet between each tunnel. Contestants must crawl as fast as they can through all the tunnels, one contestant at a time. In the spaces between the tunnels, they can get up and run. The fastest time wins.

Twenty-Foot Hop.   Mark a starting point on the ground. Then mark a finish line 20 feet away. Each contestant must stand behind the starting

line holding a paper cup full of water. On "go," the players must hop on one leg to the finish line. It does not matter how long it takes. The winner is the player who crosses the finish line with the most water left inside his cup.

Races

Ankle Race.   Everyone lines up behind a starting line. On "go," each person must bend down and grasp one of his ankles. Everyone must race in this position toward the finish line.

Backward Dash.   All the runners must line up backward at the starting line. At the signal, the runners must run backward toward the finish line.

Blindfold Foot Race.   Ahead of time, obtain two pieces of rope; each should be 12 feet long. Lay them down with about six feet between them. Two contestants may race at a time, one to a rope. Each must remove his shoes and wear a blindfold. Position each player at the beginning of a rope. At the signal, each must feel his way with his feet along the rope. Anyone who loses his way and goes off the rope is out. The first player to reach the end of his rope wins.

Box Hurdles.   Cut off the tops of seven boxes so they are the same height. Line up the boxes in a straight row, with some of the boxes linked together, and spaces between others. To set up the boxes, start with two linked boxes, followed by a space and three linked boxes. Leave another space and finish with two more linked boxes. Allow about three feet between each set of linked boxes.

To link the boxes, punch matching holes through the ends of the boxes and tie them tightly together with twine or heavy string.

Contestants must jump through each of the boxes, starting at one end, and dash across the spaces between the boxes. Make sure only one contestant runs the hurdles at a time. The fastest time wins.

Circular Track Race. Mark a large circular track around the outer edges of your yard or field. On "go," all the contestants must start the race at the same time from the starting line. The first person to run three times around the track is the winner.

Crab Race. Divide the players into two teams of equal size. Have each team line up single file behind a starting line. Leave about three feet between each line of players. This is a relay race.

To walk like a crab, each player must lean backward onto his hands and feet. Make sure no bottoms touch the ground!

On "go," the first two players race crab-style towards a goal, turn around, and race back crab-style to touch the next person in line. The next person then goes into the crab position and continues the race. The first team to finish wins.

Feather Race. Give each contestant a feather and a paper plate. Each player stands behind the starting line with the feather on his plate. At the signal, players must race toward the goal, trying to cross the finish line without losing the feather off his plate. If the feather falls off, that player must stop and pick it up before continuing. Hands cannot be used to keep the feathers on the plates. The first person to cross the finish line with the feather on his plate is the winner.

Heel-to-Toe Race In this race, everyone must walk as fast as possible toward the finish line by placing one foot forward, then putting the heel of the other foot in front of the toe of the first foot. Each time, the heel must touch the toe of the foot behind it. The first person to cross the finish line in this way wins.

Human Wheelbarrow Race. Team everyone up in pairs behind the starting line. One player in each pair must go down on his hands and knees. He is the wheelbarrow. His partner must pick up the wheelbarrow person's legs by the ankles and hold them higher than his own knees.

At the signal, the wheelbarrow person must walk on his hands while his partner steers him from behind. When the partners reach the goal, they trade places, so the pilot becomes the new wheelbarrow. The first team to return to the starting line wins.

Inner Tube Race. Separate the players into two equal teams. Have each team stand in a single-file line, with about five feet between the teams. Place an inflated inner tube in front of each team. On "go," the first player in each line jumps into the middle of the inner tube, pulls the tube over his head, and places the tube in front of the person behind him in line. The next person in line does the same thing. Each person in turn jumps into the tube and pulls it over his head. The first team to finish wins.

Kick-the-Can Race. Have two teams with even numbers of players line up behind a starting line. The goal should be about 10 feet away. Place an old tin can in front of each team. At the signal, begin the race. The first players in line kick their cans along the ground toward the goal line, cross over the line, turn around, and come back. The second player in line takes over as soon as the first player is back. Continue the race in this way, making sure the can is kicked only along the ground and not into the air. The first team to finish is the winner.

Peanut Race. For each contestant in the race, sprinkle a path of unshelled peanuts from a starting point to the goal line a few feet away. Use the same amount of peanuts for each contestant. At the signal, the contestants must crawl on their hands and knees, shelling and eating their peanuts as they go. The first person to eat all his peanuts and cross the goal line wins.

Sack Race. You will need some big burlap sacks or heavy shopping bags for this race. On "go," each player hops toward the goal line with both his feet in the bag. The first one across the line wins.

Shoe Relay Race. Divide your contestants into two equal teams. Have everyone take off their shoes and mix them up in a pile about 20 feet away from the starting line. Have each team line up single file behind the starting line. Leave about three feet between each team. At the signal, the first player on each team races toward the pile of shoes. Each player must find his own shoes, put them on, and run back to tag the next player on his team. The tagged teammate then runs to the pile to find his own shoes. The first team to finish wins the relay.

Slow Turtle Race. In this strange race, the contestants must walk *as slowly as they can* to-

ward the goal line. Any player who stops is out! The *last* person to finish is the winner!

Spider Race. Split up your players into two equal teams. Have each team line up single file behind the starting line. Leave about three feet between the teams. The first player in each line must bend forward into a spider position so only his feet and the palms of his hands are touching the ground.

At the signal, the first person in each team races toward a goal line, spider-style, then turns around and comes back the same way. When tagged, the next player in line goes into the spider position and continues the race. The first team to finish is the winner.

Teaspoon Water Race. Have the contestants choose partners. One person in each pair gets a cup of water. (Make sure all the cups contain the same amount of water.) The other person on the team gets a teaspoon. On "go," the person with the teaspoon starts feeding his partner the water in the cup. The first pair to empty the cup wins.

Three-Legged Race. Have the contestants pick partners and line up in pairs behind a starting line. The goal line should be about 50 feet away. Each pair should stand side-by-side so their bodies are touching. Tie together the inside legs of each pair of players at the ankles, using a piece of rope or a strong rag. At the signal, the pairs must hop three-legged toward the finish line.

Wild String Windup Relay. Divide your contestants into two equal teams. Line up each team in single file. Give the first player in each team a ball of string. On "go," the first player on each team wraps the string around himself once and then passes the ball to the next player in line. The second player wraps the string once around himself, too, and passes the ball along.

Players continue passing and wrapping the string until the last person in line has wrapped himself. Then the race reverses. The last person unwraps the string and passes it to the person in front of him. Each player unwraps himself in turn. The first team to finish wins.

Batik Art

Some of these projects require the use of an iron.

Crayon Batik. Use crayons to draw a picture or design on a white handkerchief. Push down hard with the crayons to make the crayon wax sink into the cloth. Next, dampen two paper towels. Lay the handkerchief between the paper towels and iron them until the towels become dry. (Have an adult help you if necessary.) Remove the towels. The melted crayon wax has now set into the handkerchief with a batik-like effect.

Paper Bag Batik. Cut open a brown paper bag to make a flat sheet of paper. Crumple the paper and rub it together over and over to make it pliable. Spread it out and color a design onto it with crayons, pressing down very hard. Place the paper on a pad of newspaper, with the crayon side facing down. Press the back of the paper with a warm iron. (Have an adult help you.) Lift to reveal a batik-like effect.

Watercolor Batik. Draw a heavy crayon design on a sheet of white paper. Wet the paper under a faucet, and crumple it well. Then open up the paper and smooth it out. Paint over the entire sheet with watercolor paint.

Bees

Beehive Art. Glue some honeycomb-type cereal pieces close together on a sheet of paper in the shape of a dome-type beehive. With crayons, color some bees flying in or around the beehive.

Egg Carton Bee. Use three connected egg carton cups to make the body of a bee. Paint the body piece yellow. At each side, cut a slot for a wing. Cut two paddle-shaped wings from colored paper. Insert the "handle" part of each paddle into a wing slot.

Make six legs by punching a hole on each side of each cup; stick a pipe cleaner through each hole. (You can make the legs look like they are covered with pollen by shaking the pipe cleaners in a bag with dry yellow tempera ahead of time.) Paint black stripes around the body, and add black pipe cleaners to the head for feelers.

Birds

Feather Bird. On a piece of lightweight cardboard, draw the outline of a bird. Cut it out. Use glue to attach real feathers to the bird.

Feather Collage. Dip some feathers into different colors of paint. Allow them to dry, and then glue them together to form a collage on a piece of background paper.

Flying Bird Mobile. Cut some bird shapes from colored construction paper. Tape a piece of string to each bird and suspend them from above to represent birds "flying south" for the winter.

Paper Bird and Nest. From a sheet of colored construction paper, cut out the shape of a bird. From brown paper, cut out an oval piece to use as the base of a bird nest. Arrange a handful of straw on top of the oval, forming it into the shape of a nest before gluing it in place. If you want to, add other materials to the nest such as string, twigs, and leaves. When the nest is dry, glue the paper bird cutout upright inside the nest. Glue a few paper eggs into the nest, too.

Paper Hanging Bird.   From paper, cut out the profile (side view) of a bird. Then in one single piece cut out a pair of wings. Cut a slit in the body piece and slip the wing piece through the slit until the wing is centered. Hang the bird from the ceiling with thread. Air currents will make the bird look like it is flying.

Paper Parrots.   Outline parrot shapes on paper and cut them out. Color or paint the parrots, and then either paste on brightly colored feathers cut from construction paper or paste on real feathers.

Paper Strip Bird.   Cut a large strip of paper. Glue the ends together to form a large ring. Then cut out another smaller strip. Glue it into a ring also. Glue the two rings together to form the body and head of a bird.

Glue a paper beak to the smaller head ring. Attach paper feet to the bottom of the body ring. If the bird does not stand up easily, fasten a paper clip to the bottom of the bird to add weight. Place the bird on a piece of green paper with ragged edges for display.

Picture Activities.   Study drawings and photographs of birds. Learn how to recognize the different kinds of birds. Cut out some of the pictures

and glue them in an arrangement on poster board.

Pinecone Birds.   Lay a large pinecone on its side. On top of this cone glue another, smaller pinecone, also in a sideways position; this cone will be the head. Glue real feathers on the body or make feathers from colored paper. Attach a beak, eyes, and wings made with paper or felt.

Plastic Spoon Bird.   Overlap and glue together the handles of a plastic fork and spoon. The bowl of the spoon is the head, and the fork tines make a tail. Glue a one-piece set of paper wings across the handles. Make a beak and eyes from paper, and glue them to the spoon end.

Birds (Science)

Bird Formations.   In the fall, watch for birds flying in formations, going south for the coming winter. How many birds do you see? What shape is the formation? Why do birds fly together?

Bird Nest Hunt.   Go on a bird nest hunt! Carry along a bag for collecting any empty bird nests you find. Look for empty nests in trees, shrubs, hollow stumps, fields, and stream banks.

If you find a nest, make sure it is an abandoned one. Then ask yourself some questions. What kind of bird made the nest? Why did the bird build its nest here? Look closely at the nest; what

Plastic Spoon Bird

materials were used to build it? Later, visit the library and read about birds.

Bird Watching. Toss some birdseed, bread crumbs, or nuts on the ground to attract birds. Hide in a spot where the birds cannot see you, but you can see them. Carry binoculars so you can get a closer look at the birds. Watch them feed. Perhaps you will see a bird building a nest or defending his territory against other birds.

Egg Observation. Did you know that birds are hatched from eggs? Crack open a chicken egg from the refrigerator. Look at the yolk and clear part. The yolk develops into a bird. The clear part, called the "white" of the egg, provides food for the bird while it is growing in the shell.

Many eggs are a good source of food. Cook an egg to see the changes that take place. If possible, compare the shells of duck, turkey, hen, and bird eggs. What are the differences? Study pictures of birds hatching, or place a fertile egg in an incubator to see if it will hatch.

Parakeet Observation. Take care of a parakeet. Notice that parakeets, like other birds, have two legs, two wings, and their bodies are covered with feathers. At least once a year they *molt*, or shed their feathers and grow new ones.

Parakeets can usually learn to say a few words. Try teaching yours to talk. You will find parakeets are easy to care for. Place them in a wire bird cage with plenty of water and bird food. Put paper on the cage bottom and change it every day. With a little practice, the bird will learn to sit on your finger.

Peanut Butter Footprints. Spread peanut butter (thinly) on a piece of cardboard. Place the cardboard outside overnight. The next day, look for bird or other animal footprints in the peanut butter.

Bird Feeders

Cereal Feeder. Thread circle-shaped cereal pieces onto a heavy string, and hang them in a tree. Look for birds feeding from the string. Also try threading cranberries and popped corn onto the string.

Doughnut Feeder. Obtain a cake doughnut and two jar lids about the same size as the doughnut. Make a hole in the center of each lid by carefully pounding a nail through the middle. Next, find a long nail that has a good head on it. Push this nail through one lid, through the doughnut hole, and through the second lid. The doughnut is now sandwiched between the two lids. Tap the nail end of the feeder lightly into a window sill or into a tree branch. When the birds finish the doughnut, replace it with a different-flavored one.

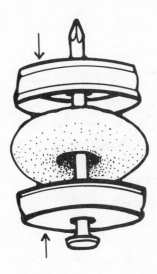

Paper Cup Feeder. Pour some birdseed into a paper cup. Fill it almost to the top. Then pour in just enough melted suet or lard to make the seeds stick together. Ask an adult to supervise the melting of the fat to avoid fire danger. Stir the mixture, then poke one end of a piece of string down into the seeds. You will need a string long enough to make a hanger for the feeder. Place the cup in a freezer. Later, remove the cup and peel away the sides to reveal the frozen mixture. Notice that the string is sticking out from the mixture and can be used to hang the feeder from a tree.

Peanut Butter Feeder. Spread some peanut butter all over the outside of an empty cardboard tube. Roll the covered tube in a plate of birdseed. Run a piece of yarn through the tube and hang the feeder outdoors.

Pinecone Feeder. Fill a pinecone with suet or peanut butter. Set the feeder on a windowsill or in a tree. Watch for the birds coming to feed.

Suet Strip Feeder. Tie a string to a suet strip. Spread some peanut butter on the strip. Then roll the strip in birdseed; hang it outside.

Tray Feeder. Use a wooden tray as a "feeding station" for birds. Put old bread crumbs, suet, or seeds in the tray and set it outside. Watch from a window to see the birds feeding.

Birthday Fun

Animal Hunt. Before the party, cut out small animals from paper. Make eight animals for each guest. Hide the animals in the party room. When it is time to play, signal "go" to your guests. The player who finds the most animals is the winner.

Birthday Throne. Turn a chair into a throne for the birthday person. Decorate it with crepe paper, wrapping paper, or a colorful tablecloth. Tie on balloons and bows.

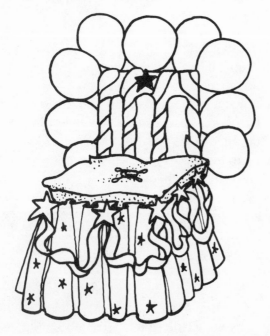

Candy Hunt. Before the party, hide lots of small wrapped candies in the party room. When it is time to play, give each guest a sandwich bag containing a piece of paper with his name on it. On "go," each guest tries to find as many candies as he can, putting them in his bag. Have a few extra candies on hand for guests who did not find many. Eat one or two candies, then put the bags away until later.

Castle Battle. Make some cannonballs by crumpling sheets of newspaper into balls. Split up everyone into two teams. Have each side make their own "castle" by moving furniture around (if that is okay with parents) or stacking cardboard boxes. Each team must stay behind its own castle, but members can jump up and down to fire the cannonballs at their opponents.

Charades. Pretend to be doing something simple, such as throwing a ball, spinning like a ballerina, or walking like a monster. The other players try to guess what you are doing. No talking allowed!

Collage Contest. Give each guest a sheet of construction paper, a pair of scissors, and these materials: a 12-inch length of string, a six-inch piece of ribbon, six toothpicks, four buttons, and some glue.

Tell the players to make a collage or picture with their materials. Who can finish their collage in five minutes?

Giraffe. A giraffe hardly ever makes a sound, right? So, in this game, everyone must be quiet like a giraffe! The first player to speak becomes "it" and tries to tease the others into talking or laughing. The first person to make a sound becomes the new "it."

Lion in the Cage. Have the players join hands and form a circle. One person is the lion and stands in the middle. He tries to get out of the circle by climbing under, over, or through the players' hands. If the lion escapes, the players chase him. The player who catches the lion becomes the new lion.

Musical Papers. This game is much like *musical chairs*, but you do not need chairs! Instead, you need a folded newspaper page for every player; one of these pages should be a comics page.

Arrange the newspaper pages in a large circle on the floor about one step apart. Have each player stand next to a page. For music, play a record or turn on a radio. When the music starts, everyone marches around the circle without stepping on the papers. When the music stops, each player tries to stand on the nearest newspaper. Only one player can stand on each paper. Anyone who ends up on the "funny paper" must do a funny trick! Repeat.

Party Favor Fishing Pond. Ahead of time, wrap small favors (puzzles, trinkets, candies, etc.) with paper and a bow. Put the wrapped favors into a large decorated box. Make several fishing poles by tying strings to rulers or yardsticks. Tie paper cups to the ends of the strings to make hooks. As your guests leave the party, invite them to "fish" for a favor by scooping one up from the box.

Pass the Ice. Split your guests into two equal teams. Ask them to line up in two single-file lines. In front of each line, place a bowl con-

taining six ice cubes. Place an empty bowl at the end of each line.

On "go," the first player in each line picks up one ice cube and passes it down the line. When the last player in line gets the cube, he puts it in the empty bowl. If a player drops the cube along the way, he must pick it up and return to his spot before handing off the cube again. The second piece of ice cannot be picked up until the first piece is placed in the bowl at the end. Each player, then, must handle all six of the cubes. The first team to pass all six cubes to the back of the line is the winner.

Pin the Tail on the Donkey. Ahead of time, draw a large donkey without a tail on a sheet of paper. Mark an "X" where the tail should be.

Tape the donkey picture to the wall so the center of it is about level with your guests' outstretched arms. Cut out a tail for each guest. Then stick a loop of tape onto the end of each tail.

Make a starting line about six feet from the wall. Give each player a tail. Bring each player up to the line one at a time. Have him close his eyes and spin him around. Lead him toward the picture. The first spot he touches with the tail is where the tail must be stuck. Let each player have a turn at sticking a tail on the donkey. The person with the tail closest to the "X" wins.

Scavenger Hunt. Beforehand, make a list of items for each guest to look for on the hunt. If you are playing outdoors, list things found outside. If playing indoors, list things found inside. Give every player a copy of the list. Set a time limit. When the time is up, the player who has found the most things on the list is the winner.

Take-Home Bags. Before the party, make some take-home bags for your guests so they can carry home their prizes, treats, and favors. Write the name of each guest on a brown lunch bag. Decorate the bags with crayons or colored paper cutouts. Or, have the guests make their own bags while waiting for the others to arrive.

Where's Doggie's Bone? Have the guests sit in a half circle. Pick one guest to be the dog. He must sit in a chair opposite the other players with his back to them. Place a small object, such as a block, under the chair to represent a bone. One player from the half circle tiptoes to the chair, takes the bone, and returns to his place. Then everyone puts their hands behind their backs to pretend they have all taken the bone. The players chant, "Doggie, doggie, where's your bone? Someone took it from your home!"

The "dog" names the player he thinks has the bone. The player who took the bone becomes the next dog and the game continues.

Blocks

Box Blocks. Collect some shoe boxes and cigar boxes. Tape the lids closed. Wrap the boxes with contact paper. Now you have lightweight blocks that are easy to stack, fun, and inexpensive!

Can and Mix-Box Blocks. Ask an adult if you can use full cans of food and full boxes of cake mix as blocks. If a mix box starts to wear out while you are playing with it, put it back on the shelf and get another one. Try it—you will probably find these are better than the blocks you buy at the store!

Milk Carton Blocks. Save empty milk cartons for making blocks. Completely open the top of each carton, then rinse and dry it.

To make a single block, you need two cartons

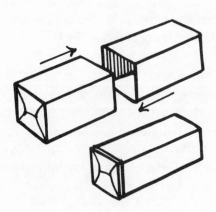

the same size. Push the open end of one carton inside the open end of the other. Keep pushing until one carton is totally inside the other. Now you have a strong, solid block! Use these for building forts, doll houses, walls, and even a play house! And if they fall on you, they will not hurt you! Have fun!

Wooden Blocks. Obtain some two-by-four-inch boards for making blocks. Saw the boards into 3-, 6-, 12-, and 24-inch lengths. (Ask an adult for help, if needed.) Sand the edges to remove splinters and make the blocks smooth. Then start building!

Boats and Ships

Boat Mural. On a sheet of butcher paper, make a mural showing many kinds of boats and ships in a harbor. Use crayons or paints to draw the boats, or cut the boats from construction paper and paste them onto the mural.

Cardboard Tube Raft. Glue three short cardboard tubes side by side to form a raft. Poke a hole into the top side of the middle tube. Stick a plastic straw into the hole to make a mast. Glue a small paper flag to the top of the mast. Place the raft on a piece of blue paper so it looks as if the raft is in the water.

Clothespin Sailboat. Remove the metal part from a clip-type wooden clothespin. Now you have two pieces! Glue the flat sides of the pieces together. See the tiny hole at one end? Glue a toothpick mast into the hole. Then glue a paper sail to the top end of the mast. Allow it to dry. Now the boat is ready for playing!

Cut and Paste Ship. Using colored paper, cut out the shape of an ocean liner. Use medium-blue paper to cut out a wavy ocean piece. Paste this piece at the bottom edge of a sheet of light-blue background paper. Now paste the ship onto the background paper so the ship rests on the ocean waves. Paint or color in other details.

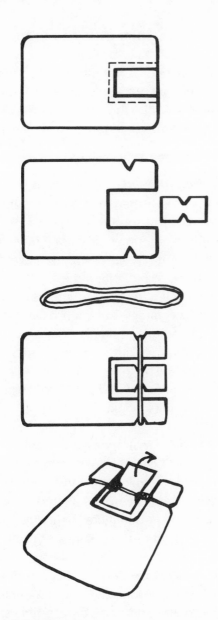

place. Insert the paddle in the cut-out space between the bands of rubber. Wind up the paddle, catching the rubber band in the paddle notches. Place the boat in water and let go of the paddle. Watch the boat move!

Milk Carton Boat. Use any size empty milk carton to make this boat. Staple the spout closed. Cut the carton in half lengthwise. Now you have two boats! These boats float well in the bathtub and will hold lightweight objects. Sail away!

Plastic Bottle Sailboat. For a hull, use a small round plastic bottle. Lay it down sideways and poke a small mast hole into the top side. Insert a pencil for the mast and tape on a paper flag.

Uncap the bottle. Add just enough sand to keep the bottle stable when placed in water. (This is called ballast.) Replace the cap and shake the sand back and forth so it lies flat along the bottom when the bottle is placed on its side. Put the boat in water and give it a push!

Popsicle Stick Raft. Place two Popsicle sticks beside each other, three inches apart. This is the base for your raft. Glue other Popsicle sticks crossways over the base, side by side as close together as possible. When the glue dries, paint the raft brown or yellow. It actually floats!

Round Lid Boat. Obtain a lid from a margarine tub and turn it upside down. Then use a wire twistie as a mast. Stick some glue on both ends of the twistie. Attach a paper flag to the top end and bend the twistie slightly outward at the bottom end. Fasten the bottom end onto the center of the lid. Allow the glue to dry. Then try your boat in a tub of water!

Walnut Shell Boat. Half of an empty walnut shell makes an excellent boat! Place a small mound of clay into the shell and poke a toothpick mast into the clay. Glue a small scrap of white cloth or a tiny piece of paper onto the mast for a sail. Float the boat in a pan of water or in the bathtub.

Meat Tray Paddle Boat. Cut away the rim from a plastic foam meat tray. For the paddle piece, cut out a small rectangle (2¼ inches long and 1¼ inch wide) from the center of one end of the tray. Set the paddle piece aside.

Enlarge the three inside edges where the paddle piece was cut by trimming away another one eighth inch from each. On each long outside edge, about half an inch from the back end of the boat, cut a small notch. Then, pick up the paddle piece and cut a small notch in the center of each end.

Stretch a weak rubber band around the boat, using the notches to hold the rubber band in

Bookmarks

Construction Paper Bookmark. From construction paper, cut out some 2-by-7 inch strips. Next, cut out small animals, flowers, designs, or symbols from contrasting colors of construction paper. Glue the cutouts to the bookmarks. When the glue has dried, cover the bookmarks on both sides with clear contact paper. Punch a hole at the top of each bookmark and loop a pretty ribbon through it.

Envelope-Corner Bookmark. Cut off the bottom corners of some envelopes. Color and decorate the corner pieces. Give them as bookmark gifts. To use the bookmarks, slip them over the corners of the pages to be marked.

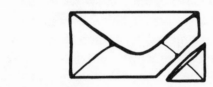

Pressed-Flower Bookmark. Collect some tiny flowers and miniature oak or maple leaves and take them indoors. Place the flowers and leaves under a heavy book for several days. Then lay the pressed items close together on a sheet of colored construction paper; overlap some of them if you want.

Cover this arrangement with clear contact paper. Flip the paper over, and cover the reverse side. Cut up the paper into any number of bookmarks; give them as gifts, and keep some for yourself.

Books and Magazines

Book Cover. Cut out a long rectangle that will fit around a book you want to cover. Finger paint over the entire surface of the rectangle. When the paint dries, fold the cover so it fits around the book.

Cardboard Book. Save some shirt packaging cardboards. When you have enough, cut them into halves or fourths to make book pages.

Cut several ring holes along the left-hand side of each page. Fasten the pages together by tying shoelaces through the holes.

On each page, paste pictures cut from magazines or catalogs. Fill each page with one large picture or many smaller ones. Or, draw your own pictures to tell your own stories. When each page is finished, cover it with a sheet of clear contact paper. Gradually, you can add more pages to your book.

Cut and Paste Magazine. Stack several sheets of 8½-by-11-inch paper. Fold them in half and staple them together along the center fold to make a booklet. Make it into a magazine by pasting in cut-out figures of people, animals, and objects from old magazines or catalogs.

Moving Picture Book. Ask an adult for an old book you can draw in. On the upper corner of every right-hand page, draw a little stick man or stick animal.

Start on the first right-hand page. Draw the figure in any position you want. On the next page, draw the figure in a slightly changed position. On each following page, make the figure move a little more. In this way, you can make him walk, dance, or jump up and down. Or you can make a face with a talking mouth or show a rocket blasting off!

When you have finished your series of pictures, flip the corners of the pages toward you, and watch the picture "move"! Make your own cartoons and movies!

Plastic Bag Book. Collect some plastic zip-lock bags, a sheet of poster board, and some old magazines. Measure the size of the zip-lock bags, then cut out some squares from the poster board to fit inside the bags.

Clip out interesting pictures from magazines and paste them to the poster board squares. Place each finished square in a bag to form a page. See how the pictures show through the plastic? Staple the bag pages together to form a book.

This is an especially good book for a toddler, because he cannot tear the pages of the book!

Zigzag Book. Find a long piece of lightweight cardboard. Fold it in half, then fold the outside edges back on themselves, forming a "zigzag" piece of cardboard. Unfold everything loosely and stand the piece on one edge. On each of the four "pages," glue a photograph cut from a magazine or draw your own picture.

Bowling

Aluminum Can Bowling. For this, you need three small balls and some empty aluminum cans or plastic bottles for bowling pins. Set up the pins on the grass outdoors. Each player has three turns to roll or throw the balls at the pins. Whoever knocks down the most pins wins.

Block Bowling. Use large cardboard blocks or regular wooden blocks for this activity. Stack the blocks in interesting ways or line them up in a triangular pattern. Try to knock all the blocks down at once by rolling a rubber ball at them.

Cardboard Tube Bowling. Save three cardboard tubes from paper towel rolls. Cut each tube in half. Set the tubes upright in a triangular pattern to use as bowling pins. How many pins can you knock down with a rubber ball?

Milk Carton Bowling Alley. Save empty, half-gallon milk cartons until you have 10. Line up the milk carton pins and place a pillow behind them for a backstop. Roll an unopened soup can to knock down the bowling pins.

Bubble Fun

Bottle Bubbles. Mix a little water and liquid soap in a clear plastic bottle. Close the lid tightly and shake the bottle to make bubbles. Add some food coloring to the bubbles if you want.

Bowl Bubbles. Mix ½ cup of water and ½ teaspoon of liquid soap in a bowl. Stick a straw into the mixture. Blow through the straw to create bubbles in the mixture. Watch the bubbles pile up! *Caution*—be sure not to suck any of the soap mixture through the straw!

Detergent Bubble Recipe. Make your own bubble mix! In a plastic cup, stir a mixture of one-half water and one-half liquid detergent. Add a little cooking oil or glycerine to help strengthen the bubbles.

When the mixture is ready, bend a paper clip into a circle and dip the paper clip into the mixture. Remove the paper clip from the solution. Notice how the soap film sticks to the paper clip! Blow forcefully and watch the bubbles fly!

Pipe Cleaner Bubble Wand. Bend an eight-inch piece of pipe cleaner at the top end to form a hook. Make the hook about one-quarter inch long. Then, bend down the pipe cleaner further from the top end and form a loop about one-half inch across. Attach the hook back to the middle section of the pipe cleaner to complete the loop.

The lower end is now a handle. Dip the loop into a bubble solution and remove it to blow bubbles. Adjust the size of the loop to make different-sized bubbles.

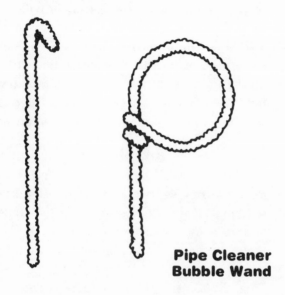

Pipe Cleaner Bubble Wand

Scissor Bubble Wand.   Dip the finger hole of a small pair of blunt scissors into a bubble solution. Blow through the finger hole to make bubbles.

Six-Pack Carrier Wand.   Clip off a ring from a plastic six-pack carrier. Dip it into a bubble solution and blow through the ring to make large bubbles. (Other bubble wands can be made from such things as deep-fry baskets and plastic strawberry baskets.)

Bugs and Small Critters

Button Bug.   Use a large button for the bug's body. Glue on small pipe cleaner pieces for legs. For a head, loop a small length of pipe cleaner into a ring and glue the edge of it to the front of the bug's body. Glue a smaller button on top of the loop to complete the head.

Clothespin Grasshopper.   To make a grasshopper body, use a round-top clothespin. Twist some pipe cleaners around the clothespin prongs to form legs and to make wings. Place the grasshopper on a sheet of newspaper and spray paint the grasshopper green.

Macaroni Bug Scene.   Glue pieces of dry macaroni to a sheet of green paper. Pretend the macaroni pieces are bugs, butterflies, and caterpillars. Draw in details and a background scene to go with your macaroni ''bugs.''

Paper Plate Beetle.   Paint or color a paper plate gray. From black and white sheets of construction paper, cut out circles and paste them on the beetle's back to make spots. Paste two paper eyes to the front end, and glue pipe cleaner legs around the plate.

Plastic Spoon Dragonfly.   Use a plastic spoon for the body of a dragonfly. Cut wings from a piece of colored cellophane. Turn the spoon upside down and glue the wings across the ''neck'' of the spoon. Paint eyes on the bowl end. Your dragonfly is complete.

Playacting.   Pretend to be a caterpillar. Act out spinning a cocoon, going to sleep, and coming out as a butterfly. Then pretend you are a spider. Crawl on the floor spider-style, spin a web, and look for bugs caught in your web. What other bugs can you pretend to be?

Playdough Bug.   Mold a piece of Playdough into a bug shape. Stick toothpicks, pipe cleaners, or paper cutouts into the body to form legs and feelers.

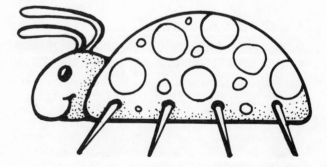

Butterflies

Blotto Butterfly. Fold a piece of paper in half and reopen it. Drop some food coloring or paint into the center, then refold the paper and press on it to spread the color around inside. Reopen and allow to dry. Draw two antennae on the top of the blotto design to make it resemble a butterfly.

Bread Bag Butterfly. Cut a plastic bread bag into squares. Tie the squares in the middle with yarn or pipe cleaners and fluff the ends to look like wings.

Clothespin Butterfly. Cut a pair of wings in one piece from colored tissue paper. Gather the wings at the center and clip a clothespin across the center between the wings. For antennae, open the clothespin again slightly and insert two pipe cleaner pieces.

Crayon-Melt Butterfly. You will be using an iron for this project. Use a vegetable peeler to shave some old crayons into bits. Then place a sheet of waxed paper on top of a piece of newspaper. Sprinkle the crayon shavings onto the waxed paper. Place another sheet of waxed paper on top of the shavings. Cover this with another piece of newspaper.

Press the newspaper for several seconds with a warm iron. (Ask an adult for help if needed.) Remove the waxed papers from the newspaper sheets. Notice that the crayon shavings have melted between the waxed paper. Cut out a butterfly from the waxed papers.

Hang the butterfly in a window so the light shines through, showing off the beautiful, brilliant colors.

Easel-Paint Butterflies. Decorate paper butterfly cutouts using cotton swabs dipped in easel paints.

Egg Carton Butterfly. From a cardboard egg carton, cut out a single connected row of four eggcups. This is the butterfly's body. Using construction paper, cut out a pair of heart-shaped wings. Cut a slot in each side of the body to hold the wings. Paint the body and wing pieces with bright colors, using tempera paints. Let them dry. Poke two small holes into the head and stick in pipe cleaner feelers. Paint a face on the head and stick the wings into place.

Mosaic Butterfly. First cut out some small squares of several colors of paper. Then draw a large butterfly on another sheet of paper. Cut out the shape. Paste the paper squares all over the body and wings of the butterfly.

Shoeprint Butterfly. Set a pair of shoes side by side on a sheet of paper. Place them a few inches apart, with the left shoe on the right-hand side, and the right shoe on the left-hand side. Using a crayon, trace around each shoe. Remove the shoes from the paper.

The shoe outlines are the wings for your butterfly. Draw a body in the space between the

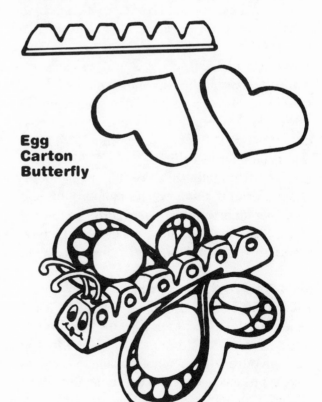

Egg Carton Butterfly

wings. Draw a head with antennae, color the butterfly, and cut it out!

Spatter-Paint Butterfly. Cut out a butterfly from black paper. Fold the butterfly in half down the middle. Open it up again. Spatter colorful pastel paints onto the butterfly. Then fold it up again. Press the wings together carefully. Open them to reveal beautiful patterns on the butterfly.

Sponge-Printed Butterflies. Cut some sponges into butterfly shapes. Dip the butterfly-shaped sponges into paint. Make butterfly prints on pieces of paper.

C

Carnival Fun

Have a carnival in your own backyard or at the local park! Plan the games and activities you want beforehand. Have your friends and neighbors help. Make prizes and awards to give to the winners of the games. Have fun!

Balloon Toss. Line up three open cartons, laundry baskets, or other open containers in single file. Make sure the containers are equal distances apart. The first carton should be fairly close to the throwing line.

Give each contestant three inflated balloons. The player must try to toss his balloons into the container farthest away. Award prizes according to the containers the balloons land in. Count the best of three throws. It is harder than you think!

Bean Bag Toss. In advance, obtain a side panel from a large cardboard carton. Fold the panel in half the short way. Set the panel on its edges so the fold is on top like a tent. On one side, cut out a large mouth, and paint on a clown face. When it is ready, have the contestants stand behind a line. Take turns tossing a bean bag or small ball through the clown's mouth.

Chair Leg Ring Toss. Ahead of time, make some throwing rings by cutting out the centers of some paper plates, or use some rubber rings from the inside of jar lids. Then turn a chair or stool upside down so the legs stick up. Stand behind a line and see how many rings you can toss onto the legs.

Clothespin Drop. For each turn, you get five clothespins. Stand over an empty oatmeal box or wide-mouthed jar. How many clothespins can you drop into the opening?

Fat Person. Dress up in clothes belonging to an older person. Stuff a pillow or newspapers under the clothes to make yourself look like a sideshow fat person.

Fish Pond. This is a game where everyone wins a prize! Ahead of time, stack one carton on top of another. (Fasten them together with tape.) Then tie a piece of string to a stick for a fishing pole. Tie a closed safety pin to the end of the string to serve as a hook.

To play, have the player lower his fishing line (with the safety pin closed) over and down behind the boxes. The fish pond operator, who is crouched behind the boxes, then sticks a bagged prize on the safety pin hook.

Floating Duck Game. Cut a piece of plastic foam into two-inch-long chunks. These are the ducks. Using a permanent, water-fast, felt-tip marker, number on the bottoms of the pieces.

To play, float the pieces in a tub of water. Make sure the numbers face down so they cannot be seen. Each player scoops a "duck" out of the water with a goldfish net. The number 1 gets no prize. The numbers 2 and 3 get another turn. The numbers 4 and 5 win prizes.

Penny Fling. Outside, use chalk or tape to mark a bull's-eye target on cement or hardtop. (If you are using the driveway or patio, check first with your parents.) If playing on grass, lay down circles of string to make the bull's-eye target.

Mark a spot nearby where the players must stand. Each player gets five pennies to toss at the target. For each penny that lands in the bull's-eye, the player earns a prize.

Penny Pitch. Place several empty dishes close together on a flat surface. Each player tries to pitch five pennies onto the dishes.

Prizes. Check out your closet or drawers for small toys you have outgrown or do not want anymore. Use them for prizes. Trinkets and small rubber animals make good prizes. Ask your friends and neighbors to help by donating more prizes.

Refreshments. Sell sandwich bags full of homemade popcorn.

Put some crushed ice into a small paper cup, and fill with some fruit punch concentrate to make a snow cone.

Tall Person. Become a sideshow tall person by walking on an empty pair of upside-down tin cans! Punch two holes on opposite sides of each tin can. Thread a long piece of strong twine through the holes. Make sure the string is long enough to reach your hands. Place one foot on top of each of the cans. Pull the strings tightly for balance while you walk on the cans. Let your guests take turns being the tall person.

Cars

Matchbox Cars. Use small empty matchboxes for cars. For wheels, glue buttons to the corners of the boxes. Paint the boxes solid colors and allow to dry. Then paint in the details.

Wooden Cars. Sand down a short two-by-four inch board to remove any splinters and make it smooth. Near the corners of both long sides, nail baby food jar lids for wheels. Glue on small pieces of wood to decorate the car with bumpers and other details. Nail two bottle caps to the front end for headlights.

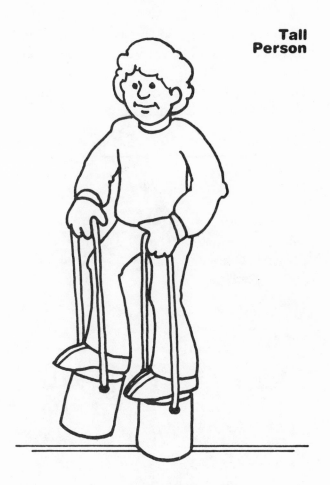

Tall Person

Caterpillars

Egg Carton Caterpillar. Cut out a single linked row of six cups from a cardboard egg carton. Paint it green and allow it to dry. (Or, if you want, paint each cup section a different color.) At the head end, paint a face. Poke two holes on top of the head and stick in pipe cleaners to make feelers. Glue on cloves or buttons for eyes.

Egg Carton Caterpillar Cocoon. Cut out two linked egg carton cups. Insert a small colored paper butterfly inside one of the cups. Fold the cups together and staple them shut. Cover the cups completely by gluing cotton over them. Later, "hatch" the cocoon to reveal the butterfly.

Construction Paper Caterpillar. On construction paper, draw a caterpillar, as shown in the illustration. Cut him out and punch a hole at the bottom of each body segment. Loop a short piece of yarn through each hole. Tie the pieces of yarn underneath to form feet.

Construction Paper Caterpillar

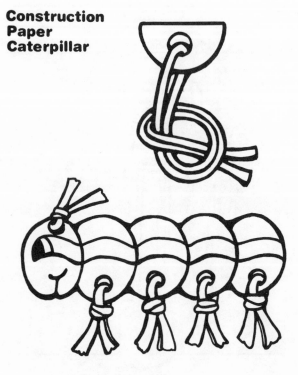

Chalk Art

Chalk Painting. Spread buttermilk, liquid starch, or liquid detergent on a sheet of paper. Using dry chalk, draw on the paper while it is still wet. Spread the colors around with your fingers. When finished, the picture will look like an oil painting with bright colors.

Chalk and Torn Paper. From scraps of colored paper, tear off pieces of different sizes and shapes. Paste the pieces on a sheet of background paper. Use colored chalk to fill in the background areas. Smooth over the chalked areas with a paper towel.

Marbelized Paper. Pour several inches of water into a large cake pan. Using a dull table knife, scrape the sides of colored chalk so the powder falls into the water. Then lay a piece of pastel construction paper in the water so it floats. Quickly pull out the paper by lifting from a corner. The chalk will stick to the paper, making a pretty marbelized effect. Wash out the pan so it can be used for baking.

Christmas

Activities

Card Sorting. Collect a large number of Christmas cards; find some saved from last year or given to you by friends. Sort them into different groups according to the pictures on the cards. See how many cards of each group you can collect (cards with Santa, angels, manger scenes, bells, etc.).

Letter to Santa. Write a letter to Santa Claus. If you need help, tell an adult what you want to say and ask him to write it for you. Tell Santa what you want for Christmas. Sign the letter and give it to an adult for mailing.

Picture "Gifts." On a large sheet of paper, use crayons to draw gift boxes of different sizes and shapes. Then, using gift catalogs, cut out pictures of things you want for Christmas, or things you think others in your family may want. Paste a cut-out gift picture inside each of the gift box outlines.

Santa's Workshop. When the Christmas season nears, you can have your own Santa's workshop. At the same time, you can help others enjoy the holiday season!

Ask friends, neighbors, and relatives for some old toys they do not want anymore. Clean and wash the toys, and, if needed, fix and repaint them. Ask an adult to help you deliver the toys to a hospital or a home for the needy. It is fun to help others!

Stories. Cut out a Christmas picture from a magazine or an old Christmas card, or draw your own picture! Paste the picture on a 12-by-18-inch sheet of manila paper. Tell a story based on the picture. Print the story underneath the picture, or have an adult print the story for you.

Story Acting. Have someone read *The Night Before Christmas* or another Christmas story to you. Act out the story as it is being read.

Wish Book. Flip through some old department store catalogs. Look for pictures of things you would like to give or receive for Christmas. Cut out the pictures. Glue them on sheets of notebook paper. Staple the papers together to form a "wish book."

Wrapping Practice. Practice wrapping packages using sheets of newspaper, old magazine pages, or paper bags. Wrap empty boxes of different sizes and shapes. Hang the smaller, prettier ones as Christmas ornaments.

Angels

Construction Paper Angel. Using construction paper, cut out an angel shape as illustrated. Fold over the outside ends so one overlaps the other and glue them into place. Now you have a cone-shaped angel! Paint on a face and robe decorations. The angel will stand up by itself.

Paper Plate Angel. Draw a cute face on a paper plate. Paste on some yarn for hair. Form a piece of pipe cleaner into a halo and with another pipe cleaner tie a handle to the halo. Glue the handle end of the halo to the angel's head. Prop the head up for display.

Paper Strip Angel. Cut out a strip of construction paper. Pinch the strip in three places to form a triangle. Glue the triangle in an upright position on a piece of paper. Then cut out a smaller strip. Glue the ends together to form a ring. Glue the ring to the point of the triangle for a head. Glue two smaller triangles to the sides of the big triangle for wings.

Pinecone Angel. Collect a medium-sized pinecone, an acorn with a cap, and a milkweed pod. Pick out a pinecone that will stand up. Glue the acorn to the top of the pinecone. (If the acorn does not stick, you might have to make a small notch at the bottom of the acorn so it will stay in place.) Split the milkweed pod and throw away the silk. Each side of the pod is now an angel

wing. Glue on the wings, and allow everything to dry.

Shape Angel.   Using colored paper, cut out a circle for a head. Cut out a large different-colored triangle for a dress, and two smaller gold-colored triangles for wings. Glue the parts together on a piece of background paper. Draw a face, using crayons or felt-tip markers.

Standing Angel.   Cut a large half circle from a sheet of construction paper. Fold the ends around and glue or staple them in place to form a cone. This will be the angel's skirt.

Then fold a round paper doily in half. Glue it near the top front side of the cone to make the outstretched arms of the angel. For wings, cut a crescent-moon shape from paper and fasten it behind the angel so the tips rise up behind both sides of the arms.

For a head, push a piece of pipe cleaner into a plastic foam ball. Insert the free end of the pipe cleaner into the small hole at the top of the cone. Bend the pipe cleaner inside the cone to hold the head in place. Glue on facial features made from paper, buttons, and sequins.

Art

Card Collage.   Gather some old Christmas cards. Cut out parts of the cards. Paste the parts on a piece of construction paper to form your own picture. Use your imagination to make a winter scene, a collage of toys, or anything else you want.

Card Mosaic.   Glue old Christmas cards on a sheet of background paper to form a mosaic. Finger paint on top of the cards with blue paint.

Card Scrapbook.   Collect some old Christmas cards. Staple together 12-by-18-inch sheets of construction paper to form a large scrapbook. On each page, glue cards having similar pictures on the front. For example, one page can display cards showing angels, and another page can display cards with manger scenes.

Christmas Banner.   Obtain a large piece of burlap or heavy fabric, about three-by-five-feet in size. Staple one end to a dowel stick.

Next, cut 15 one-foot squares from fabric scraps. On each square glue a Christmas shape cut from other pieces of fabric. The shapes can include such things as stars, bells, candles, trees, angels, etc. Make sure each shape is glued on a square of a different color.

Glue the squares in rows on the burlap banner, three squares across and five squares down. Tie string to each end of the dowel rod and hang the banner for display.

Crayon-Rubbing Christmas Scene.   Cut out Christmas shapes from thick paper, including trees, stars, bells, angels, wise men, Santas, reindeer, etc. Place the shapes under a single sheet of paper.

Using a crayon without a wrapper, rub gently over the paper with the side of the crayon. This makes impressions of the cutouts underneath! Before starting, you can arrange the cutouts beneath the paper to form a scene or arrange them in a pattern to make Christmas wrapping paper.

Frosted Picture.   Clip out a colored picture from an old magazine or a greeting card. Mount the picture on a piece of cardboard of the same size.

Dilute some white glue with an equal amount of water. Cover the entire picture with this glue solution. While the picture is drying, make a salt solution by stirring Epsom salts in warm water. Add salt until it will no longer dissolve. As soon as the picture is dry, brush the salt solution all over the picture, or brush only over the background areas or onto certain details. This creates a frosted effect when the picture dries! Glue the finished picture to the front of a homemade Christmas card or prop it up for display.

Gift Drawing.   Draw a Christmas tree on paper. Then, from a gift catalog, cut out pictures of gifts for each member of your family. Paste the cut-out gifts under the tree on the drawing.

Glitter Bell. Cut out a bell shape from thin cardboard, and paint it with glue. Place the bell in a bag with silver glitter and shake well. Remove the bell and shake off the excess glitter. Punch a hole in the top of the bell and tie a string through it. Trim the bell with odd pieces of rickrack and hang for display.

Paper Gingerbread Man. On brown paper, draw a large outline of a gingerbread man and cut him out. Glue circular-shaped cereals, buttons, and small bits of candy on the gingerbread man to form eyes, nose, mouth, and buttons down his front.

Paper Star. Cut a square of paper in half from one corner to another (diagonally). You now have two triangles! Lay down one triangle with the point facing up. Lay the other triangle on top of the first, with the point facing down. Now you have a star shape! Glue the pieces together to hold the star in place. Hang for decoration.

Paper Tube Candy Cane. On a large piece of white, lightweight paper, paint some wide, bright red stripes. Leave white spaces of the same size between the stripes. When the paint has dried, roll the paper tightly into a tube from one corner to the other. Glue down the ends. Carefully bend one end of the tube to make a crook in your cane.

Poinsettia Wash. Draw poinsettia or other red flowers on a 9-by-12-inch sheet of manila paper. Color in the flowers very heavily with red crayon. When you are finished crayoning, paint over the picture with a very thin tempera paint.

Santa Hat. Draw a Santa hat on a piece of red construction paper. Make the hat wide enough at the base so it will fit a little more than halfway around your head. Cut out the hat and lay it on another sheet of red paper. Trace around the hat and cut out the tracing. Now you have two matching hat shapes! Staple the two hat pieces together at the sides, leaving the bottom open. Glue some cotton along the bottom edges and glue a cotton ball to the top. Now you have a Santa hat to wear for Christmas!

Shape Figures. Cut out some squares, rectangles, circles, and triangles from paper, making them in different sizes and colors. Paste them together on manila paper to form a Santa, reindeer, or other Christmas figure. When dry, display or hang for decoration.

Winter Christmas Scene. Whip some liquid starch with some powdered laundry detergent. Using this mixture, paint a winter scene on blue paper.

Wintry Christmas Village. Paint some empty milk cartons to look like village buildings. To make paint that will stick to the milk cartons, add a small amount of liquid dishwashing detergent to the paint. After the paint has dried, paste on paper cutouts of doors and windows. Arrange the buildings on a large, flat cardboard base to form a village and glue in place. Paint in roads, sidewalks, etc., and then glue tufts of cotton to the board and rooftops for snow.

Candles

Cardboard Tube Candle.   Cover the outsides of a short cardboard tube with whipped soap flake snow. (See *Snow Art,* page 182, for instructions for making Soap Flake Snow.) Cover the top of the tube with a thick glob of the snow. Add a precut paper flame to the top.   *Another way to do it:* Glue a piece of construction paper around a short cardboard tube. Glue the tube in an upright position on a circle base cut from construction paper. Cut out a yellow flame and glue it on top of the tube. Glue on a paper strip handle from the bottom of the candle at the base to a point halfway up the candle.

Decoration Candle.   First make a candle holder by driving a nail through a fairly thin, flat piece of wood. (Ask an adult for help, if needed.) Then stick the bottom of a candle onto the nail. Paint the base and allow it to dry. Glue sequins to the candle, then attach a sprig of pine needles to the board. Lightly spray paint the whole assemblage gold, so the original candle and base colors show through just a little. This is a candle for decoration only; do not light it.

Juice Can Candle.   Find an empty juice, fruit, or soup can to make a candle. Remove the label, wash out the can and make sure any rough edges are sanded down.

Cut a piece of contact paper or construction paper to cover the outside of the can. Set it aside.

Next, tie a piece of string to the middle of a nail. Make sure the string is longer than the height of the can. Also make sure the nail is long enough to reach across the top of the can so it will not fall in the can from that position.

Tie a paper clip to the free end of the string to give it weight. Lay the nail across the top of the can so the string hangs straight down into the can.

Now, place some old candle pieces or paraffin into an empty coffee can. With the help of an adult, place the can in a saucepan containing a small amount of water. Then place the saucepan over medium heat and stir the candle pieces until the wax melts.

Pour the melted wax into your can and allow it to harden. Then clip off the nail that is still lying across the top of the can. Now you have a wick sticking out of the candle!

Decorate the outside of the can with the covering you made earlier. If you want, spray the finished can cover with a coating of acrylic lacquer. The candle is now ready for lighting!

Cards

Candle Greeting Card.   Using black construction paper, cut out a 3½-by-9½-inch rectangle. Fold the long side in half, forming a card which opens up from the bottom.

Make paper cutouts of a candle, a candle holder, and a flame. Color in the parts with crayon. Paste the candle and candle holder together on the front of the card.

Next, cut a 2½-inch diameter circle from aluminum foil. Glue it above the candle so the bottom of the circle slightly overlaps the candle top. Over this, paste the flame cutout so its bottom touches the candle top. Write a Christmas greeting inside.

Cut and Paste Card.   Cut out a rectangle from red construction paper. Fold it in half to form a card. Glue on a green triangle for a tree on the front. Cut out and glue small circles and other shapes to the tree for bulbs, lights, and other tree decorations. Write a message or greeting inside the card.

Frosted Card.   Mix a solution of Epsom salts and warm water. Stir constantly while adding the salts to the warm water. Continue until no more salt crystals will dissolve.

Paint a greeting card with this solution. When it dries, you will see sparkling crystals on the card, creating a frosted effect!

Glitter Card.   Fold a piece of dark-colored paper into a card. Write a greeting or draw a Christmas symbol on the front, using a paint-brush soaked in glue. While the glue is still wet, shake glitter all over the card. Leave glitter there for a few minutes. Then carefully shake off the excess glitter. Write a message inside.

Santa Card.   Fold a piece of colored paper to make a card. On the front color in blue eyes and a red nose for Santa's face. Glue curled strips of white paper along the bottom front edge for Santa's beard. Write a message inside.

Three Kings Card.   Fold a piece of colored paper to make a card. From a piece of gold paper, cut out three crown shapes. From a piece of silver paper, cut out a star. Glue the three crowns on the front of the card to represent the Three Kings. Glue the star above the crowns to represent the Star of Bethlehem. Write a greeting inside.

Decorations

Cardboard Fireplace.   Lay an empty laundry detergent box on its side in front of you. On the front side, cut away a rectangle from the bottom edge to within several inches of the top and within several inches of the sides. This makes a hearth for the fireplace. Paint the fireplace with red tempera paint.

Glue a wide red strip of paper to the top of the fireplace, from behind, for the chimney. To the top of the chimney glue a gray paper cutout to look like rising smoke.

Next, glue some small paper stockings to the outside of the fireplace above the hearth opening and below the mantle. Lay some small twigs inside the hearth, and on the inside wall behind the twigs, glue some paper cut-out flames to represent the fire.

Choir Heads.   On a six-by-nine-inch piece of white construction paper, draw and color in a picture of your own head and shoulders. When finished, cut out the head and shoulders.

Next, cut out a 4½-by-6-inch piece of red construction paper. Fold the piece over to form a miniature folder. Pinch the folder outward so it looks like an open book of sheet music. Staple the pinched-out folder over the shoulder part of your head and shoulder cutout. Now it looks like the choir head is holding the music folder!

Make choir heads for each member of your family or for each of your friends. Make an entire choir this way!

Evergreen Package.   Arrange some pine needles and other pieces of flat greenery on the sticky side of a piece of clear contact paper. Then press a sheet of colored cellophane paper over the top, and, if necessary, fasten it underneath with tape.

Golden Bird's Nest. Dig out a bird's nest you might have saved from last year. Spray it with gold paint and place small colored Christmas balls inside for eggs.

Greenery Ball. Loop a piece of red yarn around an orange crossways to form a yarn basket. Tie it at the top with a loop so you can hang it up later.

Stick short sprigs of hemlock, holly, or other greens into the orange until it is totally covered. If you want, paint the very tips of the greens gold or silver. Hang the decoration from a doorway, an overhead light, or set it on the fireplace mantle.

Greeting Board. This is an activity for the whole family. Cover a large bulletin board with red or green paper. Across the top, write the words, "We Wish You A Merry Christmas."

In the center of the board, attach several Christmas symbols, using your own paper cutouts or store-bought decorations.

Give each member of the family a paper plate and crayons. Each person draws his own face on his paper plate. When the faces are finished, fasten the portraits on and around the edges of the board. Mount the board where visitors will see it when they come to your house.

Holiday Chain. Cut some straws into one-inch lengths. Then cut out some one-inch squares of construction paper. String the straws and squares on a long piece of yarn, alternating the straws and the squares. Drape the chain across the branches of your Christmas tree.

Holly Man. Using construction paper, cut out some holly-shaped leaves. Poke small holes in the ends of the leaves. Overlap and fasten them together with paper fasteners. Attach a paper

head and draw in the facial details. Notice that the arms and legs will move. Hold the holly man by his head and make him dance!

Macaroni Chain. Add some green or red vegetable dye to a small jar of water. Drop some elbow macaroni into the colored water. Quickly stir the macaroni, remove it, and spread it on a paper towel to dry.

With a large-eyed needle tied to red or green yarn, thread the macaroni on the yarn. Make sure a large-enough knot is tied at the bottom end of the yarn so the macaroni will stay in place. When finished, hang the chain as an icicle or use it as a tree garland.

Modeling Clay Decorations. Make some simple Christmas shapes from modeling clay, including trees, bells, candles, wreaths, etc. Stick small colored beads and sequins to the clay figures to make them more colorful. Set up the figures around your house for decorations.

Paper Strip Mobile. Paste together the ends of colored paper strips to form Christmas ornaments, including teardrops, circles, and bulbs with pointed ends. Hang them by yarn from a wire mobile or tree branch.

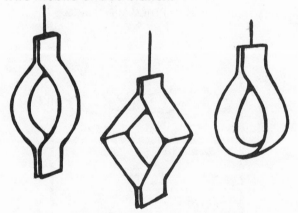

Pinecone Decorations. Paint some pinecones or eucalyptus pods with red, green, gold, or white paint. While the paint is still wet, shake the cones in a bag with some glitter. Remove, allow to dry, and then display. *Another way to do it:* Color the pinecones with white shoe polish using a sponge-tip applicator. Display them when dry.

Streamers. Cut out some 3-by-12-inch strips of white paper. On each streamer, paint a series of Christmas symbols, such as bells, trees, Santas, etc. Hang the streamers for decoration.

Tree Counting-Calendar. Cut out a large tree from construction paper. Next, cut little doors in the tree, one for each day left until Christmas. Cut the doors so they will open and close. Then mount the tree on a sheet of red background paper.

Open each door, one at a time, and mount a small paper Christmas symbol (a Christmas seal or picture cut from an old Christmas card) on the red paper inside the door. When all the door spaces have been filled with pictures, close them.

Starting at the right-hand side of the bottom row, number the doors on the outside. Starting with number 1 and counting forward, work across the row to your left. When that row is complete, go back to the right-hand side of the next row up and continue numbering the door flaps. The last door, at the very top of the tree, will have the highest number. That number should show how many days are left before Christmas on the day you make this project.

Each day, beginning at the top of the tree, open the door that shows how many days are left until Christmas. Leave it open. Each following day, open a new door, working across the rows from left to right.

Finally, on the night before Christmas, you will open the last door. At this point the counting tree is "lit," displaying all its colorful Christmas symbols to celebrate the arrival of Christmas!

Ornaments

Bell Ornament I. Cover a small paper cup inside and out with aluminum foil. Turn the cup upside down. Make a small hole in the middle of the bottom of the cup. Insert a pipe cleaner. Bend the pipe cleaner sideways inside the cup so it will not fall off the pipe cleaner. Form the top end of the pipe cleaner into a hook, and hang the ornament from a tree.

Bell Ornament II. Turn a plastic foam cup upside down. Make the bell any size you want by trimming away part of the cup's rim. Poke two holes near the center of the bottom of the cup. Loop a piece of string through for hanging.

Cut pieces of braid long enough to fit around the base of the bell and glue in place. Paint the remaining outer surface with glue. Stick on pieces of ribbon and holiday trim while the glue is still wet. Using a small spoon, sprinkle on some colored glitter, or roll the cup in a bowl of glitter. Allow to dry, then hang.

Cardboard Free-Form Ornaments. Cut any Christmas shapes you want from a piece of cardboard. Paint them or cover them with foil. Poke a hole in the top of each ornament. Hang from the tree with an ornament hook.

Christmas Balls. Cut out circles, triangles, diamonds, trees, and bells from pieces of Christmas wrapping paper. Make at least eight cutouts for each shape you choose.

Gather the eight cutouts of one shape. Fold each cutout down the middle, then spread paste on the outside of the fold. Press the pasted sides together, joining all eight cutouts to form a ball. When dried, thread yarn through the center with a long needle and hang.

Clay Ornaments. Roll out some clay about one-eighth inch thick. Cut into the clay with small Christmas cookie cutters. Punch a small hole in the top of each clay ornament. Bake at 350 degrees for about one hour or until dry. Allow to cool, and decorate with enamel paints. Tie thread through the holes on top and hang.

Clothespin Angel Ornament. Cut out a pair of paper wings in a single piece. Then cut out a circle for a head. Glue the wings across the pincher end of a wooden clothespin. Glue the circle head to the clothespin and hang the ornament from a tree.

Coffee Lid Ornament. Glue different kinds of macaroni to both sides of a plastic lid from a coffee can. Paint the ornament with Christmas colors. Glue a piece of yarn or string to the ornament and hang it from a tree.

Cottage Cheese Lid Ornament. Spread glue all over a lid from a cottage cheese carton and sprinkle on bits of red and green confetti. Press the confetti into the glue so that it sticks to the lid. Punch a hole near the edge, insert a ribbon through the hole, and hang. *Another way to do it:* Glue Christmas card cutouts on the lid and hang the ornament from the tree.

Dried Glue Ornaments. Obtain a sheet of waxed paper and a bottle of white glue with a squeeze-top lid. Carefully squeeze a line of glue on the waxed paper. Loop and bend the line of glue around in a long, thin pattern, twisting and crossing over lines already on the paper. Allow

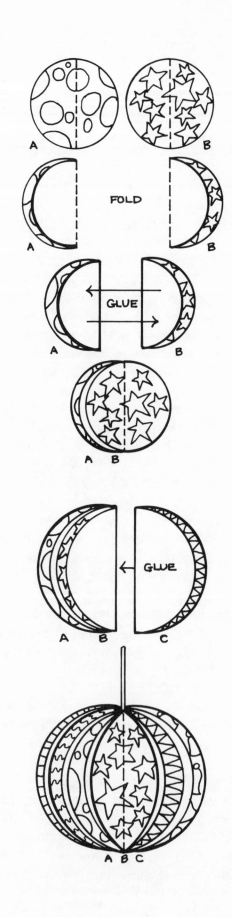

the glue to dry and harden completely. Then peel away the waxed paper. Using Christmas-colored felt-tip markers, color the dried-glue ornament. Attach a piece of yarn to the ornament, and hang it from the tree or ceiling.

Eggcup Bell Ornaments. Cut out single eggcups from a cardboard egg carton. Poke a hole into the bottom of each cup. Paint the cups with Christmas colors. Thread silver gift tie through the holes and hang the ornaments.

Foil Icicles. Cut out a circle from a sheet of paper foil. Starting at the edge, cut around the circle along the inside of the edge. Continue working toward the center, cutting the circle into a spiral pattern. When you reach the center, hold onto the end and let the design fall open. Hang it for display.

Paper Ornament I. Cut out two equal-sized circles of colored paper. Staple them together in the center. Fold each circle in half to the outside. Glue a Christmas picture on each side of the ornament and hang it.

Paper Ornament II. Cut out a number of circles from colored construction paper. Make each circle about three inches across. Punch a hole in the top of each circle. Smear glue over the surface of the circles and sprinkle glitter over the glue.

  While drying, the circles will curl up into interesting shapes. Leave them that way. Tie ribbon or string through the holes and hang the ornaments.

Pie Dish Ornament. Cut out a paper circle to fit inside the bottom of a foil dish from an individual-sized frozen meat pie. Color a Christmas scene on the circle and glue it inside the pie dish. Poke a hole in the top edge of the dish. Thread a piece of yarn through the hole and hang the ornament.

Pinecone Ornament. Mix some white or colored tempera paint in a large can until it looks like cream. Next, tie or glue a string to the top of a pinecone, and dip the cone into the paint. Cover the cone completely with paint. While the paint is still wet, place the cone in a bag of glitter. Shake the bag so the glitter sticks all over the cone. Remove the cone, allow it to dry, and then hang it.

Plastic Lid Ornament. Obtain a plastic lid from a fast-food chain drinking cup. Cut the rim away from the lid. Spread glue inside the patterns stamped in the lid. Sprinkle the glued areas heavily with glitter. Allow it to dry. Shake off the excess glitter and turn the ornament over, applying glitter to this side also. For a hanger, glue a piece of colored yarn to the top.

Sphere Ornament. Make two large paper rings and glue them one inside the other crossways at the top and bottom. Very carefully, place crushed colored tissue paper inside the ornament ball. On top, glue a third, smaller ring for a hanger.

Starched String Ornament. Dip a length of heavy string into some liquid starch and then remove it. Lay the string on a piece of waxed paper in any flat shape you want. When dried and painted, the shape will be stiff and can be hung by string from a tree.

Starched String Ornament Ball. Inflate a balloon until it is about three or four inches across. Tie off the balloon to keep the air inside.

Next, dip a two-foot length of string into a bowl of liquid starch. Wet the string completely and start wrapping it around the balloon in an interesting pattern. Set the balloon aside to dry overnight.

The next day the string will be stiff. Pop the balloon and remove it from the stiff string ball. Now you can paint the ornament red, green, or white, and hang for display.

Tiny Box Ornaments. Wrap some tiny boxes with Christmas paper. Tie them with colored string, attach a hook, and hang.

Toothpick Ornament Ball. Poke toothpicks into a plastic foam ball or cork so the toothpicks stick out on all sides. Insert a bent pipe cleaner into the ball for a hanger. Dip the ornament into thinned tempera paint. Sprinkle glitter over the ornament while the paint is still wet. Hang. *Another way to do it:* Instead of dipping the ornament into paint, spear the ball or cork all over with colored toothpicks and hang.

Toothpick and Tape Ornament. Cut a six-inch strip from a roll of masking tape. Stick colored toothpicks crossways along the length of tape. Lay the ornament down with the toothpick side facing up and place another six-inch length of tape on top of the toothpicks, matching the tape on the other side. Now the toothpicks are sandwiched crossways between the two pieces of tape!

Spread glue on the tape one side at a time. Sprinkle glitter over the glued areas. Drape the ornament over tree branches, or poke an ornament hanger through one end and hang from the tree.

Tree Cone. Roll an 8-by-12-inch sheet of paper or colored foil diagonally, beginning at one corner. Paste the leftover edge to the inside of the cone. Decorate with paper scraps, gummed stars, etc. Attach a paper strip handle to the open end and hang.

Reindeer

Paper Reindeer Head. Using brown paper, cut out a large rectangle. Set the paper in front of you so the short ends are at the top and bottom. Fold the lower corners of the rectangle together until they touch, and staple them in place. Flip the paper over, making sure the pointed end remains down. This is the reindeer's head.

From scrap paper, cut out eyes and a nose; glue them to the face. For antlers, twist pairs of pipe cleaners into antler shapes and glue them to the head.

Reindeer Puppet. Use a brown paper bag to make your reindeer puppet. Lay the bag in front of you so the folded bottom is at the top end and faces you. Cut out eyes and a nose from black paper. Glue these pieces on the folded bottom of the bag and use a felt-tip marker to draw in the mouth.

For antlers, trace around each of your hands on a sheet of brown paper. Cut along the outlines and glue them to the reindeer head.

Cut dots from white paper and glue them to the "chest" area of the reindeer. (You can make the puppet Rudolph by gluing on a red nose.)

Santas

Apple Santa Claus. Collect three large marshmallows, five toothpicks, two red jelly beans, two black jelly beans, a large red gumdrop, two cloves, a candy heart, some cotton, and one large red apple.

Cut two of the marshmallows in half sideways. For each arm, spear a toothpick through a red jelly bean and then through a marshmallow half. Poke each arm into position on the apple with the marshmallow touching the surface of the apple.

For the feet, spear a toothpick through a black jelly bean and then through a marshmallow half. Attach the feet to the apple.

For the head, glue the remaining whole

Apple Santa Claus

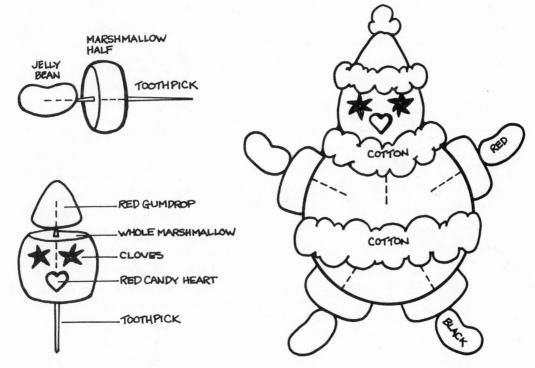

marshmallow on top of the apple. Stick cloves in for eyes, a red candy heart for a nose, and set the large red gumdrop on top for a hat.

Glue cotton around the waist and around the base of the head for trim. The apple-Santa is ready for display!

Circle Santa. Cut a circle about the size of a large coffee can lid from red paper. Paste it on a sheet of green background paper. This is the head.

For a beard, cut out eight or nine circles of white paper. Make each circle about the size of a small jar lid. Cut each of these circles into spirals. Glue the inside end of each spiral to the lower edge of the head circle. Pull out the spirals to form a beard.

Glue a small circle on top of the head for a hat pompon. Glue two half circles on the face for eyes and an upside-down half-circle for a mouth. To finish, stick a gold gummed star on each eye.

Cylinder Santa. Make a cylinder by rolling a piece of construction paper into a wide tube and stapling the ends together. Set the cylinder on its end in front of you. Staple a red triangle along

the top front of the head for a hat. Glue on strips of white paper for a beard and hair. Glue paper eyes, nose, and mouth cutouts to the face.

Paper Plate Santa. Cut out a red paper triangle. Paste it on the top part of a paper plate for Santa's hat. Color in the eyes, nose, and mouth. Glue on cotton tufts for a beard and for the trim at the base of the hat.

Santa Collage. Collect some cotton, buttons, scraps of paper, and other collage materials. Glue the materials on paper any way you want to form a picture of Santa's head.

Santa Cookie Jar. Obtain a coffee can or oatmeal box and cover it with white paper. From red paper, make a cone hat that fits down over the top of the can. Make nose, eyes, and mouth cutouts from paper and glue them to form a face on the side of the can. Glue on cotton eyebrows and a beard. Lift the hat and place cookies, candies, or other Christmas goodies inside.

Star-Shaped Santa. Cut out a large five-pointed star from a 9-by-12-inch sheet of red

Star-Shaped Santa

construction paper. This is Santa's body.

Next, from a 2½-by-2½-inch square of pink paper, cut out a circle. This is the face. Paste it on the top point of the star. Draw in facial features.

Using a black felt-tip marker, draw a belt and buckle across the middle of the star. Draw on details to make the top outside points of the star into hands. The bottom two points become boots.

To make a beard, spread some glue on the bottom of the face where the beard should go. Stick cotton on the glued area to complete the beard. Smear a little more glue on the top point of the star and stick on a small cotton tuft to make the top point above the face look like a hat.

Poke a hole above the head and string through a piece of yarn for hanging.

Stained-Glass Windows

Cellophane Window.   Cut out many small shapes such as trees, stars, candles, bells, etc., from a sheet of black construction paper. Use the entire surface of the paper, cutting the shapes fairly close to one another. Tape a piece of colored cellophane behind the sheet of paper. Fasten the sheet of paper to a windowpane with the cellophane side facing the window. Notice how the light shines through the colored cellophane shapes!

Crayon-Resist Window.   With a black crayon draw a church window on a piece of white paper. Then color heavily inside the window outline, using bright colors, to make it look like stained glass. Paint over the entire picture with thinned black tempera paint for a beautiful and effective stained-glass look.

Crayon Shavings Window.   Using a potato peeler, shave several colors of crayons onto one side of a 9-by-12-inch sheet of waxed paper. Fold the sheet and press it with a warm iron to melt the crayon shavings inside. (Ask an adult for help, if needed.)

Then fold a 9-by-12-inch sheet of construction paper in half. Hold it in front of you like a book. On the front, cut out the shape of a church window. Glue the waxed paper sheet to the inside of the window outline so the melted crayon colors show through like stained glass!

Tissue Window.   From several sheets of colored tissue paper, cut out a large number of small strips. Paste the tissue strips to a sheet of tracing paper in irregular, overlapping patterns. Cover the sheet completely with the strips. Then place the paper under heavy books until the glue has dried. Remove the sheet and fasten it to a window so the light shines through the pretty colors.

Wrapping Paper Window.   Find a sheet of Christmas wrapping paper with a stained-glass window pattern or other colorful design. Tape the paper to a window. When the light shines through, the paper will create a stained-glass effect.

Trees
Card Tree.   On a bulletin board or large sheet of background paper, pin or glue old Christmas cards in rows to form the shape of a Christmas

tree. Use five cards for the bottom row, four cards for the row above that, three cards for the next, two after that, and one card on top. Place one more card underneath the bottom row to form a tree stump.

Collage Tree. Draw the outline of a Christmas tree on a piece of white paper. Cut out odd shapes from various shades of green paper. Paste the pieces in a collage within the outline of the tree, frequently overlapping them to create a filled-in effect.

Cone Tree. Cut a half circle from a sheet of green construction paper. Decorate it by gluing on ornaments made from colored scrap paper. Form the half circle into a cone shape and staple; glue a paper star on top.

Crayon-Resist Tree. Using bright crayons, outline a Christmas tree on paper. Color in ornaments and other tree decorations. Be sure to press very hard while coloring. Brush over the entire tree with thinned tempera paint.

Cut and Paste Tree. On a large piece of paper, outline a tree. Paint in the greenery, the star on top, etc., and allow to dry.

From pieces of colored paper, cut out small ornaments and paste them on the tree. Glue on colored sequins for bulbs and short lengths of rickrack for garland.

Egg Carton Tree. Cut out several rows of eggcups from cardboard egg cartons. Make sure the first row contains six cups. The second row should contain five cups, the third row four cups, and so forth, through to the last row, which should have only one cup.

Glue the first and longest row near the bottom edge of a sheet of background paper so the eggcups are upside down. Mount the second row on the paper, centered above and next to the row below. Mount the third row in a similar way above the second row and continue adding rows until the single-cup section is mounted on top,

Egg Carton Tree

completing the shape of a Christmas tree.

Paint the protruding eggcups different colors to represent bulbs and lights. Paint the rest of the egg carton sections green. If you want, you can also glue on small colored Christmas beads and glitter. To finish, color in a brown trunk under the tree.

Felt-Board Tree. If you do not have a felt board, make one of your own. Wrap a large piece of felt around a sturdy piece of cardboard. Glue the felt to the cardboard from behind.

From a piece of green felt, cut out a large tree. Cut out decorations for the tree—ornaments, bulbs, a star, etc.—from scraps of bright-colored felt. Place the tree on the felt board. Notice how it sticks to the board! Then stick the decorations onto the tree. You can change the decorations any time you want!

Lighted Bulb Tree. Cut out a Christmas tree from green construction paper. Using a hole punch, make holes all over the surface of the tree.

Cut a piece of red tissue paper into the same shape and size as the tree. Glue the tissue paper on one side of the tree. Tie a piece of string through a hole at the top of the tree. Hang the tree in a window with the tissue paper side facing the window. When light shines through the window, the tree will appear to have lighted bulbs!

Live Miniature Tree.   Ask an adult if you can buy a small real Christmas tree to give to a shut-in or a retirement home. Make small ornaments, paper chains, and popcorn strings to hang on the tree.

Add a few pinecones that have been dipped in glue and rolled in glitter. Finish with a ribbon and bow decoration at the base. Ask an adult to help you deliver the tree.

Milkweed Pod Tree Mosaic.   This activity has to be planned well ahead of time. In the fall, collect milkweed pods that have shed their silk. This will allow them plenty of time to dry.

When Christmas nears, paint the dry milkweed pods silver, green, or gold. On a sheet of construction paper, or on a bulletin board, draw a large triangle. Pin the milkweed pods within the triangle. This tree is especially fun because you can feel it as well as see it!

Oatmeal Box Tree.   Cut an oatmeal box in half between the top and bottom. Set the top half aside and use the bottom half as a tree trunk. Glue a piece of brown paper around the trunk piece.

Form a cone from a half circle of green construction paper and place it open side down on the tree trunk. This forms the tree. Glue a paper chain to the tree around the outside of the cone.

Paper Circle Tree.   Stand an empty thread spool on end so the hole in the center is on top. Insert a full-length pencil into the spool hole, pointed end up.

Next, cut out eight or nine circles of green paper. Start by making a small circle first. Then make each following circle larger than the one before it. Mark the center of each circle with a pencil dot.

Poke the circles onto the pencil, starting with the largest circle on the bottom and ending with the smallest on top. Leave a little space between each of the circles. Decorate with felt or paper cutouts and glue on some glitter if desired.

Paper Ring Tree.   From cardboard, cut out a one-inch-wide strip. Bend it at three points to form a triangle. Glue or staple the ends of the strip together to hold the triangle in place.

Next, make paper rings of equal size in a variety of colors. Paste the rings in upright rows along the inside of the triangle. Fill the entire triangle with the rings.

For a base, glue an empty thread spool to the bottom of the triangle so the tree will stand up.

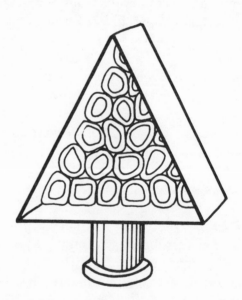

Pinecone Tree.   Paint a pinecone green so it will look like a Christmas tree. After the paint has dried, glue on small colored beads, sequins, ribbons, and glitter for decoration.

Pinecone and Grass Tree.   Prepare for this activity at least two weeks before the Christmas season. Sprinkle grass seeds on a pinecone.

Place the cone in a small dish. Sprinkle the cone with water from time to time. When the grass seeds sprout, the cone will look like a miniature Christmas tree!

Pleated Tree. Fold a piece of green construction paper into a pleated fan shape. Staple the fan together at one end.

Glue the fan facing downward on a sheet of background paper. The stapled end should be at the top to form a tree. Glue on small pieces of colored paper for decorations. Cover the stapled top of the tree with a paper star. Draw the trunk on the paper below the tree.

Spatter-Paint Tree. Cut out a Christmas tree from black paper. Spatter or drip Christmas-colored tempera paint on the tree. (Be sure to put a piece of newspaper underneath to catch the excess splatter.)

Cover the spatter-painted tree with another piece of newspaper and press down. Then remove the newspaper and sprinkle glitter on the tree.

Standing Paper Tree I. Draw or trace two identical Christmas trees on a piece of green construction paper. Cut out the trees.

On the first tree, draw a straight line from the top down to the middle of the tree. Cut a slot along this line. On the second tree, draw a line from the bottom center up to the middle of the tree. Cut a slot along this line, too.

Decorate the trees by gluing on colored paper ornaments. Fit the second tree crossways over the first tree by connecting them at the slots. Place the tree on a nut cup base.

Standing Paper Tree II. Fold two 6-by-9-inch rectangles of green construction paper in half lengthwise. Slip one inside of the other so they are matched. Staple the two rectangles together along the fold. Cut along a diagonal line from the lower outside corner to the opposite corner at the fold. Now you have a tall triangle.

Cut slashes into the longest side of the triangle,

forming a side view of Christmas tree branches. Unfold the tree. Drip glue along the edges and sprinkle on some glitter. When the tree is dry place it in a standing position for display.

Tissue Tree. Using chicken wire, make a cone about 14 inches tall. This will be the frame for your tree. Next, obtain three or four packages of green tissue paper. Take out the paper and cut it into eight-inch squares.

Wad the squares of tissue paper loosely and stuff them into the openings in the chicken wire. Keep doing this until the tree is completely filled in. Use the tree as a table decoration.

Torn Paper Tree. Fold a piece of paper in half lengthwise. Tear the paper from the top inside corner at the fold to the outside bottom corner. Open the paper to reveal a Christmas tree shape. Paste on a brown tree trunk and decorate by pasting on ornaments cut from colored paper.

Triangle Tree. Cut out three equal-sized triangles from green paper. Glue them one above the other, slightly overlapping, on a sheet of background paper. Add on a paper trunk and a base.

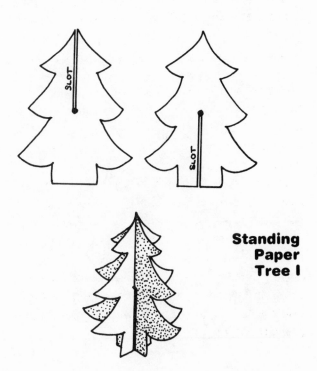

Standing Paper Tree I

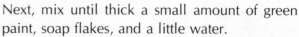

Wreaths

Crayon Wreath. With a crayon, draw a large circle on a sheet of paper. Then draw another, smaller circle inside the first one. Cut out the large circle and then cut out the small inner circle. Now you have a paper wreath! Color on some red berries and a green background.

Glitter Wreath. Draw a wreath on green construction paper. Cut it out. Spread glue over the surface of the wreath and sprinkle on a thick layer of gold or silver glitter. Press the glitter carefully all over to make sure it sets into the glue. Allow it to dry, shake off the excess glitter, and hang for display.

Macaroni Wreath. Using a paper plate as a base, glue some elbow or shell macaroni around the rim. Glue the macaroni pieces as close together as you can. Let the macaroni dry on the plate overnight.

The next day, spray the macaroni with gold or green paint. When the paint has dried, cut away the center portion of the paper plate and hang the wreath for display.

Nutshell Wreath. Cut out the center part of a paper plate, leaving a wreath shape. Glue different kinds of unshelled nuts on the wreath as close together as possible. Tie a pretty ribbon to the bottom. Hang the wreath on a door with a piece of colored yarn.

Paper Plate Wreath. First, cut out a circle from the center of a paper plate to form a wreath.

Next, mix until thick a small amount of green paint, soap flakes, and a little water.

Spread a thick coat of this mixture on the wreath. Press on colored buttons, seeds, beads, and other decorations. Allow it to dry. Make a bow from crepe paper or ribbon and glue it on the wreath.

Tissue Paper Wreath. Cut a wreath shape from a piece of poster board. Then, from green tissue paper, cut out many 2-by-2-inch squares. Wrap a square over your thumb and dip it into some paste. Next press this tissue "cap" on a spot on the wreath. Repeat this method until the entire wreath is covered.

Staple a red bow to the bottom of the wreath and tie a red string to the top. Paste a few red dots here and there for berries.

Torn Paper Wreath. From green paper, tear out four rectangular strips. Glue the strips together to form a square wreath.

For a bow, make a ring from red paper and glue it to the bottom part of the wreath. Paste a straight piece of red paper through the ring to complete the bow effect.

For a hanger, make another ring and glue one edge of it to the top of the wreath. For berries, crush small pieces of red tissue paper and glue them to the wreath. Hang for display.

Wreath Bow. Trace your hands on a sheet of red paper. Cut out the hand shapes. Place the hand shapes facing each other thumb-to-thumb. In this position, glue the hands to a wreath, ap-

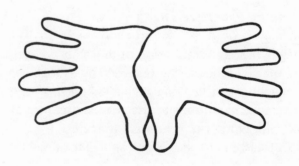

plying the glue along the thumbs of each hand-print. Allow them to dry. To add realism to the bow, bend the hand shapes outward slightly at the point where the thumbs join the hands.

Circus Fun

Activities
Circus Tray Guessing Game. Here is a game you can play with a friend! Place on a tray a number of items you might see at a circus. A clown hat, ball, popcorn box, balloon, whistle, peanut bag, and toy animal are good items. Ask your friend to study the items on the tray. Have him close his eyes while you remove one item from the tray. Ask your friend to guess which item was removed. Switch roles and play the game again.

Clown Dress Up. Turn yourself into a clown! Dress in a pair of baggy pants, a baggy shirt or blouse, and shoes that are too large for your feet. Put some makeup on your face and perform your own clown stunts.

Grandstand Play. Create a circus grandstand by setting up rows of chairs. Invite your friends to take part. Have them sit in the chairs to watch circus acts performed by you and your friends. One person can pretend he is selling popcorn, and another can pretend he is selling balloons.

Lion Tamer Act. Choose one person to be the lion tamer. The others become the lions. Give the lion tamer a yarn whip, a chair, and a hat. The tamer then orders the lions to sit, roll over, lie down, and do other tricks. Take turns being the lion tamer.

Popcorn Catch. This game requires the supervision of an adult. Place a large, clean sheet in the center of the room and set an electric popcorn popper in the middle of it. Have everyone sit in a circle around the edges of the sheet. Start the popcorn popper, leaving off the lid.

While the corn is popping, allow it to jump out of the popper. Try to catch the corn as it pops out! But be careful, sometimes the kernels might be a little hot! Eat what you can catch!

Ringmaster Game. Have everyone form a circle. Choose one player to stand in the middle as the circus ringmaster.

The ringmaster states the name of an animal. Everyone else must imitate that animal as they move around in a circle. Take turns being the ringmaster!

Tightrope Walk. Place a long piece of rope on the floor in a straight line. Try to walk on the rope without "falling off."

Art
Cardboard Circus Animals. Draw lions, tigers, elephants, and other circus animals on pieces of lightweight cardboard. Color in the features of the animals with crayons or felt-tip markers. Cut out the animals. Attach clip-style clothespins to the animals for legs, and stand them up.

Cardboard Tube Clown. Cover a short cardboard tube with a piece of white paper. Stand the tube on one end. Draw a face on the top end using a felt-tip marker. For the hair, paste paper strips or pieces of yarn around the top end. Make a small paper cone from colored paper and place it on top of the tube for a hat. Glue paper ruffles around the bottom.

Circus Wagon Picture. On a 6-by-9-inch sheet of paper, draw some circus animals, or paste on circus animal pictures cut from magazines. Cut out six strips of black paper, a half inch wide and six inches long. These strips are the bars for the circus wagon. Paste them in an upright position along the length of the animal picture so the animals appear to be behind the bars. Glue two red circles at the bottom corners of the picture. Now you have a circus wagon! Make a series of them to form a circus train if you want.

Clown-Face Balloon.   First, inflate a balloon and tie it so the air stays inside. Then, using a felt-tip marker, draw a clown face on the balloon. Make many of them if you are having a circus party.

Cut and Paste Clown Face.   Cut a large circle from a piece of white construction paper. Then, from a piece of bright paper, cut out a large triangle. Glue the triangle to the top part of the circle. Now you have a hat resting on top of the clown's head!

   From other pieces of paper, cut out funny features and paste them on the circle to finish the clown's face.

Mural.   Draw a circus scene on a piece of butcher paper or brown wrapping paper. Perhaps you can show three rings and a grandstand full of spectators. Draw in the circus acts, clowns, circus animals, etc. Do not forget the cotton candy stand!

Paper Balloon.   From a piece of paper, cut out a large round circle for a balloon. Paint it or color it with crayon. Poke a hole near the edge and tie on a string to finish. (Small paper balloons make good party favors!)

Paper Clown.   Use a paper plate for a head and a paper triangle for a hat. Glue them together and paste paper cutouts on the plate for facial features. For a body, glue together two squares of colored paper. Fasten the head to the body with a paper fastener. Fold four paper strips accordion-style, then paste them to the body for arms and legs.

Paper Plate Circus Ring.   Paint two paper plates in bright colors. When dry, glue six drinking straws around the rim of one plate. They should be upright and equal distances apart. These are the pillars for the circus ring. Glue the second paper plate on top of the pillars to make a roof. Later, play with small plastic people and animals in the circus ring.

Paper Clown

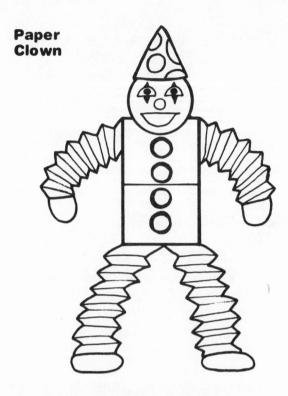

Paper Plate Circus Ring

Portrait "Balloons."   Cut out some large circles from colored construction paper to represent balloons. On another piece of paper, draw some faces. These can either be faces of people you know or imaginary faces. Cut out the faces and glue each to a paper balloon. Paste the balloon shapes to background paper and use crayons to draw balloon strings.

Shoebox Circus Wagon.   Paint a shoebox and lid with enamel paint. Paint both the inside and outside of each piece.

From heavy corrugated cardboard, cut out four wheels. Each wheel should be about 2½-inches across. Paint the wheels.

Poke a hole near each side corner of the shoebox. Fasten the wheels to the shoebox by poking paper fasteners through the wheels and into the shoebox holes.

Clay

When you work with clay, always cover your work table with newspapers. To use the clay, break up the sticks and roll the clay into balls. When you are finished, store your clay in plastic buckets with lids or keep it in plastic bags sealed with twisties.

You can pinch, roll, break, and smooth clay, but you should never strike clay against anything. Remember, always clean up when you are finished! Use a small ball of clay to pick up the tiny clay crumbs left on the table.

Some recipes for making your own homemade clay follow:

Baker's Clay. Mix 2 cups of flour with 1 cup of salt. Add about a cup of water until the dough becomes stiff. If desired, add some food coloring while mixing.

Mold the clay into an object or figure. When finished, set it aside for drying. It will harden in the air. You can speed up the hardening process by baking the clay at 350 degrees for about one hour. Time depends on the size and thickness of object.

Cornstarch Clay. Mix 1 cup of cornstarch and 1 cup of baking soda in a saucepan. Carefully add 1¼ cups of cold water. Cook over medium heat, stirring constantly, until the mixture looks like mashed potatoes. Then empty the mixture onto an empty plate. Cover with a damp cloth and allow to cool. When cooled, knead the dough.

This clay can be molded, rolled, squeezed, flattened, and shaped. When dry, the clay can be painted.

Sand Clay. Sift some sand and measure out 1 cup. In an old saucepan, mix together the sand, ½ cup of cornstarch, and ¾ cup of cold water. (Use an old saucepan because the sand might scratch it.)

Cook over medium heat for five to ten minutes, or until the mixture is thick. Stir constantly.

Place the dough on a paper towel. Cover the dough with a damp paper towel, and let it cool. Then knead the dough until it is smooth and soft.

Mold or roll out the dough as desired. When you are finished modeling, allow the clay figure to dry for about two days. Store any unused clay in an airtight container.

Sawdust Clay. Add white glue or wallpaper paste to sawdust until you have a mixture that holds together. Shape the mixture into a sculpture and allow it to dry.

Clocks

Circle Clock. Cut 12 two-inch squares from colored construction paper. Then round off the corners of the squares to form circles.

On a 12-by-12-inch square of white construction paper glue the circles to form a large circle. Number the circles like those on the face of a clock. Poke a hole in the middle of the clock face.

From black construction paper, cut two arrow-shaped strips for clock hands. Using a paper fastener, attach the hands to the center of the clock. Now you can point the hands to the time of day!

Paper Plate Clock. Paint or color in the numbers 1 through 12 around the outside rim of a paper plate to make a clock face. Cut out hands from black construction paper; fasten them to the middle of the clock with a paper fastener.

Clouds

Blotto Cloud. Fold a piece of blue paper in half and then open it up. Pour a small blob of white paint in the crease, then close the paper once more. Press the paper gently. Open again to reveal a cloud against a blue sky!

Cotton Clouds.   Spread some glue on a sheet of blue paper. Press on cotton balls or tufts of cotton and shape into clouds.

Cut-out Clouds.   Cut out cloud shapes from white, gray, and black pieces of paper. Glue them on a sheet of blue paper.

Shaving Cream Clouds.   Spread some shaving cream on a sheet of blue construction paper. Form the soapy cream into cloud shapes. For sunset clouds, sprinkle on some dry pink tempera paint. For storm clouds, sprinkle on some dry gray tempera paint. Enjoy your shaving cream clouds, because they will not last too long!

Sponge-Painted Clouds.   Dip the end of an old sponge into some white paint. Dab the paint on blue paper to form clouds.

Clouds (Science)

Clouds form in the sky when warm, moist air meets cooler air. Here are some ways to make your own clouds at home.

Breath Cloud.   On a cold day, go outdoors and blow in the air. See your breath? You have made a cloud!

Glass Jar Cloud.   Pour some hot water into a large glass jar. Cover the jar with a large chunk of ice. Watch what happens! As the warm, damp air inside the jar rises and meets the cool air near the ice, the warm air cools and turns into clouds. (Fog is formed the same way. Fog is a cloud that has come down to the ground.)

Jug Cloud.   Find a half-gallon or gallon-sized jug and a stopper that has a small hole in it. Rinse out the jug with warm water. Plug the jug with the stopper.

Now, blow air into the jug through the hole in the stopper. Blow as much air inside as you can! Then cover the hole with your finger. Do not let the air out! Next, pull out the stopper quickly. Do you see the cloud form inside the jug?

Smog Cloud.   Ask an adult to help you with this one or to watch over you while you do it. Use the same jug as in the experiment above.

Rinse out the jug once more with warm water. This time, drop some lighted matches into the jug. Quickly put in the stopper, and blow air into the jug through the hole in the stopper. Then, quickly remove the stopper.

See? The cloud is thicker than before! It has mixed with smoke to make smog. It is not good for us to breathe smog. Why? What other things mix in the air to make smog?

Collages

Collages are made by gluing flat or nearly flat pieces of material on a background. Sometimes collages can be made into a picture or design. Some collages are completed by adding drawn or painted details to the artwork.

Adhesive Materials Collage.   Use gummed stars, stickers, paper reinforcements, labels, old stamps and gummed dots to make a collage.

Alphabet Collage.   Find the initials for your name in large letters in a magazine or newspaper and cut them out. Glue them to the center of a piece of paper. Glue other, smaller alphabet letters around the initials in any way you want.

Bean Collage. Collect many different kinds of dried beans. Glue them onto cardboard to form a picture or design.

Carpenter Collage. Make a collage from wood shavings, sawdust, bits of sandpaper, and small nails. Glue them on cardboard.

Cereal Collage. Glue pieces of different kinds of dry cereal to paper, making a collage, picture, or design.

Circle Collage. Cut out paper circles in different sizes and colors. Glue the larger circles on a sheet of paper. Then glue the smaller circles on top of the larger ones. Finish with the smallest circles on top. Repeat, using different shapes.

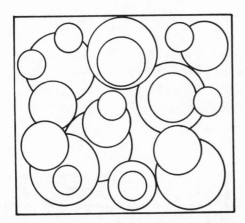

Collage Rubbing. Fold a large sheet of construction paper in half the short way, then open it up. On the right-hand side of the crease, glue together a collage of flat items such as paper clips, toothpicks, rubber bands, pennies, and bits of thick paper.

When the collage has dried, fold it back into a booklet. On the front ''page,'' rub a crayon firmly over the surface, using the flat side of an unwrapped crayon. As you rub, you can feel the objects on the page underneath. What do you see on the front when you are finished?

Color Collage. Glue scraps of bright paper into a collage on a black or dark-colored piece of construction paper.

Crazy Picture Collage. Look through some old magazines, newspapers, and catalogs for pictures of objects. But when you cut out the picture, just cut out part of it! The crazier it looks, the better it is!

Glue the bits and pieces of pictures on a large piece of paper. Try to make a complete picture from all the bits and pieces. It might look silly. It might look impossible! But it is fun!

Fabric Collage. Gather some pieces of yarn, lace, cotton balls, and different kinds of fabrics. Glue them into a collage on a piece of cardboard.

Funny Shapes Collage. Fold a piece of paper in half. Starting near one end of the folded side, cut into the crease with scissors. Cut a wiggly pattern, making sure to stay within the borders of the paper until you are done. Then cut your way out of the paper from the folded edge at the opposite end from where you started.

Unfold the paper and paste the wiggly cut-out shape on a sheet of colored background paper. Repeat this process several more times with other pieces of folded paper. Glue all the shapes to the background paper to make a collage.

Glass Collage. Collect old, worn pieces of colored beach glass that do not have sharp edges. A beach is a good place to find this type of glass. Be very careful about what you pick up. When you have collected enough, cover the inside of a plastic lid with thinned white glue. Allow the glue to set for about 10 minutes, or until the glue becomes sticky. Then arrange the bits of glass close together in the lid and allow the collage to dry.

Grass Collage. Collect blades of grass. Then go indoors and spread some glue on a sheet of construction paper. Dip the pieces of grass into paint, then press with a piece of scrap paper to the paper.

Magazine Collage. Cut colorful magazine pages into many different shapes. Arrange the shapes on a sheet of paper, forming whatever kind of design you want. Then glue the pieces into place.

Monster Collage. On a large, sturdy piece of cardboard, draw the outline of a monster. Then look around the house for things to fill in the monster outline. Egg carton cups, plastic utensils, aluminum foil balls and strips, buttons, colored paper, and bottle caps are all good materials to collect.

Glue the materials inside the outline of the monster to make him look however you want. Using your imagination, make the scariest monster you can!

Nature Scene Collage. Find a large picture of a nature scene. It can show the countryside, the mountains, the seashore, the desert, or whatever else you like. Mount the picture on a sturdy piece of cardboard.

Next, look around for things you can glue to the picture to give it realism. For instance, salt can be used for snow or cotton for clouds. Fine sand can be glued over the beach part of a seashore scene. Twigs can cover pictures of trees and dry moss can be used for tree leaves or bushes. Pieces of sandpaper can be used for desert or beach scenes. Use your imagination, and anything else you can find, to make your picture jump right out at you!

Nutshell Collage. Glue unshelled nuts of different sizes and shapes into a collage on a piece of cardboard. You can also make mosaics and sculptures with unshelled nuts.

Paper Collage. Hunt for as many different kinds of paper as you can find. Collect thin pieces, thick pieces, smooth pieces, and rough pieces. Look for candy wrappers, pieces of shiny foil, and pieces of waxed paper, tissue paper, and crepe paper. Gather the pieces in a variety of colors. Then glue them all on a large, strong piece of paper to form a pattern or picture of anything you like.

People Collage. From newspaper pictures and ads, cut or tear out pictures of people. Glue them together in any way on background paper to form a collage. *Another way to do it:* Tear out shapes of arms, legs, hands, feet, body, head, and neck from pieces of paper. Paste the parts together on a sheet of paper to form a person. You can also cut the body part pieces from magazine pictures, mix them up, and glue them back together to form people.

Pine Needle Collage. Mix some green finger paint with nontoxic wallpaper paste until the mixture is thick. Make a finger painting on a sheet of paper. While the paint is still wet, press some pine needles into the paint, forming a collage.

Popcorn Collage. Pop some fresh popcorn. Eat some of it while gluing the rest into a collage on a piece of paper.

Nutshell Collage

Ribbon Collage. From a box of scrap ribbons and gift wrap, pick out pieces of different sizes, shapes, colors, and textures. Glue them on a sheet of black construction paper. Make a beautiful collage, design, or picture this way.

Scrap Collage. In this collage, use odd bits of any kinds of material you can find! Buttons, seeds, cloth, ribbon, macaroni, beans, rice, yarn, paper, twigs, leaves, and anything else you can think of can be used. Glue the items to form a collage on a piece of cardboard.

Spaghetti Collage. Tape or pin a large piece of brown paper to a wall and spread newspapers underneath to cover the floor. Ask an adult to help you cook some spaghetti, but don't cook it all the way! When the spaghetti is *almost* done, let it cool just enough so it will not burn your fingers when you touch it.

Now, the fun starts! Throw the spaghetti at the paper on the wall, one piece at a time! Look! It sticks to the paper in crazy wiggly, squiggly ways! When it is done, allow the collage to cool. It will harden and last for a long time.

Stamp Collage. Buy some packs of colorful used stamps at a variety store, or peel off old stamps from household mail. Sort the stamps by color, using the different colors to form simple designs on a sheet of plain paper. Pink or orange stamps make good flowers. Green ones are good for leaves. Think of things to make from the other colors of stamps.

Texture Collage. Find materials with different kinds of surfaces. Paste them all together on background paper to make a design or picture. Tissue paper, sandpaper, onion paper, corrugated cardboard, plastic foam pieces, silk scraps, tin foil, carpet pieces, yarn, and wood shavings are good for starters. What other things can you think of to use?

Yarn Collage. On a large sheet of white cardboard, draw the outline of a big flower. Next,

find as many pieces of scrap yarn as possible. Glue down the pieces along the flower outline, filling in the petals, leaves, and stem.

For the middle of the flower blossom, lay down yarn in a spiral pattern within the petals and glue it into place.

Colors

Blow Painting. Ahead of time, get out three colors of food coloring—red, yellow, and blue. (These colors are called the *primary colors*.) In the middle of a piece of paper, put a drop of one of the colors. Next to that, put a drop of another color.

Aim a straw at one of the drops. Blow through the straw to make one of the drops move. Blow the drop so it runs into the other drop and the colors mix together. What new color did you make?

Repeat, blowing two different primary colors together on another sheet of paper to make a new color. Here are a few combinations you can try:

Red and Blue to make Purple
Red and Yellow to make Orange
Blue and Yellow to make Green

All the colors in the world are made from the primary colors combined in different ways!

Color Blots. Fold a piece of paper in half. Then open it up. Using an eyedropper, drop two primary colors of food coloring on the crease in the paper.

Fold the paper once more. Smooth it out to spread the colors together inside. Open it up one more time to see the new color.

Color Paste-Up Collage. Look through magazines for pictures showing a certain color. Cut out the pictures you find and paste them together to form a collage in one color. Make different collages using other colors.

Color Day. Pick out a day to be ''color day.'' On that day, select a color to be your official color for the day. Wear clothes that match the color, wash yourself with a washcloth that color, and dry yourself with a towel the same color. Use food coloring to make your food and drinks that color, and paint or color with crayons of that color.

Color Hanging. Cut a sheet of waxed paper into two equal-sized pieces. Brush some liquid starch on one side of each piece.

Sprinkle colored confetti or small pieces of colored paper on the starched side of one piece. Press the other sheet on top, starched side down.

Press the two sheets together gently, sealing them. Cut any shape you want from this paper. Poke a hole in the top. Tie a length of thread through the hole and hang it in the light where it can turn and show off its colors.

Color-Matching Worm Puzzle. Draw a large, curvy worm on a piece of paper. Cut out the worm. Then cut the worm into six equal sections, but keep him lined up in the proper order.

On each side of the first cut, color a large red dot. On each side of the next cut, color a large blue dot. On each side of the third, fourth, and fifth cuts, color in yellow, green, and purple dots.

Now, mix up the pieces. Put the worm puzzle back together again by matching the colors to each other.

Color Wheel. From an old magazine with colored pictures, cut out three circles—one red, one blue, and one yellow. Paste them equal

distances apart in a circular pattern on a sheet of paper.

Now, look through the magazine for the other colors that might fit between the three circles on the paper. Cut out circles of these colors and paste them into place so the colors gradually change in steps from one shade to another.

Finger Paint Colors. Place a primary color (red, blue, or yellow) of liquid tempera paint on paper. Spread it around with your fingers. Next, put an equal amount of another primary color on the same painting. Spread this color around into the first color. What new color is formed?

How Many Can You Find? In this game, pick out a color. Look around the room and see how many objects you can find in that color.

Tape Color Collage. Using strips of tape in different colors, make a collage on paper.

Which Color Is Gone? Play this game with a friend. Place four or five circles of colored paper in front of your friend. Make sure each circle is a different color. Remove one circle while your friend looks the other way. Ask him to guess which color is missing.

Next time, *you* guess which color is missing.

Columbus Day

Cut and Paste Ship. From a piece of dark construction paper, cut out a 9-by-4-inch rectangle.

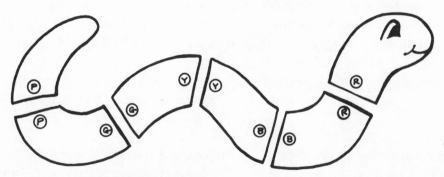

Color-Matching Worm Puzzle

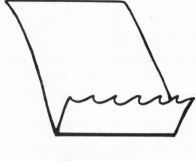

Cut away two bottom corners to form a boat.

Cut out two four-inch squares of white construction paper. Form these into sails.

Paste the boat piece on a 9-by-12-inch sheet of light blue construction paper. Paste the sails on the boat. Add a mast and other details using crayons or felt-tip markers. Draw in the ocean with waves around the ship. Draw Christopher Columbus standing on the ship.

Flat Earth or Round Earth? When Columbus lived, some people thought the world was flat! They believed that if they sailed very far out in the ocean, they would fall off the edge of the world!

Columbus proved they were wrong when he discovered America. Look at a globe (most libraries have them) and see how Columbus sailed from Portugal to America. (Have an adult show you if need be.) Read a book about how Columbus discovered America.

Playacting. Pretend you are Columbus discovering America. Act out sailing across the ocean, discovering new land, and meeting Indians. Why did Columbus call the natives he met *Indians*?

Three Ships Sailing. Fold up the bottom edge of a large sheet of white construction paper. Cut wave shapes along the edge.

On another sheet of paper, draw, color, and cut out three ships. Position them on the ocean picture so when you raise the ocean wave flap, it looks like the ships are sailing on the water. Paste the ships in place.

With crayons, color in other waves, clouds, birds in flight, and a shining sun.

Three Ships Sailing

Cooking

(Some of these recipes will require the help of an adult.)

Aggression Cookies. These cookies are made entirely with your hands! You do not have to use any spoons or mixers! And best of all, you can use all the energy you want in mixing the cookies with your hands! You will feel better afterward!

In a bowl, put the following ingredients:

3 cups oatmeal, uncooked
1½ cups white flour
1½ teaspoons baking powder
1½ cups brown sugar
1½ cups margarine (three sticks)

Mix and knead the ingredients with your hands. Continue until there are no more lumps of margarine.

Roll the dough into small balls. Place the balls on an ungreased cookie sheet. Flatten the balls with the bottom of a glass dipped in sugar. Bake for 10 to 12 minutes at 350 degrees.

Bird Nest Salad. Grate a carrot and mix the gratings with ½ cup canned Chinese noodles. Then add some mayonnaise to moisten the mixture.

Place a small mound of this salad on a plate. Press the mound in the middle with a spoon to form a nest. Add a few peas or grapes to the nest for "eggs," then serve.

Bologna-Cheese Biscuits. Obtain one roll of refrigerated biscuits, two slices of bologna, and two slices of cheese.

Cut the bologna and cheese into very small pieces. Break open the biscuits and place each one into the cup of a muffin pan.

Sprinkle the bologna and cheese pieces evenly over each biscuit. Bake at 450 degrees for 10 minutes until the biscuits rise and turn brown.

Butter Making. Pour some heavy cream into an empty baby food jar until the jar is half full. Seal the lid tightly. Shake the jar until the cream turns to butter! This takes about 15 minutes. It is fun to take turns shaking with a friend or family member. Open the jar and pour away the excess liquid. Add a small amount of salt and spread on crackers.

Cheese Chips (Nachos). This zesty Mexican side dish is easy to make! Place some taco or corn chips close together on a cookie sheet. Grate some Cheddar cheese and sprinkle over the chips. Place the chips in an oven at 350 degrees until the cheese melts. Remove and allow the chips to cool a little before eating them.

Cheese Cookies. In a bowl, mix a 5-ounce jar of processed cheese spread and three tablespoons of soft margarine.

Add ¾ cup of flour to the cheese, a little at a time. Mix well each time you add the flour. Then, on a piece of waxed paper, form the

dough into a roll about 5 inches long and 1½ inches thick. Wrap the roll of dough in waxed paper. Put the dough in the refrigerator for at least one hour. Then remove the roll and cut slices about a quarter inch thick from the roll. Place the slices on an ungreased cookie sheet.

Bake the cookies in the oven at 400 degrees for about 15 minutes, or until the edges are light brown. Remove the cookies from the baking sheet and allow them to cool.

These are better for you than sweet cookies!

Cloud Sandwich. This is a good snack for a rainy day. It is simple to make—spread some marshmallow cream between two graham crackers and serve!

Cookie Paint. Blend one egg yolk with ¼ teaspoon of water. Pour this mixture into three or four small containers.

Add a different color of food coloring to each container. Now you are ready to paint your cookies! It is easy! Just paint each cookie before you bake it using a small paintbrush dipped in your mixture. The "paint" works best on sugar cookie dough.

If the "paint" gets too thick, thin it with a few drops of water. Paint designs, pictures, faces, words, or whatever you want on the cookies. Then bake the cookies as directed.

Corn Chowder. This is especially yummy for lunch on a cold day. Carefully chop half a small onion into little pieces. Brown the onion in one tablespoon of margarine in a large saucepan.

Add 1 can of condensed cream of mushroom soup, 2 soup cans of milk, a 1-pound can of cream-style corn, and ½ tablespoon of salt. Simmer for 15 minutes, then serve in bowls.

Cranberry-Orange Relish. You will need adult help on this recipe. This is a nice dish to make at Thanksgiving or Christmas time. Beforehand, freeze a package of fresh cranberries. Cut two oranges into quarters. Be sure to leave the skins on! Discard any seeds. Then run the oranges, along with the frozen cranberries, through a food grinder. Mix in 2 cups of sugar and stir well. Chill in the refrigerator.

You can also give the relish as a gift! Divide it into several glass jars and wrap ribbons around the tops of the jars.

Crisp Noodle Chicken. Cut a whole chicken into pieces. Have an adult help you do this. Then place the chicken pieces in a shallow casserole dish in one layer.

Next, in a large bowl, mix 1 can of mushroom soup, 1 cup of sour cream, 3 tablespoons of onion soup mix, and ⅛ teaspoon of pepper. Spread this mixture over the chicken.

Bake uncovered in the oven for 1½ hours at 350 degrees. Then remove from the oven and sprinkle a 3-ounce can of chow mein noodles over the chicken. Return to the oven for 10 more minutes, then remove and serve.

Dog Kabobs. Cut up some cooked hot dogs into bite-sized pieces. Also cut up some cheese and pineapple into bite-sized chunks. Spear all the pieces with sandwich toothpicks and serve.

Easy Salad. Peel a banana and cut it into bite-sized pieces. Mix the banana pieces together with one 15-ounce can of fruit cocktail, one small can of mandarin oranges (drained), a mini-ature box of raisins, and one cup of miniature marshmallows. Serve.

Easy Soup. Assemble the following ingredients:

    1 small onion, chopped
    1 tablespoon butter
    1 can (1 lb., 13 oz.) chopped tomatoes, undrained
    1 16-ounce can of mixed vegetables
    3 cups water
    2 beef bouillon cubes
    ¼ teaspoon basil
    2 teaspoons salt

Sauté the onion in margarine over medium heat. Stir in the remaining ingredients. Mix well and bring to a boil, stirring often. Simmer for 25 minutes. Serves eight people.

Egg Twins. For this you need one hamburger bun, two eggs, two slices of cheese, two slices of tomato, and some butter.

Preheat the oven to 300 degrees. Split the hamburger bun and cut a hole in the center of each bun half. Make the holes large enough to hold one egg.

Spread butter on the buns, then lay the buns in a pan. Break an egg into the hole in each bun half. Bake for 15 minutes. Remove and top each bun half with a tomato slice and cheese slice. Then place under the broiler until the cheese melts. Serve at once.

Ironed Cheese Sandwich. You will need adult supervision to make this fun sandwich. Set up an ironing board and iron in the kitchen. Turn on the iron to a high setting. Next, spread soft butter or margarine on two slices of bread. Place a slice of cheese between the two slices of bread, but make sure the buttered sides are on the outside! Wrap the sandwich in foil.

Lay the foil-covered sandwich on the ironing board and set the hot iron onto the foil for two or three minutes. (This will toast the slice of bread facing up.) Then, lift the iron and turn the foil package over so the other side faces up. Set the iron on the foil again for two or three more minutes. Finally, turn the iron off and unwrap the sandwich. (Be careful, the sandwich is hot!) The sandwich is now toasted and ready to eat!

Macaroon Cookies. Preheat the oven to 350 degrees. Mix a 14-ounce package of shredded coconut, a 15-ounce can of sweetened condensed milk, and 2 teaspoons of vanilla. Spoon this onto a well-greased cookie sheet with a teaspoon. Bake for eight minutes.

Mixed Bean Salad. Obtain a small can of each of the following kinds of beans: green beans, yellow wax beans, kidney beans, and garbanzo beans. Drain all the beans and put them in a large bowl. Toss with some Italian dressing. Chill. It tastes even better if you make it the day before you are going to eat it!

Peanut Butter. Have an adult help with this recipe. Put a cup of shelled roasted peanuts and a tablespoon of vegetable oil in an electric blender. Replace the top and turn on the machine. Blend until the peanuts are finely chopped. Add another tablespoon of oil, if needed, and blend until the peanut butter becomes as smooth as you like it. Store any leftover peanut butter in the refrigerator—or it will spoil.

Pretzels. Mix 1 package of yeast, 1½ cups warm water, and 1 tablespoon sugar. Stir in 1 teaspoon salt and 4 cups flour.

Knead until smooth. Shape into pretzels. Brush with a beaten egg, and sprinkle on some coarse salt. Bake at 450 degrees for 12 to 15 minutes. Serve warm or cooled.

Pudding Cookies. In a bowl, mix ¾ cup of biscuit baking mix, one small package of instant pudding mix (any flavor), ¼ cup of salad oil, and 1 egg.

Shape the dough into small balls. Place them on an ungreased cookie sheet. Flatten the cookies with the bottom of a glass dipped in

sugar. Bake in a preheated oven at 350 degrees for 8 minutes. Makes two to three dozen cookies.

Pumpkin Pudding. For this you need the following: 1 pack of instant vanilla pudding, 1 cup of whole milk, and 1 cup of pumpkin pie filling.

Mix the pudding and milk according to the package directions. Stir in the pumpkin pie filling. Pour into dessert dishes. Let stand for a few minutes until firm. Then eat! (Be sure to use pumpkin pie filling, *not* plain canned pumpkin in this recipe.)

Shape Sandwich. First, find some cookie cutters in interesting shapes (animals, holiday shapes, etc.). Second, obtain a slice of bologna, a slice of cheese, and two slices of day-old bread.

With the cookie cutter, cut out the shape from the bologna, cheese, and both pieces of bread. Spread a little mayonnaise on the bread cutouts, then match all the parts together to form a shape sandwich! *Another way to do it:* Cut a sandwich into basic shapes after it has been put together. Circles and triangles are good shapes to start with. What other shapes can you make from a sandwich?

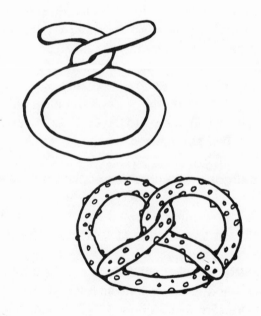

Pretzels

Shaped Cinnamon Toast. Mix 1½ teaspoons of cinnamon and ½ cup of white or brown sugar. Next, place several slices of day-old bread on a cookie sheet. Place the bread slices under the broiler so they will toast on only one side. Remove them and cut them into shapes using cookie cutters.

Spread softened butter over the untoasted sides. Sprinkle on the cinnamon mixture. Put the toast shapes back under the broiler so the untoasted sides now become toasted. Remove and enjoy!

Turtle Burger. The next time you are having hamburgers for a meal you can make them look like turtles! You need one olive and five short, raw carrot sticks for each hamburger.

Stick the carrot sticks into the sides of the bottom bun to form the feet and the tail of the turtle. Poke an olive on a toothpick and stick it into the top bun for a head. Place the meat patty in between, and dress the hamburger any way you like.

Yummy Chili. Brown 1 pound of hamburger with a tablespoon of dried onion in a pan. Drain the excess grease after the hamburger is browned.

Add in the contents of a 1-pound can of pork and beans, a 16-ounce can of tomatoes (cut up), and 2 teaspoons of chili powder. Simmer the ingredients for 10 minutes. Serves four.

Crayon Art

Banded Coloring. Wrap a rubber band around three crayons. Draw with all three crayons at the same time!

Crayon Etching. Color very heavily over a piece of paper using different colored crayons. Be sure to press hard to make dark impressions. While coloring, make any shape or design you want. Be sure one color always meets another, leaving no white space in the area to be etched.

When your design is well colored, go com-pletely over the picture again with black crayon. Be sure to press heavily this time, too! When black crayon totally covers the picture, take an open paper clip and scratch away gently so only the black crayon etches away. This allows the original coloring underneath to show through where you have etched! Etch a new picture or design, moving the paper clip with any motion you want, in any direction you like.

Crayon Pressing. Sprinkle crayon shavings onto a sheet of white drawing paper. Cover the shavings with another piece of drawing paper. Carefully place the two sheets on a pad of newspapers.

Press the top drawing paper with a warm iron. Pull the sheets apart and see the design on both sides now!

Crayon Rubbing. A crayon rubbing is made by placing something with a textured surface (such as a leaf or a coin) underneath a sheet of paper, and then rubbing over the sheet of paper to make an impression of the object underneath.

Look around for things to place underneath the paper. Try to find things with highly textured surfaces to create interesting patterns in the rubbing.

Paper cutouts, burlap, sandpaper, pegboards, weathered boards, tiles, corrugated paper, wire screen, and even cement blocks will make good rubbings!

When you are ready to rub, place a piece of paper over the rubbing material. Using a crayon with the wrapper removed, rub over the paper with the flat side of the crayon. See the pattern appear on the paper?

Cupcake Pan Crayons. Line the cups of a cupcake pan with pieces of foil and then fill with old crayon bits. Make sure all the wrappers are removed! Each cup should contain crayon bits of a similar color. Or, you can fill each cup with two or three different colors, as long as each color is clustered separately within the cup and not blended together.

When all the cups are filled, place the cupcake pan in an oven at 300 degrees until all the crayon bits have melted. Remove and allow to cool. Then, tip your new, large-sized crayons out of the cups. You will enjoy coloring with these giant crayons, especially the ones with a different color on each side. Have fun!

Melted-Crayon Designs. Dip a long piece of yarn into some liquid starch. Lay the yarn in a pattern or outline on a sheet of colored tissue paper. Carefully slip a piece of waxed paper under the tissue paper.

Next, grate or shave some old crayons (with the wrappers removed). Place the crayon shavings inside the yarn outline. When this is done, cover everything with another piece of waxed paper. On top of that put a sheet of newsprint.

Melt the crayons underneath by pressing the newspaper with a hot iron. Remove the newspaper and waxed paper before the melted crayons cool. Try to remove some of the crayons only partially melted to add depth and texture to your artwork. Trim the excess tissue from the design and hang it as a mobile in the light.

Natural Crayon Melt. Do this activity on a very hot day. Grate some old crayon stubs into fine shavings. Cut off a piece of waxed paper about 24 inches long. Fold the paper in half. Open it and lay it on a metal cookie sheet.

Sprinkle the crayon shavings on one side of the open paper. Fold the other side over the shavings. Place the cookie sheet outside in the direct sunlight. Watch what happens to the crayons after they have been in the sunlight for awhile!

Sandpaper Crayon Art. Color directly on sandpaper with old crayons, making pictures or designs. Try this using different grades of sandpaper.

Sandpaper Print. Place a piece of black sandpaper on a flat surface so the rough side faces up.

Color with crayon directly on the sandpaper. Be sure to press real hard!

Next, place a sheet of newsprint or construction paper over the sandpaper. With an iron set on medium heat, press over the newsprint paper. Lift the paper, turn it over, and see what has happened!

Crystals (Science)

Epsom Salt Crystals. Pour ¼ cup of water into a small saucepan. Heat the water on a hot plate. While this is heating, look closely at a few grains of Epsom salt using a magnifying glass. Notice the crystal shapes!

Next, drop 4 heaping tablespoons of Epsom salt into the heated water. Stir until all the crystals have dissolved. Remove the saucepan from the heat, and add two drops of musilage-type glue to the mixture.

With a cotton swab, wipe some of this mixture on a glass plate. Put the glass plate aside for about 20 minutes. Watch for the crystals to grow!

Look at the new crystals with the magnifying glass. Do they look the same as the ones you saw earlier? As the water evaporates from the glass plate, watch the Epsom salt crystals form a frost-like pattern on the glass.

Salt Crystal Examination. Sprinkle some grains of salt on a piece of black paper. Shake the paper gently to spread the salt grains apart.

With a magnifying glass, look at a grain of salt. You will see that it is actually a small crystal. Compare the shape of this grain of salt to the others on the paper. Are any of them alike? What shapes do you see?

Sugar Crystals. Set an ordinary drinking glass on the table. Cut off a length of string that is just a little longer than the height of the glass. Tie one end of the string to the middle of a pencil and tie the other end to a safety pin. Set the string assemblage aside.

Sugar Crystals

Pour a cup of water into a saucepan. With adult supervision, place the pan on a hot burner and heat the water to boiling. Slowly pour some sugar into the boiling water. Stir constantly while you watch the sugar dissolve. You should use a total of two to three cups of sugar.

Soon, you will have a pan full of hot syrup. Pour the syrup into the glass on the table. Lower the weighted string into the syrup. Lay the pencil across the mouth of the glass so the string hangs in the glass permanently.

Allow the glass to sit undisturbed for two days. Then look to see if any crystals have grown along the length of string. If they have, they will probably look something like rock candy! Study the crystals through a magnifying glass.

Designs

Colored Tape Design. Near Christmas time, stores sell colored cellophane tape. Pick up some to use year-round for making designs. Stick different lengths and colors of the tape on paper to make interesting designs. Shorter strips usually work best because they are less likely to twist and stick to themselves.

Fingertip-Painted Yarn Design. Cut some slits in several places along the edges of a piece of cardboard. Hook a piece of yarn across the cardboard, from one slit to another, forming a design.

Next, dip a finger into some paint. Make fingertip prints in the spaces created by the yarn design. Use a different color of paint in each area of the design.

Mondrian Art. When you finish this design, it will resemble paintings done by the artist Mondrian.

Cut a sheet of black construction paper into one-inch-wide strips of different lengths. Glue the strips on a sheet of paper to form a design. Glue some of them horizontally across the paper. Glue others vertically. Color in the spaces between the strips with different colors of crayon.

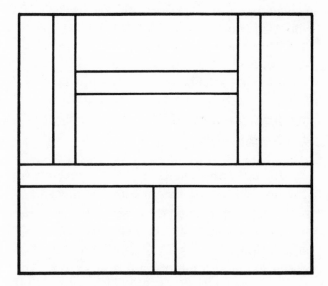

Ruler Designs. Using a ruler, draw many straight lines at random on a sheet of paper. Color the spaces between the lines with various colors of crayon.

Shaker-Top Designs. Save the shaker top from the next empty seasoning bottle. Use the top and a pencil to make dot patterns on a piece of paper.

Texture Design. Lay a piece of net, burlap, or plastic doily on a sheet of paper. With a brush, paint over the material. Then carefully lift it to reveal a painted design underneath.

Toothpick Fun. Use a whole box of toothpicks to form large designs on your patio or sidewalk. When finished, be sure to pick up the toothpicks and save for another project.

Dinosaurs

Bone Construction. Most of what we know about dinosaurs has been learned from fossils found in the ground. Scientists have figured out what the dinosaurs looked like by putting fossil skeletons back together from some of these bones.

See if you can do the same thing! Search through a book, magazine, or coloring book for a diagram or picture showing the bone pieces fitting together to form a skeleton. Trace or copy all of the bones on a large sheet of paper. Cut out the pieces.

Now mix up the bones. Without looking again at the diagram, see if you can lay out the pieces into the shape of the dinosaur! Was it hard? Just imagine how hard it is for scientists!

Cardboard Dinosaurs. From a magazine or coloring book, cut out pictures of dinosaurs. Glue the cutouts to heavy cardboard. Then cut out the dinosaurs again. Use your cardboard dinosaurs for playing, making a dinosaur diorama, or making a crayon rubbing picture.

Dinosaur Collage. Draw or trace a dinosaur shape on a sheet of construction paper. Next, crush some eggshells, wash them off, and allow them to dry. Glue the crushed eggshells all over the area inside the dinosaur outline. Paint it later if you wish.

Dinosaur Diorama. In a terrarium, plant some miniature tropical house plants. Place some stones on the ground, plant some moss, and add

a few twigs to the setting. Place some toy plastic dinosaurs or cardboard dinosaurs (see earlier project) in the terrarium. Now you have a scene of the earth as it was millions of years ago! *Another way to do it:* Set up your landscape on a table. Draw a tropical background scene on a cardboard panel, and prop up the panel behind the dinosaurs.

Dinosaur Measurements. Do you realize just how big some of the dinosaurs really were? Read a book about dinosaurs to find out. Then go outside with a cloth measuring tape and a ball of string. Mark on the ground, using the string, the length of each dinosaur. Next, measure at a right angle from the length of string to see how tall each dinosaur was. Now you can truly ''see'' how big each dinosaur actually was!

Dinosaur Pictures. Study pictures of your favorite dinosaurs. On a sheet of paper try painting or coloring your own pictures of those dinosaurs. (Keep in mind no one really knows what colors they were.) Draw a background of lush tropical fern plants, perhaps with a volcano in the distance. If you want, arrange the pictures to form a book telling a dinosaur story.

Dinosaur Puzzles. Cut out pictures of dinosaurs from a coloring book or magazine. Mount the pictures on pieces of cardboard. Cut out the pictures again. Cut each dinosaur into puzzle-shaped pieces. Scramble the pieces and see if you can put the dinosaurs back together.

Make Your Own Fossil. From a piece of corrugated cardboard, cut out a dinosaur footprint. Set the footprint shape aside to use later.

Pour some plaster of Paris into a container. Stir enough water into the mixture to make it look like heavy cream. Pour the mixture into a disposable cake or pie pan.

Press the cardboard footprint shape into the soft plaster of Paris to make a dinosaur footprint. If you have enough room, make another print. When the plaster of Paris dries, you will have your own "fossil" footprint! *NOTE:* you can also make imprints of shells, leaves, and other objects this way. *Another way to do it:* Using your own hands or a scoop, hollow out a dinosaur footprint in the ground. Place a cardboard frame around the footprint. Dust over the print with some flour. Pour some plaster of Paris into the print hollow and let it dry. Later, remove the frame, pick up the mold, and turn it over. What do you see?

Dolls

Cardboard Dolls. From clothing store catalogs or magazines, cut out pictures of people. Paste the picture cutouts on pieces of cardboard. Allow to dry, then cut out the people again. Now you can play with your cardboard dolls!

Cardboard Doll House. Find a good, heavy-duty cardboard carton to use for making a doll house. Cut one of the long side panels away from the carton so you will be able to play with the house through the back.

Carefully, use a small paring knife to cut out doors and windows from the walls of the house. (Ask an adult for help, if necessary.) You do not really need a roof, but if you want one, make it from a panel of cardboard that can be removed or put in place as desired.

To make a two-story house, leave the solid roof intact on the bottom carton and stack another carton on top. Tape the cartons together along the outside.

Cut out small cardboard panels to make room

Cardboard Doll House

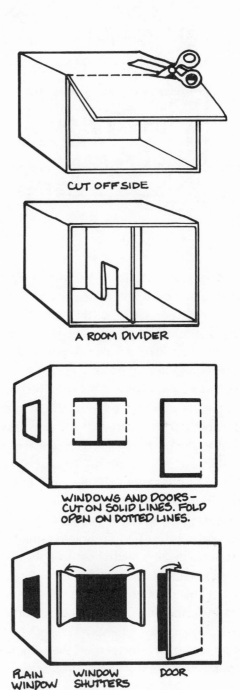

CUT OFF SIDE

A ROOM DIVIDER

WINDOWS AND DOORS—CUT ON SOLID LINES. FOLD OPEN ON DOTTED LINES.

PLAIN WINDOW   WINDOW SHUTTERS   DOOR

dividers for the doll house. Use tape to fasten the room dividers inside the house.

Paint the interior walls of the doll house with poster paints, or glue on pieces of cloth or wallpaper. Patterned contact paper also makes good wallpaper for your doll house.

Use small boxes, spools, jar lids, bottle caps, etc., for making miniature furniture. For instance, make a bed from an empty matchbox covered with a piece of cloth. Make bathtubs and tables from small gift boxes. Use fabric scraps to make rugs and curtains. Finish the doll house by painting the outside with poster paints.

Clothespin Doll. Old-fashioned, single-piece wooden clothespins with knobs at the top are perfect for making cute dolls.

Twist a pipe cleaner around the pin, just under the knob, to form arms. Wrap bits of cloth and material around the clothespin for clothes. Use a string or ribbon for a belt. Using a felt-tip marker, draw a face on the top knob.

Dancing Paper Doll. On a sturdy piece of paper, outline the parts you need for the doll—a head, upper arms, lower arms, upper legs, lower legs, feet, and hands. You can make most of these from oval shapes.

Cut out the pieces. Punch holes in each part where they are supposed to join each other. Hook together all the parts with paper fasteners. Tie a rubber band to the top of the head, and dangle the doll. Make it dance!

Doll Clothes. Here is an easy way to make doll clothes without sewing! Cut a head hole in the middle of a rectangle of cloth. Slip the cloth over the doll's head and tie the waist area with a sash. Make a blouse from a short rectangle and a dress from a long rectangle. Add pieces of ribbon for decoration, and use bottle caps or egg carton cups for hats.

Paper Boy-Girl Dolls. Cut an 8½-by-11-inch sheet of paper in half lengthwise. Take one of the halves and fold it up lengthwise, accordion-style. Leave about 2¼ inches between each pleat. (The last fold might be a little short.)

Set the folded piece of paper in front of you so the short ends appear to be on the top and bottom as you look at them. On the right-hand side of the paper make an outline of half a boy. On the left-hand side, make an outline of half a girl. Make their hands join in the middle (see illustration). Cut along the outlines, then pull the dolls open. Clip off the half doll at each end. Notice how the dolls alternate boy-girl along the strip! Make other boy-girl strips and tape them together to form a long chain.

Spool Doll. Collect three large spools, twelve small ones, and four shoestrings. Tie the four shoestrings together at one end, then string them all through a large spool (the head).

Underneath the head, separate the strings. Add three small spools to two strings for the arms. Tie a knot at the end of each arm to hold the spools on.

Now thread the other two strings through the two remaining large spools (the body). At the bottom, again separate the strings and add three more small spools to each string for the legs. Once more, tie a knot at each end to hold the spools on.

Paper Boy-Girl Dolls

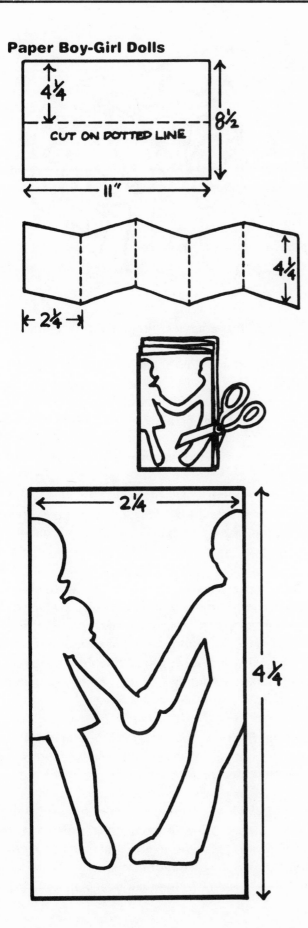

Paint a face on the top spool using water colors or nail polish.

Tissue Dolls. Crumple some pieces of tissue paper into a ball. Place the ball in the middle of a single square of colored tissue paper. Wrap the square around the ball to make a head. Make a twist at the bottom for a neck. Hold the twist in place with a trash bag twistie. Carefully mark the facial features on the head using a felt-tip marker.

Cut out a skirt from another piece of colored tissue. Wrap it around the base of the head. Fluff out the skirt, and the doll is finished!

Wooden Doll House People. You can make your own wooden doll house people similar to the ones you buy in the store!

First, collect some jumbo-sized wooden beads that have stringing holes through their centers. To make a wooden person, stack one bead on top of another, lining up the holes. Stick a short dowel inside with glue to hold the doll together. The bottom bead is the body, and the top bead is the head. Use a permanent felt-tip marker to draw hair and facial features on the head.

If you want, you can use a cylinder-shaped bead for the body and a round bead for the head. Or, you can experiment with different combinations to form dolls in all shapes!

Dragons

Chase the Dragon's Tail (Game). Every person lines up with his hands on the shoulders of the player in front of him. The first person in line is the dragon's head. The last person in line is the dragon's tail.

The lead player tries to catch the tail by running in a circle toward the tail player. The dragon's body twists and turns to keep the head away from the tail. When the head catches the tail, the head player drops out and the old tail becomes the new head. The game ends when only two players are left.

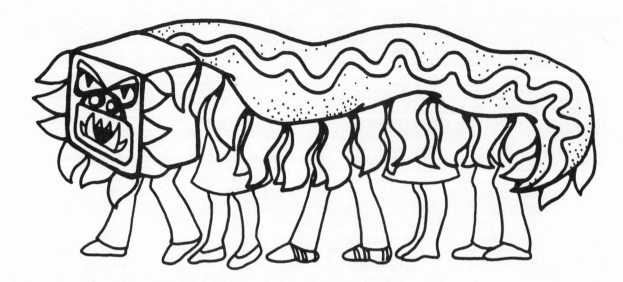

Chinese New Year Dragon. This is a large dragon you and your friends can make for a parade. Obtain a large box. On one side cut out a large mouth and eyes. Decorate the head with bright paint and colored construction paper cut-outs. Attach long curled paper strips to the head.

Next, make a tail from a very long, brightly colored piece of butcher paper. Glue one end of it from the top of the head box. Decorate the tail end with paper streamers.

When the dragon is finished, one person puts the box head over himself. The others stand under the paper tail and hold it over their heads. All together, walk the dragon in a parade!

Eggcup Dragon. Cut out a number of individual cups from a cardboard egg carton. Paint the cups green, purple, or any other colors that seem right for a dragon. Make one cup a dragon head.

Poke holes into the ends of all the cups. String the cups on a chenille stem to form a dragon. Bend the chenille stem in spots so the dragon body bends up and down along its length. Make him as long as you want!

Mashed Potato Dragon. Adult help may be needed for this project. Wash and peel some potatoes, then cook them until they become tender. Whip the potatoes, adding butter and salt. Place the mashed potatoes into a pastry bag.

Squeeze the potatoes through the bag onto a cookie sheet.

Form potatoes into a dragon shape. Add grated cheese, bacon bits, and sesame seeds to the body of the dragon. Place the dragon under a broiler until browned. It is ready to eat!

Drawing

Blind Drawing. Try drawing a picture while your eyes are closed. Do not open your eyes until the picture is done! How did your picture turn out?

Drawing to Music. Play a record or listen to music on the radio while drawing a picture or design on paper. Listen closely to the music. Does it suggest long, sweeping motions, or small, crowded drawings? Is the music happy or sad? Draw according to the type of music, and see what kind of picture you create.

Dream Picture. Can you remember something from a dream you have had recently? Draw a picture based on that dream.

Line Drawing. Draw some lines on a sheet of paper. Make some of them straight and others wavy, swirling, or zigzagged. The lines can cross each other any number of times.

Now, it is time to use your imagination. Draw

over some of the lines with a colored felt-tip marker to outline an animal, object, or any other picture you can see in the lines!

"Magic Slate" Drawing Box. Find a box about 14 inches wide, 18 inches long, and 2 or 3 inches deep. Make sure the box has a lid to fit.

Line the inside bottom of the box with dark-colored construction paper. Fill the box with enough salt to cover the bottom. The drawing box is now finished.

With your fingers, draw shapes, letters, pictures, or anything else you want in the salt so the dark-colored paper underneath shows through. To erase your picture, simply put the lid on and shake the box. Now the box is ready for another drawing!

Easter

Activities

Easter Egg Hunt. Ahead of time, dye some Easter eggs for your hunt. Ask an adult to hide them for you, or hide them yourself for your friends to find. (The hider should remember where he put the eggs. Those not found get smelly.)

You might want to set a limit on how many eggs each person may collect. This way everyone has an equal opportunity to find some eggs! Make sure everybody has a bag for their eggs. Afterward, everyone can eat some of the eggs they found.

Easter Egg Tree. Find a small, well-shaped branch from a tree. If desired, spray paint the branch white. Place the branch in a felt or paper-covered coffee can. Fasten the branch in place at the bottom of the can with sand or plaster of Paris.

Decorate the tree with decorated plastic foam eggs or real eggs! If you use real eggs, poke a

hole in both ends of a number of raw eggs with a pin or ice pick. Ask an adult to help you. Make the holes in the large ends a little bigger.

Blow out the insides of each egg through the larger hole by blowing hard into the smaller hole. (Save the insides for making scrambled eggs or use in another recipe.)

Rinse the eggshells well. Dye them different colors and let them dry. Later, decorate the eggs by gluing on rickrack, sequins, or decals from an Easter egg dye kit. Glue ribbons around the eggs to hang them from the tree branch.

Easter Egg Tree

Eggshell Flower Gift. Cut an eggshell in half and paint the outside. Fill the eggshell half with soil, and plant a single flower seed in the soil. Keep the soil moist. This makes a nice gift.

Playacting. Pretend you are an Easter bunny. Act out decorating and delivering the eggs to other children.

Stories. From a magazine or old greeting card, pick out a picture you like, or, draw your own Easter picture. Glue the picture on a 12-by-18-inch sheet of drawing paper.

Tell a story based on your picture. Either ask an adult to print the story below the picture as you tell it or print it there yourself.

Art

Broken Egg with Bunny. On colored construction paper draw an egg. Then cut it out. Next, draw a jagged line down the middle of the egg. Cut the egg in half along the jagged line.

Using white paper, cut out two circles small enough to fit within the egg halves. Paste them on a sheet of background paper, one above the other, to form the body and head of a bunny. Draw two bunny ears on the top circle and add a face.

Poke a hole near the bottom edge of the lower circle. Also poke holes in the bottom corner of each egg half. Pin all the pieces together with a metal paper fastener so you can close the egg and then open it to reveal the bunny inside.

Bunny Mask. Cut out a heart large enough to cover your face. Use white construction paper. Draw a bunny face on the front of the mask. Tape two large bunny ears to the top of the mask. Fasten a paper band across the back so the mask will fit onto your head.

Chain Basket Wall Decoration. Pin paper chains to a bulletin board or wall, forming an Easter basket shape. Cut out egg shapes and pin them on the basket.

Chalk Easter Picture. Mix one part sugar with three parts water. Pour the mixture into a shallow container.

Next, pick out some pastel chalks for your picture. Soak the chalks in the mixture for about five minutes. Then draw an Easter scene on construction paper using the wet chalks. Dip the chalks into the mixture as you go to keep them wet.

Egg-Shaped Card. Fold over a sheet of construction paper from each end so the ends meet in the center of the paper. Round off the corners to form an egg. Now you have an egg-shaped card that opens in the middle!

While the card is closed, decorate the outside to look like an Easter egg. Then open up the card and color an Easter scene on the inside center. Write your message or greeting on either of the inside flaps.

See-Through Egg Card. Fold a 12-by-18-inch sheet of construction paper in half the short way. On the front of the card draw a fairly large Easter egg and cut it out. Open the card, and on the inside right-hand page, color an Easter scene. Write a message on the inside left-hand page. The Easter scene will show through the egg-shaped hole when the card is closed.

Stained-Glass Cross. Cut out a cross shape from the center of a piece of purple paper. Discard the cut-out piece and keep the larger piece from which it was cut.

Next, using permanent felt-tip markers, color a piece of clear plastic to look like stained glass. Let each color dry before using a new one. Make sure the piece of plastic is large enough to cover the cross opening.

When the colors have dried, tape the piece of plastic behind the cross opening so the colors show through. Mount the picture on a window for display. *Another way to do it:* Using crayons, heavily color a piece of white paper. Use bright colors to look like stained glass. Tape this colored sheet to the back of the purple one.

Baskets

Construction Paper Basket. Cut an eight-inch square piece of construction paper. Fold up a two-inch border along the edges of the square. Cut the corners so you can paste the border corners together in an upright position.

From the excess paper cut out a one-inch-wide strip. Staple each end of the strip to the basket to make a handle. Fill the basket with grass made from strips of green crepe paper.

Cottage Cheese Carton Basket. Cover an empty cottage cheese carton with tissue paper, finger-painted paper, or ruffled crepe paper. Use paper fasteners to hook on a paper handle, or make a handle from pipe cleaners. Fill with green crepe paper grass.

Doily Basket. Fold a circular paper doily in half. Glue on a ribbon handle and fill the basket with paper flowers.

Eggshell Basket. Carefully break an egg in half and save half of the eggshell after it has been cleaned out. Dip the eggshell half into some dye, then glue a pipe cleaner across the top for a handle.

Carefully, place some small artificial flowers in the basket. If the basket does not sit upright easily, glue it in place on a small piece of poster board.

Milk Carton Basket. Cut off the top from a school-sized milk carton. Cover the box with construction paper. Attach a paper or pipe cleaner handle and decorate the basket.

Paper Bag Bunny Basket. At the open end of a flattened white paper lunch bag, draw some bunny ears along the outside edges. Fluff open the bag. Cut away the spaces between the ears on the sides as well as on the front and back. Staple the ears together at the top to form a pair of handles.

Flatten the bag again. On the front side draw a

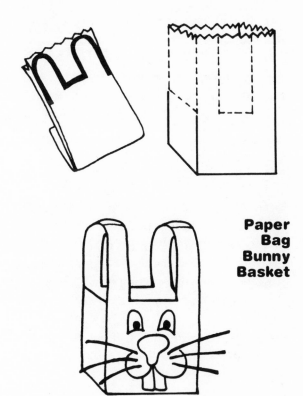

Paper Bag Bunny Basket

large bunny face. Then unfold the bag and the basket is ready to use!

Papier Mâché Basket. Mix shredded newspaper with wallpaper paste. Put the strips down in layers over an inverted bowl. Allow them to stand until dry. Then remove the papier mâché piece from the bowl and paint it with Easter colors. Glue on a handle made from poster board. Stuff the basket with commercial Easter grass.

Strawberry Container Basket. For this simple Easter basket, use a plastic strawberry basket from the supermarket. Fill it with Easter grass and attach a ribbon handle.

Bonnets

Circle Bonnet. Cut out a large circle from white construction paper. Cut around the outside edges in a scalloped pattern. On top of the circle glue a smaller circle cut from colored paper.

Cut a pair of slits through the smaller circle. Thread a crepe paper streamer through the slits. (Use the ends of the streamers to tie the bonnet to your head.) Decorate the bonnet with tissue paper bows.

Construction Strip Bonnet.   Cut out a 3-by-12-inch strip from a piece of colored construction paper. Fold it in half the short way so the ends meet. Then unfold the strip. Decorate the peaked side with tissue paper bows. Glue a paper tie to each end of the hat.

Paper Plate Bonnet I.   Turn a paper plate upside down. Cover the bottom with tissue paper flowers, ribbons, netting, sequins, glitter, buttons, artificial flowers, feathers, etc., using glue to fasten down the decorations. Attach a long ribbon to each side for a tie.

Paper Plate Bonnet II.   Cut out the center of a paper plate. Flatten some paper baking cups and staple them all around the paper plate rim. Staple a ribbon to each side for a tie.

Paper Plate Bonnet III.   Cut a paper plate in half. Discard one half and keep the other. Decorate the half plate with paper bows and paper flowers. Add a paper streamer to each corner of the bonnet and tie it under your chin.

Bunnies

Begging Bunny.   Staple two paper plates together end to end, one above the other, and slightly overlapping. On the top plate, draw a bunny face and attach paper ears and pipe cleaner whiskers.

On the bottom plate draw ovals near the bottom for feet. Glue a cotton ball tail at the bottom of the plate and a paper bow tie over the area linking the two plates together.

Bunnies in the Grass.   On a sheet of drawing paper, scribble with green crayon to represent grass. Glue cotton balls on the grass here and there to look like bunnies hiding in the grass.

Cotton Ball Bunny.   Glue two cotton balls together side by side. At the end of one ball, care-

fully glue on paper eyes, ears, and a nose to form a bunny.

Eggcup Bunny I.   Cut out a one-cup section from a plastic foam egg carton. Turn over the cup and glue a cotton ball to one end. Cut out two paper bunny ears and glue them to the other end of the cup. With felt-tip markers, draw a face on the bunny.

Eggcup Bunny II.   From a cardboard egg carton, cut out a cup section that includes two long protrusions. Cut the protrusions just enough to form bunny ears. On the outside front of the cup, draw a bunny face. Glue on pipe cleaners for whiskers.

Eggshell Bunny.   Outline the shape of a bunny on a sheet of construction paper. Spread glue over the inside area of the bunny. Press crushed eggshells over the glue, filling in the bunny. After it is dry, shake off the excess eggshells.

Fruit Can Bunny.   Cover a fruit or vegetable can with white paper. On one side draw a bunny face with a felt-tip marker. Cut some bunny ears from white paper and glue them to the top, back side of the can. Add pipe cleaner whiskers to finish.

Begging Bunny

Eggcup Bunny II

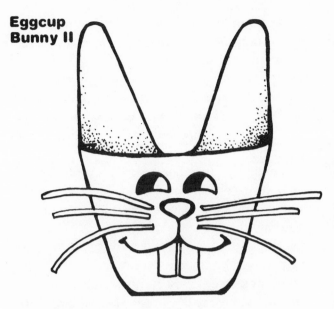

Paper Bag Bunny. Stuff crumpled paper in the bottom of a small paper sack. Tie a string around the middle for a neck. Turn the bag upside down so the stuffed-head part is on top. Draw on a face and add curled paper strips for paws and ears.

Papier Mâché Bunny. Inflate a balloon until it is soft but not quite blown up all the way. Tie a string around the middle of the balloon. Cover the balloon with several layers of paper strips dipped in diluted glue. Allow to dry.

Place the papier mâché piece on its side in front of you. One end is the head, the other end is the body. Paint the bunny and let the paint dry. Glue on paper ears and a cotton tuft for the tail. Paint on a face.

Paper Plate Bunny. Fold a paper plate in half. Glue or tape the plate together at the top. At one corner, glue on tufts of cotton for a tail. At the other corner draw a face and glue on cut-out ears.

Pocket Bunny. Fold a sheet of colored construction paper in half. While it is folded, cut out an egg shape. Now you have two eggs of the same size. Cut one of the eggs in half between the top and bottom.

Glue the bottom half of the cut egg to the bottom area of the whole egg, forming a pocket. (Glue it along the side and bottom edges only.) Then make a white bunny from two paper circles joined together with ears glued to the head piece. Insert the bunny in the pocket so just its head and part of its body show.

Chicks

Eggshell Chick. Place some yellow powdered tempera paint in a plastic bag. Drop two cotton balls inside the bag. Shake well. Remove the two yellow-colored cotton balls.

Glue the two cotton balls together to form the body and head of a chick. Glue the chick inside an empty half of an eggshell, so the chick is just peeking over the jagged edges of the broken shell.

Cut a tiny beak and eyes from paper, and carefully glue them to the head of the chick. If the eggshell half does not sit up easily, glue it to an index card or a small piece of paper.

Fluffy Chick. Drop some cotton balls into a bag with some yellow powdered tempera paint. Shake well to turn the cotton yellow. Then, draw an outline of a chick on paper. Glue the cotton balls inside the outline to form a cute, fluffy chick.

Eggs

Blow-Painted Egg. Drip different colors of tempera paint onto white drawing paper. Blow through a straw to move the paint drops in different directions across the paper, forming colorful patterns and designs. When dry, cut out a large egg shape from the painting. Display the egg.

Construction Paper Egg. Cut out an egg shape from a piece of colored construction paper. Decorate the egg with sequins, rickrack, ribbon, and other colorful items.

Crayon-Resist Egg. From a 9-by-12-inch sheet of manila paper, cut out a large egg shape. Color designs on the egg with crayons, being sure to press very hard! Then paint the egg with a light color of thinned tempera paint.

Marbelized Paper Egg. Pour several inches of water into a large cake pan. Using a table knife, scrape some colored chalk over the pan, letting the powder fall into the water.

Next, lay a piece of pastel construction paper on the water so it floats. Quickly pull it out of the water by lifting a corner. Notice how the chalk has stuck to the paper in colorful patterns! Cut a large egg shape from the paper. Rinse out pan so it can be used again.

Papier Mâché Egg. Ahead of time, tear lots of newspaper into strips. When ready, wad another piece of paper into the shape of an egg. Gather the newspaper strips together and dip them into diluted glue. Cover the egg with several layers of strips and allow to dry. Then paint the egg with Easter colors.

Starched String Egg. Inflate a round balloon and tie it closed to keep the air inside. Next, dip 12-inch lengths of colored strings into liquid starch and wrap each string around the balloon. Start at one end of the balloon and work across to the other end. Continue until the balloon is completely covered with rows of string rings. Allow it to dry.

When dried, pop the balloon with a pin, and pull it out, leaving a colorful egg made of stiffened colored string rings.

Stuffed Paper Egg. Fold a large sheet of colored paper in half. Draw a big egg on one side. Cut out the egg through the double thickness of the paper.

Sew the egg together with a piece of yarn, but leave a space open at one end so you can stuff it with crushed newspaper. Then finish sewing and decorate the egg.

Eggs (Dyed)

Easter Egg Dye. You can make your own Easter egg dye by mixing 1 teaspoon of food coloring, 1 tablespoon of vinegar, and 1 cup of hot water. Make a different color for each container available for holding the dyes. (Soup bowls make good containers.)

Spoon-dip a hard-boiled egg into the dye to color it the way you want. Try dipping some eggs into more than one color to see what new colors you get. Dip other eggs halfway in one color and halfway in another.

If you want an egg to have a special design or message, draw or write with crayon on the egg ahead of time. The crayon will resist the dye and leave your design or message visible on the egg.

You can also decorate your egg with gummed stars or Easter seals after the dye has dried.

Easter Egg Stand. Cut off a one-inch-long ring from a cardboard tube. Place the ring on its end to use as a display stand for your dyed eggs.

Felt-Tip Colored Eggs. Instead of dyeing hard-boiled eggs, color them with felt-tip markers.

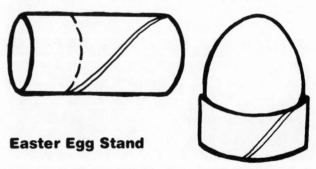

Easter Egg Stand

Marbled Eggs. Mix 1 teaspoon of food coloring, 1 tablespoon of vinegar, 1 cup of hot water, and 1 tablespoon of salad oil. Eggs dyed in this solution will have a marbled coloring.

Hats

Bunny Balloon-Ears Hat. Cut out a 3-by-13-inch strip of white cardboard. Inflate two long white balloons and tie one to each end of the cardboard strip about an inch in from the ends.

Make sure that the strings you use for tying the balloons closed are also long enough to reach under your chin. Place the cardboard strip over your head and tie the strings together under your chin so the balloons become bunny ears. *Another way to do it:* Attach a long, inflated balloon to each side of a paper plate. Cut a slit at the edge of each side of the plate near the balloon ears. Tie a length of ribbon through each slit so the ribbon ends can be tied under your chin to hold the hat on your head.

Bunny Ears Headband. Draw and cut out a pair of bunny ears from construction paper. Paste them to a headband made from a strip of paper cut to fit around your head.

Paper Sack Easter Cap. Cut off the bottom part of a small paper sack. Turn the bottom piece upside down. Paste a paper half circle to the front edge of the sack for a bill. Glue a small circle on top of the cap to represent a button. Decorate or paint the cap with Easter colors if desired.

Eggshell Art

Eggshell Artwork. Crush eggshells with your hands. Use glue to apply the eggshells to paper plates, box lids, egg carton lids, or other objects. Paint the shells lightly, using very fine brushes or cotton swabs.

Eggshell Mosaic. Dye eggs in a variety of colors. Then break off shell pieces and glue them together on paper to make a colorful mosaic.

Grass-Haired Eggshell Face. Carefully break off an egg at the top and drain the contents. Rinse the eggshell and set it upright in the cup of an egg carton. Draw a face on the shell with a felt-tip marker. Then spoon some soil into the eggshell, and sprinkle in some grass seeds. Water the soil lightly.

Keep the soil moist, but be sure not to flood it! After awhile the grass will start growing. Soon your eggshell "friend" will have grown a full head of grass hair!

Etchings

Crayon Etching. With a crayon, heavily color a piece of cardboard or a paper plate, using a single bright color. Make sure the coloring is quite solid. When finished, color over the whole area with black crayon.

Then, using a Popsicle stick, a strong toothpick, or a straightened paper clip, scratch a pattern, design, or picture into the black layer so the colored layer underneath shows through.

Waxed Paper Etching. Using a Popsicle stick or a plastic fork, etch a picture or design on a sheet of heavy waxed paper. Be sure not to tear or poke a hole in the paper!

Then mount the finished etching on a piece of black construction paper. See how well the etching shows up now?

Evaporation (Science)

Evaporation Pan. Slow evaporation cannot be seen, but it can be measured. Fill a pan with water and mark the water level. Put the pan outside where it will not get bumped.

Each morning for several days mark the new water level. What has happened each time?

Experiment I. Heat from sunlight helps water evaporate faster. To see this, make two small puddles of water on the sidewalk—one puddle in the sunlight and the other in the shade. Which one evaporates faster?

Experiment II. Wind can also help water evaporate faster. Wipe a wet sponge on a chalkboard, making two separate wet spots. Fan some air or blow on one of the spots. Which one dries faster?

Experiment III. Place two flat dishes on a table. In one dish, place a mixture of salt and water. In the other, place water only. Let both liquids evaporate. A residue is left in one of the dishes. Why didn't the salt evaporate?

Experiment IV. Pour exactly the same amount of water into two identical clear glasses. With a marking pen or a rubber band, mark the water level of both glasses. Cover one of the glasses with a piece of cardboard. Leave the other glass uncovered.

For the next several days compare the water levels of the two glasses. Which one has evaporated the most? Why?

Fall

Autumn Collage. Finger paint with green paint on a large sheet of background paper. Allow the paint to dry. Then glue on dried weeds and autumn leaves to make an autumn collage.

Autumn Leaf Picture. Go outdoors and find as many colored leaves as possible. Take them indoors and set them aside.

On a large piece of white paper, draw the outline of a tree trunk and branches. Color in the outline with brown crayon. Next, glue the leaves you found onto the colored branches and allow to dry.

Autumn Leaf Montage. On a 9-by-12-inch sheet of manila paper, outline as many leaf shapes as you can. Then dip the paper in a large pan of water. Remove and carefully drain the excess water.

Next, drip various autumn colors of paint (gold, yellow, orange, red, tan, and green) on the wet leaf outlines. Watch the colors run together to make a beautiful autumn montage!

Back-to-School Mural. From old magazines, look for and cut out pictures of a school bus, a school building, and children. Paste the pictures together on a long piece of butcher paper or brown wrapping paper, forming a mural of children returning to school in the fall. Draw in background details with felt-tip markers or crayons.

Construction Paper Scarecrow. Draw and cut out the clothes and face of a scarecrow from construction paper. Paste the scarecrow together on a cardboard strip, and prop it up for display.

Finger-Painted Leaves. Finger-paint with fall colors on a sheet of construction paper. Then cut out leaf shapes from the painting.

Football Art. Outline the shape of a football on a sheet of paper. Spread glue within the outline of the football. Sprinkle grits (colored brown with tempera paint) over the glue. Shake away any excess grits.

Football Collage. Look through some old sports magazines for pictures of footballs, football players, stadiums, officials, pennants, concession stands, goal posts, or anything else you might see at a football game. Cut out the pictures. Glue them together on a sheet of construction paper to make a collage.

Spatter-Painted Leaves. Glue some real autumn leaves on a sheet of paper. Spatter paint over the leaves first with black paint. Then spatter on some white paint. This creates a "spotty"

Stuffed Scarecrow

effect similar to that of leaves on the ground under a tree in partial light.

Stuffed Scarecrow. Stuff some old play clothes with crumpled newspapers. Tie the ends of the pants and sleeves with string to keep the papers inside.

For a head, inflate a round balloon and draw on a face with felt-tip markers. Place a hat on the head and attach the head to the body with string. Put the scarecrow in a chair or prop him up next to a wall and give him a name!

Tissue Apples. Inflate some small, round balloons just enough to make them the size of apples. Tie them closed to keep the air in.

Cover the balloons with a light coat of petroleum jelly, and stick on strips of red tissue paper that have been dipped in liquid starch. Let the balloons sit for 24 hours.

Then, pop the balloons with a needle and remove them through the openings where the balloon stems were. Hang the apples from a tree, a mobile, or window rods.

Finger Painting

Before finger painting, cover your work table with several layers of newspapers. Also put some newspapers on the floor so you can set your finger paintings there to dry. If you do not have commercial finger painting paper available, use shelf paper.

Chocolate Pudding Finger Painting. Spread some chocolate pudding on a cookie sheet. Using your fingers, draw pictures and designs in the pudding. You can even eat some of the pudding while you work! Wash off in a sink when finished.

Finger Painting the Refrigerator. If you have a white enamel refrigerator, ask an adult if you can finger paint on it! Mix a little food coloring or paint in a bowl with some liquid starch. Wet the front of the refrigerator with a sponge. Apply the paint with your hands and smear the paint around. Wipe it off with a sponge when you are finished.

Flour and Water Finger Paint Mix. Mix some flour and salt with a little bit of water. Mix it until it looks like thick gravy. Then add a little food coloring.

Now, finger-paint directly on the surface of a plastic-topped table! (Of course, you should ask an adult first!) You can change the colors as you go by adding different food colorings.

If you want to preserve your painting, lay a piece of shelf paper over it and press carefully. The paint will stick to the reverse side of the paper when you lift it up!

When you are finished, simply mop up the finger paint with a sponge.

Liquid Soap Finger Paint Mix. Mix one part liquid soap and one part powdered tempera paint. Use this for finger painting on paper.

Liquid Starch Finger Paint Mix. This is another mix to use on paper. Mix one part liquid

starch and one part powdered tempera paint to create your finger paint.

Powdered Soap Finger Paint Mix. Blend one part powdered soap, one part powdered tempera paint, and one part water. This mixture is for finger painting on paper.

Shaving Cream Finger Painting. Squirt a can of shaving cream on a cookie sheet or plastic table surface. With your fingers, draw pictures or designs in the shaving cream. Sprinkle in some food coloring if you want. To clean up, simply wash it away with water!

Fish

Fish Bowl Scene. Cut out some fish shapes from bright-colored construction paper. Cut a seaweed shape from green paper. Glue the shapes on a large piece of blue paper.

Separate a white tissue into a single ply, and lay them over the fish bowl scene. Brush over the tissue with diluted glue. When the scene dries, it will have a watery effect.

Paper Plate Fish I. Use a paper plate as the body of a fish. Glue on upper, lower, and tail fins cut from construction paper. Draw in the mouth, eye, and scales using a felt-tip marker.

Paper Plate Fish II. Obtain two paper plates the same size. Cut one plate in half. Take one of the halves and cut it in half again so you have two pie-shaped wedges.

Newsprint Flag

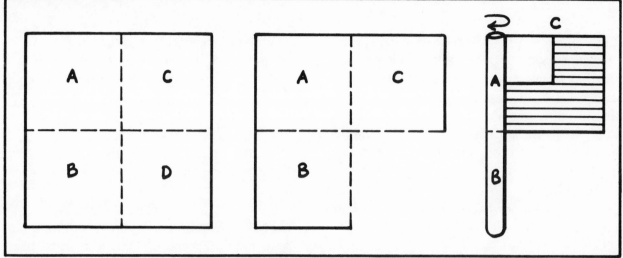

Staple the half piece to the edge of the whole plate so the curved sides meet. The half piece is the tail fin.

Staple one pie wedge to the top edge of the whole plate. Staple the other pie wedge to the bottom edge of the whole plate. These are the upper and lower fins.

Color in an eye, mouth, and scales.

Shoe Fish. Place your shoe on a sheet of paper, and outline it on the paper. Using crayons, add fins and other details to the outline to make it look like a fish.

Flags

Cloth Flag. Cut out a rectangular piece of white cloth. Paint the flag with red and blue paint. Staple the finished flag to a dowel rod. (You can design your own flag pattern if you want.)

Construction Paper Flag. Cut out a large white rectangle to use as a flag. On the upper-left corner of the flag, glue a blue rectangle to represent the star field. Glue four short strips of paper to the right side of the blue field. Glue three long red strips of paper across the rest of the flag.

Manila Paper Flag. Glue a drinking straw (the flag pole) to the short side of a 6-by-9-inch piece

of manila paper. Fold the edge of the paper loosely around the straw so it will hold. Using crayons, color in a blue star field. Then color in the red and white stripes to finish the flag.

Newsprint Flag. Fold a sheet of newsprint paper into fourths. Cut out area D, as illustrated. Roll areas A and B into a pole shape. Complete the flag by coloring in area C with flag colors.

Flowers

Baking Cup Flowers. Flatten some paper baking cups to use as flowers. Glue the flattened baking cups on a large sheet of construction paper. Glue on stems and leaves cut from green paper, or draw in the stems and leaves.

Black-Eyed Susan Flower. Cut out a circle from yellow paper. Cut fringes around the circle, then bend the fringing down. At the center of the circle glue a smaller black or brown circle. Mount the flower on a plastic straw or wire stem.

Button Flowers. Glue buttons on paper for the centers of flowers. Make petals by drawing them with felt-tip markers or gluing on petals cut from construction paper.

Candy Paper Flowers. Obtain some paper cups from boxed chocolates. Flatten the cups and glue them on paper for flowers. Add stems and leaves drawn with crayons.

Catalog Flowers. From seed catalogs and magazines, cut out pictures of flower blossoms. Cut out stems from green construction paper, and glue the stems on the flower cutouts. Place the flowers in a flower basket, or glue them to Popsicle sticks and plant them in a playdough base.

Chalk Flowers. Cover a piece of paper with a light coat of liquid starch. Draw flowers on the paper with colored chalks.

Circle Flower. Cut out circles of various colors. Make each circle slightly larger than the one before. Scallop the edges of each circle. Glue them on top of each other with the largest on the bottom and the smallest on top. Glue a drinking straw to the back for a stem.

Cotton Swab Flower. Cut some cotton swabs in half. Then cut out a two-inch paper circle. Glue the cotton swabs fairly close together around the circle, with the ends pointing outward from the center. Glue on a full-length cotton swab for a stem.

Crayon-Melt Flowers. Grate some crayon pieces (without wrappers) on a piece of waxed paper. Place another sheet of waxed paper over the crayon shavings. Then place paper towels on top and under the pieces of waxed paper.

Using an iron set at medium heat, carefully iron over the surface of the top paper towel. This will melt the crayon shavings and fuse the surrounding sheets of waxed paper.

Cut flower shapes from the melted crayon sheets and hang them in a window to show off their colors.

Cupcake Container Flowers. Insert pipe cleaners through the bottoms of colored paper cupcake containers to make flowers.

Egg Carton Tulips. Cut out single eggcups from a cardboard egg carton. Paint each cup a pretty color and punch a hole in the bottom of each. Thread pipe cleaners through the holes for stems.

Fingertip Flowers. Draw some small circles on paper to represent the centers of flower blossoms. Dip a finger into some paint. Make petals for your flowers by printing your fingertips around the circles on the paper. Use a different color for each flower.

Gumdrop Flowers. Remove the twigs and berries from a thorny barberry twig, or a twig from a similar kind of bush. Stick colored gumdrops on the thorns. Use an empty thread spool for a stand. Stick the twig of gumdrops in the top hole of the spool and display.

Imagination Flowers. Draw, paint, or color any kind of flowers. They do not have to be real flowers! Use your imagination!

Macaroni Flowers. Dilute some food coloring with a small amount of water in a jar. Quickly drop some macaroni into the jar. Put on the lid and shake the jar. When the macaroni reaches the desired color, remove the macaroni and place it on a paper towel to dry. Glue the colored macaroni on a paper plate in flower designs. Use felt-tip markers to draw in stems and leaves.

Paper Cup Flowers. Make a number of cuts from the top rim of a paper cup all the way down to the bottom of the cup. Make the cuts equal distances apart. Open the cup out. The original bottom of the cup is the center of the flower. The opened-out strips are the petals.

Make as many of these flowers as you want. Paint them in different colors. Make stems from drinking straws or pipe cleaners, and attach them to the flowers with clear tape.

Paper Sunflower. Cut a large circle from yellow paper. Cut fringes around the edges. Then cut a smaller circle of brown paper. Paste the brown circle to the center of the larger yellow one.

Paint a Popsicle stick green and allow to dry. Glue the stick to the flower for a stem.

Plastic Spoon Flower. From paper, cut out an oval shape just slightly larger than the bowl part of a plastic spoon. Cut around the edges of the oval to make a scalloped pattern.

Turn a plastic spoon upside down and glue the bowl end of the spoon to the oval. Using green paper, cut out some small leaves and glue them to the handle of the spoon.

Seashell Flowers. From a piece of green paper, cut out some stems and leaves. Glue them into position on a sheet of background paper. Glue on small seashells for flower petals.

Tissue Carnation. Open up three facial tissues and evenly stack them on top of one another. Starting at one of the short edges, fold the stack of tissues accordion-style. Put one end of a pipe cleaner over the middle of the folded tissue. Bend the pipe cleaner behind the tissue and twist it to hook around the tissue.

With pinking shears, cut off about three quarters of an inch of tissue from each side of the pipe

cleaner. Carefully, lift each separate sheet of tissue and pull it toward the center, forming a flower shape.

Use white, pink, or yellow facial tissues for making these flowers. If you want, you can gently outline the borders of the flowers with a red felt-tip marker.

Plastic Spoon Flower

Flower Baskets

Cylinder Basket. Roll a sheet of colored paper into a cylinder and seal it in place with glue. Fold the cylinder in half, bringing the open ends together side by side. Staple the touching edges together. Glue on a paper strip handle to the outside edges.

Doily Basket. Fold a circular paper doily in half. Glue on a ribbon handle and fill with paper flowers.

Paper Cone Basket. Roll a colored half circle of paper into a cone and staple or tape it together. Attach a paper strip handle.

Paper Plate Basket. Using colored paper scraps, cut out flowers. Glue the flower shapes to the back side of a paper plate. Fold the paper plate in half so the flowers are on the outside.

With the plate folded together, punch a hole through the top. Open the plate slightly and insert a pipe cleaner through the holes. Tie the pipe cleaner ends together to form a handle.

Flower Pots and Planters

Eggshell Planter. Place some cleaned eggshell pieces in a plastic bag. Crush the eggshells by rolling over the bag with a rolling pin.

Next, paint the sides of a small empty fruit juice can with glue. Spread the eggshells on a flat surface. Roll the glue-covered can through the eggshells until the can is completely covered with the shells. Allow everything to dry.

Fill the can with soil and plant a small flower or plant in it.

Margarine Tub Planter. Punch some holes in the bottom of a margarine tub. Fill the tub with soil. Plant some herbs, beans, or flower seeds. Keep the lid underneath to catch the drainage.

Painted Pots. Paint some plain clay pots with pretty flowers and colorful designs. Then plant some seeds in the pots.

Paper Cup Planter. Place some soil in a small paper cup. Plant some seeds. Keep the planter on a window sill where it will receive good light. Water it frequently. Seeds to use include grass, beans, flowers, orange, lemon, and grapefruit.

Foreign Countries

Cardboard Tube Kiosk (France). Glue some miniature-sized advertisements (drawn or cut out from magazines) to a cardboard tube. Set the tube upright to look like a French kiosk.

Fish Kite (Japan). First, tape several pieces of paper together to make a long sheet. Draw a fish shape about 2-by-4-feet in size. Cut out the fish.

Next, paint the fish with bright colors. When dried, attach colorful crepe paper streamers to the tail end of the fish. Attach a short length of string to the nose so you can run with the kite. Later, tape the kite to a wall for display.

Foreign Lands Collage. From magazines and travel brochures, clip pictures of people, activities, and objects from foreign countries. Paste them together into a collage on background paper.

Hat Dance (Mexico). Toss a sombrero or other hat on the floor. Play the "Mexican Hat Dance" or other lively music on a record player. Dance around the hat to the music.

Lunch Bag Piñata (Mexico). Fill a small lunch bag with crumpled newspaper, some pieces of candy, and a few toy trinkets. Tie the bag closed with a piece of string. Dip colorful pieces of tissue paper into liquid starch. Stick the tissue pieces all over the outside of the bag. Later, hang the piñata with string from a tree branch or ceiling fixture. With a broomstick, bat the piñata down and break it open to find the prizes.

Mexican Cakes. Remove some biscuits from a container of canned refrigerator biscuits. With a rolling pin roll out each biscuit a little until it is flattened. With help from an adult, fry the biscuits in hot oil until they are slightly browned. Remove them from the oil and quickly drain on paper towel. Before they cool roll them in cinnamon sugar. They are quite tasty!

Oriental Spirals. Cut colored paper plates into spirals. Then lay them flat on a table, and make a collage on one side with glue and confetti. Open up again and hang from a window or ceiling.

Paper Lantern (Japan). Fold a rectangular piece of colored paper in half lengthwise. At the folded edge, draw a series of lines straight across to a point about an inch from the other edge of the paper. Make the lines an equal distance apart.

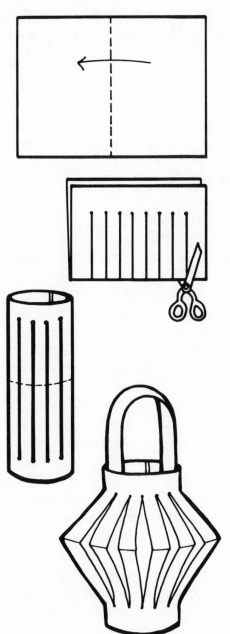

Next, cut along the lines with a pair of scissors. Open up the paper and glue the sides together, forming a lantern (see illustration).

For handles, glue the ends of a paper strip to each side of the top of the lantern.

Pottery-Making (Mexico). If you can, obtain some Mexican pottery clay from a hobby shop or an art supply store. Otherwise, use regular clay or even plain modeling clay.

Add water to the Mexican pottery clay until it is moist enough to work with. Mold the clay into a plate, a cup, or a bowl. Be sure to handle the clay carefully or it will break. You should pat the clay and not pound it.

Place your finished pieces of pottery to dry on a shelf or table overnight.

Note: The clay may leave a brown stain on your hands. This will wash away easily with soap and water.

Rice and Tea Party (Japan). Plan a Japanese tea party. Invite friends and adults to attend. Decorate the room ahead of time with cherry blossoms made from real tree branches and pink tissue paper.

Did you know Japanese children honor their parents during the Cherry Blossom Festival? In Japan it is similar to Father's Day and Mother's Day here in our country!

Cook some rice and serve it with tea at your party. Be sure to sit on the floor Japanese-style while having your snack. You might even try eating with chopsticks! End your party by serving cookies.

G

Games

Circle Games
Capture the Ball. Everyone forms a circle with one player in the middle. The person in the middle carefully tosses a ball into the air and at the

same time calls the name of a person in the circle. (Everyone can wear name tags if needed.) The player who was called then tries to catch the ball before it bounces more than once. The person who catches the ball goes to the center to throw the next ball.

Duck-Duck-Goose.   Have everyone sit in a circle, facing the center. Pick one person to be the goose.

The goose goes around the outside of the circle, lightly tapping each person on the shoulder. As he taps each person, he says "Duck" and continues until he suddenly taps one person and says "Goose!"

The person tapped "goose" jumps up and chases the goose around the circle. The goose tries to run around and sit down in the empty space before he gets caught.

If the person who was tapped does not catch the goose, he becomes the new goose. If he *does* catch the goose, the goose must tap shoulders around the circle again.

Feed the Elephant.   Roll two pieces of gray construction paper into a wide cylinder. Fasten it together with paper clips.

Have everyone sit in a circle. Explain that the

roll is an elephant's trunk, and it is now time to feed the elephant. Lay the trunk flat on the floor in the center of the circle. Aim the open end of the trunk at the player chosen to be first.

Each player, in turn, tries to toss three peanuts all the way through the trunk. As each player takes his turn, make sure the trunk is aimed toward him. Keep track of how many peanuts each player tosses through the trunk.

Hot Potato.   Have everyone sit in a circle on the floor. Roll a ball back and forth across the circle from one player to another as fast as you can. Try not to be the one with the "potato" when someone blows a whistle to freeze!

Musical Catch.   Have the players stand in a circle, facing the center. While music is playing, toss the ball from one person to the next. When the music stops, the person holding the ball is "caught." Continue the game until all players have been caught.

Poor Kitty.   Have the players sit in a circle, with one person in the center as the kitty. The kitty then approaches one of the players in the circle, and says, "meow." The person approached must pet kitty's head, saying "Poor kitty, poor kitty, poor kitty."

The kitty then tries to make that person laugh. If the person laughs, he is then the new kitty. If he does not laugh, the kitty must try to make someone else laugh.

Shark in the Sea.   Mark or draw a circle on the ground. Players stand just outside the circle. The player inside the circle is the shark and tries to tag the others as they jump in and out of the circle. The shark can tag a player only when part of that player is inside the circle.

Players must jump in and out of the circle all the time. They chant, "Shark in the sea, can't catch me!" A player who is tagged becomes a shark and joins the shark already inside the circle. Continue until everyone is a shark!

Indoor Games

Balloon-Bat. This is a game you can play by yourself. Inflate a balloon and toss it in the air. Keep batting the balloon to keep it in the air. See how long you can keep it from falling to the ground. Use your hands, arms, legs, feet, and even your head to bat the balloon! You can also play this game with a friend.

Balloon Puff-of-War. Place an inflated balloon in the middle of a table. Split up into two teams. Have each team go to one end of the table. On "go," each team tries to blow the balloon off the opposite edge of the table. Each time a team successfully blows the balloon over the opposite edge, it gets a point. You can also play this game using a feather or ping pong ball instead of a balloon.

Hot and Cold. One player is *It* and closes his eyes or leaves the room. The others then hide an object or pick out an object that is in plain sight.

It then starts hunting for the object. If he is far away from it, the other players call "cold!" As he gets closer, the players call "warmer." When he is very close to the object, the players call "hot!" *It* has three chances to name the proper object. Take turns being *It*.

Indoor Basketball. Form a hoop from a wire coat hanger by bending the hanger into a circle, leaving a length sticking out for a handle. Bend the handle at right angles from the hoop. Depending upon how tall you are, hang the loop from a doorknob or hook it on top of a door.

For a ball, use a balloon, a foam ball, or a crumpled ball of newspaper. Each time you shoot the ball through the hoop, you get two points. Take turns with your friends. See who can score the most points, taking the same number of shots from the same distances.

Indoor Hockey. Set a cardboard box on its side for a goal. Place a goal at each end of the room. Roll up a sock to use as a puck. Yardsticks or old brooms make good hockey sticks.

Each player tries to hit the puck across the room to the opponent's goal with his hockey stick. You must also try to keep your opponent from scoring into *your* goal. If you are playing on a hard, smooth-surfaced floor, play in your socks so it seems more like you are skating on ice.

Jump the Puddle. Using tape, outline the borders of a puddle on the carpet or floor. Line up in single file behind a player chosen to be the leader. One person is in charge of a record player.

While music is playing, players must follow the leader in jumping across the puddle. Jump to the rhythm of the music. When the music stops, whoever is stuck over or in the puddle must drop out of line and play the record player. The person who was playing the music beforehand then joins the game.

Kitty in the Corner. Play this game with four friends. Pick one to be the kitty. He must stand in the middle of the room.

The rest of you must each stand in a different corner of the room. When kitty says, "Kitty wants a corner," everyone runs for a different corner. Kitty also runs for a corner!

The person left without a corner is the new kitty and goes to the middle. If the same person ends up being kitty more than three or four times in a row, let him go to a corner and pick someone else to be the new kitty.

Musical Chairs. Line up some chairs in a single row. Use one less chair than the number of people playing. While someone plays a record, the players move in a circle around the line of chairs. When the music stops, everyone scrambles to sit down in the nearest chair available! The person who is left out leaves the game. The players then stand in a circle again, and another chair is removed. Repeat the game. One more person drops out and another chair is removed. Keep playing until only one player is left!

Shadow Mystery. Stretch a large sheet across the room. Set a lamp behind the sheet so the light shines through. Split up everyone in two teams.

One team goes behind the sheet. One at a time, the players on that team wiggle, dance, jump, move around, and change their positions as the lamp light casts their shadows upon the sheet.

The team members on the front side of the sheet, of course, can only see the shadows! They must try guessing which players on the other team are making the shadows. When all the players on the performing team have had a turn making shadows, the teams switch places. The team to make the most correct guesses is the winner.

Tag Games
Arm Tag. Play this game with one friend. Stand facing each other, about an arm's length apart. Try to tag each other by moving your arms and bodies only. You cannot move your feet, but you may twist, duck, and bend to avoid being tagged. If you move your feet, you lose that round.

Basic Tag. Pick out a spot to be home base. No player may be tagged when he is on home base.

Choose one player to be *It*. As other players run to avoid him, *It* must try tagging them with his hands. When a person is tagged, he becomes the new *It*.

Circle Tag. It is better to play this game with only four or five friends. One person is chosen to be *It*. The others hold hands and form a circle. *It* stands outside the circle and points to a person he wants to tag.

It then runs around the circle, trying to tag the person he pointed to. At the same time, the players make the circle spin around and around, trying to avoid the tag. When the player is tagged, he becomes the new *It*.

Shadow Tag. Play this game on a sunny day. The player chosen as *It* tries to jump on the shadow of the other players as they run to avoid him. When *It* steps on a shadow, he calls out the name of that player. That player then becomes *It*.

Stoop Tag. Play this game just like basic tag, but do not have a home base. A player is safe from being tagged only when he stoops. However, each player can only stoop three times during the game. *It* tries to tag the players as they run and stoop to avoid the tag. When a player is tagged, he becomes *It* and the game starts over.

Walking Tag. Play basic tag, but instead of running, you must walk. It is harder than you think!

Outdoor Games
Bounce the Ball. Stand six feet away from a bucket. Try to bounce a ball into the bucket. The ball must bounce once on its way before landing in the bucket. Take turns with your friends. Later, try the game standing 10 or 12 feet away.

Grandmother's Footsteps. Choose one person to stand so his back is towards you. This player is "grandmother." The rest of you stand in single file some distance away from grandmother, behind a starting line.

Try to creep up on grandmother without being seen. Each time grandmother turns her head, everyone must instantly freeze. If grandmother sees anyone moving, the person who was caught must return to the starting line. The first person to reach grandmother is then the new grandmother.

Jump the River. Mark off the banks of a river with two long pieces of rope. Make one end of the river narrow, the other end wide.

Starting at the narrow end, take turns jumping forward and backward across the river. Work your way toward the wide end as you jump. Anyone who lands in the river gets "wet" and falls out of the game. Continue until everyone has become wet. (You can pull the ropes wider apart if needed.)

Leap Frog. Split up into two equal-sized teams. Have each team line up single file. Everyone must squat down close to the ground.

On "go," the last player in each line jumps over the line of squatting players, one at a time. (Be sure there is enough room between players!) When he reaches the front of the line, he squats down there. Then the next player from the back starts "leaping the frogs." Continue until the original "leaper" is again at the end of the line. The first team to finish wins.

Red Light, Green Light. One player is chosen to be *It*. The others line up single file about 20 feet away.

It turns his back to the group and says "green light." The players in line start running toward *It*. Meanwhile, *It* counts quickly to 10. Then he calls "red light" and whirls around.

The players must freeze when they hear "red light." If *It* sees anyone moving, he sends him back to the starting line. The game continues until a player gets close enough to tag *It* before he can call "red light." This player is then the new *It*.

Simple Simon. This is a very old game, but just as fun as ever. One player is the leader and faces the others. He says something like this: "Simple Simon says put your hands on your head!" and performs the movement himself. The others must copy the movement, putting their hands on their heads, too.

But sometimes, to trick the players, the leader will give an order *without* first saying "Simple Simon says . . ." For instance, he might just say, "Put your finger on your cheek!" Anyone who follows the order is then out!

Take turns being the leader.

Statue. The person who is *It* twists and turns each of the other players into different positions and then lets them go. Each person must freeze in that position like a statue. After all the players have become statues, *It* chooses the one he thinks is the funniest or best. That person becomes the new *It*.

Gardens

Artificial Flower Garden. This activity is especially fun in the winter months. "Plant" plastic flowers and fabric flowers in pots, window-sill planters, and coffee cans. You can also use the flowers to make a pretty centerpiece for your table.

Birdseed Bowl Garden. Fill a small bowl half full with moist soil. Sprinkle some birdseed in it and cover with some more moist soil. Watch for sprouts!

Bulb Garden. Plant several bulbs in a wide, shallow dish. Put sand or gravel around the bulbs to hold them in place. Then add some water. Crocus, hyacinth, narcissus, tulip, lily, daffodil or jonquil bulbs all make good gardens.

Cactus Garden. Visit a plant store and buy some tiny cactus plants in pots. Place the potted cactus plants next to each other on a tray to form a garden. Water them once in awhile and watch for blossoms.

Crystal Garden. Mix 4 tablespoons of salt, 4 tablespoons of water, and 1 tablespoon of ammonia.

Place three or four pieces of charcoal close together in a disposable foil pie plate. Pour the mixture over the charcoal. Drop several colors of food coloring onto different parts of the charcoal. After awhile, crystals will form on the charcoal. Some crystals will form immediately, others will take about a day to appear. Try not to disturb the dish once the crystals start growing.

Eggshell Garden. Clean some empty egg shell halves and fill each with some soil and potting mix. If you want, place the half shells in an egg carton to help them stand upright. Plant a few seeds in each half shell. Keep the soil moist. When the seedlings have grown between one and two inches tall, transplant them into larger containers.

Moss Garden. Look around in a park or forest for some moss. It usually grows near the shady side of trees. Dig up a small clump of the moss and take it home.

Fill the bottom of a large, flat dish with water. Place the moss in the water. Add water only once a week!

Name Garden. Obtain some seeds that will grow into very small plants. Ask an adult which ones to get. Split up the seeds into piles for each letter in your name.

Clear away a patch of fine soil for your seeds. With a stick, draw your name in the soil. Carefully lay the seeds in the grooves of the letters. Then cover the seeds with more soil.

Make sure the patch stays watered. When the plants grow, they will spell your name!

Sponge Garden. Punch a hole in the end of a sponge and tie on a piece of string to hang it later. Then dip the sponge in water. Sprinkle some parsley seeds on the sponge.

Hang the sponge in a sunny window and keep it wet. Soon the seeds will grow and cover the sponge. (You can keep the sponge garden watered using an atomizer or an old spray bottle.)

Spring Garden. Springtime is the best time to plant seeds. Ask if you can plant a garden outdoors. If not, plant some seeds indoors using flower boxes or coffee cans for containers. Seeds that grow the quickest include bean, corn, pumpkin, marigold, zinnia, and four-o'clocks.

Surprise Garden. In wintertime, when plant growth has stopped in the ground, cut out a

Surprise Garden

3-by-3 inch slab of soil that is frozen solid.

Take the slab indoors and place it in a dish or on a tray where it will get sunlight. Water the slab as needed to keep it moist.

Watch the slab over a period of time to see what kinds of plant life spring up. If the slab was taken from rich soil, you might get grass. If it was taken from a vacant lot, you might get weeds! What kinds of surprises do you find?

Vegetable Garden. Following the directions on seed packets, plant any kind of vegetables you want for your own garden. You will enjoy the fresh, homegrown taste later and have a lot of fun at the same time!

Vegetable-Top Forest. Cut off the tops from carrots, turnips, beets, or parsnips. Make the cuts about an inch from the top of each vegetable. Clip back the leaves so they are just half an inch or so tall.

Next, place the tops in a shallow bowl or plate. Fill with just enough water to come a quarter inch up the vegetables. Place the bowl in a warm, sunny spot, and keep up the water level.

After several weeks, the leaves will grow quite tall! You can add beauty to your vegetable-top forest by surrounding the vegetables with colored pebbles at the bottom of the plate.

Gasses (Science)

Experiment I. You can actually make some gas and see it forming! Place a funnel into the opening of an empty bottle. Pour 2 tablespoons of baking soda and ½ cup of vinegar in the bottle.

See the bubbles forming? That is carbon dioxide gas! Remove the funnel and *quickly* cover the bottle mouth with your hand. Feel the pressure against your hand? The pressure is caused by new molecules of gas forming in the bottle. *Another way to do it:* Instead of placing your hand over the bottle top, quickly plug the bottle's mouth with a cork. What happens?

Experiment II. In this experiment, you can inflate a balloon without blowing it up! It also shows that gas can expand and take up space.

Stretch the end of a balloon onto the mouth of a pop bottle. Then take it off. Stick the bottom of a funnel into the balloon. Pour in 1 tablespoon of baking soda. Set the balloon aside.

Now put the funnel into the bottle. Pour in ¼ cup of vinegar. Pick up the balloon again. Stretch the balloon back onto the mouth of the bottle. Hold it up with your hand so the baking soda inside the balloon falls into the bottle. The baking soda will now mix with the vinegar inside the bottle.

Watch the balloon inflate from the gas forming inside!

Gifts

Autumn Leaves Placemat. Arrange a selection of dry autumn leaves on a 12-by-18-inch sheet of construction paper. Carefully cover the arrangement with a sheet of clear contact paper. When the contact paper is sealed firmly over the leaves, fold the excess contact paper under the edges of the construction paper. Make a set of these placemats to give as a gift.

Bath Salts. Mix some Epsom salts, several drops of food coloring, and a few drops of cologne. Place the mixture in clear plastic bags, tie with ribbons, and give as gifts.

Bottle Cap Trivet. Find a strong, square piece of cardboard to use as a base for your trivet. Collect some soda bottle caps and glue them in rows on the cardboard base. (Use plenty of glue.) Place some heavy books on top of the trivet while the glue is drying. Then remove the books and coat the trivet with enamel paint. You can apply the paint with a brush or use a spray can.

Bud Vase. Find a plastic or glass tube that comes with a new toothbrush. Make a stand from modeling clay and paint it with bright enamel paint. Also paint the top of the toothbrush tube with a design matching the color of the clay stand. Insert the "vase" in the stand and put a flower bud in the vase.

Burlap-Covered Gifts. Use pieces of burlap to cover objects given as gifts. Cut enough burlap to fit the item you want to cover. Paint the object with glue using a paintbrush. Press the burlap over the glued surface. Clip off any excess burlap, and wipe away excess glue with a damp cloth. Use brightly colored braid or cream-thick poster paints to make designs on the burlap surface.

Objects to cover with burlap include juice cans (for pencil holders), jars (for kitchen storage), and round ice cream cartons (for wastepaper baskets).

Button Box. Paint a pint-sized ice cream carton or cover it with a piece of contact paper. Cover the lid also. Glue a button on top of the lid to finish.

Car Litter Box. Use an empty rectangular cracker or cereal box to make a litter box for the car. Cut off the top flaps. Then cut a piece of construction paper to fit around the outside of the box. Next, using a brush, spread glue over the surface of the box so you can stick on the construction paper. Allow it to dry.

Punch a hole at the top end of each narrow side of the box. Attach the ends of a 15-inch length of yarn to holes to make a handle for the litter box.

Decorate the outside of the box with crayons or paper cutouts. Write the words "Litter Box" on the front, and it is finished!

Clothespin Holder. Obtain an empty one-gallon plastic bleach bottle. Ask an adult to help you cut through the bottom of the handle. This makes a slit so the holder can be slipped over a clothesline.

Cut away the top half of the bottle on the side opposite the handle. Use felt-tip markers to decorate the holder or glue on felt designs.

Coiled Rope Hotmat. Soak a length of sisal rope in diluted white glue. Working over a piece of waxed paper on a flat surface, roll the rope tightly into a coil that is about 10 inches across. Cut away any excess rope.

Lay another piece of waxed paper on top of the coil. Put a heavy weight on top of this. The weight will prevent the mat from warping as the glue dries. Later, remove the waxed paper, and give the hotmat as a gift.

Cork Hotmat. Cut a medium-sized circle from a sheet of thin cork. Paint a design on the hotmat with poster paints. After the paint dries, ask an adult to help you coat the hotmat with clear varnish. After it is dry, give it as a gift.

Corsage Box. Use a cylinder-shaped ice cream carton for making this corsage box. Make sure the box is clean and dry. Cover the box and lid with pieces of colored construction paper cut to fit. Fasten on the pieces with glue.

Punch a small hole on each side of the carton. Run a ribbon through each hole. Tie a knot in each ribbon on the inside to keep it from slipping from the hole. Place the lid on the box and tie the ribbons to each other on the outside to form a handle.

Cotton Ball Sachet. Drip a small amount of perfume on a cotton ball. Fold a small paper doily in half, and place the cotton ball inside the doily. Staple the doily closed, then staple a bow to the top of it. Give the sachet as a gift.

Decorated Can Opener. Spread waterproof glue around the handle of a metallic can opener. Before the glue dries, add sequins, glitter, spangles, or rhinestones for decorations. You can use a pair of tweezers to set the decorations in place.

Desk Caddy. Cut off the lid of a cardboard egg carton. Paint the lid inside and out with tempera paint. Allow the paint to dry.

From the bottom part of the carton, cut two sets of four cups, including the center cone. Trim these sections neatly. Cut the tops off the center cones. Paint the sections a color contrasting the color of the lid. Allow to dry.

Glue the cup sections to each end of the lid. Store paper clips, thumbtacks, etc., in each section. Pencils can be inserted in the center cones.

Desk Pad. Stick leatherette corners on each corner of a piece of blotting paper. Decorate the blotting paper, using a felt-tip marker or crayons. Mount the blotting paper on a piece of cardboard the same size.

Doily Corsage. Wrap strips of colored tissue paper around a pencil so they become curled. Glue the ends of the curled strips to the middle of a paper doily so the curled ends face outward in a circle around the center of the doily. Fasten a pin to the back of the doily and give as a gift.

Egg Carton Snack Server. From a plastic foam egg carton, cut out a square section containing four cups. Poke a hole in the center of the four cups. Poke both ends of a pipe cleaner through the hole, leaving a loop handle on top. Bend both ends of the pipe cleaner sideways underneath to keep the handle in place.

Father's Day Greeting Card. Cut out a 6-by-9-inch rectangle from a piece of red construction paper. Fold it in half lengthwise, making a tall, narrow card.

Next, draw the outline of a necktie, about eight inches long, on gray construction paper. Cut out the tie and glue it to the front of the card. Print a greeting inside.

Finger-Painted Placemat. Finger paint on a rectangular or oval piece of shiny white cardboard. Allow to dry. Then cover both sides of the cardboard with a coating of shellac.

Handprint Gift. Mix one color of tempera paint with a small amount of liquid detergent. Press your hand into the paint or paint the palm of your hand with a brush. Then, make a handprint on a plastic foam meat tray, plastic lid, or paper plate. Give it as a gift.

Ice Cream Carton Wastepaper Basket. Obtain a clean, dry five-gallon ice cream container. Cover the outside with a mosaic of pictures cut from magazines, using glue to fasten the pictures in place. When the glue has dried, cover the pictures with a sheet of clear contact paper cut to fit around the container.

Jewelry Box. Paint a cardboard egg carton and allow it to dry. Glue a cotton ball in the bottom of each cup for the jewelry to rest on. Decorate the box by gluing on bits of broken jewelry.

Juice Can Pencil Holder. Cut a piece of paper to fit around an empty frozen juice can. Decorate the paper with finger paint, then glue the paper around the can. Allow it to dry.

Key Pin. Ask an adult for a discarded key. Cover one side of it with glue, then sprinkle on a thick coat of glitter. Allow everything to dry, and shake off the excess glitter.

Turn the key over. Cement a pin clasp on the back side of the key.

Magnetic Picture Noteholder. Find a picture of yourself or someone else in your family. Place a small plastic lid over the face of the person in the picture. With a pencil, trace around the lid and onto the photograph. Lift the lid and cut out the circle you traced.

Spread glue around the top of the lid. Glue the photograph circle to it. Then turn the lid upside down. Glue a small magnet inside the lid. Allow everything to dry.

The magnet will hold notes to your refrigerator door.

Masking Tape "Leather-Look" Gifts. Cover a gift object completely with small strips of masking tape. Rub brown paste-type shoe polish all over the taped surface. Wipe away any excess polish. Now the gift object looks like it is made of leather!

Some suggestions: a vase (a small glass jar or cola bottle covered with tape); a pencil holder (a juice can covered with tape); and a bookmark (a strip of paper covered with tape).

Milk Carton Book Ends. Cover a pair of small milk cartons with paper and pictures cut from magazines. (Use glue to do this.) Fill the cartons with sand for weight. Glue the cartons shut. Clamp the top with clothespins until the glue is dry.

Milk Carton Paperweight. Cut off the tops of two milk cartons. Cut them down so that when one carton is inserted into the other, a cube is formed.

Fill one carton with sand or plaster, and cover it with the other carton, forming the cube. Cover the cube with a single layer of papier mâché. Then cover the entire cube with scraps of colored magazine pictures.

Mitten Bean Bags. Cut off the end of an old mitten below the thumb. Fill loosely with beans. Sew the opening shut, and your bean bag is complete. An old sock can be used, too.

Mother's Day Greeting Card. Fold a 9-by-12-inch sheet of colored construction paper in half the short way, forming a card.

On the front of the card, paste a flattened paper cupcake container. In the middle of the cupcake container, paste a circle that is two inches in diameter. On the circle, write the words, "Best Mother in the World." Cut two short ribbons from crepe paper, and glue the ribbons directly below the cupcake container to look like a blue-ribbon prize. Write a greeting inside.

Nut Bags. Crack some nuts, then fill some small plastic bags with the nuts. Tie the bags with pretty ribbons and give them as gifts.

Mother's Day Greeting Card

Orange Sachet Ball. Press some whole cloves into an orange, covering the entire surface. Place the orange in a bag with a small amount of cinnamon and allspice. Shake well.

Make a hanger by pinning on a loop of ribbon. The orange will dry out and retain a nice smell for a long time. The person who receives this gift can hang it in a closet (or elsewhere) to keep the closet smelling nice.

Painted Drinking Glass. With a brush and enamel or plastic paint, make a picture, greeting, or design on the outside of a tall jelly glass. You can paint a colored band or two around the bottom also. Allow it to dry, and give as a gift.

Papier Mâché Bowl. Dip strips of newspaper into diluted paste and completely cover the outside of a bowl. Make at least three layers of newspaper. Allow it to dry. Remove the bowl-shaped papier mâché, paint it, and give as a gift.

Picture Paperweight. Place a snapshot of yourself, face up, under the bottom of a glass furniture coaster (the kind used under the legs of chairs and tables). Hold the picture in place by putting a larger construction paper circle over the picture and gluing the circle to the coaster.

Plastic Foam Pin Cushion. Cover a plastic foam ball with a piece of fabric cut to fit. Pin the fabric on the ball at the bottom.

Next, obtain a plastic lid (the kind that goes with a spray can). Turn the lid upside down and set it on a flat surface. Press the bottom side of the plastic foam ball into the lid so it will nest firmly in the lid. You might have to fiddle with the ball a little to help it fit into the lid because of the fabric covering the ball.

Salad Fork Recipe Holder. Bend a salad fork into the shape shown in the illustration. Next, find a twist-on type jar lid to use as a base. Then sand off the top of the lid where the fork will be attached. Stick the fork onto the lid with epoxy glue. Spread some more epoxy glue over the rest of the lid's surface and apply small colored beads and sequins for decoration. The fork tines will hold a recipe card so it can be read easily when using the recipe.

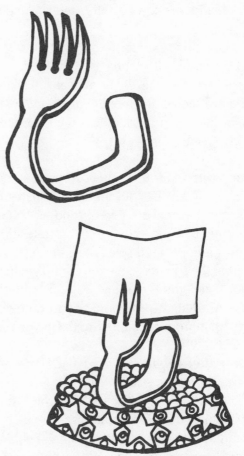

Sand-Covered Vase.   Obtain a brown-colored bottle or jar. Then line the bottom of a large pan with some waxed paper and put some sand into the pan.

Using a brush, spread glue all over your bottle or jar. Then roll the glue-covered jar in the sand until sand covers the outside of the jar. Allow the jar to stand until the glue dries. Pick out some flowers or dried weeds to place in the vase, and give as a gift.

Satin Sachet Bag.   From a piece of satin, cut 2 three-inch squares. With a needle and thread, sew the satin pieces around some sachet tablets. Decorate the bag with lace and other trim. Ask an adult to help you with this, if necessary.

Shell Pin.   Glue a pin clasp to the back of a small seashell or shell macaroni. Turn the shell over and paint it any color with a small water-color brush. While the paint is wet, sprinkle the pin with glitter. Allow it to dry, and shake off the excess glitter.

Soap Balls.   In a mixing bowl, blend a little water with some soap flakes. Use an eggbeater to do the mixing. Let the mixture dry partway, then mold it into soap balls. Allow them to harden, and give as gifts.

Spice Rope.   From fabric scraps, cut out 3 six-inch squares. Lay out the three squares on a flat surface. Place a different kind of spice on each square. Cinnamon sticks, whole cloves, and allspice are good spices to use.

Gather the squares at the edges and tie them at the top with string, forming sacks. Tie the three sacks on a length of ribbon or yarn about two inches apart from each other to finish your rope.

Stone Paperweight.   Find a flat stone about the size of a big potato. Also, look for some small, colorful pebbles (or shells, if you live near the beach) to use as decorations.

Clean the large stone and the small pebbles or shells. Place the stone on a piece of paper. Coat the sides and top of the stone with a strong glue. Press the pebbles or shells into the glue, covering the stone completely with the pebbles or shells. Make sure the pebbles are placed close together!

When the glue has dried, have an adult help you spray over the entire paperweight with a clear varnish.

Tin Can Flowerpot.   Obtain an empty can that is three or four inches deep. Make sure the rim is smooth. Paint the can with any color enamel paint and allow it to dry.

Stick straight clothespins all around the edge, as close together as possible. Paint the clothespins in a contrasting color from the can, and let them dry.

Next, tie a pretty ribbon or cord around the clothespins to help keep them in place on the flowerpot. Fill the pot with soil and plant some seeds or a bulb inside.

Tiny Treasure Boxes.   You can make empty matchboxes into bright, pretty storage containers! Cover matchboxes with felt scraps, pieces of paper, or paint. These boxes are handy for storing coins, beads, paper clips, and other small items.

Toddler Toy.   Cut out two fabric circles big enough to cover the ends of a short cardboard tube. Glue one circle over one end of the tube.

Put an old golf ball inside the tube. Glue the remaining circle over the open end.

Glue fabric scraps over the rest of the tube. The toy will stand on end, but if placed on an incline, it will tumble end over end!

Tug-of-War Pet Toy. Cut off the legs of two pairs of old nylon panty hose. Tie three of the leg pieces together at the toes. Braid them tightly. Tie them again at the top. Now you and your pet can play tug-of-war!

Waxed Paper Placemats. Place a placemat-sized rectangle of waxed paper on a sheet of newspaper. Set a number of materials on top of the waxed paper, such as small flowers, crayon bits, small pieces of colored tissue paper, leaves, and weeds.

Next, place another rectangle of waxed paper on top of the materials. Then place a sheet of newspaper over that. Press the top piece of paper with a warm iron. Remove the newspaper to reveal a colorful waxed paper placemat!

Wooden Decorated Spoon. Stain a wooden spoon with brown shoe polish. Glue some tiny straw flowers close together inside the bowl part of the spoon.

Tie a pretty ribbon around the spoon just above the bowl. Ask an adult to help you put a hook in the handle to hang it.

Gravity (Science)

Gravity is.a strong force that pulls objects toward the earth. It keeps things on the earth from falling off into space.

Demonstration. Toss several objects in the air. Notice that they always come back down! Gravity pulls the objects back to the earth. If you jump up, you will fall back to the ground also.

Next, stand on a chair and drop two objects at the same time from the same height. One of the objects should be heavy (such as a bean bag) and the other light (such as a pencil). Notice that both objects hit the ground at the same time, even though one is heavier than the other!

Experiment. There is one case wherein a lighter object will fall back to earth slower than a heavy object. This happens when the lightweight object is built so that it catches air currents while falling. The air currents slow down the fall of the object. Parachutes and gliders take advantage of that fact to avoid fast downward descents.

You can do an easy experiment yourself to see how this happens. Stand on a chair and drop two objects at the same time from the same height — one of the objects should be a crayon and the other, a sheet of typing paper. Which one lands on the floor last? Why?

H

Halloween

Activities

Costumes. Use laundry bags, burlap sacks, or large brown paper bags to make costumes. Cut out holes for your head and arms. Draw or paste designs on the sacks. Make a mask to go with your costume.

Creepy Feely Box. Cut a hole in one side of a cardboard box large enough for an arm to reach through. Paint the box black. When dry, place creepy-feeling objects and Halloween objects inside. Have your friends reach into the box to feel the contents. Can they identify the objects they touch?

Here are a few suggested objects for your feely box: a rubber bat, plastic false teeth, a small plastic jack-o'-lantern, an eye mask, a rubber spider, pumpkin seeds, an apple, and a popcorn ball.

Ghost Favors. To make ghost favors for your Halloween party, you need round lollipops and some white napkins. Cut the napkins in half along one fold. Put a sucker in the center of this half napkin. Fold the napkin over the lollipop and tie a string under the candy. This makes a cute little ghost-shaped favor to give to your friends! Use a felt-tip marker to draw eyes on the head.

Makeup. Mix one part shortening with two parts cornstarch. Add a few drops of food coloring. Blend until creamy. Now color your face with the makeup. Use other colors of makeup as desired. To help the makeup set, dust your face with talcum powder.

Playdough Fun. Make your own playdough (see recipes in the *Playdough* section) colored with orange or black tempera paint. Make Halloween figures such as cats, bats, pumpkins, etc., from the playdough.

For an interesting effect, start with plain, un-

colored playdough. Knead in some red and yellow powdered tempera, and watch the dough turn orange as you work it!

Pumpkin Fun. Feel, smell, and taste a pumpkin as you carve it to make a jack-o'-lantern. Wash the seeds you saved and set them aside to dry. When you finish with the jack-o'-lantern, it can be cut up and cooked. (If you keep it overnight, be sure it is refrigerated.) Save a few pieces of the uncooked pumpkin to compare with the cooked pumpkin. Later, with the help of an adult, you can make pumpkin pies, bread, cookies, and ice cream. For winter greenery, you can plant pumpkin seeds in flowerpots.

Roast Pumpkin Seeds. After you have carved your jack-o'-lantern, save the pumpkin seeds. Rinse them off and allow them to dry. Then mix 2 cups of the seeds in a bowl with 2 tablespoons of melted butter and ½ teaspoon of Worcestershire sauce.

After mixing, spread the seeds in a shallow pan. Shake a small amount of salt on the seeds. Place the pan in an oven at 300 degrees for one hour. Open the oven once in awhile and stir the seeds. The seeds are done when they are crispy and brown.

Sound Effects. Play a Halloween sound-effects record. What sounds seem the scariest? How do you think the sound effects were created?

Art

Black Cat Bookmark. From black construction paper, cut out a ¾-by-5-inch rectangle. At one end, cut a ½-inch-deep fringe in the paper. At the other end, glue on a cat's head cut from black paper. Glue eyes, nose, and mouth pieces cut from green paper to the head.

Charcoal Halloween Drawing. Draw Halloween symbols, such as bats, cats, and witches, working with black charcoal on orange paper.

Black Cat Bookmark

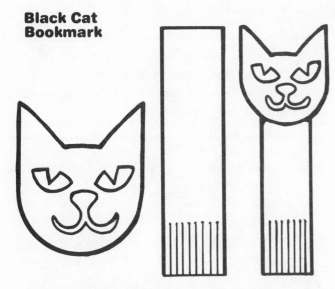

Crayon-Resist Scene. Using black crayon, draw a scary picture on a sheet of paper. You might show a witch flying on her broomstick, a haunted house, or a spooky graveyard. Be sure to color very heavily with the crayon!

Complete the scene by painting over it with red, yellow, and orange watercolors, making wide stripes across the paper. This creates a fine silhouette effect!

Crayon Rubbing Halloween Shapes. Cut out Halloween shapes such as cats, pumpkins, owls, ghosts, bats, and witches. Place the cut-out shapes under a sheet of paper. Rub over the surface of the paper, using a crayon without the wrapper. This makes impressions of the cutouts underneath!

Creepy Picture. Brush clear water on a piece of construction paper until the paper is quite wet. Then dab or drip some ink or paint on the wet surface, creating strange shapes.

Cut and Paste Spooky Picture. From scraps of yellow, orange, and white paper, cut out some "scary" things. Glue the pieces on a 9-by-12-inch sheet of black construction paper to make a spooky picture.

You can make a ghost for the picture by wrapping a sheet of facial tissue around a wad of paper. Fasten a rubber band at the base of the tissue ball to form a ghost head and body. Glue the ghost on the black paper.

Ghostly Painting. Brush clear water on a piece of dark-colored construction paper until the paper is very wet. Then mix one part liquid bleach with three parts water. Use this solution to paint a Halloween picture on the wet paper. At first you will not see anything, but when the paper dries, the picture will appear!

Night Scene. Using black crayon on black paper, draw a Halloween night scene (a witch riding on a broomstick, the full moon in the sky, bats flying, etc.). Lightly brush over the picture with white tempera paint, or use a cotton ball to dust the picture with dry white tempera. Watch the picture appear!

Placemats. Lay a placemat-sized rectangle of waxed paper on newspaper. On top of that, lay some Halloween shapes cut from black and orange paper. Sprinkle with black and orange crayon shavings.

Place a second rectangle of waxed paper on top of the shavings and cover with another sheet of newspaper. Press with a warm iron, then remove the newspapers to reveal a colorful Halloween placemat!

Pumpkin Seed Collage. Obtain some pumpkin seeds from a health food store, or use seeds removed from a jack-o'-lantern. Glue the seeds together on background paper to make a collage or mosaic.

Self-Portrait. Draw a picture of yourself showing how you will look on Halloween.

Trick-or-Treat Collage. On background paper, glue empty candy wrappers to make a collage.

Window Display. Cut out various Halloween shapes from black, orange, and white pieces of tissue paper. Place the shapes between two

**Witch
Greeting
Card**

you cast a spell on me!

FOLD

FOLD

**Construction
Paper Bat**

sheets of waxed paper. Then put the waxed papers between two pieces of newspaper. Press over the top newspaper with a warm iron. Remove the picture and hang it up in a window so the light shines through it.

Witch Greeting Card. From construction paper, cut out a shape as shown in the illustration. Write a Halloween message inside the shape. Then fold over the edges as illustrated. When the witch's arms are opened, the message will be revealed.

Bats

Construction Paper Bat. Fold a 9-by-12-inch sheet of black construction paper in half. Lay the folded sheet in front of you like a book. On the front, outline half of a bat, as shown. Cut out and unfold to reveal a full bat.

Hanging Bat. Fold a 9-by-12-inch sheet of black construction paper in half lengthwise. Now you have a double 9-by-6-inch rectangle. Draw a bat on the front side of the folded rectangle, as illustrated. Cut out the bat through the double thickness of the rectangle. Punch a hole in the top center of the head. Tie a piece of thread or yarn through the hole and hang your decoration.

Paper Plate Bat. Paint a paper plate black, then glue on some facial features cut from colored paper. To make wings, cut an 8-by-8-inch square of black paper in half from one corner to another. Glue the wings so they are spreading out from the back of the paper plate, the freshly cut edges down. Tear along the bottom edges of the wings to create a ragged effect.

Cats

Arched Cat. On a 9-by-6-inch sheet of black construction paper, draw and cut out a large, wide arch. This is the body of your cat. From the cut-away scraps make a head and a tail. Attach the head to one side of the arch and the tail to the other. Glue it to a sheet of orange background paper.

Standing Cat. Fold a sheet of construction paper in half lengthwise. From the unfolded side, cut away an arch. The remaining shape forms a cat body with four legs.

From the pieces that were cut away, make a head and a tail. Then, on the top, folded side of the cat, cut two slits. Make one slit about an inch away from the left-hand edge. Make the other slit an inch away from the right-hand edge. Slip the head piece into one slit and the tail piece into the other slit. Display your standing cat.

Paper Strip Cat. Form a strip of black construction paper into a bulge, then glue down the ends on a piece of cardboard so the "bulge" faces up. This standing "semi-circle" is the cat's body. To one side glue a head made from a paper ring. To the other side glue a short, curled strip for a tail. Glue a pair of ears to the head and then display.

Decorations

Balloon Mobile. Inflate several orange balloons. Draw spooky faces on the balloons using a black felt-tip marker. Suspend the balloons with string from wire hangers.

Balloon Table Decoration. Use a white, black, orange, or yellow balloon to make a "head" centerpiece for your table.

Glue black or orange cutouts to the balloon to make a face. Make hair by gluing paper strips to the top. You can also make a collar from paper strips. Using a small cardboard frame as a base, set the decoration in the center of your table.

Construction Paper Chain. Cut strips of orange and black construction paper. Form interlocking loops to make a chain, alternating the colors. Hang for decoration.

Shrunken Head. Peel a potato, then carefully carve out a mouth and eyes. Since the potato will

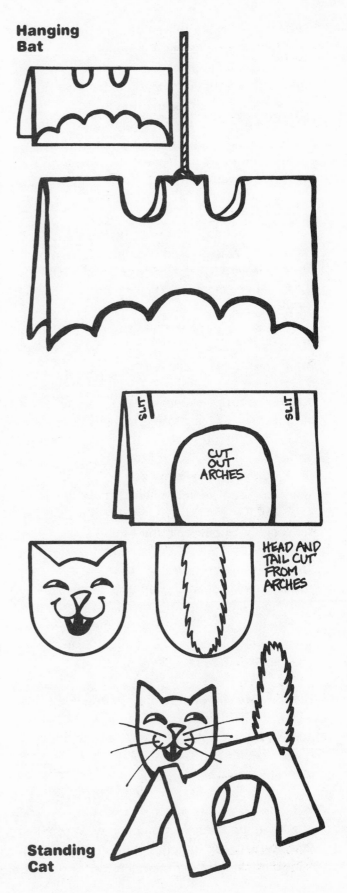

shrink later, make the mouth and eyes a little bigger than you would otherwise. Push large, colored, plastic-topped pins into the eye sockets. Push a paper clip into the top of the head. Tie a string through the clip.

Find a dry, warm place to hang the potato. (A closet is a good place.) Hang the potato there until it shrinks and hardens. After it dries, glue on some black yarn for hair. Display.

Games

Apple Bobbing Without Water. First, tie strings to the stems of all your apples. Then hang the apples from a tree branch or door frame. Make sure the apples are hung at the mouth level of your guests.

Players must place their hands behind their backs and try to get a bite from an apple while it gently swings back and forth.

Apple Fishing. Ahead of time, make some fishing poles by tying strings to the ends of some sticks. Attach cup hooks to the free ends of the strings.

Next, obtain some more cup hooks and screw one into each apple. When you are ready to play, put the apples into a bucket of water. Try hooking the apples with the fishing poles.

Jack-O'-Lantern Bean Bag Toss. Beforehand, make pumpkin-shaped bean bags of orange felt. Decorate each bag with facial features made from felt scraps. Stand a short distance away from a wastepaper basket. See how many bean bags you can toss into the can.

Pin the Mouth on the Pumpkin. Play this game just like *Pin the Tail on the Donkey*, except try to pin a paper mouth on a large drawing of a pumpkin. You can also play *Pin the Tail on the Cat.*

What Is This? Before the game starts, put a number of unusual objects on a tray. When it is time to play, ask the players to sit in a circle. Turn out the lights and pass the tray of objects around the circle. The players should feel the objects on the tray while the tray is in their hands. After the tray has been passed to everyone, take it out of the room. Turn the lights back on. The players then try to guess some of the objects that were on the tray.

Objects to put on the tray can include a lump of sugar, a wet tea bag, a toothpick, a wishbone, a feather, a bar of soap, a key, a walnut, a grape, a piece of plastic foam packing material, and an egg carton cup.

Who Was Here? Ahead of time, cut out some gigantic footprints from sheets of paper. Tape the footprints to the floor, up the walls, and if you can manage it, upside down on the ceiling!

When your guests arrive, show them the footprints. Ask them to guess who was there. What did he look like, why did he come, and where did he go? Have your friends draw pictures and make up stories about their ideas.

Witch's Brew Treasure Hunt. Give each guest a paper bag. Show them samples of the ingredients used for making a witch's brew. (Display a twig, an acorn, a leaf, a dead flower, and a pebble.) Ask your friends to hunt for the items you have shown. The first person to find each of the items is the winner.

Ghosts and Goblins

Blot Spooks. Fold a sheet of black paper in half, then open it up. Drip a blotch of white paint on the crease. Carefully fold the paper in half again and press down on the paper. Then open it once more to see the spook inside.

Crayon Rubbing Ghost. Lay a 9-by-12-inch sheet of white paper on a flat surface. Then lay a piece of string on the paper, outlining the shape of a ghost. Carefully lay another 9-by-12-inch sheet of white paper on top of this. Fasten the sheets together with paper clips.

Using the side of a crayon without a wrapper, rub over the entire surface of the top sheet. The outline of the ghost will appear magically!

Ghost Puppet. Stuff the bottom of a small white paper bag with crumpled newspaper. Turn the bag over and tie a string around it to form a neck. Make sure to leave enough room inside the neck to insert your middle finger.

Cut a hole on each side of the front part of the bag so your first and third fingers can be placed through for arms. Draw or paste on the facial features you want.

Ghost Tree. To make a tree outline, trace your hand and arm up to the elbow on a piece of paper. Paint the inside of the outline. Cut out spooky eyes, a nose, and a mouth from dark paper. Glue the pieces onto the tree to form a ghostly expression.

Goblin Tree. Draw a leafless tree on a large sheet of drawing paper. Use dark crayons to create an eerie effect. Fasten the drawing to a bulletin board or a wall.

Next, draw and cut out some goblins, ghosts, jack-o'-lanterns, bats, spiders, etc., from scrap paper. Staple each cutout to a short length of yarn. Then staple the lengths of yarn to the drawing so the cutouts appear to be hanging from the barren tree limbs. Prop up the picture for display.

Papier Mâché Goblin. Cut newspaper into 1-by-6-inch strips. Dip the strips in diluted paste or liquid starch. Crisscross the strips around a crumpled piece of newspaper. Make three or four layers.

When everything is dry, coat with thick green paint. After the paint has dried, paste on colored construction paper pieces for the eyes, nose, mouth, and any other features you want.

For carrying or hanging the goblin, staple an elastic band to the top.

Paper Napkin or Tissue Paper Ghost. Spread a white paper napkin or facial tissue flat on the table. Then wad another napkin or facial tissue into a ball. Place the ball in the center of the open piece and wrap up the ball to form the head of your ghost.

Insert a Popsicle stick into the head for a handle. Then tie the head around the handle with string or a rubber band. The rest of the ghost will hang down to cover the stick. Finish by drawing a face on the ghost using a felt-tip marker.

Torn Paper Ghost. Tear out some ghost shapes from white paper. Paste the shapes on a piece of black paper. Add features to the ghosts with felt-tip markers or crayons. Then draw in a Halloween background.

Hats
Construction Paper Witch Hat. Fold a 12-by-18-inch sheet of black construction paper into a cone. Then, from orange crepe paper, cut out many two-inch squares. One at a time, wrap the squares over your finger to form caps. Dip the caps into paste and press them over the entire surface of the hat.

You also can make the cone hat from orange construction paper and the cap decorations from black crepe paper.

Devil Horns. From red construction paper, cut out a one-inch-wide strip. Make it long enough to fit around your head.

To make horns, cut out two large triangles about 11 inches wide at the base and 8 inches tall at the points. Bend the bottom corners of each triangle together and staple them to form cone horns.

Glue the horns to the headband (you can flatten the horns at the bottom) and decorate them with a felt-tip marker.

Halloween Crown. From orange construction paper, cut out a wide strip of paper long enough to fit around your head. Form it into a crown by cutting points along the top rim. Decorate the crown by gluing on Halloween shapes cut from black paper.

Newspaper Witch Hat. Form a cone from a sheet of newspaper and glue it in place. Paint on some Halloween designs. Cut out some strips of newspaper, curl them on one end (by wrapping them around a pencil), and glue them around the bottom rim of the hat for hair.

Wizard Hat. Fold a thick sheet of paper into a cone and glue the sides together. Cut the bottom to make it even. Then decorate the hat with stars, crescents, and other magic symbols.

Jack-O'-Lanterns and Pumpkins
Animated Pumpkin. Obtain a paper plate and a circle of colored paper the same size. Cut out openings in the paper circle for jack-o'-lantern facial features. Then glue the circle to the back

side of the plate. Through the openings in the circle, draw the eyes, nose, and teeth on the plate. Suspend the jack-o'-lantern from a piece of string. As the air currents cause the jack-o-lantern to stir, its eyes will seem to move!

Bag-O'-Lantern. Turn a paper bag upside down and cut jack-o'-lantern features into it. Gather the open end of the bag around the lighted end of a flashlight. Tie the bag so it will not slip up or down the flashlight, but make sure to leave the switch uncovered! Simply turn on the flashlight to make the bag-o'-lantern come alive.

Finger-Painted Jack-O'-Lantern. To form the jack-o'-lantern, finger paint a single vertical line in the center of a piece of paper. Add gradually arching lines to the left and right of the center line. Keep adding the arch lines until you have a pumpkin shape. When the paint has dried, glue on colored paper cutouts of eyes, nose, and mouth.

Hanging Pumpkin. Outline a pumpkin on a sheet of construction paper, then cut it out. Also cut out the eyes, nose, and mouth. Glue a sheet of colored tissue paper behind the face.

Glue a large rectangular hat to the top of the pumpkin. Cut a hole at the top of the rectangle and hang the pumpkin with string.

Jack-O'-Lantern Mosaic. Get some pumpkin seeds from the store or save the seeds from your jack-o'-lantern. On a sheet of black construction paper, draw the outline of a jack-o'-lantern. Glue the pumpkin seeds along the lines. Then fill in the entire area of the jack-o'-lantern with seeds placed as close together as possible.

Paint the seeds in the eye, nose, and mouth areas black. Paint the rest of the seeds orange. Cut away the excess paper that is sticking out from behind the jack-o'-lantern. Mount the mosaic to the wall or prop it upright for display. (You can tape a piece of string to the paper backing to hang it.)

Paper Bag Jack-O'-Lantern. Crumple some newspaper and stuff it into a large grocery bag. Twist the bag at the top to make a stem, holding it in place with a rubber band.

Paint the bag orange up to the stem, and paint the stem green. When the pumpkin has dried, paint on black facial features. If you want, you can make your pumpkin from a lunch-sized paper bag instead of a large one.

Paper Jack-O'-Lantern. Cut out two pumpkins of the same size and shape from two sheets of orange paper. Also, cut out spaces for the eyes, noses, and mouths from both pumpkins so they match.

Cut out a circle of red tissue paper just slightly smaller than the pumpkins. Glue the two pumpkins together to match, with the red circle sandwiched between them. Tape the pumpkin piece to a window so the light shines through the tissue paper features.

Papier Mâché Pumpkin. Stuff a paper sack with wads of newspaper. Form the stuffed bag into a pumpkin. Twist the bag near the top and wrap several strips of masking tape around the twist to form a stem that will stay in place.

Next, tear some newspaper into one-inch-wide strips. Dip the strips in diluted glue and layer them around the stuffed pumpkin bag. Make several layers of strips until the pumpkin is smooth. Make the last layer in paper towel strips, so paint will stick to the pumpkin easier.

Allow the papier mâché pumpkin to dry for several days. Then paint the pumpkin orange and the stem green. After the paint dries, paint on a jack-o'-lantern face.

Paper Plate Jack-O'-Lantern. Paint a paper plate orange. Let the paint dry. Cut out eyes, a nose, and a mouth for jack-o'-lantern features from black paper. Glue the features to the paper plate and glue a green paper stem to the top.

Paper Strip Pumpkin. Cut out a strip of orange construction paper. Paste the ends to-

Paper Strip Pumpkin

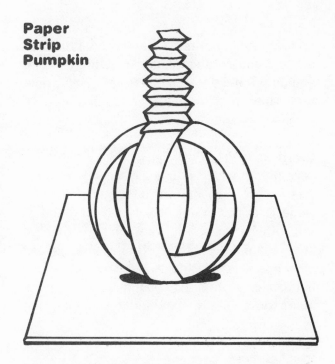

gether to form a ring. Then make another ring the same size. Glue one ring inside the other at right angles, forming a pumpkin. Glue the pumpkin to a piece of yellow paper in a standing position. For a stem, accordion-pleat a short green strip of paper and glue it to the top of the pumpkin where the strips cross.

Potato Pumpkin Prints. Cut a potato in half. From the freshly exposed surface of one of the halves, cut away the edges to leave a pumpkin shape. Dip the printing surface into orange paint, and print the pumpkin shape on black construction paper.

Pumpkin Patch Picture. First, roll some cotton balls in a shallow pan filled with orange powdered tempera paint. Then set them aside.

Next, spread some glue over the surface of a brown piece of construction paper. Then twist several lengths of green yarn around the cotton ball pumpkins. Press the yarn and pumpkins down on the glue-covered paper to represent a pumpkin patch.

Pumpkin People. Cut out a pumpkin from orange construction paper. Then cut out paper strip arms and legs. Fold the strips back and forth to make accordion-pleated arms and legs. Glue the arms and legs to the pumpkin. Using a felt-tip marker, draw on facial features. Add some newspaper strips for hair, and attach a piece of yarn for hanging.

Pumpkin with Wiggly Eyes.   Make a jack-o'-lantern with a pair of triangle-shaped holes for eyes from orange construction paper. Then cut a vertical slash on the outside of each eye. Guide a strip of white paper through one slash, behind the eyes, and out through the slash next to the other eye. With the strip centered behind the eye holes, draw a pair of eyes on the strip through the holes. Move the strip back and forth to make the eyes wiggle!

Masks
"Boo" Mask.   One advantage of this mask is that it does not cover your entire face. On a thick piece of colored paper, print the word "BOO" in large, thick letters. Make sure the letters touch each other at many points.

Cut out the word in one piece. Also cut out the centers of the "O" letters. Glue the "B" edge of the word to the top end of a dowel or thin stick. Add long strips of colored paper to the top of the stick for decoration.

When you want to be "scary," hold the boo mask to your face and peek through the two O's.

'Boo' Mask

Box Mask.   Find a deep box that will fit over your head. Turn the box upside down and decorate one panel with an eerie face. Cut out large holes for eyes, and glue on hair made from paper strips. Cut half circles from the side panels so the box will fit over your shoulders. Finish the mask by painting on any other details you want.

Cardboard "Hold-Up" Mask.   This is called a "hold-up" mask because you hold it up to your face when it is finished! To make it, you need two pieces of lightweight cardboard and a Popsicle stick.

Cut ovals the size of your face from both cardboard pieces so they match. Discard the oval cutouts and keep the matching cardboard frames. Glue the frames together with the end of the stick poking out from between them at the bottom. The stick is your handle.

Decorate the front side of the cardboard mask in any way you want. Glue a large pair of ears to the side or a pair of antennae to the top. When you are ready, hold the mask to your face and peer through the oval face hole.

Construction Paper Mask.   Pull a 12-by-18-inch sheet of construction paper over the edge of a table several times. This will give the paper a curve.

Hold the paper so the 12-inch sides are on the top and bottom. Cut fringes in these top and bottom edges about one inch apart. Slightly overlap and staple the top corners to each other. Then do the same with the bottom corners. This will shape the mask into an oval.

Add features cut from pieces of scrap paper. Attach an elastic band so the mask will stay on your face.

Foil Mask. Place a piece of foil over your face. Press the foil, following the shape of your face. Remove the foil, and poke in eye holes big enough so you can see through them clearly. Remember to poke a nose hole for breathing! Paint over the surface of the mask. (Powdered tempera mixed with liquid soap will stick to the foil.) Allow it to dry. Poke a hole on each side edge of the mask, and tie through a piece of yarn to hold the mask on your face.

Paper Bag Mask. Turn a large paper bag upside down. Decorate it with a nose, ears, mouth, and other features cut from pieces of paper. Cut out a large pair of eyes and then paint the mask.

Paper Plate Mask. Make a Halloween face on a paper plate, and add hair made from paper strips. Use buttons for eyes. Glue a Popsicle stick to the bottom of the plate and hold the mask to your face.

Witch Mask. Glue a long, thick rectangle to the base of a paper triangle to form the brim of a witch's hat. Make eyes from two squares that have large eye holes cut from the centers. Glue the eye pieces so they hang from the rectangular brim of the hat. Add some newspaper-strip hair to the brim and then staple on a paper-strip band to go around your head.

Noisemakers
Cardboard Roll Noisemaker. Obtain an empty cardboard ribbon roll. From black construction paper, cut out a circle to fit one end of the spool. Glue the circle to one of the spool ends.

At the open end, drop a few beans into the spool. Then cut another circle, this one with peaked ears added to make a cat's face. Glue this circle to the open end of the spool, sealing the beans inside.

Glue a paper nose and mouth on the cat face. Draw on whiskers with white crayon. To make shiny eyes for the cat, glue on a pair of green sequins. Let everything dry, then shake away!

Rattle Box. Make a simple noisemaker using a small, empty box. Put a few pebbles inside, then tape the box shut. Decorate the box and fasten it to a stick or carry it in your hand.

Pie Plate Shaker. Obtain two disposable aluminum foil pie plates of the same size. Place a few beans or some gravel in one of the pie plates. Smear glue on the rims of both plates. Turn the empty plate upside-down and press its rim to the rim of the one with the beans. Fasten the plates together tightly with clothespins or rubber bands until the glue dries. Then remove the clothespins or rubber bands.

Decorate the shaker with Halloween stickers. Poke a small hole through the plate rims and thread a piece of string through for a handle.

Owls
Oval Owl. On paper, draw an oval to form the body of an owl. Inside the top part of the oval, draw a heart. This will be the owl's face. Draw two large circles for eyes inside the top part of the heart. Then draw in a triangular-shaped beak. Make two small ovals on top of the head for ears. Connect a series of semicircles along the bottom edge of the owl to create the look of feathered feet. Draw a branch underneath so it looks like the owl is perched on the branch.

Owl with Egg Carton Eyes. From a 9-by-12-inch piece of light-brown construction paper, cut out an owl. Cut out a beak and feet from scrap paper. Draw some feathers on the owl.

Next, cut out two cups from a cardboard egg carton. Glue the cups right side up on the owl over the spots where the eyes should be. Paint a dark circle on the inside center of each cup to finish the eyes. Complete the owl by gluing the beak and feet in place.

Paper Bag Owl. This owl can be used either as a decoration or as a puppet! Flatten a lunch-sized brown paper bag so the bottom flap is facing you when the bag is placed flat on a table. The flap area will be the owl's head.

From scrap paper, cut out shapes for the owl's eyes, beak, ears, and wings. Glue them in position on the bag. Use crayons to add feathers or any other features to the body.

To use the owl as a puppet, put your hand inside and work the flap to make the owl talk.

To use the owl as a decoration, stuff crumpled newspaper inside and tie the owl closed at the bottom. Cover the bottom with short strings of yarn. Then hang the owl from the ceiling or from a light fixture.

Party Food

Bubbling Witch Cauldron (Apple Cider Punch). Combine 1 gallon of apple cider with the following: 3 large cans of pineapple juice, 6 cups of apricot nectar, 4 cups of orange juice, 4 teaspoons of whole cloves, and half a box of broken cinnamon sticks.

Simmer everything until warmed. Serve it warm from a kettle or punch bowl. The spices will float on top of the punch.

Cookie Spider. Cut eight licorice sticks into spider legs. Slit and bend them in the middle for joints.

For each spider body, use a frosting-filled, sandwich-type cookie. Fasten the legs to the body by sticking them into the layer of frosting in the middle of the cookie.

Cookie Spider

Use frosting and chocolate chips to make the eyes and a nose on top of the cookie. Eat your spider right away or make a group of them to serve at a Halloween party!

Ghost-Face Cheeseburgers. Have an adult buy some round cheese slices at the grocery store, or cut some regular cheese slices into hamburger-sized circles. Using a plastic knife, cut a spooky face in each circle of cheese. Place each circle on a cooked hamburger pattie. Place the patties under a broiler for a few seconds and remove them. Serve the ghost-faced patties open face on buns.

Ice Cream Cone Witch. Place a single scoop of ice cream in a paper cupcake container. On top of the ice cream place a large cookie. Press the cookie into the ice cream so it will not fall off.

Use frosting to fasten a cone-shaped sugar ice cream cone upside down on the cookie. The cone and cookie form a witch's hat! The ice cream scoop is the witch's head!

Decorate the ice cream face with frosting, candies, nuts, and raisins. Place the witch in the freezer until served.

Sugar Wafer Gravestone. Stand a large sugar wafer on end next to the top edge of a cookie. Use frosting to make the wafer stand up. Print a name on the "tombstone" with frosting.

Snack Fun. For a fun way to have a Halloween snack, obtain a black licorice stick. Cut off the ends so the licorice stick is hollow all the way through. Use the stick as a straw for drinking orange juice. Serve with slices of cheese cut into pumpkin shapes.

Skeletons

Accordion-Fold Skeleton. Cut a skull-shaped head from a three-inch square of white construction paper. Then cut out a 3-by-4-inch skeleton.

Cut out four strips of white, lightweight paper. Make each strip ½-by-6-inches in size. Accordion-fold the strips to make pleated arms and legs.

Glue the skull head to the body. Then glue on the arms and legs. Use a black felt-tip marker to draw features on the skull. Hang the skeleton for decoration.

Coat Hanger Skeleton. Obtain 11 wire coat hangers to make this seven-foot skeleton. Ask an adult to help you put it together if necessary.

Bend the first hanger into a skull shape. Then cut the same shape from a piece of white construction paper. Draw skull features on the paper and set it aside.

Use tape to fasten the rest of the skeleton together. Make a rib section by hooking four hangers together, one above the other, so they hang down in a single row. Use tape to hold the pieces in place.

To make arms, legs, and feet, use six hangers that have been pulled straight. Fasten a single straightened hanger to the right corner of the top rib hanger to make one arm. Fasten another straightened hanger to the left corner of the top rib hanger for the other arm. The hooks at the ends are the hands.

To form each leg, link two straightened hangers lengthwise. Then fasten these to the bottom rib hanger with each leg about four inches inside of a corner. Form the feet by bending out the lower leg pieces at the bottom. Spray paint the skeleton white.

Cut out large feet and hands from white construction paper. Glue them in place on the arms and legs. Glue the paper skull in place, too. Hang "Mr. Bones" by the hook on top of the skull.

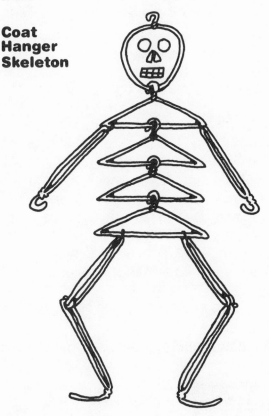

Coat Hanger Skeleton

Hinged Skeleton. From white poster board, cut out the parts for a skeleton: a skull, the legs and arms, the body, the feet and hands.

Punch holes in the ends of the parts where they should join. Hook the skeleton together with paper fasteners. Draw additional features on the skeleton with a black felt-tip marker. Hold the skeleton up, and see the different ways you can make him dance!

Paper Skeleton. Cut out a 4-by-18-inch rectangle from white paper. Then, from a 10-inch square of paper, cut out a body. From an 8-by-10-inch sheet of paper, cut out a head and draw in the facial features.

Glue the rectangular piece across the top of the body piece to form shoulders. Then glue the head on top of the shoulders.

Now cut out six circles from white paper, making each circle six inches wide. Then cut each circle into a spiral. These pieces will make the arms and legs.

Glue two spirals together end to end for each leg. Glue the legs to the body. Finally, glue the other two spirals in place for the arms. The skeleton is now ready for hanging!

Plastic Foam Packing-Piece Skeleton. For this skeleton, you will need 10 plastic foam packing pieces, the kind that are almost S-shaped.

Glue the pieces into a skeleton shape on a 5½-by-9½-inch piece of black construction paper. Use two pieces for the body, two pieces for each arm, and two pieces for each leg. At the top, glue a small skull cut out from white construction paper. With a black felt-tip marker, draw in skull details. Set up the skeleton for display.

Spiders
Paper Plate Spider. Obtain a paper plate which has a slightly curved rim. Paint both sides of the plate black.

When dry, turn the plate upside down. Cut away segments of the rim on each side to leave four legs on each side.

From another, smaller paper plate, cut away the rim entirely. This leaves a small circle to use as a head. Paint it black. When it is dry, glue the circle to the body.

Make sure the body plate is still upside down. This way the rim legs are curved down, elevating the spider from the surface. Crimp the middle of each leg slightly to make leg joints and raise the spider even more. Add paper cutouts for eyes and antennae, and the spider is done!

Spider Mobile. From black construction paper, cut out any number of small and large circles. Glue the small circles (heads) to the large ones (bodies) to make spiders. Attach black paper strips for legs.

When complete, glue different lengths of string to the spiders and hang them close together from the ceiling as a mobile.

Spider and Web. Using white paper, cut out a circle about one inch across. Glue eight toothpicks on the circle in a sunburst pattern from the center of the circle. Make sure the inside tips of the toothpicks almost meet in the middle of the circle. Notice how the toothpicks stick over the edge of the circle!

After the glue dries, weave a long piece of white yarn in and out through the toothpicks, around in a circle, over and over, until a web is formed. Fasten the end of the yarn to one of the toothpicks with glue. Using black paper, cut out a small spider and glue him to the center of the web.

Trick-or-Treat Bags
Oatmeal Box Trick-or-Treat Container. Cover the outside of an oatmeal box with orange paper. Decorate it with stickers, paper cutouts, or marking-pen drawings. Punch holes on opposite sides near the rims. Tie the ends of a 12-inch piece of rope through the holes for a handle.

Paper Sack Trick-or-Treat Bag I. Fold down the top of a large paper sack two times. Staple a poster board strip across the top for a handle. Decorate the outside of the bag with stickers, paper cutouts, or drawings.

Paper Sack Trick-or-Treat Bag II. Paint a lunch-sized paper bag black. Then cut out a large number of two-inch squares from orange crepe paper. Wrap the squares around your fingers to form caps. Dip them into some glue, then stick the paper caps to the outside of the bag. Continue applying them until the whole bag is covered and allow it to dry.

If you want, you can paint the bag orange, and make the caps from black crepe paper. Attach a poster board strip across the top for a handle.

Pillowcase Trick-or-Treat Bag. Using waterproof marking pens, draw Halloween pictures on a pillowcase. Then the pillowcase is ready to use as a trick-or-treat bag!

Witches

Apple Witch. Use a round apple for the witch's body. Cut out a paper head shape with a witch hat on top. Then cut out hands, arms, and a pair of boots.

Draw facial features on the head. Glue each of the paper cutouts to the end of a toothpick. Then insert the toothpicks into the apple, properly positioning the arms, boots, and head.

For a broom, use a toothpick with paper bristles glued to one end. Fasten the handle end of the broomstick to one of the hands.

Broomstick Witch. On construction paper, draw a witch and cut her out. Then glue the witch to a long paste stick.

Draw the straw end of a broom on construction paper and cut it out. Glue it to the end of the paste-stick broomstick. Cut fringes in the straw end to finish.

Cone Witch. From a nine-inch square of black construction paper, cut out a half circle and roll it into a cone. Seal it with glue. Then cut out a doughnut shape from black paper. Fit this shape

over the tip of the cone so it comes to rest just below the top of the cone. The top part of the cone now forms the witch's hat and brim.

Cut out a round face from colored scrap paper (yellow, green, or blue), add crayon features, and glue the face to the cone under the hat brim.

Form arms from pipe cleaners and glue them to the sides of the witch. She is now complete!

Paper Doll Witches. Fold a piece of paper in half three times. Draw half of a witch's body along one folded edge. Make sure the witch's arm extends across and joins the other folded edge.

Cut along the outline of the witch, leaving the end of the hand intact with the folded edge. Then unfold to reveal four witches with joined hands! Make several more sets of witches and tape them together to form a long chain.

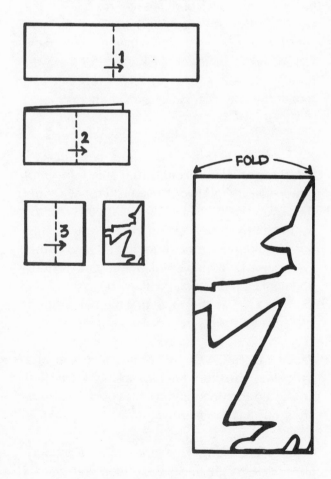

Paper Plate Witch. Use a paper plate for the face of a witch. To make a hat, cut a triangle from a piece of black construction paper. For the hair, cut strips of purple paper. Glue the hair and hat to the top part of the plate, then draw in facial details. Color the face a light green by softly rubbing a crayon sideways across the face.

Rocking Witch. On black paper, draw and cut out a witch about six inches high. Round the bottom of the witch's skirt. Stand the witch up and glue a one-inch section of a cardboard tube to the back of the skirt, and at the bottom, so the witch and the attached cardboard tube touch the surface at the same place. Put a marble inside the cardboard roll and glue it shut with a paper circle cut to fit. The witch will now rock from side to side when nudged!

Triangle Witch. From black construction paper, cut triangles of different sizes to form the witch's body, arms, legs, and hat.

Using green construction paper, cut out a face. Cut smaller triangles of black paper for the eyes, nose, and mouth. Glue the parts together and mount the witch on background paper.

Hats

Newspaper Hat. Fold a full-sized sheet of newspaper in half two times, first crosswise and then over. (Paint it ahead of time if you want to.) Set the folded newspaper in front of you as illustrated. Fold over corner A to point B, and corner C to point D, as indicated by the dotted lines. Then fold up the bottom flaps on both sides, forming a hat as shown. Staple the hat at opposite ends to make sure it holds its shape.

Paper Bag Hat. Cut down the open end of a paper bag, then turn the bag upside down. Roll or fold up the open end a little to form a brim. Try it on! Paint it if you want.

Paper Plate Hat. From the edge of a paper plate cut a straight line to the center. Pull the two

Rocking Witch

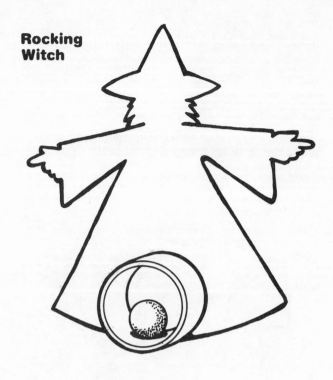

Newspaper Hat

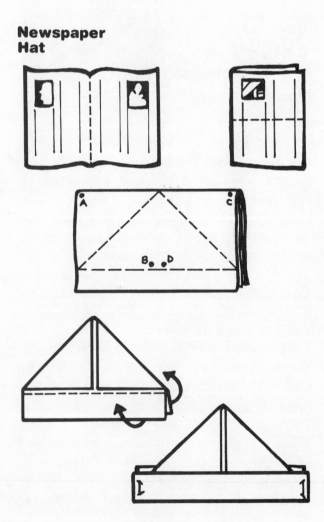

edges of the slit toward each other so they over-lap. Glue the edges in this position to form a slightly cone-shaped hat. Poke holes at opposite sides, then tie pieces of yarn from the holes so you can tie the hat on your head.

Plastic Bottle Hat. Cut off the top half of an empty plastic bleach bottle that has been thoroughly rinsed and dried. The bottom half will be your hat. You can have a deep hat or a shallow one. Decorate it with paper or fabric scraps, gummed stickers, yarn, and ribbons. Poke holes at opposite ends for tying the hat onto your head.

Illusions

Bent Spoon Illusion. Pour a glass half full with water. Place the glass so your eyes are level with it. Stick a spoon in the water. Notice how the spoon appears to bend under the water! Remove the spoon. Is it really bent?

Color Illusion. Using blue and yellow crayons, make dots on white paper. Make the dots each a little larger than the head of a pin and close enough together so they almost touch. Alternate the colors blue-yellow, blue-yellow, filling up a space about the size of a half dollar. Then hold the paper at arm's length, at a slight angle. What color do you see?

Color Wheel I. Cut out a cardboard circle. With a pencil, draw three lines toward the center of the circle. Make the lines an equal distance apart. Now you have three pie shapes of the same size!

Paint one pie wedge red, paint another one yellow, and the third blue. Poke a hole in the center of the circle and thread a piece of string through the hole.

Tie one end of the string to something sturdy. Then pull the free end of the string tightly so the color wheel can spin on the string. While keeping the string tight, spin the wheel rapidly so the colors blend. What color do you see?

Color Wheel II. Cut out a cardboard circle about 3½ inches across. Draw lines on the circle to split it up into six equal pie wedges. Starting at the top wedge and going around the circle clockwise, color each wedge in order as follows: red, orange, yellow, green, blue, and violet.

Poke a pin through the center of the circle. Spin the circle around the pin, faster and faster. Watch all the colors blend together. What color do you see?

Spiral Illusion. Cut out a cardboard circle about 3½ inches across. Using a red felt-tip marker, draw a spiral onto the circle starting at the outside edge and ending in the center. Poke a pin through the middle of the circle. Spin the circle around the pin. What does the spiral seem to do?

Independence Day

Cardboard Firecracker. Glue a circle of heavy construction paper to the bottom of an empty, short cardboard tube.

Next, cut a piece of red paper to fit around the sides of the tube and glue it in place. Then cut out another circle to fit over the open end of the tube, but this time attach it with a hinge made from tape so the circle opens and closes like a trap door.

Poke a small hole in the center of the hinged circle. Insert a few inches of string through the hole for a firecracker wick. (Bend and tape the wick a little underneath the lid to hold it in place.)

Decorate the outside of the firecracker with Independence Day seals or stickers. When finished, you can store candy or other treasures inside your firecracker.

Cardboard Tube Roman Candle. Obtain two long cardboard tubes. One tube should be slightly smaller in diameter so it can fit inside the other tube.

Color both tubes with red, white, and blue crayons. Put some cotton balls inside the larger tube, then shove the smaller tube through the larger one to fire the cotton balls into the air.

Crayon Rubbing Holiday Impressions. Using thick paper, cut out some Fourth of July symbols, such as firecrackers, flags, the Liberty Bell, and the heads of U.S. Presidents. Lay the cut-out shapes on a flat surface. Cover them with a piece of paper. Using a crayon with the wrapper removed, gently rub over the paper, coloring with the flat side of the crayon. This makes impressions of the cutouts underneath.

Flag Cookies. Stick tiny flags (available at party supply stores) into frosted cookies to help decorate your Fourth of July table.

Fourth of July Parade. Invite your friends to a neighborhood Fourth of July parade. Make flags to fasten on dowel rods. Decorate your bikes with red, white, and blue crepe paper streamers. Make some red and blue newspaper hats. Wear bright clothes, and march with rhythm instruments. Perhaps you can have a backyard barbeque when the parade is over!

Paper Bag Firecracker. Inflate a small paper bag and twist the top tightly closed to keep in the air. Now smash the bag between your hands or on the ground to make a loud pop!

Indians

Activities

Indian Circle. Make a large floor mat by cutting open some paper bags, taping them together, and laying them on the floor. Draw a large circle on the mat.

Next, draw some large Indian symbols inside the circle. Use symbols found in books about

Indians or make up your own. Color in the circle with crayons, and use the circle as a meeting place for you and your friends.

Indian Language. Look through a book about Indians for some symbols they used in writing on rocks and animal skins. Then, try to draw them on a 9-by-12-inch sheet of paper. You can also invent your own picture-symbols, drawing them on paper too.

Indian Names. Indians often named their children after the first thing seen following the birth of the babies. In this way, Indians received names like Falling Star, Full Moon, Big Bear, Running Squirrel, and Little Fish. Now, pretend that your own baby has been just born. What is the first thing you see? What would you name your baby?

Navajo Groaning Stick. From a wooden fruit or vegetable crate or wood shingle, cut out a rectangle of wood about six inches long and two inches across. (Ask an adult to help you do this). Drill or hammer (using a nail) a hole centered on the wood, about one inch from one end. (Be careful not to split the wood). Tie a three-foot length of heavy twine to this end, through the hole. If you wish, paint the wood with Indian designs. Twirl the stick over your head to create a buzzing sound. (Navajo Lightning Dancers did this to create the voice of the Thunderbird. According to mythology, the Thunderbird would flap its wings to make wind and thunder, and blink its eyes to make lightning. The sticks were often used to summon rain).

Art

Cardboard Carton Pueblo.

Create a make-believe pueblo by piling several cardboard cartons on top of each other, on their sides, so the open parts face you.

For a ground-floor pueblo apartment, use a large carton. Stack smaller cartons on top for the upper floors. Make rafters by gluing painted cardboard tubes across the ceilings of the rooms. Cut out door and window openings in the walls. Using felt-tip markers or paint, draw details on the inside and outside walls, including ladders going from one floor to the next.

Construction Paper Tepee.

Using white or tan construction paper, cut out a circle. Decorate it with Indian designs. Then cut a straight line from the outside edge directly to the center of the circle. Pull the two edges together until they overlap, and staple them in place. This will pull the circle into a cone, or tepee shape. Stand the tepee up to display.

Construction Paper Tepee Scene.

Fold down the two top corners of a 9-by-12-inch sheet of construction paper, as illustrated. Decorate the flaps with Indian designs. Then color the space behind the flaps to resemble the inside of a tepee, and include the Indians inside. Fold back the bottom strip so the tepee will stand up on a flat surface.

Indian Ponies.

Cut out pony shapes without legs from cardboard. Color them with crayons. Clip a clothespin at each end for the legs.

Mural.

On a long piece of butcher paper or brown wrapping paper, draw tepees with women working nearby. Show braves hunting, and draw in horses and crops. You might show Indians holding a pow-wow, doing a rain dance, or drying animal skins in the sun.

Paper Bag Indian Vest.

Turn a grocery bag upside down and cut arm holes in the sides near the closed end of the bag. Cut an opening all the way up the front. On the top of the closed end, make a neck hole.

"Potato-print" some Indian designs on the vest. To do this, cut a potato in half. Carve away parts of the freshly cut ends leaving Indian designs raised above the rest of the potato. Dip the potato ends into a shallow pan of paint and print the designs on the vest. Allow paint to dry. Your vest is ready.

Paper Indian Corn.

First, look at some real Indian corn to see what it looks like. Then, obtain a piece of graph paper with half-inch squares on it. With red, blue, green, and dark yellow crayons, color the squares to make a checkered pattern.

When the squares are colored, cut out ears of corn from the paper. Finish the ears by gluing on green or tan construction paper leaves.

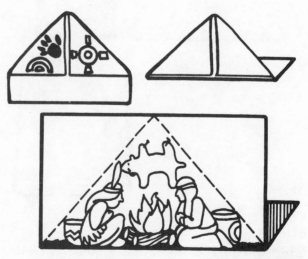

Construction Paper Tepee Scene

Sand Painting. To make colored sand, place a little sand in a jar. Add several drops of food coloring and shake well. Place the sand in the sunlight to dry.

To use the sand for painting, spread glue on a piece of paper where a particular color is desired. Sprinkle the areas with the colored sand. Allow to dry, and shake away the excess sand.

After the first color has dried, make some more sand with the next color, and repeat. Continue with different colors until you finish the design.

Sleeping Indian in Blanket. From construction paper, cut out a half circle. On another sheet of construction paper, draw the head of an Indian baby. Make sure the neck is extra long!

Cut out the head. Glue the neck portion to the rounded top of the half circle so the head seems to rest just on the top edge of the circle.

Fold over each end of the half circle in front of the neck, one at a time, so it looks like a baby is wrapped in the blanket. Fasten the ends into position with glue.

Blankets
Cloth Indian Blanket. Tear a piece of cloth into a 22-by-30-inch size. Fold down the piece to one quarter size. Using crayons, draw Indian designs on the top section.

When the first section is completed, turn and refold the cloth so a new section is on top. Color it with more designs. Continue until all sections are filled in. Then open it up and color a border around the blanket by alternating X's and O's. The crayon design can be made washable by pressing it with a warm iron. (Ask an adult to help you.)

Newspaper Indian Blanket. Paint designs for an Indian blanket on a double sheet of newspaper. (Use the classified section.) Hang the "blanket" on a wall for display.

Cooking
Dried Fruit. Many Native Americans, and especially the Pueblo peoples, dried fruits so they would last through the winter months. To make your own, gather some fruits such as apples, apricots, peaches, pears, blackberries, blueberries, raspberries, or cherries. Thoroughly wash them, completely removing any stems, leaves, or pits. If the fruits are large, cut them into 1/2-inch slices. Squeeze lemon juice on the slices so they won't turn brown. Then, cover a flat wooden board or tray with cheesecloth, and spread the fruits and slices out, so none are touching. Cover with another layer of cheesecloth. Each day, over a period of two to six days, place the board and fruits outside in a sunny spot. Bring in each night, or bring in if it rains. When the fruits are dried, store in a covered jar, vacuum sealed plastic bag, or in the refrigerator, and eat when desired.

Navajo Fry Bread. In a bowl, mix together 2 cups all-purpose flour, 1 tablespoon baking powder, and 1 teaspoon salt. Use a spoon to push a well (hole) in the middle of the mixture. Pour 3/4 cup water and 1 tablespoon vegetable oil into the well. Stir together with a fork to form soft dough. Put the dough on a lightly floured surface and knead with your hands until smooth. Divide the dough into six equal portions. Shape each portion into a ball, then flatten with hand or roll out to make a six or seven-inch circle. With an adult's help, heat 3/4 inch of salad oil in a pan large enough to hold the circle. Fry circles one at a time in the hot oil until puffy and golden brown, turning once. Remove and drain on several layers of paper towels. Serve one of two ways: dribbled with honey and sprinkled with powdered sugar, or topped with refried beans and salsa (hot sauce).

Nut Butter. Since nuts were easy to store, Native Americans would save them for use when other food sources were scarce. This recipe shows you how to make butter from nuts. Place a cup of shelled nuts (such as almonds, beechnuts, hazelnuts, peanuts, pecans, or walnuts, or any combination) into a blender and mix them into a fine powder, or "nut flour." Pour this flour into a bowl and gradually add 1 to 3 tablespoons of sunflower oil or peanut oil, until the mix turns into a spreadable butter. Taste, adding some honey for a sweeter flavor. Scoop out the butter with a spoon, cracker, or tortilla, or spread onto crackers or bread.

Drums and Shakers
Oatmeal Box Tom-Tom. Make an Indian drum or shaker from an oatmeal box or salt box with a lid. (If you want to make a shaker, drop a few beans inside.) Seal on the lid with tape. Glue on a piece of colored paper to cover the box. Make Indian designs with crayons or a felt-tip marker.

Tin Can Drum. Obtain a large restaurant-sized tin can with the contents removed. Turn the can upside down. While you are sitting, hold the can between your knees. Play the drum with your hands.

Feathers
Feather Fan. Cut a paper plate in half. Take one piece and decorate the bottom side with Indian designs. Fold this piece in half again, so the designs are on the outside, to form a fan shape. Open up the piece again and spread glue over the opened piece. Lay the shaft ends of some large feathers into the area on the right side of the fold, so when you close the piece the feathers will project outward from the fan shape, forming a feather fan. Add more glue if necessary, and place under a heavy book so the feathers will fasten strongly. The feather fan is finished when dry.

Feather Painting. Fasten a feather alongside a craft stick (to give it strength) and use the feather instead of a paint brush to create interesting paintings.

Necklaces and Ornaments
Bean Necklace. Tint some water with food coloring. Soak some dried beans or whole dried corn in the water to soften and dye them. (This will take some time, maybe all day or overnight). Remove beans. Thread a needle with heavy thread and carefully string the beans to form a necklace. Tie together for desired size, and allow to dry. The beans will shrink. Paint with shellac if desired.

Forehead Ornament. Cut out two same-sized circles of cardboard, a size that would fit across your forehead. Lay one circle on a table in front of you. Over this lay a length of yarn, so that the circle is centered underneath. Squeeze glue over the circle and yarn, and lay the second circle on top, so it matches the first circle and sandwiches the yarn in between. When dry, glue a shiny coin, small shells, or tiny feathers to the top circle. Wear the ornament on your forehead, tying the yarn behind your head.

Macaroni Necklace. First, drop some food coloring into a container of water. Add some large-sized macaroni and stir carefully for a short time. Remove the macaroni from the water and set it on a cookie sheet for drying. Repeat this process for each color of macaroni you want.

When it is dry, thread the macaroni on different lengths of insulated wire to make necklaces and bracelets.

Tongue Depressor Bracelets. Beforehand, soak a few tongue depressors in water for about 24 hours. Then remove them. While they are still wet, punch a hole in both ends of each depressor. Place them in an empty glass so they become curved along the inside of the glass. Leave them there until they become totally dry.

Then, remove the depressors. Notice they are now stiff and curved into bracelet shapes. Paint them with Indian colors, and tie them around your wrists with ribbon.

Pottery

Baker's Clay Beads. Form small balls out of baker's clay. Stick a round toothpick through the center of each ball to make a hole. Allow the balls to dry, then paint them with enamel or acrylic paints. Thread the beads on string to make necklaces or bracelets.

Papier Mâché Pottery. Cut a well-rinsed, quart-sized plastic bleach bottle until only the bottom third remains. Using one-inch-wide strips of newspaper dipped in diluted glue, cover the bottle piece with several layers. Allow it to dry. Then paint with either a brown or tan color. When the paint has dried, paint on some Indian designs in a contrasting color.

Insects (Science)

When you study insects, you will notice certain things about them. They have six legs and three main body sections. They can crawl, swim, fly, and appear in many sizes and colors. They can be either helpful or harmful.

Activities

Bug Hunt. Go on a bug hunt outdoors! See how many different kinds of insects you can find. Take along a magnifying glass so you can look at

some of them up close. Carry along some containers to hold the insects you catch. Release the insects later.

Cocoon-to-Caterpillar Changes. Place a caterpillar in a container covered with a perforated lid. Also place a little soil in the container. Keep the soil damp. Feed the caterpillar leaves from the plant on which he was found. If the caterpillar was found on the sidewalk, try different leaves until you find the ones it likes.

Watch the caterpillar spin a cocoon or chrysalis. Do not disturb the cocoon or chrysalis until a beautiful moth or butterfly hatches!

How Far Can a Grasshopper Jump? Catch a large grasshopper and measure with a ruler to see how long it is. Then put the grasshopper on the floor or ground and let it jump. Mark the takeoff and landing points with chalk or tape. Measure the distance jumped.

Find out how many times its own length the grasshopper jumped. Then measure your own length. How far would you have to jump in order to jump as many times your length as the grasshopper did? (Ask an adult to help you figure this out, if necessary.)

Insect Zoo. Catch some insects using nets or paper bags to capture them. Put them in small jars (baby food jars are good) covered with caps having air holes poked in them. Watch how the insects behave, and look at them with a magnifying glass to see how they look up close. Then release them.

Observation Square. Mark off a one-foot square on the ground using string. With a magnifying glass, study the area within the square closely. How many different kinds of insects do you see? Keep a notebook listing your discoveries and draw pictures of the insects.

Temperature Reactions. Place a small jar into a larger jar. Surround the smaller jar with ice, and place an insect inside.

With a thermometer, measure the temperature in the test tube (jar). How does the insect react to the dropping temperature? Then remove the insect and watch how it reacts as it warms up.

Observation Cages
Ant Farm. Partly fill a large jar with loose, moist soil. Also put a little bit of sugar in the soil. Place a few large ants in the jar and cover the top with a fine wire mesh screen.

Wrap a piece of black paper around the outside of the jar. Make sure it reaches all the way to the bottom and sticks up just a little higher than the level of the soil.

When you want to observe the ants, push up the black paper to allow a good view. Watch the ants build tunnels and carry small pebbles around. Release them after a week or so.

Milk Carton Cage. Cut large windows on opposite sides of a milk carton. Place some twigs and grass in the carton. Add some bugs to the carton and swiftly push the carton into the toe end of a nylon stocking. Twist the stocking at the top and seal it with a wire twistie.

Observation Box. Place some insects, twigs, and grass in a shoe box. Cover the top with clear plastic kitchen wrap. Poke air holes in the sides of the box, and watch how the insects behave. From time to time, feed the insects leaves, seeds, and dead bugs.

Jewelry

Button Jewelry. String buttons together to make bracelets and necklaces. Thread the string through only one hole in each button. (To make the threading easier, stiffen the end of your string by dipping it into shellac or nail polish.) After stringing, tie the ends together to keep the buttons from falling off.

Button Ring. Find a colorful, flashy button to use for your ring. String the button on a piece of wire or a twistie. Tie the ring to your finger with the button on top.

Clay Ring. Form a piece of clay into a thin roll. Wrap it around your finger and pinch the ends together underneath to form a ring. Remove any excess clay. For a gem, press a bead, button, or small pebble on the top of the ring.

Earring Loops. Many different things can be used to form loops from which you can make your own earrings. Pipe cleaner pieces, twisties, rubber bands, and ribbon all make good loops. For earrings, use shapes cut from bright papers and cardboard, buttons, foil, curtain rings, paper clips, and pipe cleaners.

Envelope Bracelets. Seal the flap on a new envelope. Color both sides of the envelope with a heavy design, using crayons. Cut off one end of the envelope.

Then cut up the rest of the envelope into half-inch-wide strips, cutting from one folded edge to the other. Notice the strips will open up into ring shapes. Wear the ring shapes as bracelets.

Foil Ring. Twist a piece of aluminum foil into a thin roll. Wrap it around your finger for a ring.

Ice Cream Lid Wristwatch. Paint a wristwatch face on a lid from a school-sized ice cream container. Punch holes on opposite edges and tie a ribbon or yarn through them for a watchband.

Paper Strip Ring. Cut a small strip from a piece of stiff paper and glue the ends together to make a ring. Glue on pieces of dried colored macaroni, small shells, dry rice, or small silver balls for decoration.

Pipe Cleaner Ring. Firmly twist a piece of pipe cleaner around a small pebble. Then twist the rest of the pipe cleaner around your finger to form a ring. Cut away any leftover pipe cleaner.

Yarn Bracelet. Cut a ½-by-7-inch strip of cardboard. Curl the strip forming a bracelet. Tape it closed at the ends.

Cut a long strand of colored yarn. Tape one end of the yarn along the inside of the bracelet. Starting at one end wrap the yarn around and around the cardboard crossways. Wrap the yarn close together until the cardboard is completely covered. At the end, tuck in the ends of the yarn.

Jewish Holidays

Chanukah

Chanukah, or the Festival of Lights, occurs in late November or December. It commemorates a great victory of the Jewish people more than two thousand years ago, when they recaptured their temple from the Syrians.

When they purified and re-dedicated their temple, the Jewish people found there was only enough oil to light the lamps for one day. Miraculously, the lamps burned for eight days. Today, this joyous festival is celebrated for eight days. Families light a menorah, or candlestick, with special candles and recite blessings of thanks every evening. Gifts are exchanged and special potato pancakes called *latkes* are often served.

Driedel Game. A driedel is a cubical top children use for playing a game during Chanukah. The four Hebrew letters on the sides, N̄un, Ḡimel, H̄ey, and S̄hin, stand for the words "A great miracle happened there."

When playing the game, the letters mean the following:

N = Nothing. You don't get anything from the pot.

G = All. You get all the beans in the pot. The other players then add two beans each to the pot.

H = Half. You get half of the beans in the pot.

S = Put In. You must add two beans to the pot.

Each player begins with 10 beans. (You can also use buttons, pennies, nuts, raisins, or small candies.) Each player puts one bean into a pot (a bowl or hat.) Then take turns spinning the driedel to see which side lands up. You win or lose the spin depending on which letter faces up! The player to win all the beans is the winner of the game.

(See *Milk Carton Driedel* and *Pencil Driedel* for instructions on making your own driedels.)

Festival of Lights Playacting. Eight people pretend to be candles on the menorah. Pick one to be the candle that lights the others.

Darken the room. Give each participant a flashlight. Then the player who lights the others chooses a player to be the candle for the first day of Chanukah. That player then lights his flashlight and stands on the first spot chosen as the menorah.

The candle lighter continues "lighting" each candle, until all eight players have been lit to symbolize the eight days of Chanukah.

Latkes (Potato Pancakes). With the help of an adult, peel and shred some potatoes. Then mix them with egg, water, and a little salt. Drop spoonfuls of this mixture into hot frying oil. Allow to brown on both sides. Serve with applesauce.

Menorah on Paper. For candles, glue nine straws upright in a row on a sheet of construction paper. Glue the middle straw slightly higher than the rest.

To make candle flames, drop nine cotton balls into a paper bag with dry orange tempera paint inside. Shake the bag to turn the cotton balls

orange. Remove the cotton balls and stretch them out into the shape of flames. Glue the flames into place above the candles.

Use felt-tip markers or crayons to draw the menorah base under the candles.

Milk Carton Driedel. Obtain an empty half-pint milk carton. Fold down the spout to form a box. Cover the box with tissue paper.

Poke a pencil or dowel all the way through the center of the box. On each side panel of the box, write one of the following letters: N, G, H, and S. Spin the driedel to see which side lands up. (See earlier game instructions.)

Pencil Driedel. Cut out a four-inch square of cardboard. Draw a diagonal line from one corner to the opposite one. Then draw a line between the two remaining corners. In the space between two of the lines, write the letter N. In each of the next three spaces, write the letters G, H, and S.

Poke a small hole in the middle of the square where the lines crisscross. Stick a sharpened pencil through the hole. Spin the pencil and see which side of the driedel falls face up.

Room Decoration. Decorate a room blue and white using streamers and paper cutouts. Blue and white are the colors of the Israeli flag.

Spool Menorah. On a piece of wood, or on a cardboard strip, glue eight wooden spools of equal size in a row. Leave a space in the middle of the row. In that space glue a larger spool.

Spray paint the menorah gold or silver. Stick candles into the holes of the spools. With adult supervision, light this menorah during the eight days of Chanukah, using new candles every night.

Star of David. Obtain one blue 9-by-12-inch sheet of paper and one white 9-by-12-inch sheet of paper. From each sheet, cut out a triangle that is equal on all sides. Set one of the triangles in front of you in an upright position. To form a star, glue the other triangle upside down on top of the first one.

Passover

Passover, a festival of freedom, celebrates the Exodus of the Hebrew people from Egyptian slavery. It occurs in March or April.

Bedikat Hametz Game. Have someone hide pieces of bread in the room. Everyone else hunts for the bread and puts it into a lunch sack. Share the bread when finished.

Charoses. Mix ¼ cup of firmly chopped walnuts, 1 finely chopped or grated apple, ¼ cup grape juice, and 1 teaspoon of cinnamon. Traditionally, this is eaten on unleaven bread (Matzoh).

Purim

Purim is a festival commemorating the time good queen Esther delivered the Jewish people from a massacre planned by a wicked man named Haman. It occurs in February or March.

Paper Cup Gregger. To make this shaker, use a white paper cup that has a plastic lid. Decorate the cup with felt-tip markers. Drop a few beans into the cup and put the lid back on. For a handle, tape a Popsicle stick to the side of the cup. The Gregger is used to drown out Haman's name when the Book of Esther is read in the synagogue.

Pin the Hat on Haman—Game. To represent Haman, tape a picture or a drawing of a man on the wall. Close your eyes and try pinning a cutout of a three-cornered hat on Haman's head.

Sukkot

Sukkot is a festival celebrating harvest time. It is also a commemoration of the Exodus, when the Jews wandered in the desert. The holiday occurs in September or October.

Milk Carton Succah Centerpiece. Cut the top off of a milk carton. Then cut away one side. Glue Popsicle sticks over the rest of the carton.

Next, cut small strips from tissue paper and cut flower pictures from magazines. Decorate the succah with the cutouts.

Paper Torah Scroll. Cut out a strip of paper as wide as the length of a Popsicle stick and 11 inches long. With crayons, color a picture on the strip. Then glue a Popsicle stick at each end of the strip. Allow to dry. Roll both sticks toward the center to form a scroll.

Room Succah. Cut out some small paper flowers and fruits. Glue the cutouts to some paper streamers. Decorate the corner of a room with the streamers to form a succah (a shelter).

Lady Bugs

Egg Carton Lady Bug. Cut a single eggcup from a cardboard egg carton. Turn it upside down and paint it red. After the paint dries, paint on several large black dots. Punch two holes on top of the head, and stick a short piece of pipe-cleaner into each one for feelers. Paint a cute face on the front of the lady bug.

Magnetic Moving Lady Bug. Paint half of a walnut shell red. Allow to dry. Then paint on some black spots.

Glue three wire twisties across the bottom of the shell, and let the glue dry. Then bend down the twistie ends to form legs.

Place the lady bug on top of a cardboard box. Hold a magnet underneath the cardboard and move it around directly under the lady bug. Watch the bug move, following the pull of the magnet!

Leaves

Cut and Paste Leaves. From fall-colored sheets of construction paper, cut out leaf shapes. Paste the cutouts on a piece of wallpaper.

Leaf Collage. Collect different kinds of fallen leaves. Glue them together into a collage on a piece of poster board.

Leaf People. Glue several leaves on a sheet of background paper. With felt-tip markers or crayons, draw heads, arms, and legs on the leaves to make them look like people.

Poster-Painted Leaves. Draw a leaf on a piece of manila paper. Dip the paper in water and allow the excess moisture to drain away. Then dot the leaf with red, yellow, and orange poster paints. Turn the paper around in different ways so all the colors run together.

Sponge-Printed Leaves. Draw the outline of a tree on paper. Then cut out small leaf shapes from sponges. Dip the shapes into paint and print the leaves on the tree.

Starched Leaves. Cut out leaves from fall-colored paper. Dip them into starch. Curl and shape the leaves and allow them to dry.

Waxed Paper Leaves. Place leaves between two sheets of waxed paper. Sandwich this packet between two sheets of newspaper. Press with a warm iron, sealing the leaves inside. (You may need adult supervision.) Remove the newspaper and hang the decoration in a window for display.

Wax Dipped Leaves. Find some colored leaves that have stems. Then pour two or three inches of water into a pan or coffee can. Heat the water on the stove. Drop in some wax candles or paraffin.

When the wax has melted, hold the leaves by their stems and dip them into the wax. Set the wax-covered leaves on paper to dry. Over a period of time the leaves will still turn color. But they will not become wrinkled, and they will not dry out!

Leaves (Science)

A Walk in the Leaves. Walk through some fallen leaves. Notice how dry they are! Listen to them crunch under your feet! Why did they fall from the tree? Take some of the leaves home to study.

Leaf People

Leaf Classification.   Collect different kinds of leaves to examine. Compare the colors and shapes and look at the veins in the leaves. Look closely at the leaves through a magnifying glass. Then sort the leaves into piles of big and small, smooth and rough, and thick and thin. What other ways can you classify the leaves?

Watching Leaves Fall.   In the autumn, watch the wind blowing leaves from the trees. The stems are dry and brittle at this time of year, which makes it easy for the wind to snap the leaves off the branches. The green color of the leaf has disappeared because the leaf has stopped making food for the tree. Count how many leaves fall in a five-minute period.

"Watch" Tree.   Pick out a tree near your home to be your "watch" tree. Observe the tree at different times of the year to see the changes that take place in the leaves. Make drawings of the tree several times during the year to note the changes you see.

Light (Science)

Colors in Light.   Did you know light is made of many colors? Put a small mirror in a glass of water. Position the glass of water so sunlight will reflect off the mirror and onto a wall.

Look—you will see the colors of the rainbow! These colors are coming from the sunlight! The sunbeams bounce off the mirror through the water and separate into the colors you see. This is similar to the way a real rainbow is formed!

Flashlight Experiment.   In the daytime, darken a room and shine a flashlight in it. The beam of light shows up easily. Now go into a sunlit room. Shine the light again. Why is it hard to see the light?

Light and Objects.   Light can pass through some objects, but not others. In the dark, shine a flashlight through glass, clear plastic, or plastic kitchen wrap. Notice how a certain amount of light passes through each one of these! Then try shining the light through a solid object. What happens?

Light Reflecting on Dust Particles.   Watch a ray of sunlight shining through a small opening into a darkened room. The sun's rays let you see particles of dust floating around in the air. The particles are always there, but cannot always be seen unless the light is just right.

Sunlight and Shadows.   Anything solid placed between the sun and the earth blocks some of the light and leaves a shadow. On a sunny day, go outside to see your own shadow. Make the shadow long, then make it short, and, finally, try to run away from it! Stand on the sidewalk at different times of the day and have someone draw around your shadow each time. Notice that as the sun changes position, the shadow changes its size and shape!

Next, go inside the house and find a flashlight. Also gather a few small toys, dolls, and action figures. Stand the toys on the floor, and make the room dark. Pretend the flashlight is the sun, rising low, moving over the earth, moving overhead, and then setting again. As you move the flashlight, watch the shadows of the toys below. Notice that the shadows are always on the side opposite the light, and that the shadows move and change shape as the light moves. They are short when the sun is high and long when the sun is low.

Sunlight Warms the Earth.   Light is warm! To prove it, place two metal objects that are exactly alike outdoors. Place one in the direct sunlight. Place the other one in the shade. Leave them there for awhile, then go back and touch each one. Which one is hot? Which one is cool? Why?

Lincoln's Birthday

Corrugated Paper Log Cabin.   Cut out the front side of a cabin from a piece of corrugated cardboard. Paste it on a sheet of construction paper with the corrugated side facing up. With crayons and felt-tip markers, add details to the cabin.

Lincoln's Top Hat. Using a sheet of black construction paper, form a tube 8 to 10 inches tall and wide enough to fit on top of your head. Tape or staple the tube so it holds together.

Stand the tube on another sheet of black construction paper. Using a pencil, trace around the base of the tube to form a circle on the paper underneath. Cut out this circle. Then fasten the circle to one end of the tube by taping it from inside.

To make a brim, trace another circle on black construction paper. But this time, measure two inches from the outside of the circle and make a dot. In this way, make dots all the way around the circle. Then connect all the dots to form a larger circle. Cut out the larger circle, then cut away the original inner circle. This leaves a doughnut-shaped brim for the hat.

With black tape, fasten the brim to the base of the hat. Glue a one-inch-wide strip of white paper around the hat, just above the brim, for a hat band.

Milk Carton and Pretzel Log Cabin. Obtain a can of ready-to-use frosting and an empty 8-ounce milk carton.

Cover the milk carton with the frosting. Press stick pretzels into the frosting to represent logs. Cover the whole milk carton with pretzels to resemble a log cabin.

Paper Cup Lincoln Face. Beforehand, mix 1 pint of black tempera paint with ¼ cup of dishwashing detergent. Then set the mixture aside.

Turn a paper cup upside down in front of you With a felt-tip marker, draw a face on the lower part of the cup.

Next, from a six-inch square of black paper, cut out a doughnut shape for a hat brim. Make the inside hole of the doughnut just a little larger than the closed end of the cup. Slip the doughnut on the cup so it rests just above the face. The

Paper Cup Lincoln Face

doughnut brim and the part of the cup above it represent the hat. Paint those areas with the black tempera mix you made earlier.

Below the face, attach some small paper strips for a beard.

Rolled-Paper Log Cabin. From brown wrapping paper, cut out six 5-by-9-inch rectangles. Roll each rectangle into a log and hold in place with glue. Allow the glue to dry.

Next, set a 12-by-18 inch sheet of drawing paper in front of you. Create the front of a log cabin on part of the paper by lining up rows of horizontal logs. Glue the logs on the paper, making sure they are close to one another.

Cut out a door, window, and chimney from scrap paper. Glue them in place on the log cabin. Draw in a background landscape.

M

Magnetism (Science)

Changing Face. On a square of heavy cardboard, draw a clown's face. Place some iron filings on the cardboard. Cover the cardboard with a sheet of clear plastic. Tape the plastic in place around the edges to keep the filings inside.

Hold a magnet underneath the piece of cardboard. Notice that when you move the magnet under the cardboard, the filings move also! Move the magnet around so the iron filings make eyebrows, a mustache, a beard, and hair on the clown's face!

Dueling Magnets. Place a nail on a flat surface between two magnets of equal strength. Make sure the nail is exactly between the magnets! Notice that the nail does not move. (The pull of the magnets in opposite directions cancel out each other.)

Now move one magnet slightly closer to the nail. What happens? Move both magnets around a little, creating a "duel" to see which one keeps control of the nail!

Magnetic Transfer. Did you know magnetism can be transferred to other objects containing iron? To do this, rub a nail or the metal part of a screwdriver with a bar magnet. Be sure to stroke in the same direction each time, using the same end of the magnet while rubbing. Make about 30 strokes. Then try picking up some nails with the magnetized nail or screwdriver.

Magnetism Through Water. Fill a jar half full of water. Then put some metal objects, such as bobby pins, paper clips, and safety pins, into the water.

Using a very powerful magnet, try to attract the objects in the water by holding the magnet next to the outside of the jar. If the magnet is strong enough, the objects will be attracted!

Compare these results with those of a much weaker magnet.

Magnets Attract Iron. Mix some nails and sawdust in a pile. With a magnet, try to attract the nails from the sawdust. Why doesn't the magnet pick up the sawdust?

Next, place the following objects on a table: nails, pins, copper pennies, pencils, aluminum cans, dimes, and other small objects made of different materials.

Touch a magnet to each object, one at a time. Watch the results. Notice that the magnet attracts iron and steel objects, but will not attract things made of wood, copper, silver, or anything else not containing iron!

Magnets Attract and Repel. Every magnet has two "poles," a north one and a south one. Place two magnets on a flat surface, with their north poles almost touching. What happens?

Now place the magnets so the north pole of one almost touches the south pole of the other. What happens this time?

Unlike poles attract, and like poles repel.

Make a Magnet. Some magnets can be made by using electricity. With the help of an adult, wrap an insulated copper wire around a large spike, store bolt, or screwdriver. Then connect the ends of the wire to a dry-cell battery. Try picking up different objects with the spike magnet.

Simple Magnetic Compass. Before you start, obtain a commercial compass to use for comparison. Then get an old cork and a sewing needle. From the cork, cut away a cross-section slice that looks somewhat like a coin. Cut a straight groove across the cork piece so the sewing needle can rest in the groove. Rub one end of the needle with a magnet, making sure to rub only in one direction. Rub the needle about 30 times. When the needle is magnetized, lay it in the groove on the cork slice.

Float the cork in a shallow dish of water.

**Simple
Magnetic
Compass**

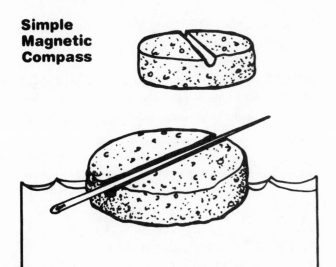

Watch—see the cork turn in the water? The magnetized needle is pointing toward the earth's North Pole!

Set the commercial compass next to the one you have made. Notice the needles of both compasses point the same way! What makes the needles point to the north? What can you use a compass for?

Magnification (Science)

Commercial Magnifying Glass. Obtain a commercial magnifying glass. Notice that when you look through it, objects underneath appear larger! Use the magnifying glass to study rocks, shells, fabrics, leaves, your skin, or anything else you find interesting.

Microscopes and telescopes also make things look larger. Microscopes make very small things appear larger, and telescopes make things far away look closer. If you can, look through a microscope and a telescope and learn about worlds smaller and larger than yourself.

Glass Jar Magnifier. Pour some water into a glass jar. Then place a spoon in the jar. Look at the spoon from the side of the jar through the water. Notice that the spoon looks bigger!

Now take out the spoon and place it outside the jar on the side away from you. Look at it

through the water in the jar. This time the spoon looks even larger!

Try enlarging the appearance of other objects by placing them in the water or behind the jar.

May Day

Cone-Shaped May Basket. Roll a half circle of colored paper into a cone. Staple it together and attach a handle made from a strip of paper. Fill with flowers.

Marshmallow May Basket Favors. Here is a way to make marshmallows look like miniature May baskets! With the help of an adult, use a pair of tongs to dip the top of a marshmallow into boiling water. Then quickly remove the hot marshmallow. Dip the top of the marshmallow into a shallow dish filled with small cake-decorating candies. The candies will stick to the marshmallow.

When the candies have dried in place, make a small handle from a wire twistie. Poke the ends of the handle into the marshmallow, and the miniature May basket is finished!

May Pole. Make a real May pole by sticking a large dowel stick into the ground. Tape long pieces of colored streamers to the top of the pole. Invite your friends to each take hold of a streamer. Play music and walk in a circle around the pole, weaving the streamers around the pole as you go!

Miniature May Pole. Glue an empty paper towel tube upright on a paper plate base. Glue colored yarn streamers from the top.

Mobiles

Animal Mobile. From magazines, cut out pictures of animals, or draw your own animals on paper. Cut out the animals and glue them on lightweight cardboard. Then cut out the animals again. Hang the animals close together from the ceiling or a fixture with string.

Flower Mobile. Thread a piece of yarn through a drinking straw. Tie the ends of the yarn above the straw to form a hanger. Attach real or paper flowers to various lengths of string. Hang the flowers from the straw.

Leaf Mobile. Punch holes in dry leaves and hang them from twigs stuck in a clay base to form a leaf mobile.

Plastic Bottle Mobile Hanger. From a well-rinsed, gallon-sized plastic bleach bottle, cut out a ring shape. Punch holes around the ring and tie nearly equal lengths of string from each of the holes. Tie lightweight objects, such as paper cutouts, to the other ends of the strings. Then tie equal lengths of string to the opposite ends of the ring, and tie them together to make a handle for the hanger!

Plastic Glass Mobile. Knock out the bottoms from some disposable plastic glasses. Using permanent felt-tip markers, color the outside of these plastic circles. Then melt them in the oven under low heat. (Ask an adult to help you.) Allow to cool. Poke a hole at one edge of each circle and hang them together as a mobile.

Shape Mobile. From heavy colored paper, cut out some squares, circles, rectangles, and triangles. Hang them together as a mobile.

Simple Mobile. This is the easiest mobile of all to make! From lightweight paper, cut out a single shape for your mobile. (It can be an animal, object, or design.) Hang a long piece of thread from a fixture, then attach the cut-out shape to the free end. Watch the mobile move in different ways due to the air currents in the room!

Starched String Mobile. Dip a length of heavy string or yarn into thick starch. Next form a design or shape with the string on a piece of waxed paper. Allow to dry. Then hang the stiffened design on a length of string!

Wire and Nylon Mobile. Bend a wire coat hanger at the bottom and top so it becomes diamond shaped. Slip a section of nylon stocking over the hanger. Pin things such as ribbons, paper cutouts, and leaves to the nylon and hang.

Monsters

Collage Monster. Draw the outline of a scary monster on paper. Fill in the outline with collage materials fastened on with glue. Crushed eggshells, paper scraps, small pebbles, buttons, plastic foam bits, and bottle caps are just a few of the materials you can use!

Egg Carton Monster. Cut up several cardboard egg cartons into different-sized pieces and shapes. Glue the pieces together any way you want to form your own monster. Paint the pieces with different colors, and finish with a scary painted face.

Funny Monster. On a sheet of paper, draw or color your own funny-looking monster. Make him look as silly and ridiculous as possible! Give him a name. Does he make you laugh?

"You" Monster. This is one way to bring out the monster in yourself! Lie down on a long sheet of butcher paper or brown wrapping paper with your arms and legs extended. Have a friend outline your entire body, using a crayon or felt-tip marker. Then get up. Color in crazy, funny, or scary details to turn your outline into a monster! (If you want, add things such as horns, wings, claws, scales, fangs, and a tail. You might also want to add extra eyes, legs or arms, or even an extra head!)

Mosaics

Aquarium Gravel Mosaic. On a piece of lightweight cardboard, draw a simple object, animal or design. Spread some glue on a small portion of the picture, then sprinkle some colored aquarium gravel over the glue. Allow to set, then carefully shake the cardboard to remove the excess gravel.

Spread some more glue over the next area, then add a different color of aquarium gravel over that part. Shake off the excess. Continue in this way until you have finished a pretty, colored-gravel mosaic!

Dimensional Assemblage. Make a free-form, three-dimensional mosaic by gluing some of the following items on a cardboard surface: eggshells, sand, pebbles, lima beans, peas, buttons, ceramic pieces, plastic tile remnants, bottle caps, egg carton cups, bits of broken plastic toys, or anything else you can think of.

Macaroni Mosaic. On a sheet of construction paper, draw a design or picture. Glue dry macaroni pieces on the design or picture, filling in all the spaces.

If you want, you can color the macaroni ahead of time by dipping it quickly into a mixture of food coloring and water. Let the macaroni dry on waxed paper before you start the picture. In this way, you can use more than one color in your mosaic!

Seed Mosaic. On cardboard, draw the outline of a flower, animal, object, or design. Spread glue inside the outline. Cover the glued area completely with seeds. (You can also use popcorn kernels, beans, dried peas, etc.) When the mosaic has dried, paint the seeds to complete the picture.

Straw Mosaic. Cut drinking straws into different-sized pieces. Glue the pieces on paper to make pictures or designs. Use a combination of straws that are white, colored, and striped.

Mother's Day

Handprint Gift. Pour some white tempera paint in a shallow dish. Dip your hand into the paint and then print your hand on a sheet of blue construction paper. Wash and dry your hands. Then write your name and a message underneath the handprint.

Jewel Box Gift. Paint and decorate a long egg carton, inside and out, to make a jewel box gift.

Paper Bouquet. Cut out a triangle from colored paper for a bouquet base. Hold the triangle so the flat base is on top. Then glue the edge of a paper doily to the top of this base. Cut out some paper flower blossoms and glue them on the doily.

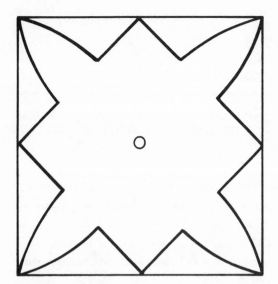

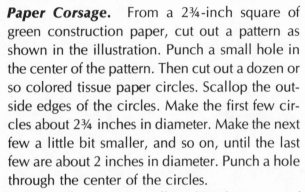

Paper Corsage. From a 2¾-inch square of green construction paper, cut out a pattern as shown in the illustration. Punch a small hole in the center of the pattern. Then cut out a dozen or so colored tissue paper circles. Scallop the outside edges of the circles. Make the first few circles about 2¾ inches in diameter. Make the next few a little bit smaller, and so on, until the last few are about 2 inches in diameter. Punch a hole through the center of the circles.

Center the cut-out, scalloped circles on top of the pattern you cut out earlier with the largest circles on the bottom and the smallest on top. Attach the circles to the pattern with a paper fastener to complete the corsage.

Paper Flower Greeting Card. Fold a rectangle of white construction paper into a card. On the front of the card, draw the stem and leaves of a flower with a green crayon.

To make the flower petals, cut out about a dozen circles from colored tissue paper. Make the first few flower circles large, then gradually make them steadily smaller. Glue the circles, on top of each other, into position on the flower stem on the front of the card. Glue the largest circles on the bottom and finish with the smallest circles on top. Write a message inside the card.

Paper Plate Lazy Susan Gift. Obtain two paper plates, one large and one small. Decorate each with crayon designs or pastel cutouts. With the help of an adult, shellac the surface so it can be wiped clean when used.

Glue a brightly painted spool upright in the center of the large paper plate. Glue the small paper plate on top of the spool. The lazy Susan is now complete!

Plant Gift. Decorate an empty tuna can. Fill it with potting soil. Plant a succulent or other small plant in the planter for a gift.

Silhouette Gift. Tape a piece of black construction paper to the wall, level with the height of your head. Stand next to the paper with your side facing the wall. Have someone shine a flashlight at you so the profile of your face is cast on the paper as a shadow. Have someone else trace your profile on the paper. Then cut out the profile and glue it on a 12-by-18-inch sheet of white construction paper for a gift.

Wall Plaque Gift. Glue shells, leaves, colored beads, etc., on a cottage cheese carton lid. Allow the lid to dry. Then spray the lid with gold paint, attach a hook to the back, and give as a gift.

Music

Experiencing music will help you learn to be creative. Do not be afraid to respond to the music with body movements and playacting. Invent your own songs or chants based on things that have happened to you in the past. Make up stories to go with the music you hear, or create a dance to fit a story. Make your own tunes to go with words you know, or substitute your own words to go with tunes you already know. Paint or draw while listening to music, and use rhythm instruments to help you interpret songs and music.

Activities

Playacting to Music. While music is playing, use your imagination and try acting out the music you hear. You might pretend to be a raindrop falling, a sunbeam dancing, an airplane flying, a horse galloping, a tree blowing in the wind, or a wave crashing onto the beach. Listen to the flow of the music and express the meaning you get from it!

Play-Along Music. Play a record and try to keep the beat on a rhythm instrument. Ask your friends to join you.

Scarf Dancing. While playing music, dance around the room with a colored scarf in each hand. As you follow the rhythm of the music, wave the scarves in large circles and around your body.

Story Sounds. While someone reads or tells a story to you, use a rhythm instrument to dramatize the story. For instance, use a triangle to represent a tiptoeing fairy, a drum for the heavy steps of a giant, or woodblocks for galloping horses.

Statue Game. Move and dance around to music. When the music stops, everyone must "freeze" into a statue.

Art

Drawing to Music. On a large sheet of paper, draw, color, or paint as music is being played. Draw your picture or design according to the moods or feelings the music seems to suggest. Use different strokes or colors to show what the music means to you.

Music Sheet Collage. Collect some old music sheets. Cut them into odd-shaped pieces. Glue the pieces on a piece of cardboard to form a collage of notes and other musical symbols.

Potato Print Notes. Cut some potatoes in half. From the freshly cut surfaces, cut away more of the potato to make the shapes of music notes raised above the rest of the surface. Using black paint, print the note shapes on white construction paper.

Instruments

Aluminum Can Mariachis. You can make this basic Mexican rhythm instrument by filling two empty aluminum pop-top cans with about ½ cup of pebbles apiece. Seal the pop-top holes with tape, and bend the cans slightly in the middle. Cover with papier mâché. Allow it to dry, and paint with bright, colorful designs. Shake to play.

Balloon Shaker. Pour 1 teaspoon of rice, sand, or beans into a deflated balloon. Next, inflate the balloon and tie it closed. Shake the balloon to music or use it in a rhythm band.

Bleach Bottle Bongo Drums. Find two empty plastic bleach bottles, one large and one small. Be sure they have been well rinsed. Remove their lids and set them on the table with a block of wood between them.

Tape the two bottles together, with the wood block still between them, or fasten them together with a large rubber band. Turn the bongos upside down. Sit down and hold the bongos between your knees. Play them with your fingers and hands.

Bottle Cap Shaker. Ask an adult to help you nail a number of pop bottle caps along the sides of a thick piece of dowel pole. Leave enough space between the head of the nail and the dowel so the caps will rattle when shaken.

Brush and Screen Rhythm Instrument. Rub a wire brush up and down on a grease screen to make different kinds of sounds.

Cardboard Tube Blow Horn. Cover one end of an empty cardboard paper towel tube with a piece of waxed paper, holding the paper in place with a rubber band. Poke five small holes in a row along the side of the tube. Hum or blow into the open end of the tube while putting your fingers over the holes.

Cardboard Tube Rhythm Sticks. Hit or rub two cardboard tubes together to create sounds and rhythms.

Cardboard Tube Shaker. Obtain a short cardboard tube. From heavy paper, cut out two circles, one to fit on each end of the tube. Glue a circle on one of the ends.

Drop a few beans through the open end into the tube. Then glue the second circle on the open end, sealing the beans inside the tube. Allow to dry. Shake to create rhythms.

Chair Harp. For harp strings, find some very large rubber bands. Or make your own strings by cutting strips from old inner tubes. Stretch the harp strings across the back of a straight chair. Tie them at each end. Pull the harp close to your shoulder and pluck away!

Chair Harp

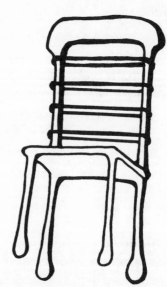

Coconut Woodblocks. With the help of an adult, start to saw a coconut in half. Stop sawing when milk starts running out of the coconut. Drain the milk into a bowl and finish cutting the coconut in two. Using a kitchen knife, cut out the coconut meat. (Be careful!) Smooth off the outsides of the coconut halves with sandpaper. Knock them together to make woodblock sounds! (They make excellent horse-hoof sounds!)

Coffee Can Tom-Tom. Cover an empty coffee can with a plastic lid. Beat on the lid end with your hands or a spoon.

Comb Hummer. Fold a piece of tissue paper around a pocket comb. Press it against your mouth and hum!

Egg Carton Bells. String a series of small bells across a cardboard egg carton and shake to make jingle sounds.

Flour-Sifter Rhythm Instrument. Drop some dry macaroni into a flour sifter. Tape a piece of paper over the top of the sifter and shake away!

Flower Pot Xylophone. Hang several small clay flowerpots of different sizes from strings that are attached to a board. To make music, tap the pots with a piece of dowel rod.

Foam Cup Shaker. Obtain two plastic foam drinking cups. Pour a few beans into one. Tape together the open ends of the cups and shake!

Hubcap Gong. Loop a piece of wire through the air valve hole of an old hubcap. Hold the hubcap in the air and strike it with a stick. (For soft sounds, cover the end of the stick with cotton, cloth, or a piece of inner tube.)

Gourd Shaker. Using a saw, cut off the top quarter of a gourd. Clean out the gourd. Place the hollowed gourd and seeds in an oven for one hour under moderate heat. When completely dry, place the seeds back into the gourd. Tape the top of the gourd back in place and shake!

Mitten Bells. Have an adult help you sew a string of bells to a pair of mittens. Put the mittens on, and clap your hands to make the bells jingle!

Nail Triangle. Tie a short length of string to a large nail. Hold the nail by the string and strike it with another nail to make triangle sounds.

Oatmeal Box Drum. Use an empty oatmeal or salt box for a drum. Beat on it with your hands or use pencils as drumsticks.

Paper Bag Maracas. Pour ¼ cup of rice or corn kernels into a paper bag. Then pour the same amount into another paper bag. Twist the open ends of each bag shut. Hold a bag in each hand by the twisted end, and shake them.

Paper Megaphone Trumpet. Roll a large sheet of thick paper into a cone, leaving a small hole at the pointed end. Staple the cone together. Hum through the small end to amplify your humming!

Paper Plate Guitar. Cut a round hole in the bottom of a paper plate. Make a circle of glue on the rim of another paper plate. Glue the two plates together face to face. Allow to dry.

For a handle, glue the end of a paint paddle to

Paper Plate Guitar

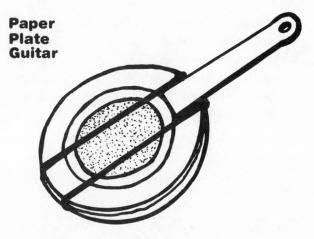

the plate that has the hole, and let the glue dry. Then put rubber band "strings" around the paper plate, in line with the paint paddle, so the strings stretch across the cut-out hole. Strum away!

Paper Plate Rhythm Instrument. Rub your fingernails quickly or slowly along the fluted edge of a paper plate to make sounds.

Paper Plate Tambourine. Place some beans between two paper plates and staple together face to face. Tape some jingle bells around the edge of the plates. Tap the sides of the tambourine with your hands or shake it.

Pie Tin Rhythm Shaker. Tape together two small frozen pie tins face to face with some beans or pebbles placed inside. Shake.

Pop Bottle Tunes. Fill some pop bottles with different amounts of water. Blow across the openings of the bottles to produce sounds or strike the bottles with spoons. Create tunes by blowing across or tapping the different bottles one after another.

Rubber Band Instrument. Tautly stretch a rubber band around a glass from the bottom and up over the mouth. Pluck the part of the rubber band that is over the mouth to make a sound. To vary the pitch, lift the rubber band slightly over the mouth, using a pencil, and run the pencil back and forth while plucking!

Sandpaper Woodblocks. Obtain two 4-by-6-inch blocks of wood. Smooth any rough edges with sandpaper. Then, from a new sheet of sandpaper, cut out two 4-by-6-inch pieces. Staple or glue one of the sandpaper pieces to each woodblock.

To play the blocks, brush them against one another, with the sandpaper sides facing each other. Play the blocks to make rhythms or to create sound effects.

Saucepan Lid Cymbals. Clang two saucepan lids together for cymbals.

Shoe Box Guitar. Stretch some rubber bands across the length of an empty, lidless shoe box to make a guitar.

For each rubber band you want to stretch across, make a pair of notches at each end of the box directly across from one another. Loop a band through one pair of notches at one end, then stretch it across the box and loop it through the opposite pair of notches. Repeat to make more strings. Play by plucking the rubber bands.

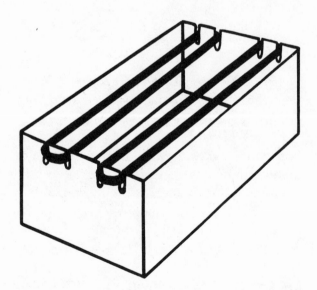

Silverware Chimes. Tie a knife, a fork, and a teaspoon to three pieces of string. Hang all three from a ruler. Play the chimes by holding the ruler in the air and striking the chimes with a tablespoon.

Spoon Castanets. Clack two metal spoons together to sound like castanets.

Tennis Ball Shaker. You may need adult help with this project. Using a knife, carefully cut a 1½-inch slit into an old tennis ball. Squeeze the ball to open the slit. Place four bottle caps inside. Relax your squeeze, and the tennis ball will close up. Hold the ball in your hand and shake it.

Tin Can Bell. Tie a one-inch-wide metal washer to a 12-inch piece of string. Then punch a hole in the center of the bottom of an empty tin can. Thread the washer string up through the hole so the washer hangs to strike the open edge of the can. Re-tie the string so it cannot slip out of the can. Hold the can from the top edge and make the bell ring.

Washboard Rhythm Instrument. Place a metal thimble on your forefinger. Rub the thimble over the surface of a washboard to make sounds and rhythms.

Wild Grass Whistle. Find a six-inch length of tall, wide-blade grass. Hold it firmly between the thumbs of both hands, leaving a small space between the thumbs. The blade should be pulled tightly in this space.

Place your lips to the blade and blow hard on its edge. At the same time, hold your hands in a cupped position with the fingertips slightly touching. This will make a high, screeching whistle sound or a low, blurred sound. You may have to practice this a few times to get it right!

Wild Oat Whistle. Find a wild oat. Then pull out a section of the hollow stem, and bite or cut off a two-inch length. Pinch one end together until its sides begin to crack. Then, blow into the hollow end as you would with a toy whistle.

Wooden Spoon Striker. Use a wooden spoon for striking pots, pans, cans, and lids. You can also use it as a drumstick.

N

Nature Art

Collection Display. Here is a way to display the small rocks or shells you have collected. Pour white glue into a plastic foam meat tray, to a depth of ¼ inch. Place the rocks or shells in the glue. Let the glue dry and harden. (It might take several days.)

Desert Diorama. Place some sandy soil in a rectangular cake pan. Add a few rocks, some cactus plants, and a few succulents.

Dried Flower Arrangement. First, find a container for your arrangement. A conch shell, clam shell, wooden basket, margarine tub, or even a large tin can will work fine. Press a piece of oasis (a light plastic foam sold at florist stores) or playdough into the bottom of the container.

Now, gather enough dried materials to make an arrangement. Weeds, twigs, flowers, and different-colored grasses are good. Stick the materials into the oasis to form the arrangement.

Leaf Prints. Place a lump of clay on a flat surface. Flatten the clay with a rolling pin. Lay a leaf on the clay. Again with a rolling pin, roll over the leaf and the clay at the same time. Lift the leaf to reveal a leaf print underneath. Let the clay dry, then paint it with tempera or acrylic paint.

Nature Castings. For this activity, you need the kind of clay that does not get hard when you work with it. Flatten the clay with a rolling pin. Next, collect some nature items such as twigs with buds, leaves, stems, seeds, and rocks. Place the items on the rolled-out clay.

Roll the rolling pin over the nature items so they sink into the clay and make an impression. Remove the items carefully. Then, cut a two-inch strip of cardboard and set it up tightly around the clay to act as a fence.

Mix some plaster of Paris until it resembles pudding. Pour it over the fenced-in clay. Allow the plaster to harden. Then take away the cardboard fence and remove the clay from the hardened casting. Paint the casting and display!

Nature Painting. While taking a nature walk, pick up various nature materials you find along the way. Look for things such as feathers, leaves, palm fronds, pebbles, weeds, grasses, etc. Take them home to use as painting tools.

Pour several different colors of tempera paints into small pie tins. Dip the nature materials into the paints and use them as "brushes" and paint on pieces of construction paper.

Rock Figures. Collect some rocks of different sizes, shapes, and colors. Pick out one of the larger rocks for a body. Use smaller rocks for the legs, arms, head, and other body parts.

Stick the rocks together with white glue to form animals and people. (To help the rocks stick better, put a little piece of glue-dipped cotton between the larger rocks.) Add features with felt-tip pens.

Twig Art. Gather as many odd-shaped, funny-looking twigs as you can find. Old, gnarled twigs are especially good. Lay out the twigs to form letters, designs, or pictures. Use the natural bends and twists of the twigs to help form the shape you want.

If you want to save your twig art, find an old, flat section of board. Clean and smooth the board with sandpaper. Then lay out your twig art on the board and glue down the pieces.

Twig and Bark People. Hunt for interesting pieces of twigs and bark. When you get home, glue colored beads to the pieces to make faces on them. Create people and animals this way, using the natural bends and twists in the materials to give the creatures personalities.

Nature Walks

Ant Tracking. Look for an ant trail the next time you take a nature walk or play outside. Locate a single ant in the trail, and follow that ant to see how far you can track him. Is the ant carrying anything? Where did it go?

Beach Walk. Carry a pail at the beach so you can pick up interesting things along the way. (But be sure not to pick up live animals.) Look for shells, sand dollars, seaweed, unusual rocks, polished pieces of beach glass, and other surprises.

Stop at a tide pool to see if you can spot any crabs, barnacles, or tiny fish. Smell the salt air and listen to the sounds of the ocean. Look for bird tracks in the sand.

When you get home, tell someone about your experiences. Visit the library and read some books about your beach walk discoveries.

Bush Life. The next time you visit the park or take a nature walk, sit down underneath a bush that has branches and leaves hanging all the way to the ground. Sit very still. Watch for and listen to the life in the branches above you.

Duck Pond Visit. Ask an adult to take you to a duck pond. Take along a bag of bread crumbs to feed the ducks. Be careful not to tease or scare the ducks. Later, go to the library and read a book about ducks.

Listening Walk. Take a walk through the woods, meadow, or park. Listen to the different sounds—the wind blowing, the birds singing, or water trickling in a brook. On a note pad, write down the sounds you hear, or, if possible, take along a tape recorder to preserve the sounds from your walk.

"Looking" Walk. Take a walk "looking" for bugs, birds, leaves, or anything in general. Be sure to take binoculars, a magnifying glass, and a bag to collect the interesting things you find.

Melting-Snow Walk. When the snow is melting, take a special walk to explore the things beginning to show from underneath the snow. Look for new green plants, rocks, and even lost toys. Did you see any animals? Make a list of the surprises you find!

Nature Crawl. Crawl among the bushes and flowers to get a close-up look at the miniature life on the ground. Be careful not to crush any plants or flowers!

Look for creatures crawling on the ground or climbing up plants. Watch for other creatures flying and jumping between the plants. Take along a magnifying glass. What things do you see?

Pond Walk. Go to a pond and take along some tin cans or milk cartons, a net, and a magnifying glass. Skim the net along the bottom of the pond and see what kinds of things catch in the net.

Look for weeds, insects, algae, small fish, tadpoles, and water plants. Look at them under the magnifying glass. If it is not against local laws, take some pond water home to study.

Puddle Walk. Go on a walk right after a heavy rain. Look for interesting puddles, raindrops on plant leaves, worms on the ground, and enjoy the fresh, wet smell of things.

Spider Walk. Go outdoors to look for different kinds of spiders and spider webs. Webs are most often found on or under bushes, trees, fences, old boards, in corners, or in the grass. Look for webs of different shapes. But remember—do not touch any spiders you see!

In the early morning, you might find large webs strung between trees and bushes and other webs sparkling with dew, reflecting the morning sunlight. What kinds of spiders do you see? Do you see any baby spiders?

Necklaces

Cardboard Square Necklace. Cut out small cardboard squares and punch a hole in the center of each one. String the squares on a length of yarn or cord and tie the ends together for a necklace.

Cereal Necklace. For this, use dry cereals that have holes in the centers. Slide the cereal on a piece of cord and tie the ends to make a necklace.

Foil Necklace. Roll aluminum foil pieces into balls of any size, but do not roll them too tightly! String the balls together to make necklaces, bracelets, and rings, using an embroidery needle and thread. (Ask an adult for help if needed.)

Hardware Necklace. String nuts, bolts, and metallic washers on heavy thread to make necklaces. Braid copper wire to make bracelets and chokers.

Pond Walk

Macaroni Necklace. String pieces of dry macaroni on string, ribbon, or cord to make a necklace.

Paper Clip Necklace. Hook paper clips together into a chain for a necklace. You can also make bracelets and belts this way!

Pipe Cleaner Necklace. Cut some colored pipe cleaners into shorter lengths and loop them together to make a chain necklace.

Plastic Foam Packing-Piece Necklace. Gather some small plastic foam packing pieces. String the pieces together, using a plastic needle and a long piece of yarn. Gather more pieces than you think you will need because some will crack and break when you push the needle through.

Pumpkin Seed Necklace. Thread pumpkin seeds on a string to make a necklace, using a large-eyed needle.

Ring Necklace. Find some old rubber jar rings or curtain rings. Tie short pieces of string between each ring to form a necklace.

Shoelace Necklace. Tie together several long shoelaces. String on things such as loop cereals, macaroni, colored straw segments, and wood beads. Tie the shoelaces at the ends to form a necklace.

Spool Necklace.   String colored spools on a shoelace and tie the ends together for a necklace.

Vegetable Necklace.   Make an unusual necklace from a potato and a carrot! Cut the potato into thin slices. Cut the carrot into cubes. Then thread a two-foot length of dental floss on a plastic needle. String the vegetables onto the floss, alternating the pieces to make a necklace. Hang the necklace in a dry, airy place. (It may take up to six weeks to dry out.) Look at the necklace each week. See how the vegetables are shrinking and turning dark!

When the necklace is dry, brush it with varnish to help it last longer. Can your friends tell what the necklace is made from?

Outer Space

Balloon Moon.   Using a felt-tip marker, draw craters on a round, inflated balloon. Hang with string from the ceiling.

Cardboard Tube Telescope.   Paint a long mailing tube or wrapping paper tube to make a "pretend" telescope.

Construction Paper Space Helmet.   Gently bend a 12-by-18-inch sheet of white construction paper so the short ends come together. But do not make a crease in the middle! To make an opening for the upper half of your face, draw a quarter circle in from the "fold." Use this line as a guide and cut through both thicknesses of paper. Then open up the sheet to reveal the full opening. With a felt-tip marker, draw dots around the face opening to represent rivets.

Now glue or staple together the short ends of

Construction Paper Space Helmet

the paper to form a tube. From another piece of white construction paper, cut out a circle to tape on as the helmet top. Staple a small aluminum pie plate to each side of the helmet for ear pieces. Staple a nut cup below the face opening for a microphone or an oxygen valve. Finish by stapling a pipe cleaner at the top of each side for antennae.

Crayon-Resist Solar System.   Draw a picture of the planets in our solar system, making heavy, dark impressions with crayon. Draw the sun in the middle, with the planets circling around the sun.

Brush over the picture with thinned black or dark blue tempera paint.

Crayon Rubbing Space Shapes.   From construction paper, cut out stars, planets, rockets, comets, and other space shapes. Place the shapes underneath a sheet of paper. Using crayons without wrappers, gently rub over the paper with the flat surface of the crayon. Watch impressions of the shapes take form on the paper!

Cut and Paste Rocket to the Moon Scene.   Cut out the shape of a rocket from white paper. Paste the rocket on blue background paper. Also paste on the cut-out shape of a yellow moon.

Egg Carton Moon Buggy. From a cardboard egg carton, cut out a section two cups wide and three cups long. Then obtain two drinking straws and two large empty thread spools.

Poke one of the straws through a spool. Center the spool on the straw. Fold up each end of the straw, making it even with the end across from it. Repeat this with the second straw and spool.

Tape the ends of each wheel assembly to the outside corners of each end of the egg carton. The moon buggy is ready to roll!

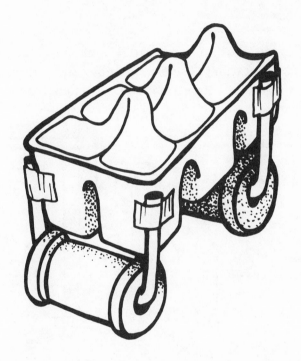

Jupiter Finger Painting. On a large sheet of shelf paper, paint a very large circle. Within the circle, and off center toward the bottom, use red finger paint to make an oval shape for the "red spot" of Jupiter. Fill in the rest of the planet by painting yellow, orange and red streaks from one side to the other. This creates the "banded" look you see in pictures of this giant planet.

Life-Sized Martian. Lie down on a large sheet of brown wrapping paper. Have someone outline your body, using a crayon or felt-tip marker. Get up and color in your outline. Make it into a "Martian" by adding strange things such as a tail, horns, scales, antennae, or anything else you can think of!

Moon Landing Diorama. From a cardboard egg carton, cut out a number of eggcups. Glue them to a large, flat piece of heavy cardboard for rocks and craters. Glue some open side down for rocks, and others open side up for craters. Cut jagged edges in the crater pieces. When all the glue has dried, paint the entire surface gray.

To make a rocket, fasten a single eggcup over the top end of an upright cardboard tube. Cover the rocket with aluminum foil. Then stand it up in the middle of the moon scene. (To help it stand firmly, make short cuts in the bottom end of the rocket and bend out the edges.)

Night Sky Drawing. On a sheet of black construction paper, paint hundreds of tiny white dots over the entire surface of the paper to look like the night sky full of stars.

Oatmeal Box Planetarium. Punch a number of small pinholes into the solid end of an oatmeal box. Each pinhole is a star. When you are finished making the pinholes, turn out the lights in your room. Aim the solid end of the oatmeal box at the ceiling, and shine a flashlight up inside the box. Look at the ceiling and see a beautiful night sky full of shining stars!

If you want, poke the shapes of constellations into the solid ends of other oatmeal boxes, or poke holes in a spiral pattern to make a spiral galaxy!

Other Worlds Scene. Use your imagination to draw a picture of what you think it might look like on another world. Remember that other planets might be totally different than ours! If you want, draw what the people, animals, and plants on your planet look like.

Paper Bowl Moon. Turn a paper bowl upside down. Glue some tiny objects on the outside surface of the bowl. Then cover the bowl and objects with some heavy-duty foil. Dab on some black paint here and there to finish the moon.

Paper Plate Flying Saucer. Glue or staple together two paper plates face to face to form a flying saucer. With black paint or a black felt-tip marker, make portholes around the dome of the flying saucer. Toss the saucer back and forth.

Paper Plate Moon Collage. From magazines, clip out pictures of the moon taken through a telescope. Then place a paper plate upside down in front of you. Paste portions of the pictures on the paper plate to make a collaged moon surface. Hang for display.

Papier Mâché Earth. Blow up a balloon and tie it to keep the air inside. Cover the balloon with several layers of newspaper strips dipped lightly in glue. When the papier mâché has dried, paint land areas with brown and green paints. Paint ocean areas with blue paint. Allow it to dry and then put your "globe" on display.

Plastic Bottle Space Helmet. Find a well-rinsed gallon-sized plastic bleach bottle that will fit over your head when the neck and handle are cut away. In the remaining bottom section, cut away a large square on one side where your face will be. Punch some air holes into the helmet. With a permanent felt-tip marker, draw rivet marks, a mouthpiece, and other details.

Round Carton Play Rocket. Here is a way to make a rocket that is big enough to play in! Obtain a very large, round cardboard carton—the kind used by packing companies. Turn it upright so the solid end is on the ground. Remove the lid if the carton has one.

Cut a doorway in one side so you can crawl in and out of the rocket. Leave the door connected on one side so you can open and close it. On the inside walls, use a felt-tip marker to draw some instrument panels and other details. If you want, cut out several portholes that can open and close easily. On the outside draw rivets, and along the bottom draw engine details. You can also write the name of your spaceship on the outside of the carton.

Make a nose cone from a large piece of poster board. Blast off!

Sky Map. Make a simple sky map on a 12-by-18-inch sheet of sky-blue construction paper. Cut out several circles from colored paper and paste them on the map for planets. For stars, stick on a number of small gold or silver gummed stars, or draw the stars yourself. Form some of the stars into constellations like the big or little dippers. Use your map to "chart your course" through the stars when you play inside your play rocket.

Sky Mobile. Cut out any number of stars, moon crescents, comets, and other sky figures. Hang them by string from the ceiling to represent the nighttime sky.

Space-Age Collage. From old issues of aircraft, astronomy, and science fiction film magazines, cut out many different photographs and illustrations of rockets, missiles, stars, planets, comets, satellites, astronauts, galaxies, and other related space-age items. Glue them together into a giant collage on a 12-by-18-inch sheet of construction paper.

Spacecraft Control Panel. With very strong tape, fasten together three large cardboard panels. Set the panel assembly upright in front of you with the two outside panels bent slightly toward you. This is how you will set up the panels when everything is finished.

Now lay the panel assembly down in front of you. To make knobs and instruments for the panel, glue on painted pop bottle caps, juice can tops, cottage cheese carton lids, spools, plastic tops of soft drink cups, and other similar things. For lit and unlit indicator lights, glue on large red and black gumdrops.

On a piece of white paper, draw some dials and meters. Cut them out and glue them directly on the cardboard or on some of the instruments you have already glued to the panel.

Set up the panel assembly in front of you. Now you are ready to chart your course and navigate your spacecraft through the stars!

Outer Space (Science)

Day/Night Simulation.   Obtain a globe or a basketball to represent the earth. Use a flashlight or lighted bulb to represent the sun. Darken the room and shine the light on the globe or the ball so half the globe is light and half is dark. This is similar to the day and night sides of the earth!

Stick a small piece of tape on the globe or the ball to represent where you live. Rotate the globe to see what happens to your "home" as the earth turns. Which way does earth face when it is nighttime for you? Which way does it face when it is daytime? Notice that when it is daytime on one side of the earth, it is nighttime on the other!

Follow the Sun.   The turning of the earth causes night and day. During the day, then, the earth is turning in relation to the sun. This causes shadows to be short when the sun is high and long when the sun is low. The shadows change shape as the earth rotates while the sun stays relatively still.

Go outside in the morning and mark the spot where a shadow of a fencepost falls. At noon, make another mark where the shadow falls. Then, in late afternoon, mark it again. What does this mean?

Globe Examination.   Our earth is a planet. It is round like a ball. The next time you visit the library, look at a globe. This is what the earth looks like from space! Look closely for areas of land and water. Look for lakes, rivers, and mountains. Find where you live. Step outside and look around. How much of the earth do you see? It is a big world!

Meteor Watch.   On a clear, moonless night, lie down outside to watch the sky for meteors. Ask permission from an adult. Most meteors last just a few seconds and look like stars that "fall" and quickly disappear. (That is why some people call meteors "falling stars.") Once in awhile you might see one that is much closer and streaks across the sky!

Meteors are stones falling toward the earth from outer space. Their great speed causes them to burn up in the air. Very rarely, a meteor will fall all the way to the earth, making a crater.

Check the newspaper to find out when the next meteor shower will take place. (You can see meteors almost any night, but you see many more of them during a shower.)

Moon Observation.   Look at the moon through a telescope or a pair of binoculars. Can you see the craters? Later, look at pictures of the moon and compare them to what you saw. Look at a map of the moon to see what parts you saw.

Rocket Power. Look at a picture of a rocket blasting off. How does it lift off from the earth? To find out, inflate a balloon and then let it go. Watch it shoot up into the air! With the balloon it is the force of the escaping air that pushes the balloon up. With a rocket, it is the force of the escaping fuel which powers it upward. The fins help the rocket go straight.

Satellite Watch. Satellites are man-made craft circling the earth. Most of them are very large and can be seen as moving pinpoints of light on a clear night. Check the newspaper to find out when the next satellite is due to pass overhead, and watch the skies for it at the proper time.

Stargazing. On a clear, moonless night, spread a blanket on the grass and lie down to look at the stars. (Ask an adult for permission.) It usually takes about 20 minutes for your eyes to adjust to the darkness so you can see the stars very well. Look for bright stars and constellations, and see if you can spot any planets. Perhaps an adult will help you locate these objects in the sky.

What are stars? They are giant balls of hot gas just like our own sun. They only look so small because they are very, very far away! Later, read some books about astronomy, and learn more about the stars and planets.

Telescope Observations. If you do not have a telescope of your own, see if you can borrow one from a friend or neighbor. If you still cannot find a telescope, use a pair of binoculars.

Look at the moon through the telescope. The best time to look is when the moon is only one quarter full. Then there are shadows on the craters, giving depth to the images you see on the moon. Consult a current astronomy magazine at your local library to find out what planets are visible and where to locate them in the sky. Ask an adult to help you find a planet in the sky, such as Mars, Jupiter, Venus, or Saturn. Moonless nights are best for looking at the planets. Even with binoculars, you should be able to see the rings of Saturn and a few of the moons of Jupiter. Through the telescope, notice that the planets no longer look like pinpoints of light but like flat disks. The planets are actually round like the earth!

Next, look at a star through the telescope. Notice that it still looks like a pinpoint of light! That is because the star is much, much farther away than any of the planets!

Warning: *Never, never* look at the sun through a telescope or a pair of binoculars, or even with the naked eye! It could blind you!

Painting

Before painting, it is a good idea to spread some newspapers over the area where you plan to work to catch the splattered paint. Wear something over your clothes to keep them clean, and be sure to clean up when you are finished!

Painting Easel. You can make a table-top painting easel by cutting a cardboard box as shown, forming a triangular-shaped piece. Cut slits in the top so you can insert clothespins to clip your painting paper into place.

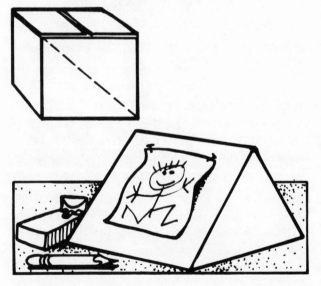

Paint Smock. Before painting, put on an old shirt to use as a paint smock. You can decorate it ahead of time, if you want, using designs cut out of iron-on tape.

Blotto Painting. Fold a piece of paper in half, then open it. Spoon a thick glob of tempera paint on the crease. Again fold the paper and press carefully. Open to see the pattern that has formed!

Blow Painting. Dribble one color of paint on a sheet of paper. Blow on the paint through a straw to move the paint. Blow on the paint from the sides or from above. See what different effects you can make in the paint. (If you get dizzy while blowing, stop to rest for awhile. You can reduce the chances of becoming dizzy by blowing through a straw that is cut in half.)

Dot Painting. On a large sheet of paper, paint a colored dot. Make many dots, using different colors, all over the paper. Then, with black paint, connect the dots. See what kind of a pattern develops.

Fingertip Painting. Soak a paper towel with tempera paint. Then touch your fingertips to the towel. "Walk" your fingers across the paper to make prints. Use a different color of paint for each finger if you want. Make patterns or pictures this way.

Fork Painting. Quickly paint all over a sheet of paper with thick tempera paint. Then drag a plastic fork over the painting to make a design.

Glue Painting. Add some food coloring to some white glue inside a plastic bottle. Squeeze the colored glue onto construction paper, forming a pattern or picture. Use a different bottle for each color of glue you make. *Another way to do it:* Squeeze white glue from a squeeze bottle onto a piece of cardboard to form a design or picture. Allow to dry overnight. Paint over the dried glue to finish the painting.

Ice Painting. Sprinkle some dry tempera on a sheet of glossy paper. Wrap an ice cube with a paper towel and hold the ice over the paper. Rub on the ice, so it melts and drips on the paper, creating an interesting, random painting.

Magic Window Painting. Cut a sheet of waxed paper about 24 inches long. Fold it in half, then open it. Dab various colors of thinned tempera paint on one side of the paper. Fold the paper in half again.

Using your fingers along the outside of the paper, gently squish and spread the paint around. (If the paint gets near the edge, squish it inward again.) When finished, do not unfold the paper. The painting will show through easily!

Marble Painting. Find an empty shoe box and line the bottom with paper. Then place some tempera paint in a shallow container. Roll a marble in the container so it becomes covered with paint. Spoon the marble into the shoe box. Tilt the box back and forth so the marble rolls around in the box, making a design on the paper. *Another way to do it:* Use an old golf ball instead of a marble.

Milk Painting. Pour some milk into a bowl and add a few drops of food coloring. With a new or very clean paintbrush, paint on white bread with the colored milk. When finished, toast the bread and eat it!

Oil Base Pastels. Use these paint sticks when you want to create luminous colors. The paint sticks are oily, making them good for many kinds of surfaces, including waxy and slippery ones.

Redi-Mix Paint. Mix 1 cup of dry tempera paint, 1 teaspoon of liquid starch, 1 heaping tablespoon of white paste, and a few drops of oil of cloves. Then add water until you have a paint mixture that looks creamy. (Store in an airtight container when not in use.) For daily painting, use a small amount of "redi-mix," adding a little water each time to thin it.

Resist Painting.   Draw a picture on a piece of white paper with crayons. Press very hard when you draw! When finished, paint over the picture with thinned tempera paint. (Black or dark-colored paint works best.) Poster paints work well also. The crayon resists the paint, creating a surprising effect!

Sand Painting.   Spread glue on a sheet of paper. Sprinkle some sand over the glued areas. Allow to dry, then shake off the excess sand. Paint a picture or design on the sand.

Scrape Painting.   Spoon several different colors of thickened paint onto paper. With a stiff piece of cardboard, scrape, twist, swirl, and zigzag the paint around the paper to make designs.

See-Through Painting.   Stretch a sheet of clear plastic wrap over a wooden frame and attach it with clear tape. Set the frame upright indoors or outdoors so you can see through it. Then, paint right on the clear plastic wrap! Paint the background that you see through the frame! Try to use colors similar to those you see in the background.

Snow Painting.   This is a winter snowtime activity where you will actually paint on the snow outside! First, while indoors, mix some powdered tempera paint with water in unbreakable containers. Mix until it looks like light cream. Make a container of paint for each of the primary colors — red, blue, and yellow.

Then take the paints outside. Using a small house-paint brush, paint directly on the snow! Make letters, pictures, or strange shapes! You might even try some dribble or spatter painting in the snow. Watch some of the colors combine in the snow to make new colors!

Soap Bar Painting.   Using a potato peeler, make some shavings from a bar of white, mild soap. With an eggbeater, whip the shavings with a little warm water to make a lather as stiff as egg whites.

Spread the lather on dark-colored paper. Try making scenes including snowmen, clouds, ghosts, or anything else that is white. When finished, be sure to handle your picture with care because the lather becomes fragile when dry.

Soap Flake Painting.   Pour ½ cup of hot water into a pan. Beat with an eggbeater and gradually add soap flakes or powder (not detergent) until the mixture looks like whipped cream.

Dip your hand or a brush into the mixture and make designs or pictures with it on paper. (If you want, you can add food coloring or dry tempera while mixing to make different colors.)

Spatter Painting.   With one hand, hold a piece of wire screen above a piece of paper. With the other hand, dip a toothbrush into thin tempera paint and gently rub the brush across the screen. This causes the paint to spatter on the paper below!

If you want, cut out paper shapes ahead of time and lay them on the paper to be spattered. Spatter paint over the shapes and allow them to dry. Then lift up the shapes to reveal their outlines surrounded by spattered paint.

Spill Painting.   Spoon thin paint onto paper. Hold the paper in your hands and slowly tilt it in all directions. This allows the paint to form patterns across the paper. Watch the paint design change as you move the paper!

You can also try this with two colors, each color on a different part of the paper. See the colors mingle as you tilt the paper!

Sponge Painting.   Dip a small sponge into paint and use it as a brush. Be sure to use a different sponge for each color you use.

Squeeze Painting.   Mix 1 cup of liquid starch with 1 tablespoon of powdered tempera. Put the mixture in a squeeze bottle. Squeeze the paint on paper to form a picture or design.

Suds Painting.   Mix some soap flakes or liquid detergent with a very small amount of water. Beat and stir the mixture until it is stiff. Place the mixture in a pail and go outside. With a paint-brush, paint things such as the fence, sidewalk, or side of the house. When finished, wash it all away with the hose!

Tempera Painting. Tempera is a dry powder paint that works best when mixed with water until it looks smooth and creamy. If you want, you can dilute the paint more to make it last longer. One way is to mix the dry paint with equal amounts of hot water and liquid starch. Then add two tablespoons of liquid soap for every pound of dry tempera used. Tempera also comes in liquid form, ready to use, but it costs much more than the dry kind.

Tissue Paper Painting. Tear colored tissue paper into small pieces and place them over manila paper. With a wet brush, carefully brush the tissue pieces to wet them. Allow to dry. Lift the tissue pieces to reveal colored stains under each one! Outline the stains or draw a picture over them.

For variety, draw a picture first with crayons, then use the tissue papers to color stain the picture.

Track Painting. Pour a thin layer of paint on a piece of scrap paper. Roll a toy car over the paint so the wheels absorb some of the paint.

On another sheet of paper, roll the car in different ways to make track patterns. When the paint begins to wear off, roll the car in paint again and continue making tracks.

Use a different car for each color you want to add. Make your entire design or picture using only car tracks!

Transfer Painting. Make a finger painting on a cookie sheet. Place a blank sheet of newsprint over the painted surface. Press gently, allowing the paint to stick to the underside of the paper. Starting at one end, carefully lift the paper to reveal a reverse painting on the other side!

Watercolors. These paints can be purchased in a set that includes a brush. The paints usually come in cake form and must be thinned with water before using. You can buy special water-color paper, but any rough-textured paper will work. Watercolors are especially good for painting backgrounds for your crayon drawings.

Yarn Painting. Dab a long piece of heavy rug yarn in tempera paint and drag it across a blank piece of paper, leaving a painted trail. Make patterns or designs this way, or drag the yarn across a paper that has been finger-painted.

Paper Art

Paper Chains. Cut a piece of paper into strips about half an inch wide and four inches long. Paste or tape together the ends of each strip to form a ring. Slip another strip through the first ring and fasten the ends of the second strip together. Now you have two rings linked together! Continue linking the rings to form a chain. Make it as long as you want. Use different colored strips to make holiday chains.

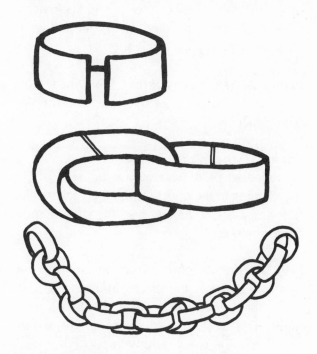

Paper Patterns. Find a large sheet of thin paper and fold it in half as many times as you can. With scissors, cut off the corners and make any other cuts you want along the edges. Open to reveal a pattern. Color it if you want.

Torn Paper Pictures. From different colors and types of paper, tear out many designs and shapes. Paste the torn pieces on a large sheet of construction paper, making a picture or collage. After the paste dries, you can outline the shapes with a felt-tip marker.

Papier Mâché

There are two basic types of papier mâché. Strip papier mâché is applied over a base or mold. It is good for making piñatas, bowls, trays, masks, and similar objects. Pulp papier mâché is usually modeled without using a base. It is good for small objects such as puppet heads or play food.

Papier Mâché Cooked Paste. With the help of an adult, mix 1 cup of wheat flour and ¼ cup of sugar in a saucepan. From a quart jar of warm water, stir in just enough water to make paste. Slowly add the rest of the water, stirring constantly to avoid lumps. Bring to a boil, still stirring constantly. Cook until clear and thick. (If too thick, thin with cold water.) Use while still warm for strip or pulp papier mâché.

Papier Mâché Easy Paste. Mix wheat flour and water to make a soupy paste. Use for strip papier mâché.

Papier Mâché Wallpaper Paste. Use a brand of wallpaper paste without insecticide in it. Mix it according to the directions on the package. Do not worry about lumps. Use for strip or pulp papier mâché.

Pulp Papier Mâché. Tear newspaper into small pieces. Put the pieces into a large pan. Cover them with water and let them soak overnight. The next day, squeeze out the excess water. Mix the paper pulp with cooked or wallpaper papier mâché paste until it reaches a modeling consistency.

Model the pulp into the desired shape. (Try to avoid thick objects, because the pulp may be-

come moldy if it cannot dry out completely.) Allow several days to dry, then paint.

Strip Papier Mâché. Tear pieces of newspaper into long strips. If you are making a large object, tear wide strips. If you are making a small object, tear narrow strips.

Pull the strips through a bowl of paste. Then remove the excess paste by pulling the strips through your fingers. Apply the sticky strips to a base, such as a balloon, rolled newspaper, wire frame, or anything else you choose.

To make a bowl or tray, first pick out a bowl or tray for a mold. Grease the mold with petroleum jelly. Apply the strips in layers, with each layer crisscrossed over the layer underneath. Apply three or four layers altogether. Allow several days for the strips to dry, then remove the papier mâché shape, and paint.

Paste Recipes

You may need adult help with these recipes.

Cooked Paste. Mix ¼ cup of flour and ¼ cup of sugar in a saucepan. Gradually add 1 cup of hot water, stirring to prevent lumps. Turn on the heat and cook until the mixture is thick and smooth. Then remove from heat and stir in ¼ teaspoon of oil of cloves. Allow to cool. When not in use, store in a covered jar in the refrigerator.

Cornstarch Paste. Mix ¾ cup water, 2 tablespoons light corn syrup, and 1 teaspoon white vinegar in a saucepan. Bring to a full boil.

Mix ½ cup cornstarch and ¾ cup water and add slowly to the boiled mixture. Stir constantly to avoid lumps. Add oil of wintergreen to preserve the mixture. Let the mixture stand overnight before using.

Diluted Glue. Mix three parts white household glue with one part warm water until it is well blended. The unused diluted glue may be saved in a screw-top jar.

Quick No-Cook Paste. Mix 1 cup flour and ½ cup water in a bowl until everything is gooey. Use immediately for pasting paper together.

Physical Exercise

Balance Beam. Ask an adult for a long, narrow piece of board to use for a balance beam (a two-by-four board is fine). Lay the board in a flat area outside. Pretend to be a tightrope walker, and see if you can walk along the board without touching the ground or falling off. Try walking frontward or backward. Hop over the board, jump off of it. If you have friends with you, play "Follow the Leader" on the board.

Follow the Leader. Pick one person to be the leader. Have everyone else line up single file behind the leader. The leader can make any movement or stunt he wants. The others must follow him and copy him. The leader might hop, skip, jump, bend over, roll over, do a somersault or a cartwheel, and the others must do the same things. Take turns being the leader.

Paper Punching Bag. Find a medium-sized paper or plastic bag and stuff it with crumpled newspaper. Tie the bag firmly with a piece of heavy string that is also long enough to use in hanging the bag.

Hang the bag from a clothesline, a basement pipe, or a hook. Or hang it from your ceiling with a piece of heavy tape if your ceiling is smooth. Now, go to it! Punch away at the bag until it breaks or you get tired!

Rubber Man. Pretend you are a rubber man and that you can stretch yourself a long way. Bend your arms, legs, and body in different ways while you are standing. Then lie on your back and move your arms and legs up and around in various positions. Also, pretend you are a metal man made of hinges. See how many different ways you can bend yourself from your "hinges!"

Touching Line. Make a circle with string or tape. (The tape works well on carpeting.) Have your friends stand with you around the circle. Take turns telling what part of the body must touch the line. Everyone must try what was suggested. Try touching the line with your nose, elbows, knees, ears, hair, etc.

Tumbling Mattress. Find an old mattress or old set of cushions to use for tumbling. Ask an adult to watch over you while you try doing somersaults, cartwheels, and other tumbling stunts. Perhaps the adult will show you how to do some of these stunts.

Pictures

Bean-Drop Picture. Drop a dozen small beans on a piece of drawing paper. Pick them up one at a time and make a crayon dot where the bean landed. Connect the dots to make a picture.

Bottle Cap Picture. From an old magazine, cut out a tiny picture. Glue the picture to the inside of a bottle cap. Now you have a miniature, framed picture!

Bumpy Picture.   Paint a picture or design on the bumpy side of a piece of corrugated cardboard.

Photograph Continuation Art.   From a magazine, cut out a small part of a black and white photograph. Paste the photograph part to a sheet of white background paper. Using a felt-tip marker, continue the lines from the edge of the photograph onto the white paper, creating a very unique design!

Punch Picture.   Put a piece of black construction paper on top of a cardboard box. Using a straight pin, poke holes in the paper to form patterns or a picture. When your punch picture is finished, hang it in the window so the light shines through the holes.   *Another way to do it:* Use a hole puncher instead of a straight pin to make the holes.

Toothpick Picture.   To make this picture use either plain or colored toothpicks. Use colored construction paper for a background. Glue the toothpicks down as you go to form a picture, or lay them out first and then glue them down.

Picture Frames

Ham Can Picture Frame.   A ham can makes an interesting, deep picture frame if an adult will help you by first sanding the edges of the can with sandpaper to make the edges smooth. Then draw or paint a picture to fit inside the can. (Or you can cut out and glue magazine pictures inside.) Paint the outside of the can, or glue on a paper cover cut to fit. This is an especially nice frame for Christmas or Easter pictures.

Plastic Foam Frame.   The next time you need a picture frame, use a plastic foam meat tray! Cut your picture to fit the bottom of the tray and glue it in place. Paint the rest of the tray with acrylic paint. Tape a paper clip to the back of the frame for a hanger.

Plants (Science)

Examinations and Observations
Bark.   Collect some bark from different kinds of trees. Look at the differences in strength, thickness, and appearance of the bark pieces. What kinds of trees did the bark come from?

Buds.   Take apart a bud and examine the outer scales that fall off as the leaf or flower grows. What time of year do buds usually appear?

Changes on Film.   Take photographs of a deciduous tree (a tree that loses its leaves in the winter) in the fall, winter, spring, and summer. Save the pictures to compare the changes that take place on the tree.

Corn.   Look closely at an ear of corn. Grind some dry corn between two flat pieces of stone to make cornmeal. Collect pictures of foods that are made from corn.

Cotton.   Some plants are used to make cloth for the clothes we wear, including cotton. If possible, examine a real cotton plant and look at the fibers. Next look at some clothing made of cotton and compare the two.

Edible Plant Parts. Examine some fruits and vegetables to find out what parts can be eaten. Here are some examples of plant parts, followed by those that can be eaten:

Flower buds (broccoli)

Fruit (apples, grapes, oranges, peaches)

Leaves (cabbage, lettuce, spinach)

Roots (beets, carrots, radishes, turnips, white potatoes)

Seeds (beans, coconut, corn, cucumbers, peas, pepper, rice)

Stems (asparagus, celery)

Examine the actual plants or pictures of them in books and magazines to compare the differences in size, shape, and color. Can you find a plant food that is not grown from a green plant?

Flowers. Buy some flowers from a florist or pick some from your own garden. Observe the different shapes, sizes, colors, and odors of the flowers. Later, plant some flower seeds in small containers. Petunia, marigold, and zinnia seeds are good to start with.

Kinds of Plants. Cut out pictures of many different kinds of plants. Then separate the pictures into piles according to what kind of plant it is—a vegetable, flower, grass, vine, weed, etc. How many of each kind can you come up with? Next, classify the pictures according to whether or not the plants can be eaten.

Plant Parts. Examine a number of different kinds of plants to see that most of them have basically the same parts. Study the parts and what they do. Use the following as a guide:

Roots: Roots hold the plants in the soil and bring food and water up from the ground.

Stems: Stems bring the food and water up to the leaves of the plant and support the leaves and flowers.

Green Leaves: Green leaves produce food from sunlight so that the plant can grow.

Flowers: Flowers produce seeds for the plant.

Seeds: Seeds contain baby plants. A new plant will grow from the seeds.

Buds: Buds are the part of the plant from which new flowers and leaves grow.

Trees. During a nature walk, stop to look closely at a tree. What kind of leaves does the tree have? Do they provide shade? Look to see if any of the tree's seeds are on the ground. What happens when the seeds are planted? Touch the bark. What does it feel like?

Wheat. If you can, examine a stalk of wheat. Take out the grains and try pounding them into flour. Did you know flour is a part of many foods you eat, including bread and cake? Wheat is also used as food by certain animals.

Experiments

Following the Sun. Place a plant in the window for a few days. Notice which way the plant leans. Then turn it around. Before long, the plant will lean toward the sun again!

Measuring Plant Growth. Pick out a young plant to use for growth measurement. Then cut off a strip of construction paper equal to the height of the plant. Paste the strip for this day's measurement to a larger sheet of construction paper.

Once a week, measure the plant with a new strip of paper cut to match the plant's height. Paste each week's new strip next to the one from the week before. In this way, you can see how much the plant grows from week to week. Watch for periods of slow growth and periods of rapid growth.

Plants Drink Water. Did you know that plants "drink" water? To show this, put several drops of red food coloring in a glass of water. Notice how the water turns red so you can see it better! Then place an untrimmed stalk of celery (with its leaves on) into the water root end down. Watch how the colored water goes through the "veins" of the stalk! In plants, these veins are called *capillaries*. The capillaries carry water and mineral nourishment to the leaves of the plant!

Plants Need Air. Grow two plants at the same time in two separate small cans. Make sure both plants receive equal amounts of water and light. When you are ready to do the experiment, place one of the plants in a glass jar. Make sure the lid is sealed to keep any more air from getting inside.

Leave the other plant as it is. Place both plants side by side to receive the same amount of light. Over a period of time, what happens to the plant cut off from the air?

Plants Need Light I. Place one plant in the sunlight and put another in the dark. After several weeks, compare the two plants. Notice that the one in the sunlight is bright green and healthy, and the one in the dark is yellow and weak.

Plants Need Light II. Sprinkle some grass seeds or birdseeds on a damp piece of cloth or a sponge. Cover with a glass dish and place on a sunny windowsill. Water the seeds a little every day.

After the seeds sprout, remove the glass dish and replace it with a solid plate to block the light. Check the seed sprouts again a few hours later. What has happened? Plants need light in order to produce food for growth!

Plants Need Room for Growth. Grow 10 or more plants in a single, small container. At the same time, grow only one or two of the same kind of plants in another container. Over a period of time, notice that the crowded plants will not grow as tall as the ones that have plenty of room to grow.

Plants Need Water. Plant two beans, each one in its own pot of soil. Water one, but not the other. Compare the growth in the two pots over a period of time.

Plants Transfer Moisture. Fill a glass with water. Cover the glass with a piece of cardboard containing a small hole in the middle. Place the stem of a plant in the hole so it reaches down into the water.

Then place a second glass upside down on top of the cardboard and over the top of the plant. Watch—moisture soon gathers inside the top glass! This shows that the plant transferred the moisture from the bottom glass to the top one! All plants lose moisture to the air this way. In fact, plants will dry up and die if they do not take in as much water as they give off!

Soil Contains Air for Plants. Fill a glass half full of water. Drop a small rock into the jar and notice that no air bubbles rise. Next drop a small lump of soil into the jar. Watch the air bubbles rise until all the air spaces in the soil are filled with water! The roots of plants use these air pockets in the soil to help the plant "breathe" and grow!

Soil Has Minerals for Plants. Plants must have minerals from the soil to obtain energy for growth. Here is a way to see that there are minerals in the soil.

Shake some soil into a jar of water and let the soil settle. When it settles, pour the clear water into another jar. Let the remaining water evaporate. See the white sediment left over? That is what remains of the dissolved minerals from the soil!

Growing Plants at Home

Acorn Growth. Find some acorns and lift off their tops. Place the acorns in a large glass jar and crumple newspaper around them. Water the acorns as you would a plant. Because they are seeds, the acorns will grow into small trees right in the jar!

Avocado Sprout. Stick three toothpicks into and around an avocado pit, roughly equal distances apart, and about one-third of the way down from the flat end of the pit.

Position the pit, flat end down, into the mouth of a glass, using the toothpicks for support. Pour water into the glass until the lower part of the pit is covered. Roots will start growing in a few weeks. From time to time add water to keep the seed moist.

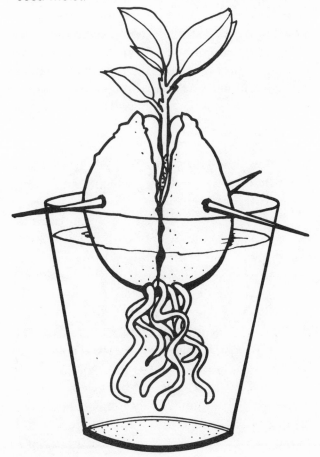

Baby Fruit Trees. Obtain some seeds from grapefruits, lemons, oranges, or tangerines. Soak the seeds in water overnight. The next day, put soil and potting mix into a pot and plant three or four seeds in the pot. Make sure the seeds are planted about half an inch deep. Place the pot in a warm, lighted place, and keep the soil moist. (Do not water every day—once or twice a week is enough.)

In about eight weeks the seeds will sprout. When the plants begin to grow, remove all of them except the one that looks the strongest. Soon this one will grow into a small tree with dark, glossy leaves!

Bud and Leaf Growth. In late winter or early spring, bring in a freshly cut twig from a deciduous tree (a tree that loses its leaves in winter). Place the twig in water, and watch for growth and development of buds and leaves.

Bulbs. Some plants grow from bulbs. To see this, plant a few narcissus bulbs in pebbles. Add water. Then place in darkness and keep moist. After several weeks, bring the bulbs back out into the light and warmth. Keep them moist and watch the flowers grow.

Also plant a few onion seeds and onion bulbs at the same time. Maintain them for a month and see which comes up first. (The onion bulb will probably grow faster because it has more stored food than the onion seed.)

Growth Revival. In the winter, dig under the snow for a piece of frozen sod. Take it inside and place it inside a terrarium. Watch for growth.

Lima Bean Growth. Lay a wide-mouth jar on its side. Then put several dry lima beans on a clump of damp cotton. Place the cotton in the jar so the seeds are pressed next to the glass. Stuff the jar with crumpled paper towels so the cotton remains pressed against the jar.

Set up the jar. Notice you can see the seeds pressed next to the glass. Add enough water to dampen the paper towels. Keep the towels damp, and watch daily for the growth of sprouts, stems and leaves from the lima beans.

Onion Flowers. Stick three toothpicks into the bottom portion of an onion, and suspend the onion by the toothpicks over the rim of a small glass filled with water. Make sure that only the very lowest part of the onion is actually in the water.

Place the glass on a sunny windowsill and add water as needed. The onion will sprout and soon grow green leaves and a flower!

Pineapple Plant. Cut the top off of a fresh pineapple, two inches from the top. Let this piece dry out for about a week. Then put it into a pot filled with damp, sandy soil. Make sure the soil stays moist. Several weeks later, notice how the pineapple piece has sprouted roots! Then transplant it into a larger pot, give it plenty of light, and keep it watered. It makes a great indoor plant!

Plants from Cuttings. Some plants will grow from cuttings taken from the parent plants. Outdoor geraniums, ivy, begonias, and different succulents make good cuttings. To obtain a cutting, use a sharp knife and cut on a slant. (Ask an adult to do this for you if necessary.) Remove most of the leaves from the cutting, but not all of them. Place in moist sand or water to see the cuttings sprout!

Stem Growth. Some plants grow from stems! To see this happen, place an old white potato in a dark but warm place. Keep it there for several months. During this time, many sprouts will appear. These sprouts (stems) will grow into a new potato plant!

Play Activities

Clothespin Constructions. Collect a batch of spring-type clothespins. Attach one clothespin to another to build any kind of construction you want. How many things can you make?

Gravel Fun. See if you can obtain a bag of gravel or marble chips to play with outdoors. Pour the gravel in a pile. With a toy dump truck, load, haul, and dump the gravel. Make gravel roads, and use pieces of gravel to outline houses and streets on the ground.

Indoor Hike. Pack a picnic lunch bag for a "pretend hike" through your own house. If your friends are with you, have them pack a lunch, too. Then start on your hike.

Pretend that steps are the sides of a mountain and that the dining room chairs are a giant forest. A crawl underneath the sofa chair can become a crawl through a cave or tunnel, and a jump over a footrest can be a leap over a fallen log!

Finally, pick a spot for your picnic (the bedroom?) and, if your friends are with you, sit in a circle for the picnic meal. When you are finished, pick up your papers and scraps, put them in the bag, and hike to a trash can to throw them away!

Newspaper Battle. Crumple newspaper into balls for "ammunition." Make forts from cardboard boxes of furniture, then start your battle! No one can get hurt, and everyone has a good time!

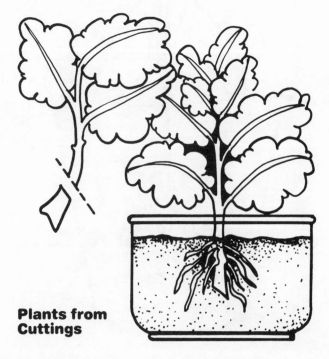

Plants from Cuttings

Pitch 'n Catch Game. To make the equipment for this game, you need two paint paddles, a pingpong ball, some white glue, and two plastic foam cups. Glue the bottom of a cup to each paddle. Allow them to dry.

Put a pingpong ball in your cup and pitch the ball from your cup toward your friend. He must try to catch the ball in his cup. Pitch the ball back and forth with each of you trying to catch the ball.

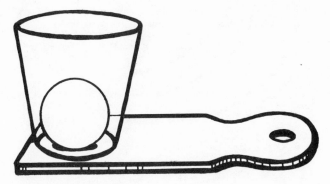

Rope Fun. Lay out a piece of rope in a curved or zigzagged pattern. Try to walk the whole length of the rope without stepping off the pattern.

Sandpaper Playboard. Glue a piece of rough sandpaper to a piece of heavy cardboard. Leave the rough side facing up. Then cut several lengths of different-colored yarn and stick them to the sandpaper board to make a design. When you want to make a new design, just pull off the old one and start again.

Shadow Theater. String a line across the room and use clothespins to hang a sheet from the line to make a screen. Shine a strong light on the back side of the sheet. The people behind the sheet are the actors; the ones in front are the audience.

The actors act out nursery rhymes or skits so their shadows are cast onto the sheet. The audience tries to guess the story being acted out.

Shadow stories can also be acted out using figures cut from cardboard or by using puppets. Whichever way you do it, let everyone take turns acting!

Tape Roads. On the kitchen floor or backyard patio, lay out strips of masking tape to make roads. Drive your toy cars and trucks along the roads. Make roadside houses and stores from cardboard boxes and milk cartons.

You can also use tape to outline your own large, play houses on the floor.

Trash Container Horse. Tip a clean, large, empty heavy-gauge metal trash container on its side. Straddle the container and "ride" it like a horse!

Playdough

Candy Playdough. This playdough is especially fun for two reasons. First, you can model with it, just as you can with any other playdough. Second, you can eat what you have modeled when you are finished!

Beforehand, wash your hands. (Avoid this activity if you have any open cuts on your hands.) Blend the following: ⅓ cup margarine, ⅓ cup light corn syrup, ½ teaspoon salt, 1 teaspoon vanilla, and some food coloring. As you blend, add 1 pound of sugar to the mixture. Knead the mixture until it becomes smooth. Add more sugar as needed to make the playdough pliable and nonsticky. Have fun!

Fast-Cook Cornstarch Playdough. With adult supervision, mix 1 cup of cornstarch and 2 cups of baking soda in a saucepan. Add 1¼ cups of cold water and several drops of food coloring. Cook this mixture for about four minutes over medium heat. Stir it continuously until it thickens.

When the mixture looks like moist mashed potatoes, remove it from the heat. Cover with a damp cloth, allow it to cool, and then knead. It is now ready to use!

This dough will dry without baking. It can be molded easily. It is also good for rolling out with a rolling pin and for cutting with cookie cutters. It works especially well for making Christmas tree ornaments. Store leftover dough in an airtight container.

Flour Playdough. Mix together 2 cups flour, 1 cup salt, and 1 tablespoon of oil in a bowl. Then put a few drops of food coloring in a cup of water and slowly add the water to the flour mixture, stirring while you pour.

When the dough starts to form, finish by mixing it with your hands. You can roll, push, pull, squeeze, flatten, and stretch this playdough into different shapes. It can be used for sculpturing animals, objects, play foods, and many other things.

Hot Water Modeling Dough. Thoroughly mix 1 cup flour, ½ cup salt, 1 tablespoon of powdered alum, and 7 ounces of boiling water. Stir until a ball is formed. Then add 1 tablespoon of salad oil. Knead. When not in use, store the dough in a covered container.

Sawdust Modeling Compound. Mix one cup of wallpaper paste as directed on the package. (Be sure to use a brand containing no insecticide.) Mix in some fine sawdust and knead into a doughlike consistency.

The amount of paste and sawdust will vary according to how coarse the sawdust is. To obtain fine sawdust, which works best, sift the sawdust through a mesh screen.

This compound makes very good puppet heads. After modeling the objects, allow several days for them to dry.

Play Food

Cardboard Cake. Bend a strip of white cardboard into a ring and fasten it at the ends with tape or staples. Next, glue the rim to a solid piece of white cardboard and allow to dry. Finish by turning over the assembly and cutting away the excess cardboard so it makes a round top for the cake. Paint the cake so it looks like it is covered with icing.

Cardboard Food. Cut out pictures of many different kinds of foods from magazines. Glue the pictures to cardboard and allow to dry. Then

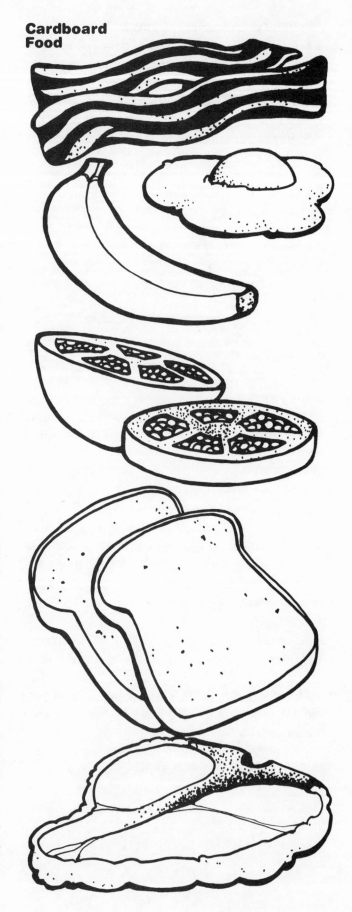

Cardboard Food

cut out the pictures from the cardboard. Make cupboards, refrigerators, and dinner tables from cardboard boxes to go along with your play food. Serve the play food on paper plates or empty frozen dinner trays.

Paper Lettuce and Cabbage. Paint several large pieces of newsprint with green paint. When dry, crumple them to look like cabbage or lettuce heads.

Papier Mâché Cupcakes. Fill some paper cupcake baking containers with crushed newspaper. Cover with papier mâché strips and allow it to dry. Paint the top to look like frosting.

Play Boxed Foods. Save empty boxes from cereals, cake mixes, pizza mixes, salt, sugar, meat pies, frozen dinners, and other frozen foods. Stuff the boxes with newspaper, if you want, to make them sturdy. Now you can set up a play supermarket or grocery store!

Play Bread. Stuff a bread bag with crushed newspaper. Close the end with a wire twistie. *Another way to do it:* Place a shoe box inside the bread bag and seal it at the end.

Play Canned Food. Save empty food cans for making a collection of toy foods. Make sure the cans are opened from the bottom, and cleaned before using. With the help of an adult, sand any rough rims and be sure to leave the labels in place.

Play Pie. Turn an aluminum pie pan upside down on a sheet of tan construction paper. Trace around the pan to make a circle. Cut out the circle and glue it to the rim of the pie pan. When the glue has dried, turn the pie upright and paint "cuts" into the paper crust.

Play Popsicle. Cut out a rectangle from a piece of construction paper or cardboard. Glue a Popsicle stick to one end of the rectangle.
Before painting the Popsicle stick, add a little

lemon, vanilla, or peppermint extract to the paint. Now the play Popsicle will have a "flavor scent" when painted!

Playdough Food. Mold fruits and vegetables from playdough. Also try making cookies, cakes, doughnuts, hot dogs, hamburgers, and many other foods from playdough.

TV Tray Dinners. Cut out pictures of ready-to-eat foods from magazines. Glue the pictures into empty frozen food dinner trays, and serve your own meals!

Play Houses

Box House. Obtain a large cardboard box for making your house. (Sometimes a new neighbor or appliance warehouse has extra boxes.) Have an adult cut a door and windows in the box. Make curtains with scrap materials and windowpanes with clear plastic wrap. Make a milk carton window box, and cut out magazine pictures for wall decorations. Draw inside and outside wall details on the cardboard with felt-tip markers.

Card Table Play House. Set up a card table to use as a play house. The rest is simple—cover the table with an old sheet or a blanket so the sides of the table are covered, and there you are!

Picnic Table Play House. If you have a picnic table in your backyard, you can easily turn it into a play house! Simply cover the sides and one end of the table with old blankets or sheets. Leave one end open for a doorway!

Tape Play House. Outline your own play house with strips of masking tape on the floor. Use the tape strips to form the inside and outside walls of the house. The tape will stick to practically any kind of surface (including carpeting) and can be picked up when you are finished playing! To make a similar house outdoors, use string instead of tape.

Play Kits

Announcer/Reporter Kit.   Make a press card from an index card, and carry a note pad and pencil to take notes. For a microphone, tape a dowel rod to a juice can. Attach a string to the end of the dowel rod for a power cable. Announce the news, weather, and sports over the microphone. Perhaps you can interview a friend!

Baker's Kit.   Gather a cookie sheet, muffin tins, bowls, measuring cups, measuring spoons, and eggbeaters and pretend you are a baker. Make a chef's hat by placing a white paper sack upside down on your head. Make baked goods from playdough.

Cobbler Kit.   Collect some old shoes to lace and "repair." Draw and cut out some paper soles to fasten to the shoes. Shine the shoes with polish. Wrap the repaired shoes in newspaper.

Doctor/Nurse Kit.   Gather some cotton balls, strips of sheeting, an adhesive bandage box filled with paper bandages, and *empty* medicine bottles to play doctor or nurse. Use raisins for pills. Weigh your friends on a scale and make charts to measure how tall they are.

Make a doctor's headband by covering a large cut-out circle with foil. Staple a paper strip band to the circle and put it on.

For a nurse's armband, use a wide strip of plain white paper and paint a large red cross on it.

To make a stethoscope, fit the end of a small metal funnel into the end of an 18-inch length of rubber tubing. Put the mouth of the funnel against a friend's chest. Put the open end of the tubing to one of your ears. Make sure it is quiet around you, and listen for your friend's heartbeat.

Fireman's Kit.   Make a paper hatchet and use a wagon for a fire engine. A stepladder makes a good fire-fighting ladder. For a hose, cut a three- or four-foot length from an old garden hose.

Grocer Kit.   Make a store using cardboard panels, plywood sections, or furniture for walls. Set up a shelf for your food products, empty food cartons and cans. Have paper bags on hand for your shopping friends, and set up a box for a cash register, using play money for the sales you make.

Gypsy Kit.   Wear a long, full skirt and a white, full-sleeved blouse. Put on as much jewelry as you can find. Wear a kerchief on your head, and put on a pair of sandals. Turn a rounded fish bowl upside down to use as a crystal ball.

Medieval Knight Kit.   Collect several pieces of cardboard. Outline a shield shape on one of the pieces of the cardboard. Cut it out and decorate it on the front with paint. Make the handle by taping a strip of cardboard on the back. You can also use a lid from a galvanized trash can for a shield.

For a weapon, cut out a sword shape from cardboard. Decorate the hilt (handle) with paint. Wrap the blade part with aluminum foil.

Draw a helmet visor on cardboard and cut it out. Decorate with paint, and poke a hole at each end. Pull a length of string through the holes to make a tie.

For armor, pull off two long sheets from a roll of aluminum foil. Have someone help you place one sheet against your chest and the other against your back. Scrunch them together at the shoulders, something like an old-fashioned sandwich board! Tape the pieces together, and your armor is complete!

Pirate Kit.   Cut off a pair of old jeans, just below the knees. Fringe the bottom edges by cutting up three inches all around. Put the jeans on and tie a bandanna around your waist, knotting it at the hip. Tie another bandanna around your head, and knot it over one of your ears.

For earrings, fasten a paper clip to each of two curtain rings. Slide a clip over the lobe of each ear. You can also make earrings by cutting ring shapes from the end of an empty cardboard tube.

**Medieval
Knight Kit**

Cover each of these rings with foil, and tie a short piece of yarn through each ring. Loop each piece of yarn over an ear to hang the earrings.

Make an eye patch from a piece of black paper and string. Make a cutlass from cardboard and cover the blade portion with foil. Use an eyebrow pencil to draw a beard and mustache on your skin.

Plumber's Kit. Collect wrenches, pipes, screwdrivers, tubing, and rulers and pretend you are a plumber.

Police Detective Kit. To make a badge, draw a badge on a piece of cardboard. Cut it out and cover it with foil. Pin or tape the badge to your shirt.

For a night stick, roll up several thicknesses of newspaper or paint an empty paper towel tube.

Carry a magnifying glass to hunt for clues and some talcum powder to use for fingerprint dusting. Simply sprinkle the powder over glass and blow it off to reveal any fingerprints. Also carry a

roll of clear tape so you can lift a suspect's fingerprints onto the sticky side. Carry a magnet to pick up small metal objects without disturbing the fingerprints.

Use a flashlight for clue hunting in the dark. Keep an eyebrow pencil handy so you can disguise yourself with fake scars, a beard, or a mustache. You can also wear an eye patch to help disguise yourself.

Take along a soft lead pencil and a notepad so you can make notes and pass messages to friends.

Post Office Kit. Use a large refrigerator box or furniture carton to make a post office. Have an adult cut out a window, a door, and a mail slot. Use cancelled stamps, envelopes, rubber stamps, and a stamp pad to run your office.

Make a delivery pouch by cutting down a brown paper bag to about 12 inches in height. Staple a twisted brown paper strip to each corner of the pouch for a handle. Write "U.S. Mail" on the outside of the pouch.

Play Money

Cardboard Coins.   Find three or four coins and place them under a thin sheet of paper. Rub over the paper with a soft pencil, so the patterns of the coins appear on the paper. Make as many coins as you want.

Then, cut out the coins and glue them to a piece of thin cardboard. Cut them out again. If you want, make a rubbing for each side of the coin.

Foil Coins.   Place coins on paper and trace around them. Cut out the coin shapes and wrap them with foil.

Paper Bills.   Place a dollar bill on a sheet of green paper and trace around it. Repeat, making as many bills as you want. Draw a face and dollar amount on the bills and cut them out.

Printing

Art Eraser Prints.   Cut away part of an art eraser to leave a raised design. Dip the design end in paint and then print the design on paper or any other material you want printed.

Clay Printing.   Form some clay into a ball or cube. Press a design onto the flat side with a pencil, paperclip, or other object that will leave an impression. Lightly paint the flat portion with thick tempera, leaving the depressed areas untouched. Press the flat side on paper several times until all the paint is used. Add more paint and repeat, continuing until the paper is covered with prints.

Cloth Printing.   Find some old bed sheets or pillowcases that can be printed on. Cut them into any size you want. Using old blocks, beads, bottle caps, sponges, Popsicle sticks, cardboard tubes, or fruits and vegetables dipped into paint, print over the surface of the material. Turn the finished product into a piece of clothing, a curtain, or a pretty hanging for your play house.

Corn Cob Printing.   Dip an ear of corn into some tempera paint. Then roll the ear across a sheet of paper to make an interesting print. You can also try making a print using a cob from which all the corn has been removed.

Flyswatter Printing.   Make a design on a flyswatter by gluing on yarn in any pattern. When the glue is dry, dip the flyswatter into some paint and swat the pattern down on a large sheet of paper. Watch out for splatter!

Gadget Printing.   First, make a paint pad by wetting a paper towel. Fold the towel and put it in a shallow pan. Pour some thick tempera paint on the towel.

Now you are ready to find some things to print with, such as bottle caps, buttons, corks, paper clips, sink stoppers, spools, or anything else you can find with interesting shapes. Press the gadget onto the paint pad, then print it on a piece of paper. Try to make designs. This is a good way to make your own gift wrap!

Inner Tube Printing.   From a rubber inner tube cut out various-sized squares. Then cut each square again to form a design or symbol. Glue each shape to a wooden block or a piece of heavy cardboard to make a stamp. Brush tempera paint over the stamp, and press it onto the desired surface.

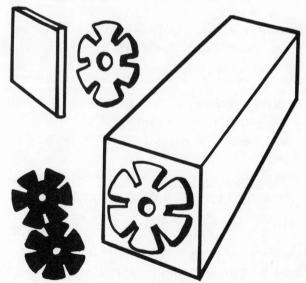

Marble Water Print. Pour some water into a 9-by-13-inch pan until the pan is one third full. In a separate container, mix some thinned tempera paint and a few drops of oil-based paint. Add a few drops of salad oil.

Gently pour some of this mixture into the pan of water so it floats on the water. Gently blow on the mixture until it forms a design. Set a piece of paper on top of the water for just a second. Quickly remove the paper and look at the marbled print on the bottom! Allow it to dry.

Blow a new pattern on the mixture and repeat with another piece of paper.

Meat Tray Printing. Remove the edges from a plastic foam meat tray so that just a flat piece remains. Turn the piece upside down so the bottom side faces up. Using a pencil with a dull point, make a drawing on the foam. Then go over the lines with the pencil to make them a little deeper.

Next, obtain a glass pane or piece of formica to use for a rolling surface. From a tube of water-soluble ink, squeeze some ink on the glass pane. Roll out the ink across the pane evenly with an ink roller. Set the roller aside.

Press the designed side of the foam piece onto the inked surface. Remove and place inked side up.

Select a piece of construction paper that is cut slightly larger than the piece of plastic foam. Place the paper on the plastic foam. Make a fist and firmly rub over the paper. Lift the paper to reveal a print underneath!

Monoprint. Paint dots on a cookie sheet. Place a piece of paper over the dots. Rub the top of the paper with your fingertips. Pull off the paper to reveal the printing transferred to the reverse side!

For variety, finger-paint a cookie sheet. Gently place a piece of paper over the painted surface. On top of this paper draw a picture with a crayon. Carefully lift the paper. What do you see?

Potato Printing. Cut a potato in half cross-

Potato Printing

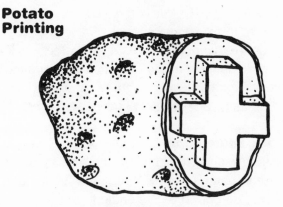

ways. Then cut away parts of the exposed surface area to leave a raised design or picture. Dip the exposed surface into paint and print it on paper.

Soap Printing. Cut designs in a bar of soap. Dip the soap in paint and transfer the pattern to a sheet of paper.

Sponge Printing. Cut up some sponges into simple shapes of animals, objects, or symbols. Press each sponge onto an ink or paint pad. Then transfer the designs by pressing the sponges on paper. You can make different shapes to create a scene or make patterns on paper for gift wrap.

String 'n Tube Printing. Wind some string around an empty cardboard tube. Fasten the string to the tube with white glue and allow it to dry.

Roll the tube in some tempera paint. Insert a dowel pole or strong pencil through the center of the tube, and lift the tube onto a piece of paper. While holding each end of the dowel rod, roll the tube along the paper to make a printing.

String Squiggle Printing. Cut a 10-inch length of yarn or string. Dip the string in a shallow pan of tempera paint. Carefully lift out the string and place on a piece of paper. Push or pull the string to make a design.

Puppets

Bandage Finger Puppet. With a crayon or felt-tip marker, draw a face on the front of an adhesive bandage. Stick the bandage on your finger to form a finger puppet.

To have two puppets talk to each other, make another puppet to fit a finger on your other hand. Perhaps you can make an entire family of bandage puppets, one for each finger!

Bleach Bottle Puppet. Clean and dry an old plastic bleach bottle to use for making a puppet. Turn the bottle upside down. Glue felt features on the side opposite the handle to make a face. Tie a piece of fabric to the bottle neck to form a body. Use the handle to hold the puppet and make it move.

Box Puppet. Cut a half-pint milk carton or small cereal box across the middle on three sides, leaving the box hinged along one wide side. Bend back the box on itself from the hinge, so that half the box is on top and half is underneath. Slip two or three fingers into the top half with your thumb in the bottom half. Move your fingers and thumb up and down to make the box "talk." Cut out some felt facial features and glue them on the box to make a cute puppet.

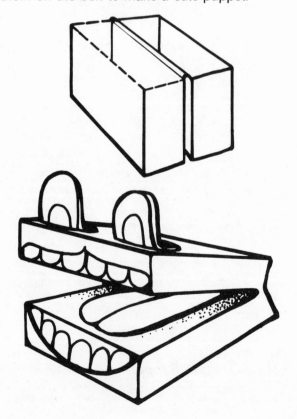

Cardboard Tube Puppet. Puppets with long faces are easily made from cardboard tubes. Draw a face on one end and glue a Popsicle stick to the other end for a handle.

Eggcup Puppet. From a cardboard egg carton, cut out two linked eggcups. On the hinged side, poke a finger hole above and below the hinge. By putting a forefinger and thumb into the holes, you can make the cup sections move up and down like a mouth.

Paint the cups any color and allow them to dry. Then paint a face above the mouth. Glue on some paper ears and yarn for hair. Cut along the mouth rims to make teeth if you want.

Finger Puppets. Items such as old glove fingers, thimbles, and the ends of balloons make good finger puppets. Draw faces on them or glue on tiny bits of paper to make features.

Fist Puppet. Make a fist, then paint on eyes, nose, and lips as illustrated, using an eyebrow pencil, a lipstick, or a water-soluble felt-tip marker. Make the mouth talk by moving the thumb.

Glove Spider or Monster Puppet. Make a yarn pompon and glue it to the back of a glove. Glue on felt eyes. Insert your hand and walk your fingers across a table to make the spider, or monster, move!

Lady Bug Finger Puppet. Paint half of a walnut shell on the outside to look like a lady bug. Allow it to dry. Then turn the half shell upside down. Cover half of the bottom with a piece of felt cut to fit, using glue to fasten it on. Turn the shell upright and slip it on a finger. Wiggle your finger to make the puppet come to life.

"Nosey" Cup Puppet. Turn a paper or plastic foam cup upside down. Poke a hole large enough to fit your finger in the side of the cup. Your finger is then the puppet's nose! Draw or glue on felt features to form the rest of the face. Glue a yarn pompon on top for hair.

Fist Puppet

Paper Bag Puppet I. Open a paper bag and stuff it with crumpled newspaper. Tie it closed with string to make a neck. Be sure to leave enough room inside, though, to put three fingers up through the neck. Position the bag so the head end is up and the neck end is down. Draw or glue on facial features. If you want, glue on paper arms and legs. Put your hand in the puppet and your fingers in the neck to control it.

Paper Bag Puppet II. With this puppet, the fold in the bag becomes the mouth. Draw a face on the bottom of the bag, then insert your hand into the bag to make the mouth open and close. Lunch-sized bags work best for making this puppet.

Paper Figure Puppets. Cut out figures of people or animals from magazines or catalogs. Glue the figures on light cardboard and cut them out. To make a handle, glue a Popsicle stick to the back of each figure. Hold the puppets by their handles and wiggle them around to make them move.

Paper Plate Puppet. Using felt-tip markers or crayons, draw a face on a paper plate, or cut the features from construction paper and paste them on the plate. When finished, glue a Popsicle stick handle to the plate.

Peanut Marionettes. Paint some unshelled peanuts to look like people, using acrylic paints. Tie a piece of string from the middle of each peanut. Dangle the peanut marionettes from above to make them spring to life!

Peanut Shell Finger Puppets. Use large peanut shells to make cute puppets to fit over your fingers. Paint faces, clothes, and other details on the puppets with acrylic paints.

Pop-Up Puppet. Cut out a small paper circle. Draw a face on it and then glue it to the end of a straw.

Punch a hole in the bottom of a paper cup. Insert the bottom end of the straw into the cup and through the hole. Hold the cup in one hand and push the straw up and down with the other to make the puppet pop up and down from the cup.

Sock Puppet. Find an old sock to use in making a puppet. Sew or glue buttons near the toe end for eyes. Glue on a cotton ball nose or any other features you want. Insert your hand all the way into the toe end. Make a mouth by moving your four fingers together up and down above the thumb. (To make the mouth more distinct, hook a rubber band on the outside of the puppet between the fingers and thumb. Stretch the rubber band from there back over the top of the puppet and fasten it in place with a safety pin.)

Stick Puppets. Paint faces and clothing on the tops of Popsicle sticks. You can also paint on mixing sticks, tongue depressors, and other sticks. *Another way to do it:* Cut out paper figures and glue them to the end of each stick.

Stuffed-Toy Puppet. Cut a slit in the back of an old stuffed animal. Remove enough stuffing to insert your hand. Use your hand to make the puppet move around.

Talking Clothespin Puppet. Cut out a face from paper or lightweight cardboard. Cut the face in half along the mouth line. Glue the upper

Talking Clothespin Puppet

half of the face to the upper pinching end of a spring-type clothespin. Glue the lower half of the face to the lower pinching end. Make sure the face parts are lined up so they meet when the clothespin is closed. Make the puppet talk by squeezing the handle end of the clothespin.

"Thumbelina" Baby Puppet. Draw a fact on your thumb with a water-soluble, felt-tip marker. Drape a handkerchief over the face and around the "chin" so it faces outward.

Pussy Willows

Chalk Art Pussy Willows. Draw a stem on paper and draw the blossoms with white chalk.

Cotton and Paper Pussy Willows. Draw some branches on paper. Paste dabs of cotton over the branches to make pussy willows.

Paper Pussy Willows. Cut out pussy willow branches from black paper. From white paper, cut out pussy willow blossoms. Glue the parts together on colored background paper.

Puffed Wheat/Puffed Rice Pussy Willows. On a sheet of blue or gray paper, draw several pussy willow branches. Glue puffed wheat or puffed rice cereal to the branches to represent pussy willow blossoms.

Twig and Cotton Pussy Willows. Glue dabs of cotton onto real twigs and branches to look like pussy willows.

Puzzles

Body Part Puzzle. Lie down on a large piece of brown wrapping paper. Stick out your arms and legs. Have a friend trace completely around your body with a felt-tip marker. Get up and color in your face, hair, and clothing with crayons.

Cut out the outline from the sheet of paper. Then cut the outline into body parts, such as arms, legs, head, etc. Glue the separate pieces to cardboard and allow to dry. Then cut out the pieces again. Now you have a giant puzzle to put back together!

Face-in-Place Puzzle. Draw a face, except for the eyes, on the bottom of a plastic foam meat tray. In place of the eyes, set two buttons on the tray. Tilt the tray back and forth to try making the buttons slide into position for eyes.

Suggestion: Use cellophane to cover the tray, with the buttons inside. Now you can also shake the tray to make the buttons move!

Jigsaw Puzzle. From an old magazine or catalog, cut out a full-page color picture. Glue the picture on a thin piece of cardboard. When the glue is dry, cut up the picture into puzzle-shaped pieces. Mix up the pieces and put the puzzle back together.

To make a double-sided jigsaw puzzle, glue a picture to both sides of the cardboard before cutting it into pieces. This two-in-one puzzle is a little harder to put back together, but twice the fun!

Rain

Painted Rain Scene. Draw a rain picture by streaking gray paint on paper with fine brushes or cotton swabs. Allow it to dry. Next, cut umbrella shapes from construction paper and make umbrella handles from pipe cleaners. Glue the umbrella parts together on the picture.

Rain Painting. Do this activity on a rainy day. Drop a few blobs of paint or food coloring on a plain paper plate. Be sure not to mix or smear the dabs of paint.

Put the plate out in the rain. The raindrops will quickly splatter the paint into a painting! Watch carefully. When you like the way the painting looks, bring it inside to dry.

Raindrop Painting. Fill four or five containers with water. Drop a few pinches of powdered tempera or food coloring into each container, putting a different color in each container. With an eyedropper, pick up water from one of the containers and drip it onto a sheet of construction paper. Drip on other colors, also, to make a colorful raindrop painting.

Rainy Day Scene. Use a sheet of blue construction paper for a background. At the top of the scene, glue on plastic foam packing pieces or cotton tufts for clouds. Glue on pieces of rickrack for lightning. With felt-tip markers or crayons, draw raindrops. Complete the scene any way you want.

Spatter-Paint Rain. Dip a toothbrush into some gray paint. Then hold the toothbrush over a sheet of blue paper and run your fingers along the toothbrush bristles to make spatter-painted rain.

Watercolor Raindrops. From a sheet of white paper, cut out some large raindrops. Paint the raindrops with watercolors. Paste the raindrops on background paper.

Rain (Science)

Rainwater comes mostly from the earth's oceans. Warm sunlight makes this water evapo- rate and rise into the air, forming clouds. It rains when the tiny water drops get heavy enough to fall.

Make a Puddle. Mix several drops of food coloring and ¼ cup of water. Lay a sheet of waxed paper on a flat surface. With an eyedropper, pick up some of the colored water. Drop some water on the waxed paper. Then aim another drop on top of the first drop. Keep adding "raindrops" to form a small puddle! With a drinking straw, "lead" some of the water away from the puddle to form a small stream.

Making Rain. Place a tea kettle of water over a burner. Bring the water to a boil. Watch a steam cloud form above the spout. This is caused by water vapor cooling as it leaves the spout. Then it evaporates quickly into the air.

Next, hold a can of ice water in front of the spout. See the water droplets forming on the can. As they grow larger, they will fall from the can. This is what happens in the sky when it rains!

Rain in a Jar. Create a miniature "rainfall" inside a covered jar or covered terrarium. Pour water into the container until it is several inches deep. Cover the container and place it near sunlight or strong lamp light. Leave it there so you can look at it from time to time.

Watch water droplets form underneath the container cover. As they get heavy enough, they will fall back down! The warm air inside causes some of the water to evaporate and condense on the lid where it stays until it gets heavy enough to fall. This is what happens in the sky when clouds form and rain falls!

Rain Measurement. Make your own rain gauge from a tall, see-through container that has straight sides (some olive jars work well). Tape a plastic ruler to the side of the jar so the ruler reads from the bottom to the top. Place the jar outside where it can collect the rain. After the rain is over, look at the ruler to see how much it rained!

Rainbows

Crayon Rainbows. Using the flat sides of stubby crayons (without the wrappers), draw a large rainbow on a 12-by-18-inch sheet of construction paper.

Crystal Colors. In a sunlit window, hang a cut piece of crystal. Watch as the sun shines through the window and the light bounces off the crystal. Little parts of rainbows will dance around your room! This happens because the colors of the rainbow are mixed together in the sunlight and the crystal helps to split up the colors.

Oil Puddles. Look around for a puddle with some oil in it. Or, make your own! Pour some water into a hollow in the ground. Then add a little oil or paint thinner. Look for swirling, rainbow-like colors in the water.

Paper Plate Rainbow. Cut out the center of a paper plate so the outer rim comes off in a complete ring. Then cut the ring into two semi-circles. Each rim piece now forms the basis for a ''rainbow'' that can be painted or colored with crayons.

Rainbow Bubbles. Use some extra-soapy water solution to blow some large bubbles. Look at the rainbow-like colors in the bubbles.

Sheet Rainbow. Cut or tear out a 12-by-15-inch section from an old bed sheet. Then fill some plastic spray bottles with water. Mix several drops of food coloring in each bottle. Make each bottle a different color.

Starting with one color and continuing with another, squirt rainbow bands in an arch across the sheet. When the rainbow is finished, allow it to dry. Then hang it up for display!

Water Rainbow. Place a small mirror in a glass of water. Set the glass in a window so the sun shines on the mirror. Put a piece of paper under the glass and watch for the rainbow to appear.

Water Spray Rainbow. Go outdoors on a sunny day. Turn on the hose and stand with your back to the sun. Spray the water into the air. You should see a rainbow in the spray!

Rainy Day Activities

Balloon Fun. Inflate a round balloon and tie it at the end to keep the air inside. Then find a short cardboard tube. Blow at the balloon through the tube to see how long you can keep the balloon in the air!

Bonk the Box. Stand up three or four small cardboard boxes on end and paint a crazy face on each one. Line them up in a row on a table. Next, tie a handkerchief into a knot or roll up a pair of socks to make a ball. Stand back from the boxes. Take aim, and see how many boxes you can knock down with one throw! Make sure there are no breakable objects nearby!

Bottle Drop. Find a wide-mouthed bottle and remove the lid. Place the bottle on the floor and stand directly over it. Try dropping objects such as clothespins, bottle caps, or buttons into the bottle. How many objects can you drop in the bottle in 10 tries?

Card Toss. Put down a bowl in the middle of the room. Stand about four feet away and try flipping cards one at a time into the bowl. Throw 12 cards on each turn. How many did you flip in the bowl?

Costume Box. For rainy day dress-up fun, start saving old worn-out or discarded clothing from others in your family. Old jackets, pants, evening dresses, hats, purses, shirts, and shoes are good things to start with. Keep your "costumes" stored in a special box. Get them out for playacting the next time it rains.

Hit the Hat. Tie a broomstick to the back of a chair with the broom end pointing down. Balance an old hat on top of the broomstick. Crumple up some newspaper into balls. Stand back and try to knock the hat off the broomstick!

Junk Mail. Ask an adult to save for you some of the junk mail he does not want. When you have collected enough pieces, have fun opening the envelopes, sorting the contents, and sealing the envelopes again. Cut up some to use for pasting.

Lady Bug Dash. Make two walnut shell lady bugs (*see Lady Bugs section*). Set both lady bugs at the top end of an inclined board. Place a marble under each shell and let go of both bugs at the same time. The marbles will roll downward, pulling the lady bugs with them. Which lady bug wins the race?

Magazine Marking. Look for a magazine that has pictures of famous people. Be sure to use an old magazine that you can mark up. Have fun changing the way people look by drawing in eyeglasses, beards, mustaches, or new hairstyles!

Mother Goose Acting. As someone reads Mother Goose rhymes to you, act out the rhymes.

No-Hands Game. See what time it is on the clock, or set a timer for 10 minutes. For the next 10 minutes, do anything you want—but do not use your hands! Use only your head, nose, teeth, elbows, feet, or toes! Try doing things such as reading a book, eating, or balancing an object on your head. Any time you use a hand, you get one out. If you get three outs before 10 minutes have passed, the clock wins!

Obstacle Course. Ask an adult if it is okay to move the furniture to make an indoor obstacle course. Set up tables, chairs, and cushions for climbing over, under, and around!

Penny Magic. Clean some dirty pennies by dipping them into a mixture of salt and vinegar. Rub them with a paper towel and the pennies will be shiny again!

Penny Snap. Cut out a section, two cups long and two cups wide, from a cardboard egg carton.

Put the cup section on a table or bare floor. Collect 10 pennies or buttons to use as tokens.

Press the edge of one penny against the edge of another so that the pressed penny will leap forward. In this way, try to get all the pennies into the cups. If you want, you can write numbers in the bottoms of the cups and keep track of the points earned.

Pick-Up Straws.   Drop a handful of straws on a table. Try to pick up as many straws as you can without moving any other straws. Continue playing until you accidentally bump a straw.

Count one point for each straw you pick up. (To make the game harder, use toothpicks instead of straws.)

Pretending to "Be".   For special fun, try play-acting some very strange things: be spaghetti, before and after it is cooked; be limp as a rag doll; be hinges; be the heaviest thing you can think of; be stiff as a board; be as small, tall, wide, or skinny as possible; be animals or machinery; be gently falling snow; be suddenly full of jumping beans; be soft, fluffy clouds floating in the air; be happy, sad, frightened, or thoughtful. Think of many other ways to "be," and act them out!

Silly Names Art.   Obtain some crayons and a sheet of paper. Make up some silly names, such as *Dirty Doug, Big Bill, Long Tall Tony, Big Foot Bob, Circle Cindy,* and *Flathead Fred.* Draw a picture of how you think each character should look based on his silly name.

Spool Contest.   Set out a basket full of empty thread spools. Who can hold the largest number of spools in the palm of his hand?

Table Hockey.   Give each player a long cardboard tube (from a paper towel roll) to use as a hockey stick. Find a plastic lid to use as a puck, and clear off a large table for your field of play.

One player should stand at each end of the table. If four are playing, then two should stand at each end. Using your cardboard tube sticks, bat or shove the puck back and forth across the table. If a shot goes off of your opponent's edge of the table, you get a point. If his shot goes off of your end, then he gets a point.

Toe-Marble Game.   All you need for this game is two flat dishes, some marbles, and bare feet! Put all the marbles in one dish. Try to pick up each marble with your toes and transfer it to the other dish.

Twenty Ways to Get There.   Select a way to move across the room and back, such as hopping, skipping, jumping, or crawling like an animal, or flapping your arms like a bird. See if you can go back and forth across the room in 20 completely different ways!

Reptiles

Cardboard and Eggshell Turtle.   From a piece of cardboard, cut out the flat shape of a turtle. Be sure to include four thick legs, a small tail, and a large, bulby head. Bend up the head and bend down the feet so the turtle stands up.

Paint the turtle green and allow it to dry. Then paint on the turtle's eyes and toes. To make his shell, clean and crush some eggshells into small pieces. Glue the eggshell pieces on the turtle's back. Paint over the eggshells with another coat of green.

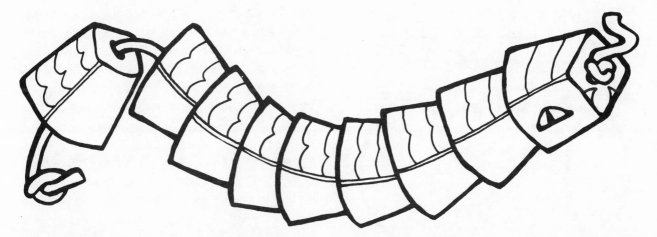

Eggcup Snake. Cut up a cardboard egg carton into individual cups. Thread the cups together with string through the ends of each cup. Paint each cup a different color or in stripes. Leave a short length of string at the front for a tongue and at the back for a tail. Tie knots at each end to keep the snake together.

Eggcup Turtle Toy. Cut out a single eggcup from a cardboard egg carton. Turn it upside down. Poke a hole in the top and thread a long piece of string through the hole. Tie a paper clip inside the hole to hold the string in place. Paint the turtle shell green, and set it aside to dry.

On a piece of construction paper, outline a flat turtle including the head, legs, and tail. Make the body about the same size as the base of the eggcup. Cut out the turtle and glue the base of the eggcup shell on the body piece. Make the turtle move by pulling him by the string!

Paper Plate Spiral Snake. From the outside edge of a paper plate, cut a spiral pattern all the way to the center of the plate. The outside edge is the tail and the center is the head of the snake. Color in eyes and body markings and add a paper tongue to the head. Pull up the snake by the head to make it unravel. Notice that the snake will stand up on its side!

Paper Plate Turtle. Place two paper plates together face to face to make a body. Cut out the head, tail, and feet from construction paper.

Slide these pieces into position between the plates and staple them in place. Paint the turtle green.

Spool Snake. Collect some empty thread spools and thread them together on a piece of string or yarn. Tie a big knot at each end of the string to hold on the spools. Paint each spool a different color, and paint a face at one end.

Rockets

Balloon Rocket. Inflate a long balloon to stretch it, and then let out the air. Next, poke a straw into the open end of the balloon and tie it to the balloon with a rubber band. Inflate the balloon rocket by blowing through the straw. Pinch the straw to hold the air in, and aim the balloon into the air. Let it go and watch how far it goes!

Box Rocket. Obtain an oatmeal box, a plastic straw, and some string. Remove the lid and cut off the bottom of the oatmeal box. Pull a very long length of string through the straw. Then tape the straw along the side of the oatmeal box. (Make sure it is taped on straight.)

Tie one end of the string to a doorknob; tie the other end to a piece of furniture. Make sure the string is tightly stretched and is level all the way across! Notice that the oatmeal box rocket is now suspended along the string by the straw!

Now, inflate a balloon. Stuff the balloon into

Box Rocket

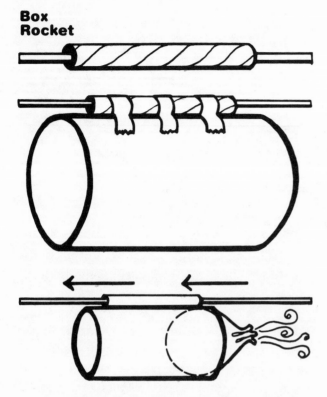

one end of the oatmeal box, keeping the neck pinched to keep in the air. Then let go of the balloon and watch it push the rocket off along the string!

Cone-Cup Rocket. Turn a cone-shaped paper cup upside down on a flat surface. Using a felt-tip marker, draw on rocket details such as a nose cone, portholes, and rocket engines at the bottom.

From the rim on one side of the cup, cut out a very narrow triangle. Cut out another triangle the same size on the opposite side of the cup. Stretch a piece of string between your hands and balance the rocket on the string through the triangular notches. Pull sharply on the string, making the string snap upward against the rocket. Watch the rocket blast off!

Play Cardboard-and-Chairs Rocket. Set up five or six chairs in a circle. Surround the chairs with cardboard panels or wrapping paper. Leave space somewhere for an entrance! Now you and your friends can "navigate" your play rocket through space!

Potato Chip Can Rocket. Paint an empty potato chip can white or silver, or cover it with white construction paper. Paint on some black circles for portholes. For a rocket nose, form a cone from a half circle of white paper and glue it on top of the can. Glue four spools upright beneath the can for engine boosters.

Shape Rocket. Cut out a large rectangle, a large triangle, and two small triangles from colored paper. Glue the pieces together on paper to form a rocket. The large rectangle is the main part of the rocket, and the large triangle is the nose cone. The two small triangles are engine boosters.

Tube Rockets. Make rockets from short or long cardboard tubes. Paint them white or silver. Paint on portholes and other details later. Glue a paper cone to the top for a nose cone.

Potato Chip Can Rocket

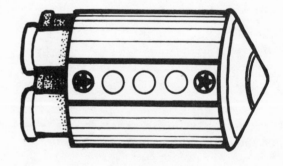

Rocks (Science)

Fizzing Rocks. Pour some soda pop over several kinds of rocks, including a piece of limestone. What happens when the pop is poured over the limestone?

Granite and Pumice Comparison. Place a small granite rock and a large pumice stone in a tub of water. Notice that the granite rock sinks to the bottom even though it is small. But see how the pumice floats even though it is big! That is because the pumice, a volcanic rock, is light and porous. It contains many air bubbles to help it stay afloat. The granite comes from a volcano, too, but it is solid and has no air bubbles to help it float.

Rock Classification.   Collect as many different kinds of rocks as you can find. Then sort them into groups according to color, size, weight, texture, and shape. What other ways can you classify them? Read a book about rocks and find out how scientists classify rocks.

Rock Color.   As you can see for yourself, most rocks are colored on the outside. But did you know they are also colored on the inside? To see this, first wash off a rock to see that the color does not wash away. Then place the rock inside a paper bag. Pound on the rock with a hammer so it breaks up inside the bag. Open the bag and pull out the pieces of rock. Does the color grain run through the inside of the rock?

Sandstone Examination.   Smooth off a piece of sandstone by rubbing it against a harder material. Notice how the rough surface becomes smooth! In this way, many kinds of rocks are changed to make walls, bridges, streets, and buildings. Look around your home and neighborhood for examples of rocks that have been converted for man's use.

Roots (Science)

Digging up Roots.   In the winter, dig up a plant that looks like it has died at the top. Notice that the roots are still alive! What will happen to the plant in the spring? Replant it to find out!

Roots Absorb Water.   Find a shallow dish that has a glass cover to fit. Place a piece of paper towel in the bottom of the dish. Pour some water in the dish and let it soak into the paper towel. Then pour off the excess water.

Next, put several radish seeds on the moist paper in the dish. Place the glass cover over the dish. Set the dish in a warm, dark place. Check the dish from time to time for moisture and to let air inside.

After a week or so, the roots should be about an inch long. At this point, study the roots through a magnifying glass. Notice the tiny root hairs! These hairs are the part of the root that absorbs water into the root.

Place some red food coloring into some water and moisten the paper towel again with this water. Lay the radish roots on the paper towel. Watch! Over a period of time, the root hairs will slowly turn red as they absorb the red water!

Root Circulation.   Once moisture enters a root through the root hairs, it is circulated through the root on its way to the rest of the plant. To see this, use a carrot, which is itself a root!

Place the carrot in water that has been colored with red ink. Keep it in the sunlight for about four hours. Then remove the carrot and first cut it crosswise near the crown and then lengthwise. Notice the red lines! These show how the water has circulated within the root!

Root Growth.   Fill a glass about one third of the way with water. Then poke some toothpicks around a sweet potato and suspend the potato by the toothpicks over the rim of the glass. Adjust the potato so the root end of it is half covered with water. Place it in a sunny window. Over a period of time, watch roots and leaves grow from the potato!

Sandboxes

Indoor Birdseed ''Sandbox.''   Instead of sand, use birdseed to fill your indoor sandbox. It is fun and also different!

Indoor Salt or Oatmeal "Sandbox." Fill a large, rimmed cookie sheet with salt or oatmeal. Play at the kitchen table or in the basement. If you spill some sand, be sure to pick it up afterward with a vacuum cleaner or broom and dustpan. Play as you would with a regular sandbox, or draw in the salt or oatmeal with your fingers.

Rainy Day Sandbox. Make a small sandbox to save for indoor fun on a rainy day. Find an old plastic dishpan or a sturdy, shallow cardboard box to use as a sandbox. Fluff open a small plastic trash bag, and set it upright in the box. Pull down the top of the bag and line the box with the outside edges of the bag. Pour in several inches of sand.

When it rains, you can enjoy your sandbox on the back porch, in the garage, or on the kitchen floor. Just be sure to pick up any spilled sand when you are finished! To store the sand, simply pick up the bag, tie it with a twistie, and keep it in a dry place.

Wading Pool Sandbox. For an easy-to-make sandbox, simply fill a plastic wading pool with sand. When it is not in use, cover it with a tarp to keep out dirt, rain, and cats.

Wood Frame Sandbox. Obtain four 2-by-4 boards, each four feet long. With help from an adult, sand the boards to remove any splinters. Nail the boards into a square frame.

Choose a spot for your sandbox, and set the frame there. Fill the frame with sand, and you are ready to play! Make sure to find a piece of tarp to cover the sandbox when it is not in use.

Sand Play

Ice Cream Container Sand Bucket. Paint the outside of a round, gallon-sized cardboard ice cream container with an outdoor scene, if you want. Then punch holes on opposite sides of the container near the top. Tie a rope handle through the holes. Now you have your own, homemade sand bucket!

Mud Pies. Pack wet sand into an aluminum foil pie plate, gelatin molds, and other utensils. Turn the molds upside down and carefully lift them up to reveal formed cakes and pies.

Plastic Scoop. Lay a well-rinsed empty plastic bleach bottle on its side. Cut away a portion diagonally from the bottom of the bottle. Be sure to leave the handle intact. Now you have a homemade sand scoop!

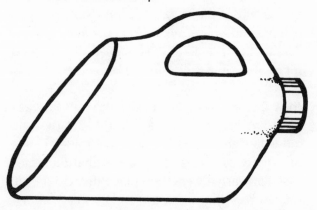

Sandcasted Footprint. First, dampen some sand. Then pack it down and smooth it out. Press your bare foot or hand firmly into the sand. Then carefully lift it straight up. The print should be at least one inch deep.

Ask an adult to help you mix some plaster of Paris with water. When the mixture is as thick as cream, pour it into the print. Allow the plaster to get dry and hard. This usually takes about one hour. Then carefully lift the plaster print out of the sand. Brush the loose sand away from the casting. (Some sand may stick to the casting anyway.)

If you have any plaster left over, throw it away. Do not pour it down the drain because it will clog up everything if you do!

Sand Castles. In damp sand, build castles, houses, towers, or even complete cities. Use buckets, cups, and plastic glasses for molds to make your structures.

Sand Sifter. Make your own sand sifter by poking holes into the bottom of an aluminum foil pie pan. Fill it with sand and sift away!

Wet Sand Fun. For a different way to play in the sand, make it wet! Make lake beds and river beds in the sand, then pour in water to form lakes and rivers. Float toy boats in the water near a make-believe shore. Make dams across the river, and form the dampened sand into hills and mountains with roads.

Scrapbooks

Paper Bag Scrapbook. Cut up some brown paper bags to make this small scrapbook. Cut out fifteen 6-by-10-inch pieces and stack them. Fold the stack in half to form a book and staple the pieces together along the crease. Now you are ready to paste anything you want into the scrapbook!

Spiral-Bound Scrapbook. Obtain an inexpensive spiral-bound notebook from the store. Use it for a scrapbook.

Typing Paper Scrapbook. Stack six pieces of typing paper so the edges are even. Staple them near the top and bottom edges on the left-hand side to form a book. If you want, add a construction paper cover to your scrapbook.

Scribble Art

Crayon and Paint Scribble Art. Make some scribbles on paper with tempera paint. When the paint has dried, color heavily with crayons, filling in the spaces within the scribbles with many bright colors.

Cut and Paste Scribble Art. Draw some scribbles on a sheet of paper. Then cut out shapes from various colors of paper and paste the shapes on the scribble lines.

Scribble Drawings. Using light or heavy pressure, as desired, draw in a round-and-round motion on paper, moving your hand along slightly while drawing. Create an animal, a plant, a person, or an object from this circular, scribble-like motion.

Scribble Drawings

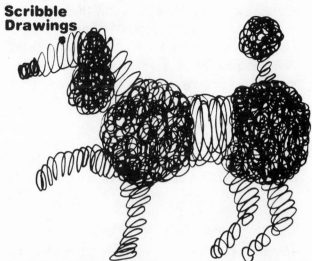

Scribble Picture Mosaic. On a large sheet of paper, draw a single, long scribble picture using just one color. Next, fill in the empty spaces within the scribbles with various shapes cut from colored construction paper, felt scraps, and pieces of yarn.

Sculpture

Bag and Plaster Sculpture. Pour some plaster into a plastic bag. Tie it tightly shut. When the plaster begins to thicken, squeeze the bag with both hands. "Hold" the squeeze to make it keep its shape. Form the shape you want. When dry, peel off the bag.

Box Sculpture. Collect a variety of boxes, cartons, tubes, cardboard panels, colored papers, and some paint. Then gather some scissors, glue, paper fasteners, clips, string, pins, tape, and other items for hooking the boxes together.

Assemble the boxes and other pieces to make animals, objects, and other creations. When assembled, decorate with paint or pieces of colored paper.

Cardboard Sculpture. Collect some panels and pieces from corrugated cardboard boxes. Insert the panels and pieces one at a time into a vise. Using a hacksaw with adult supervision, cut the pieces into smaller ones. When you have enough, tape them together into a sculptured figure or abstract shape.

Cork Sculpture.   Save as many pieces of cork as you can. If you have trouble finding enough corks around the house, buy a bag of assorted corks at a hardware store. Using toothpicks and glue, build people, animals, designs, and other objects with the corks.

Egg Carton Sculpture.   Cut off the lid of a plastic foam egg carton. Use either side for a base. Cut out the cups and form a sculpture by stacking the cups. Use glue or hook them together with toothpicks.

Hanging Yarn Sculpture.   Mix some glue in a pan containing a small amount of water. Dip a long piece of yarn into the glue mixture. Soak the yarn thoroughly.

   Lift out the yarn and lay it down in a pattern on a piece of waxed paper. Make sure that the yarn overlaps often. Allow it to dry, then lift the stiffened yarn sculpture from the waxed paper. Hang it with string for display.

Junk "Scrapture."   Hunt around the house for small scraps and pieces of "junk" to use for building your junk scrapture. Look for such things as small empty frozen juice cans, short cardboard tubes, egg carton cups, small boxes, bits of paper or cardboard, pieces of yarn, small plastic pieces, straws, Popsicle sticks, bottle caps, spools, etc. Glue them together on a flat piece of cardboard to create a fantastic, towering display of "junk"!

Marshmallow Sculpture.   Form a sculpture by sticking large marshmallows together with toothpicks, creating an animal, an object, or a strange shape. Also, you can use gumdrops instead of marshmallows.

Newspaper Animal Sculpture.   Roll a half sheet of newspaper into a tube. Bend the tube in two spots to form a body. To form legs, roll another tube from newspaper and cut it in half. Glue each leg piece over the body and bend them down on the sides. Form the head by

Newspaper Animal Sculpture

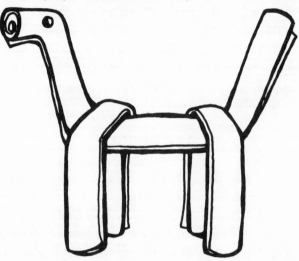

bending one end of the body piece outward a little. How many different kinds of newspaper animals can you make?

Paper Sculpture.   Flat pieces of paper can be used in many different ways to make sculptures. Here are some of the things you can do with paper to make sculptures: roll it, curl it after cutting (a pencil helps to curl it), make the paper wavy, pleat the paper accordion-style, twist the paper, cross pieces together, and cut scallops and fringes into the edges of the paper. Use some of these ideas to create your own sculptures!

Paper Strip Sculpture.   Cut out any number of paper strips. Glue together the ends of some of the strips to form rings. Pinch some of the rings in three or four places to make triangles and squares. Glue the pieces together to form animals and objects.

Plaster of Paris Panel Carvings.   Mix some plaster of Paris in a can of water until the mixture becomes a thick paste. Next, grease the inside of a shallow tin pan. Then pour the plaster of Paris "paste" into the tin pan until the pan is full. If needed, smooth the top area of the plaster. Allow it to harden overnight.

   The next day, find an old blunt knife to carve with, or use the point of a skewer as a carving tool. Have an adult supervise you. (Before you start carving, you might first want to draw a pattern, design, or picture on the plaster with a soft pencil.) When the carving is finished, color the panel with poster paints. Carefully ease the panel out of the tin pan when the paint has dried.

Soap Carving. Using a kitchen knife or potato peeler, carve various objects out of soap bars. Be very careful, though, not to cut yourself! Have an adult nearby while you work.

Soap Flakes Sculpture. Mix a little bit of water with some soap flakes to make a soapy clay. From this clay, create objects and figures. Toothpicks can be used to fasten sculptured pieces together. Later, the completed sculpture can be used as a bar of soap for the bathtub! (If you want a colored sculpture, add food coloring while mixing the soap flakes.)

Stone Sculpture. Look around for some interesting stones and pebbles to use for your stone sculpture. Gravel roads, dried stream beds, rock piles, and seashores are good places to look for stones with pretty colors, odd shapes, and interesting markings.

Glue the stones together to form animals, figures, objects, or anything else you want. (You can make a much easier sculpture by pushing stones into a ball of modeling clay to form figures.)

Toothpick and Clay Sculpture. First, make a base from colored modeling clay. Then poke some toothpicks into the base to begin the sculpture. Stick small rolled balls of clay to the top ends of the toothpicks. Then add toothpicks to these balls. Continue to build up and out, forming an unusual abstract sculpture.

Wax Carving. Ask an adult to melt some old candle bits in a coffee can over hot water. Have him pour the melted wax into a milk carton. When the wax has cooled, peel off the carton, leaving a block of solid wax. Carve a figure from the wax with a table knife or a fingernail file.

Wire Sculpture. For a base, use a 3-by-3-inch piece of plastic foam. Then bend and twist a length of soft wire or pipe cleaner into the desired shape. Poke one end of the wire into the plastic foam base for display.

Wood Sculpture. Collect some small-to-medium-sized pieces of scrap wood. Look for pieces with interesting shapes. When you have a good supply, spread them out and choose the ones you want to use.

Using a fast-drying glue, assemble the pieces to form any kind of sculpture or design. When you glue several pieces together, you might want to let the glue dry before gluing on any more pieces. If you want, use felt-tip markers to "stain" or color the pieces while you are waiting for the glue to dry.

Sea Life and the Ocean

Finger-Painted Ocean. Using blue colors, finger paint an ocean on glossy shelf paper. Make waves by rolling a soft drink bottle cap edge across the painting before the paint dries. Then, when dry, paste on cutouts of ships, clouds, and the sun.

Margarine Tub Octopus. Draw a spiral on green paper. Cut out the spiral, and cut it into shorter lengths for octopus legs. Using a felt-tip marker, draw spots along the legs for suction cups.

Turn a margarine tub upside down, and draw

a pair of octopus eyes on the side of the tub. Then place the lid from the tub upside down on the table also. Tape the octopus legs around the rim of the lid. To finish the octopus snap the margarine tub down onto the lid.

Sandy Starfish. From colored construction paper, cut out a starfish. Coat one side of the starfish with glue. While the glue is still wet, sprinkle it with sand. Allow it to dry, then shake off the excess sand.

Stuffed Sea Creatures. Fold a piece of brown wrapping paper in half. On one side, outline the shape of a sea creature (fish, shark, whale, etc.) and cut it out. Now you have two matching shapes!

Staple together the two pieces along one edge with the ends matching. Paint on the desired outside details. Then stuff the shape with crumpled newspaper and staple it closed along the remaining edge.

Undersea Stabile. Stick pieces of pipe cleaners into a clay base. From colored paper, cut out small fish, shells, crabs, seaweed, and coral. Glue these on the pipe cleaners.

Underwater Crayon-Resist Scene. On white paper, draw an underwater scene, including fish, sea plants, coral, etc., using bright crayons. Press hard with the crayons while drawing!

When the scene is complete, paint over it with blue or green poster paint. The crayon will resist the paint, making an interesting underwater effect!

Seashore Art

Beach Rock Paperweight. Look around the beach for a smooth, white rock. Take it home. Paint a seashore scene on the rock with enamel paint. Use the rock for a paperweight or a doorstop.

Beach Sand Collage. Collect samples of different kinds of beach sand in small containers.

Take the sand home. Then cover a sheet of paper with glue. Sprinkle the different kinds of sand into designs on the glue. Allow it to dry and shake off the excess sand.

Decorated Shells. Hunt for some medium-sized clam, scallop, or other kinds of seashells to use for decorating. Also collect some very tiny shells, stones, and pieces of colored beach glass. (If you do not live near the beach, obtain these items from a hobby shop.)

Brush glue over the surfaces of the larger shells, and decorate them by sticking on the smaller shells, stones, and pieces of smooth beach glass. If you want, add small plastic pearls, seahorses, and tiny starfish. Make the decorated shells into candy dishes, earring holders, pin holders, and many other items.

Fish Mobile. Obtain a green plastic net bag, the kind from the grocery store. Turn the net bag upside down and hook on a pipe cleaner to use for a hanger.

Next, cut some short hooks from pipe cleaners and fasten them around the lower, open edges of the "fish net." Cut out some fish shapes from construction paper. Make mouths on the fish using a paper puncher. Hang the fish by their mouths from the hooks. Then hang the entire mobile for display.

Flashing Lighthouse. Place a flashlight so it is facing out from the center of a lazy Susan or revolving kitchen cupboard platform. Turn on the flashlight.

Set the lazy Susan on a cardboard box. Build up blocks around the lazy Susan to form the shape of a lighthouse building. Have windows on several sides so the flashlight can shine through. Also leave space at the bottom of one side so you can reach in with your hand and turn the lazy Susan around, causing the light to "flash" through the lighthouse windows.

Lighthouse Scene. Draw a picture of a lighthouse on a piece of cardboard. Paste small pebbles over the outline of the lighthouse, and paste on sand for the beach. Paste on large pebbles for a cliff.

Seashell Wall Hanging Plaque. From a cardboard, cut out a rectangle about 5-by-8 inches in size. Cover it with woodgrain-print contact paper. On the back side (which does not have to be covered) staple both ends of a six-inch length of yarn for a hanger.

On the front side, glue on small shells to form the outline of a fish, or glue on shells to form a mosaic. Allow it to dry and hang.

Seashell Wind Chimes. Find some thin, flat shells. Ask an adult to help you punch or drill a small hole in the center of each shell. Tie equal lengths of thread through each hole. Then hang the shells close together in a place where the breezes blow. Listen to the shells tinkle as they brush against one another in the breeze!

Seashore Diorama. Put some sand and water in a shallow metal pan. Sprinkle in short pieces of grass for seaweed or beach grass, and add some small plastic seashells and toy boats to the scene.

Shell Pictures. Glue one of your favorite snapshots to the inside of a clam shell. You might want to glue a piece of cotton or felt inside the shell first as a background for the photograph.

Seashore (Science)

Grunion Run. Watch the newspapers for announcements of the next grunion run. Ask an adult to take you to see the grunion come up on the beach. If local laws permit, catch a few of the fish in a bucket. Look at them closely and then let them go.

Ocean Box. Pick out a box to be your "ocean box." Use it for storing shells, dried seaweed, driftwood, beach sand, and other seashore treasures you have found. Now you can study these objects any time you want or have them on hand for making art arrangements.

Sand Formation. Have you ever wondered how the sand on the beach was formed? Most of it was made by the waves crashing onto the rocks, wearing down the rocks into sand over a long period of time. You can imitate this by rubbing pieces of chalk or limestone together. See the sandlike material formed by the rubbing? This process of sand formation is called *erosion*.

Shell Collecting. The next time you visit the beach see how many different kinds of shells you can find. Collect them in pails so you can take them home. Even blemished shells are good to collect because they show how shells are altered by the sand and tide action.

At home, carefully look at the shells. Remember that each shell once contained a living animal. Read a book about shells, and compare pictures in the book with the shells you have collected.

Display your best shells. Keep collecting shells to find examples of each kind. Save the others for sandcasting, for decorating boxes, and for making buttons, jewelry, and Christmas ornaments.

Stone Collecting.   Search the beach for many different kinds of stones, pebbles, marbles, and bits of beach glass worn smooth by the waves. Look for stones with unusual colors, shapes, and textures. Take home some stones to start a collection. Read a book about stones and try to collect as many kinds as you can.

Tidepools.   Investigate a tidepool when the tide has gone out. Look for small plants and animals in the pool. How many kinds do you see? Carry a magnifying glass so you can look closely at some of the life. Perhaps you will see some tiny fish or crabs. How did the animals get caught in the tidepool?

Secret Things and Places

"Hidden Compartment" Book.   Find an old hardcover book or thick paperback that is at least one inch thick. Make sure it is okay to cut it up! Then cut away a cube section from the middle pages of the book to make a compartment for hiding things. When you close the book, it looks normal! Hide special treasures and secret messages in the book.

Invisible Painting.   Cover a piece of white drawing paper with a sheet of heavy waxed paper. Using a dried-up ball-point pen, etch a design, picture, or message onto the waxed paper. Then remove the waxed paper from the drawing paper.

To make your invisible drawing appear on the drawing paper, paint over the entire paper with watercolor paint. Watch the drawing magically appear!

Invisible Writing.   Obtain an ink pen with a nib and some lemon juice. Check the pen to make sure the nib is clean. Use the lemon juice as "ink" for writing a secret message. Watch— the message disappears as you write it! To make the message return, simply hold the paper over an electric light bulb!

Secret Name.   Pick a secret name you like and share it only with one or two other people. Have them choose secret names also! Call each other by your secret names only!

Secret Place.   Choose a place to be your "secret" place that only you and a few of your friends know about. Use this place as a spot for trading secret messages or holding special meetings. Just make sure it is a safe, open place, such as under a tree, behind a bush, or alongside a big boulder in a field.

Seeds (Science)

Lima Bean Examination.   Soak some lima beans in water and then remove the outer covering of the beans. Pull a bean apart and look at the small plant (embryo) inside. Notice that the rest of the inside part of the bean is actually the food for the embryo!

Lima Bean Growth.   Line the inside of a glass jar with blotting paper or a paper towel. Then fill the jar with sand and place some dried lima beans between the paper and the glass. Make sure the sand stays damp. After several days, the beans will sprout!

Seed Classification.   Collect seeds from many different plants. Separate and classify them in the following ways: seeds from trees, seeds from fruits, seeds from vegetables, and seeds from flowers. How are they alike? How are they different? Can you classify the seeds in any other ways?

Seed Comparisons. Gather or buy seeds from pumpkin, watermelon, apple, peach, orange, avocado, pomegranate, and grape plants. Also collect some from a variety of flowers. Look at the seeds carefully. What colors are they? What shapes? What sizes? After studying the seeds, plant them and watch to see the different kinds of plants they produce.

Seed Growth Experiment. Most seeds need good soil to grow well. To see this, put one bean seed in a jar of stones; put another in a pot of sand, and another in a pot of soil. Water each as needed. Which seed grows best? Why?

Seed Search. Set a cucumber, a tomato, a bell pepper, and a cantaloupe in front of you. Cut open each one and search for seeds. Compare the seeds you find.

Seed Transportation. In order to produce a new plant, many seeds need a way to get from one place to another. Seeds depend on many interesting different ways for being transported from the parent plant to a new spot that is just right for growth.

Some seeds travel by sticking onto animals and people and later falling to the ground. To demonstrate this for yourself, stick a burr to your clothing and walk around for awhile. Did the burr fall off somewhere along the way?

Other seeds are transported by floating in water. Place different kinds of seeds in a pan of water to see which ones float.

Wind is probably the best seed transporter of all. On a breezy day, obtain a milkweed pod, a cattail, and a dandelion plant. Open the milkweed pod and break the cattail into pieces. Blow on the dandelion plant. Watch the wind lift the seeds into the air, carry them along for a

Seed Transportation

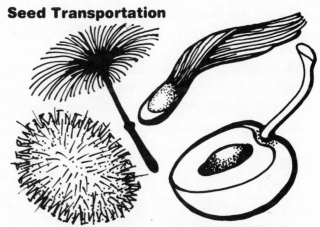

while, and then let them fall to the ground. Some of these seeds will soon take root where they have landed and will grow into new plants.

The Senses

Hearing

Hearing Walk. Take a walk and listen to the city or the country sounds. Take along a pocket tape recorder, if available, and later listen again to the sounds you heard on your walk.

Listen and Identify! Sit very quietly. Close your eyes and listen to the sounds you hear. Try to identify these sounds. Are they made by people, animals, machines, or the weather?

Then have a friend join you. Ask him to make sounds while your eyes are shut. These sounds can include crumpling soft paper towels, striking a spoon on a glass, tapping a ruler on wood, pouring water into a glass, pouring rice into a pan, bouncing a rubber ball, rubbing together two pieces of sandpaper, etc. See if you can identify the sounds your friend makes. Then switch places and *you* make the sounds for your friend!

Sound Cans. Collect some empty cans. Put a different kind of noise-making material into each can. Some of these materials can be beans, popcorn kernels, liquids, marbles, noodles, nuts, rice, salt, pins, and buttons. Cover the cans. Shake them one at a time and describe the sounds produced.

"Who Am I?" Listening Game.   Play this game when you have some of your friends over. Have all your friends close their eyes. Then touch one of them on the head. This person must then say, "Who am I?" With their eyes still closed, the others must try to guess who asked the question.

Sight

Changing Viewpoints.   Look at an object, first covering one eye and then covering the other eye. Did you notice any change between the two views? The slightly different angles of vision from each eye allow us to see depth in our field of vision!

Look and Remember Game.   Place four or five different objects on a tray. Study them for a moment and then cover them up. While your eyes are closed, have someone remove only one of the objects from the tray. Then uncover the objects. Which one is missing?

Magnified Views.   Examine a variety of objects through a magnifying glass, including rocks, shells, leaves, and insects. Also look at the print on a magazine page or the dots that make a newspaper photograph. The magnifying glass makes things look closer and larger than they really are, allowing you to see more details than you would normally.

Peep Box.   To see, it is necessary to have light. To demonstrate this, make a peep box from a shoe box. Cut a small hole at one end for peeking. Decorate the inside of the box with a painted scene. Look into the box when the lid is on, shutting off the light. Then look into the box when the lid is off. Compare the results.

Pupil Observation.   Your eyes will adjust to the amount of light available. To observe this, sit down facing a friend. Watch each other's eyes to see the pupils get larger or smaller in reaction to the amount of light in the room. To see the pupils contract (get smaller), have your friend glance quickly at an electric light bulb and then look back at you. You will see your friend's pupils first contract and then grow larger again!

Reading Display.   Every day we use our eyes to read. Make a display showing the many things you read—books, magazines, newspapers, pamphlets, posters, comics, booklets, and advertisements.

Sight and Distance.   Look at an object that is far away. See how small it seems? Now walk toward the object and notice how it appears larger as you move closer.

Sight Helpers.   We use many things to help us to see things better. Make a display showing eyeglasses, binoculars, a magnifying glass, a microscope, and telescope. (Use pictures of these objects if you do not have real ones.) Also make a display of things that help us see in the dark, including a flashlight, a lamp, a lantern, and a candle.

Smell

Close Your Eyes and Guess Game.   While your eyes are closed, have someone put some objects in front of you. Without touching them, smell the objects to try to identify them. Oranges, onions, apples, bananas, lemons, peanut butter, etc., are good things to start with.

Guess What is Cooking.   At dinner time, try to guess what is cooking without peeking to see. You will have to use your nose!

Imagine This! Using facial expressions and body movements, playact your own reactions to these imagined smells: cinnamon toast, a Christmas tree, sauerkraut, rotten tomatoes, smoke, roses, gasoline, perfume, pepper, fresh air, and a skunk.

Smell Board. Dip cotton balls into a variety of liquids. Then glue the balls in rows on a piece of cardboard. You and your friends can then sniff the cotton balls to try to identify their smells. Some suggested liquids for dipping are: almond, camphor, coffee, cola, cologne, lemon, lime, pepper sauce, strawberry, vanilla, and vinegar. Can you think of others?

Smell Bottles. Collect some empty plastic yogurt containers to use as "smell bottles." Punch some air holes in the lid of each container. Then place a different-smelling item into each "bottle." Place the lids back on and then mix up the containers. Sniff through the air holes to see if you can tell what the items are in each bottle. Suggested items are: almond, banana, camphor, cedar, cinnamon, cloves, cocoa, coffee, cologne, cucumber, flowers, garlic, lemon, lime, onion, orange, peppermint, strawberry, vanilla, and vinegar.

Smell Cards. Brush white glue on cards and then sprinkle a different spice on each card. Include such things as cinnamon, pepper, nutmeg, cloves, and chili powder.

Taste
Blindfold Test. Blindfold yourself, then hold your nose while someone gives you a piece of potato or a piece of onion to taste. Can you tell which piece your friend gave you?

Sweet and Sour Comparison. Taste the following items to determine which are sweet and which are sour: a bite-sized piece of pickle, a small sugar cube, a sip of unsweetened lemonade, and a square of bread with jelly.

Taste Comparison. Prepare several different kinds of simple foods for cooking. Taste each one before it is cooked to see what it tastes like when it is raw. After cooking, taste each kind of food again to see how the taste has changed. Apples, broccoli, cranberries, cauliflower, pears, and mushrooms are good foods to try.

Taste Game. One player closes his eyes or is blindfolded. The other player then feeds him tiny bites of food, which the blindfolded player must try to identify. Use small bites of bananas, apples, cheeses, raisins, cookies, or crackers. Think of other things to taste. Then change places so the other player has a chance to try.

Taste Identification. With your eyes closed, dip your fingers into some different-tasting liquids and solids (placed in open containers). Taste these things to see if you can identify them. Things to use include catsup, honey, peanut butter, pudding, salt, spices, sugar, syrup, and vinegar. Ask someone else to put them out for you so you do not know what is in each container.

Touch
Feely Box. Pick out a large box to use as a "feely box." Cut an arm hole in each side of the box so you can reach inside to feel the contents. Fill the box with many different things to touch: button, comb, toothbrush, pencil, adhesive bandage, fork, spoon, shoelace, washcloth, screw, scissors, sponge, soap bar, pliers, cotton swab, sock, cup, ball, thimble, and anything else you want. Cover the box so you cannot see inside. Take turns with your friends reaching into the box. Can you identify the objects just by touching them?

Feely Footpath. Normally, we feel most things with our hands. But for fun, let us try feeling some things with our feet!

To start, line up any number of dishpans, shallow boxes, and other containers large enough to step in. Put only one kind of material into each container. Suggested materials are: sawdust, thick foam rubber, smooth pebbles, sand, pinto beans, sandpaper, macaroni, twigs, cut grass, plastic foam packing pieces, and carpet samples. Be sure not to use anything sharp! What other items can you think of?

Set up a path of filled containers. Then take off your shoes and socks. Step through the containers, one after the other, feeling the materials under your feet!

Hot and Cold Sensations. Our sense of touch tells our bodies if something is hot or cold. To experience this, obtain three glasses. Fill the first with hot water and the second with cold water. Feel each glass with your fingers, and describe how it feels. Dip a thermometer into each glass to measure the temperatures.

Then, pour some water from each of the first two glasses into the third glass. What happens to the water in the third glass? Measure the temperature of the water in that glass to find out.

Sidewalk Touching. Touch a sidewalk on a bright, sunny day. Then touch a part of the sidewalk that is in the shade. Describe the differences.

Texture Book. Use a spiral notebook for your book. Look around for some different-textured material to glue in the book. Hunt for materials that are soft, smooth, bumpy, scratchy, hard, spongy, sticky, slick, etc., including such things as cotton, plastic kitchen wrap, waxed paper, sandpaper, corrugated paper, tape, Popsicle sticks, fabric pieces, shiny shelf paper, etc. Feel the various textures in your book and describe how they feel.

Texture Walk. Carry a crayon and some blank newsprint with you on a texture walk. Use the crayon and paper to make rubbings over various surfaces you see on your walk, including bricks, chain-link fences, screen, leaves, pavements, tree bark, rocks, etc.

"What Is It" Game. Hold your hands behind your back. Have someone place a simple object in your hands. Try guessing what the object is by touching it. Take turns playing this game.

Sewing

Sewing Squares. Cut an eight-inch square from a piece of loosely knit material. Practice sewing with a blunt darning needle or tapestry needle, lacing in and out of the material. Ask an adult to help you if necessary.

Shoestring Sewing. On a 9-by-12-inch piece of poster board, punch any number of holes with a hole punch. Then obtain a long shoelace and "sew" it through the holes to make a pattern or a picture. Tie several shoestrings together if needed. To sew the card again in a different way, unlace the shoestrings and start over.

Simple Sewing. Draw a simple design on a piece of drawing paper. Then transfer the design to a piece of burlap by slipping a sheet of carbon paper under the pattern. Place this packet over the burlap and retrace the pattern on the burlap. Then thread a large-eyed needle with multicolored crochet cotton and begin sewing along the outline on the burlap. Ask an adult to help you if needed.

Tomato Basket Sewing Cards. Cut some plastic tomato baskets into rectangles. Then "sew" long strands of yarn through the plastic webbing to make designs and pictures. Stiffen the ends of the yarn with masking tape to help in "threading" the yarn through the webbing.

Shapes

Colored Paper Shape Pictures. Cut up some colored paper into various shapes, including circles, triangles, squares, rectangles, and strips. Paste the shapes on background paper to form designs, patterns, or pictures.

Sandpaper Shapes. Cut different-sized circles, squares, rectangles, and triangles from rough sandpaper. Glue the shapes to a piece of heavy cardboard. Close your eyes and feel the shapes with your fingers. Can you identify the shapes?

Shape Art. Draw many different-sized circles on a sheet of paper. Make the circles fill the entire area of the paper and touch all four edges of the paper. Keep drawing smaller circles inside the original circles. Continue until all the circles are filled with a number of smaller circles. Display when finished. (Try using squares, triangles, or other shapes for this art.)

Shape Collage. Paste colored paper shapes together on a piece of background paper, overlapping them to make a nice collage.

Shape Cookies. Cut out and bake cookies in the shapes of circles, squares, rectangles, and triangles. Enjoy them!

Shape Drawing. Using only circles, make a drawing of an animal or a person on paper.

Later, make a drawing using only squares, rectangles, or triangles.

Shape Mobile. Paste the ends of paper strips together to make paper strip ornaments in the shapes of circles, squares, triangles, or rectangles. In each case, start with a circle ring. Pinch the ring in three places to form a triangle, or in four places to form a square or a rectangle. Hang the shape ornaments as a mobile.

Sick-Day Activities

Alphabet Pictures. With a pencil and note pad, draw letters of the alphabet to see how many pictures of animals, people, or objects you can make from the letters. (You can also do this activity with numbers.)

Bed Exploration. If you have to stay in bed, ask someone to bring you a magnifying glass. From your bed, examine everything you possibly can through the magnifying glass. Look at your own skin, your bed clothes, a piece of hair, the patterns in your sheets and blankets, and even the food served to you!

Bed Sailing Ship. When you must stay in bed, but are not feeling very sick, pretend that your bed is a sailing ship! Your pillow can be a life preserver, a broomstick an oar, and a paper plate the pilot's wheel. Tie a handkerchief to the bed-post for a flag. Imagine that you are out to sea, chasing pirates, weathering a storm, exploring new water passages, or watching whales.

Bedside Bulletin Board. On the wall beside your bed, or at the foot of your bed, tape or tack a piece of heavy cardboard. Use this as a bulletin board for displaying artwork you have done while you were sick or letters and greeting cards you have received in the mail. You can also pin up pictures from newspapers and magazines.

Bedside Fishing. Attach a string to a stick or a ruler for a fishing pole. At the end of the string, tie a paper clip and bend it to form a hook.

Then, place some "fish" in a basket on the floor beside your bed. Your "fish" should be things that have handles or holes, such as bracelets, cups, key rings, jar rings, etc. See how many "fish" you can hook with your fishing pole. *Another way to do it:* If all your "fish" are made of metal, then tie a small magnet to the end of your line and use the magnet as a fishhook.

Bedside Mural. Tape a large sheet of butcher paper or brown wrapping paper to the wall next to your bed. With crayons or felt-tip markers, draw your own mural on the paper.

Book-Balancing Game. Try this game when you have to stay in bed! Put a book on your head. Then try to keep the book on your head while touching your knees with your hands. After that, try touching your toes while bending your knees. Can you keep the book on your head?

Five Senses Game. This is a fun game to play by yourself when you are sick in bed. Glance around your room for five things that are brown (or any other color you choose); listen carefully for five sounds coming from other parts of the house, or from outside; try to sniff and identify five different smells; touch and feel five different objects or materials; and when eating, try to taste five different flavors.

Indoor Bow and Arrow. Obtain an elastic band, a pencil, and a small piece of cardboard. From the cardboard, cut out an arrow. Make a notch at one end of the arrow and a point at the other end. The arrow should be at least one inch wide.

To fire the arrow, wind the elastic band around the pencil two times. Hook the arrow through the loop of the second wind of elastic. Pull the arrow back against the elastic by holding the notched end and pulling. When it is stretched back enough, let it go!

Neaten Your Drawers. A sick day is a good time to straighten out one of your dresser draw-ers. Use an empty box to put away the things that do not belong in your drawers.

Paper Clip Fun. Have someone bring you a bunch of paper clips. Try making designs and pictures with them by linking them together! You can also make bracelets and chains from the paper clips.

Picture Letter. The next time you are sick in bed, try this interesting way to write a letter! "Write" the letter using pictures instead of words! Cut out some of the pictures you need from magazines or draw your own pictures with crayons. Glue the pictures in the proper order on a sheet of paper.

Room Picture. When you must stay in bed, try drawing a picture of your own room. Draw it as you see it, or draw a floor plan of it, showing where different objects in your room are located. Do not forget to show yourself in bed!

Scrap Bag Pictures. Cut up small pieces of colored cloth and scraps of yarn to make flowers and designs over a sheet of paper. If you want to save your work, paste the pieces onto paper.

Silly Meal. This is especially fun when you have to eat in bed. Ask if you can eat your meal using a different kind of utensil, such as a mixing spoon, measuring scoop, spatula, or chopsticks! It might be a little messier than usual, but it is fun! Also, try eating your meal in reverse order! Start with your dessert, and finish with your meat, potatoes, and drink.

Sock Toss. Place a wastepaper basket near your bed and see how many rolled-up socks you can toss into the basket. If you want, you can tie a long string to a sock and then pin the other end of the string to your bed sheet. This way, you can pull the sock back after tossing it!

String Pictures. Obtain a piece of string about 10 inches long. See how many pictures you can make by simply laying out the string in different patterns on paper.

Snacks

Applesauce Party. Place cut-up apples into a pan and add a small amount of water to prevent sticking. Cook until the apples become mushy. If you want, cinnamon candies may be added while the apples are cooking. Serve your finished applesauce with graham crackers to your friends.

Autumn Tasty Mix. Mix the following ingredients in a large bowl: 1 cup of popcorn, ½ cup of candy corn, ½ cup of raisins, and ½ cup of cocktail peanuts. Serve to your family and friends.

Candy Mints. Mix the following ingredients well: 4 ounces of softened margarine, 1 egg white, 1 pound of powdered sugar, some green food coloring, and some mint flavoring.

Knead the mixture until it is ready to form into shapes. Roll into balls and then flatten each ball with a fork. Serve.

Cupcake Cones. Preheat the oven to 400 degrees. Make some cupcake batter from a pack-

Cupcake Cones

aged cupcake mix following the directions on the box.

Next, set a number of flat-bottomed ice cream cones on a cookie sheet. Fill each cone no more than one half full (about ¼ cup) with batter. You want just enough batter so it will rise to a rounded peak in each cone. Bake for 15–18 minutes at 400 degrees, remove, and allow to cool. Decorate with frosting and sprinkles.

Frozen Peas Snack. For an unusual snack on a hot day, pour some frozen green peas into a little bowl and enjoy!

Frozen Pops. Mix 1 pack of gelatin and ½ cup of sugar. Dissolve the mixture in 1½ cups of boiling water. Add 2 cups of orange juice. Then pour into Popsicle containers or paper cups and freeze. (If using paper cups, stick a Popsicle stick into each cup before freezing. When ready to eat, peel away the paper cup and hold the pop by the stick!)

Fruit Cubes. Ask an adult for some colorful fruits to use when making your cubes. Cherries, pineapple chunks, strawberries, and peach slices are perfect. Spoon your fruit pieces into the cube sections of ice cube trays or into individual gelatin molds. Pour some juice over the fruits, and place the trays in a freezer.

Next, make some interesting ice cubes by pouring water into some gelatin molds or other unusually shaped containers. Freeze.

Before serving, set out cups for each of your guests. Place some fruit cubes and ice cubes into each cup. Pour some juice or another drink over the cubes and serve.

Fruit Sandwich Dessert.   Have something different for dessert—a sandwich! Spread mayonnaise or salad dressing on bread slices. Cut one ring of canned pineapple in half. Cut one banana lengthwise. Fill the sandwich with a pineapple and banana slice on each side. Cut the sandwich in half, and it is ready to eat!

Ice Cream.   First, you need to make an ice cream maker! To start, cut off the top part from a half-gallon-sized milk carton. Then place a metal can (that has a matching lid and will fit in the milk carton) inside the freezer for awhile until it becomes very cold. Then take the can out and put it in the center of the milk carton container. Put the lid on the can.

Fill the carton all around the can with ice and rock salt. Then remove the lid from the can and pour in your ice cream mixture. (For your ice cream mixture, blend ¼ cup of half-and-half, 2 teaspoons of sugar, and ¼ teaspoon of vanilla flavoring.)

With a large spoon, stir the mixture in the can for five or six minutes. Watch the ice cream as the ice melts and frost forms on the outside of the can. At this same time, the ice cream will start to freeze. Serve when ready!

For other flavors of ice cream, add any of the following ingredients to your ice cream when first mixing it: 1 tablespoon of frozen grape or orange juice concentrate, 1 tablespoon of canned juice, mashed fruit (bananas or straw-berries), or chocolate syrup or chocolate chips.

Ice Cream Cone Clown.   Beforehand, scoop out well-rounded balls of ice cream onto a tray

lined with waxed paper. Place in the freezer to set. When firm, use the balls to make your clowns.

For each clown, flatten a colored paper baking cup upside down in a dish. Place the ice cream ball "head" on top of the flattened baking cup. For a hat, set a pointed ice cream cone upside down on top of the ball.

Make the clown's eyes, nose, and mouth with a selection of maraschino cherries, chocolate chips, nut pieces, gumdrop bits, or cut-up fruits. Serve.

**Ice Cream
Cone Clown**

Marguerites.   Spread some peanut butter on saltine crackers. Put a marshmallow on top of each cracker. Slit each marshmallow and stick a small pat of butter into each slit. With adult supervision, place the snacks in the oven and broil until the marshmallows melt, and serve.

Orange Sherbet.   Mix 1 cup of whole milk, 1 cup of granulated sugar, the juice from 1 orange, and some finely grated orange rind. Blend the ingredients well and pour into ice cube trays. Freeze thoroughly and serve on a hot day. (You can make lime or lemon sherbet by substituting a lime or a lemon for the orange.)

Peanut Butter Honey Balls. Mix 1 cup of honey and 1 cup of peanut butter. Gradually add 2 cups of dry milk. Make sure everything is well mixed. Then roll the mixture into small balls. Allow the balls to stand in a cool spot until they become firm, then serve!

Popcorn Roundup. First, spread a large clean sheet on the floor. Then have your friends sit around the edges of the sheet. Put a popcorn popper in the center of the sheet, and let the popcorn pop away—with no lid on the popper! (Ask permission from an adult.)

Watch as the corn pops high into the air, and see how far it pops from the popper! Collect all the popcorn and put it into individual paper cups along with a little salt and butter. (Remember, the popper is hot! Stay away from it until it cools.)

Raisin Game. The next time you have raisins for a snack, play this game. Roll a dice and count out the same number of raisins to eat. Keep rolling until you have had a fair-sized snack!

Snack Mix. In a large bowl, mix some popped popcorn, peanuts, raisins, chocolate chips, pretzel sticks, and goldfish crackers. Use a paper cup for measuring each of the ingredients into equal amounts. That is it! The snack is ready to eat! Take it with you on trips, picnics, nature walks, and to the playground.

Snow Cones. Firmly pack some crushed ice into paper cups. Pour some fruit punch concentrate over the ice and serve. *Another way to do it:* Mix 6 ounces of frozen orange juice concentrate with ¾ cup of water. Blend well and pour the mixture over the ice.

Sweet Fruit Snack. Peel an orange and cut it into small chunks. Next peel and slice a banana. Mix the orange and banana pieces in a bowl. Pour 2 tablespoons of honey over the fruit and mix again to coat all the fruit with honey. Serve.

Snow Art

Bottled Snow I. With a hole puncher, punch out some holes from a sheet of waxed paper. Scoop up the little punched-out holes and put them in a jar full of water. Seal the lid tightly. Shake the jar to create the effect of a snowstorm inside!

Bottled Snow II. Take the lid off of an empty baby food jar and set the lid upside down on the table. Place some household cement on the inside of the lid. Next, stick some green plastic leaves (each about an inch long) into the cement. Let the cement dry.

Then, fill the baby food jar with water. Add one or two teaspoons of silver glitter to the water. Spread a thick layer of glue along the inside rim of the lid, and spread some more around the outside rim of the jar. Tightly screw the lid on the jar and allow the glue to dry, making the jar watertight.

Once the glue has dried, turn the jar upside down. Shake the jar to watch it ''snowing'' over the ''treetops.''

Confetti Snow. Cut out confetti pieces from white paper, or use plastic foam packing pieces for snow. Toss these into the air to create a snowfall effect.

Frosty Construction Paper Window. Draw a window on a sheet of construction paper. Spread glue on the windowpanes of your drawing. Sprinkle glitter on the glued areas and allow it to dry. Shake off the excess glitter and display.

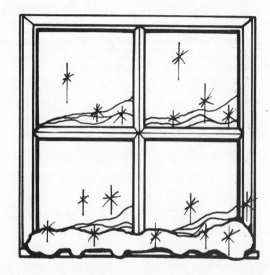

Glittery Snowflake. Cut out a paper snowflake. Then cover the snowflake with diluted glue. Sprinkle on glitter and shake off the excess. Display after the glue has dried.

Snow Scene. Make a three-dimensional snow scene using salt, rocks, and driftwood.

Soap Flake Snow. Pour just a little water into some soap flakes and beat with an eggbeater in a mixing bowl. (Ask an adult to help if needed.) Add flakes or water as necessary to make the snow thick (½ cup water to 1 cup soap flakes usually works). Thicker snow can be used like clay for shaping snowmen and other sculptures. Thinner snow can be used like finger paint to make excellent snow pictures.

Soapsuds Snow Picture. Using soapsuds, create a snow picture on gray or blue background paper.

Spatter-Painted Snowflake. First, cut out a big circle from black or blue construction paper. Fold the circle in half. Crease it along the fold, and then open up the circle.

Next, thin some white tempera paint by mixing it with some water. Dip a brush into the paint, and hold the brush over the paper circle. Carefully shake some of the paint onto the paper.

Finally, fold the circle again along the original crease. Press the two halves together firmly. Open once more to reveal a balanced snowflake design.

Sponge-Painted Snowstorm. On dark paper, use sponges dipped in white paint to create a snowstorm scene. Later, paste on snow figures cut out from other pieces of paper.

Tabletop Snow Scene. Cover the inside of a large gift box lid with cotton. Place a mirror in the middle of the cotton for a pond. Overlap the edges of the mirror with cotton so it looks like the snow is falling right to the edges of the pond.

Place small twigs and evergreen branches in the scene for trees. Make a marshmallow snowman and some playdough animals and other figures for the scene.

Torn-Paper Snow Pictures. Make snow pictures and scenes entirely from shapes torn from paper and paste them on background paper.

Wintry Night Resist Painting. Draw snowflakes or a snowman on a piece of white paper with white crayon. Press very hard as you draw. When the drawing is done, paint over it with black poster paint. The crayon will resist the paint, and the black color against the white crayon will create a wintry night effect.

Snow (Science)

Snow is actually frozen water vapor. Each snowflake that falls is different from all others, except that each has six sides or points. Snow can fall gently or come down as a snowstorm or a blizzard. Birds, animals, people, and machines leave tracks in the snow.

Melted snow turns back to water. But when snow is still moist, it sticks together and can be molded into balls and snowmen.

How Much Water Is in Snow? Go outside and put some snow in a glass measuring cup. Then go inside and mark the snow level on the outside of the cup. Allow the snow to melt in the cup. Then mark the water level in the cup and compare it to the original snow level. How much water was in the snow?

Melting Experiment. Take two equal-sized containers outside and put the same amount of snow in each one. Bring the containers inside. Evenly spread the snow from the first container over the entire surface of a 9-by-13-inch cake pan. Put the snow from the second container in a 9-by-13-inch pan also, but this time shape it into a tightly packed mound. Which container of snow melted faster? Why?

Snowflake Examination. When it is snowing, step outside with a magnifying glass and a sheet of black construction paper. Collect some snowflakes on the paper. Then look at the captured snowflakes through the magnifying glass. Study their shapes. What do you see?

Snowflakes Art

Paper Snowflake I. Fold over an 8½-by-11-inch sheet of white paper four times. Cut or tear away the corners, then unfold it. Paste the resulting snowflake on blue background paper.

Paper Snowflakes II. Cut out six-inch squares of white paper and fold each in half two times. Then cut out designs or shapes in the paper. Open up the flakes and glue them separately on eight-inch squares of colored paper.

Paper Snowflakes III. Cut circles from white paper, and fold them into fourths or eighths. Cut

Paper Snowflakes III

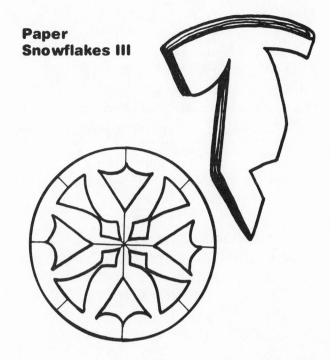

out small pieces from the area within the folds and open them to reveal snowflake patterns.

Snowmen

Chalk Snowmen. On blue or black construction paper, draw a snowman with chalk. Next dip a cotton ball into white dry tempera paint and pat this against the background paper to create a snowy effect around the snowman.

Circle Snowmen. Cut out circles and paste them in the shapes of snowmen on background paper. Glue on paper straws for arms. To make a frosted effect in the background, shred cotton into tiny pieces and glue onto the background paper.

Clay Snowmen. Using modeling clay or playdough, construct some snowmen. Decorate them with sticks, buttons, and bits of cloth.

Cotton Ball Snowman. Glue three cotton balls on top of each other to form a snowman.

Marshmallow Snowman. Stack three large-sized marshmallows on top of each other. Fasten them together by sticking a toothpick down the center of all three. Toothpicks also make good arms. Use a bottle cap for a hat. Draw a snowman face with a felt-tip marker.

Paper Bag Snowman. Stuff a white paper bag with crumpled newspaper, and close the bag at the top with staples. Tie a string around the middle, forming a snowman body and head. Glue on buttons and other objects, including paper cutouts, for the remaining features.

Papier Mâché Snowman. Crumple tissue paper into balls and cover each ball with paper towel strips dipped in diluted paste. Stack the balls on top of each other to form a snowman. When dry, paint the snowman white. Paint on facial features and other details as desired.

Paper Plate Snowman. Staple two or three paper plates together at the edges to form a snowman. For buttons, glue on some raisins in a vertical line on the body plate. Use buttons for eyes and a carrot square for a nose. Glue on raisins in the shape of a smiling mouth.

Paper Strip Snowmen. Cut out some white paper strips in various lengths. Glue together the ends of each strip to form rings. Use a larger ring for the bottom of each snowman and a smaller ring from each head. Glue the rings together to form snowmen. Add small straight strips for arms. Glue the snowmen upright on a piece of blue paper for display.

Popcorn Ball Snowmen. Mix some popped popcorn with melted butter and miniature marshmallows to make popcorn balls. (The directions are included on the back of most marshmallow bags.) Make large, medium, and small balls.

While the balls are still warm, stick the large, medium, and small balls on top of one another to form snowmen. Use toothpicks or Popsicle sticks for arms and gumdrops for buttons. Display for awhile or give as gifts. These snowmen are edible!

Popcorn Snowman on Paper. Draw an outline of a snowman on a sheet of heavy paper. Fill in the outline with glue. Then press popped popcorn over the glued areas to fill in the snowman.

Real Snowman. Make a real snowman outside in the snow. Roll a large ball of snow, then a medium ball, and a small one. Stack them on top of each other to form a snowman.

Use rocks or charcoal for eyes, a carrot for a nose, and pebbles for a mouth. Put an old hat on his head and wrap a scarf around his neck. Use sticks or branches for arms. Can you think of other ways to decorate him?

Sponge Snowman. On a sheet of paper, draw the outline of a snowman. Dab a small piece of sponge into thick tempera paint and fill in the snowman's outline. After the picture has dried, paint in the eyes, buttons, a scarf, and other details.

Tapioca Snowman. On a sheet of construction paper, lightly draw the outline of a snowman, using a pencil. Then paint the inside area of the snowman with glue. Shake pearl-shaped tapioca lightly over the glued areas. When dry, add details with scrap materials.

Snow Play

Birdseed Snow Designs. On a snowy day, take a bag of birdseed outside and sprinkle it on the snow, forming designs and pictures. When finished, leave the seeds for the birds to eat.

Cardboard Snow Sled. From a panel of corrugated cardboard, cut out a piece about the right size for your own sled. Curl up one end slightly for the nose of the sled, and then try it out!

Indoor Snow Play. If you cannot go out to play in the snow for some reason, then do the next best thing—bring some of the snow inside! Put some snow in various containers, and then play in the snow with measuring cups, spoons, pails, shovels, and spoons. To make things even more interesting, add a few drops of food coloring to the snow!

Monster Prints. Cut out monster footprints from cardboard. Poke holes in the footprints and loop strong cord through them so you can tie the footprint pieces to your feet. Go outside and make monster prints in the snow. See what your friends think when you show them monster tracks around your house!

Snow Angels. Lie down on your back in the snow. Place your arms straight out from your body and rest them in the snow. Then wave your arms back and forth over the snow, making angel wing patterns. Get up carefully so you do not destroy the angel print you made in the snow.

Snow Ice Cream. With an eggbeater, mix 1 beaten egg, 1 cup creamy milk, ½ cup sugar, 1 teaspoon vanilla, and a pinch of salt in a large bowl. Ask an adult to help you if necessary.

Go outside with another large bowl and col-

lect about half a bowl of clean, freshly fallen snow. Add the snow to the bowl of ingredients and stir well. Enjoy it!

Snow Print Tracking Game. This is a fun game you can play with several of your friends. First, each of you place a snack in a plastic bag and wrap it up tightly.

Now go out into the snow. Each of you start at the same point, but go in different directions. Leave a footprint path behind you in the snow. Go around trees, under fences, and over sandboxes, making your trail as interesting as possible. When you find a good ending spot, bury your snack bag right there in the snow. Then turn around and step into your own footprints as you walk back to the starting point.

When each person has returned, trade trails and follow someone else's path until you find the buried treat!

Snowball Target. You need an old sheet and a clothesline to play this game. Indoors, make a large target by drawing some large circles inside each other on the sheet, using permanent felt-tip pens. When finished, carry the sheet outdoors and attach it to a clothesline so it hangs with the target facing you. Now throw snowballs at the target, scoring points for hitting the different circles.

Tree Branch Snowstorm. Take ahold of a low tree branch that is covered with snow. Shake the branch and watch your own miniature snowstorm fall underneath it!

Sounds (Science)

"Seeing" Sound Vibrations. Place a handful of sand on the head of a drum. Strike the drum head sharply with your fingers, and see the sand jump to the vibrations of the drum head!

Sounds Are Waves. Did you know that sounds are actually vibration waves in the air? To better understand this, drop a small object into a bathtub full of water. Watch the circular waves spread outward from where the disturbance took place. This is just the way sound waves travel when the air is disturbed! One difference is we cannot see the waves in the air. *Another way to do it:* Strike a tuning fork so it vibrates and then stick the fork in water to create waves.

Sound Through Wood. Hold a watch as far away from your ear as you can and listen. Then put the watch on a wooden table. Place an ear on the table, and see if you can hear the watch ticking. Then move as far from the watch as possible and put your ear on the table again. Can you still hear the watch?

You can hear the watch more easily on the table because sounds travel better through wood than they do through air!

Tuning Fork Experience. See if you can obtain a tuning fork. Rap it on a hard surface and listen for the sound it makes. Then, rap the fork again and quickly stick it into a tub of water. Notice how the tuning fork makes vibration waves in the water.

A tuning fork makes similar vibrations in the air, but we cannot see the air vibrations. Our ears, however, react to the air vibrations, allowing us to hear the sounds produced.

Vibrations Make Sounds. Vibrations in the air create sounds. There are many different ways to demonstrate this. Pull a grass blade tightly between your fingers and blow across the blade to make it vibrate. What kind of sound does it make?

Place a yardstick near the edge of a table so one end is sticking out over the edge. Pull down on the extended end, then release while still pressing the other end firmly against the table. This allows the free end of the yardstick to vibrate. Watch the vibrating motion and listen to the sounds produced.

Pound a nail into each end of a two-foot-long board. (Ask an adult to help you.) Stretch a heavy rubber band between the two spikes. Pluck the

rubber band and watch it vibrate, producing a sound. Then pluck the rubber band again, and quickly stop the vibrations. The vibrations will be felt through the board and nails!

Voice Funnel. Roll a piece of paper into a funnel. Now talk through it. Does your voice sound louder? That is because the funnel transmits the sounds in only one direction instead of many.

Voice Sounds. Remember, sounds are created by vibrations! With that in mind, hold your hand over your throat and talk. Feel the vibrations produced by your talking?

Spiders
(See also Halloween section for additional spiders.)

Eggcup Spider. Cut a single cup from a cardboard egg carton. Paint it black. Punch holes on each side of the cup. Insert pipe cleaner legs into each hole on one side and thread them through the opposite holes on the other side. Bend down the pipe cleaners on the outside ends to complete the legs. Paint a face on the front of the eggcup to finish.

Plastic Foam Spider. Obtain a plastic foam ball and a plastic foam cone. Cut off one inch or so from the pointed end of the cone. Glue the ball to this flattened end. Lay the pieces down sideways to represent the head and body of the spider. Attach pipe cleaners along each side of the cone, and bend them into spider legs. Stick toothpicks into the head for antennae. Poke beaded pins into the face for eyes. Glue on paper cutouts for other features.

Spider Web. On a piece of cardboard, place thumbtacks in various locations to use as posts in forming your spider web. Wrap yarn around the thumbtacks in a webbed pattern. Then, using a circle cut from black paper, along with pipe cleaner pieces for legs, make a spider to put in the web.

Spider Web

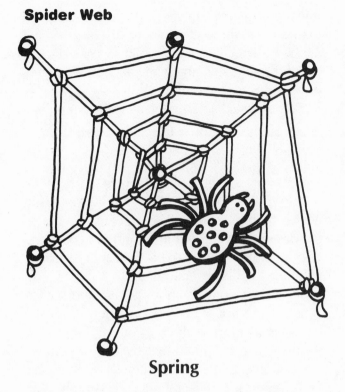

Spring

Art Show. Make paintings and drawings of a springtime scene or subject. Ask your friends to join in, making drawings and paintings on their own. Then string a clothesline across the room low enough for everyone to reach.

Ask all the participants to put their names on their pieces of art. Then hang the pictures and drawings on the clothesline for display. Have a show, letting everyone admire the artwork!

Baby Oval Animals. Cut out ovals from colored paper. Then paste the ovals on background paper. Turn each oval into a baby animal by adding eyes, wings, bills, tails, and feet with felt-tip markers. Chicks, squirrels, ducklings, birds, and butterflies are good animals to start with.

Chicken Wire Tissue Scene. Beforehand, staple a large rectangle of chicken wire to a wooden frame of the same size and shape. Have an adult help you with this part if necessary.

Then, weave an outline of a peach tree, grass, and sky on the chicken wire. Next cut four-inch squares of tissue paper in various shades of green, pink, blue, white, and brown. Push the middle of these squares partially into the holes of the chicken wire to fill in the scene. Use green for grass and tree leaves, brown for the tree trunk, shades of pink and white for tree blossoms, and blue and white for the sky.

If you want, invite your friends to help you, and complete this as a group project. Hang for display when finished. Later, use this method for making other scenes.

Cotton Paste-up Art. Paste cotton and cotton balls on background paper to form bunnies, lambs, and clouds.

Crayon Rubbing Spring Scene. From paper, cut out flowers and place them underneath another sheet of paper. Using crayons that have had their wrappers removed, gently rub over the top paper with the flat sides of the crayons. This will create impressions of the cutouts underneath.

Use other spring cutouts, such as birds and butterflies, to add to the scene.

Cut and Paste Collage. Cut out pictures of springtime symbols and scenes from old greeting cards, flower and seed catalogs, and magazines. Paste them all together on background paper to form a collage.

Finger-Painted Mural. Make pastel finger paint by mixing white tempera paint with a dark-colored tempera paint. Then finger-paint the sky, the grass, and a stream or lake on the paper. Finish by adding painted or pasted flowers and the sun to the scene.

Hand-Wing Butterfly. Fold a 9-by-12-inch sheet of bright construction paper in half to form a double-thick 6-by-9-inch rectangle. Place your hand on the rectangle so the base of your palm rests over the folded edge of the paper. Using a dark crayon, trace around your hand with the fingers tight together and thumb extended, as illustrated.

Hand-Wing Butterfly

Then cut out the hand outline and unfold it to reveal the wings of a butterfly. Set this piece aside.

Next roll a 6-by-9-inch piece of black construction paper into a tight tube. Staple it quickly to keep it from unrolling. Glue the wing piece to the tube body and glue pipe cleaner antennae at one end.

Rainy Day Cut and Paste Scene. Gather some plastic sandwich bags, some clothing catalogs, pipe cleaners, paper baking cups, some pink and green strips of tissue paper, and a 12-by-18-inch sheet of construction paper.

Cut out pictures of people from the clothing catalogs and glue them on the sheet of construction paper. Using the plastic sandwich bags, cut out raincoats to fit the people and glue them over the people.

Make umbrellas for the people by cutting the paper baking cups in half, and make handles from pipe cleaners. Glue the umbrellas into position on the construction paper.

Use construction paper scraps to cut out trees and bushes, using the pink and green tissue paper strips for blossoms.

If more detail is desired, use wallpaper pieces for houses and sandpaper pieces for sidewalks. Draw falling rain on the scene.

Shiny Paint Spring Storm Picture. Ahead of time, prepare shiny paint by mixing one part white liquid glue with one part tempera paint of the desired color. Store in an airtight container until ready to use. Make a container of shiny paint for each color you need.

On paper, draw a stormy springtime scene. When the picture is complete, paint over it with the desired colors of shiny paint.

You can make raindrops by dripping shiny paint from a toothpick. Gray clouds are made by first rubbing a lead pencil on a separate sheet of paper and then rolling cotton balls back and forth over the pencil markings to absorb the gray color. Shape the cotton balls into clouds and paste them on the picture.

Be sure not to touch the painting until it has dried. When it does dry, it will present a wet, rainy look. Be sure all the paint is used soon after the containers are opened.

Shoe Box Diorama. Using a shoe box for a display case, create a springtime scene inside. Place blue construction paper in the background for the sky and green along the bottom for grass. Paste in cutouts of children, trees, flowers, etc., in upright positions so they stand up to make a three-dimensional diorama.

Sponge-Painted Blossoms. Draw some tree trunks on paper with crayons. Then dip one sponge into pink paint and another into green paint. Sponge paint the colors on the tree branches to represent blossoms and leaves.

Spring Lambs. Cut out lamb shapes from thin cardboard. Then cover the lambs with tufts of cotton or short white yarn, using glue to hold on the materials.

Spring Plants Collage. Collect various kinds of spring growth, including seeds, twigs, soft maple and elm pods, and leaves. Glue together into a collage on background paper.

Springtime Clothesline. On paper, draw two posts at opposite ends. Then glue a length of string between the two posts for a clothesline. Glue tiny pieces of cloth to the string to represent clothes hanging in the springtime breezes.

Springtime Spray Painting. On paper, outline a bird, a birdhouse, flowers, butterflies, and other springtime symbols. Cut them out and lay them on a 9-by-12-inch sheet of white paper. Completely spray over the layout with thinned tempera paint, using a garden sprayer. Allow to dry. Then remove the loose cutouts. Color in the portions underneath that remained white.

Umbrella Picture. Cut a number of flattened paper baking cups in half to represent umbrella tops. Glue them randomly to a sheet of construction paper. For handles, glue on pipe cleaners or draw them in with crayons. Draw or paint falling raindrops over the entire picture.

St. Patrick's Day

Collage Shamrock. Cut a shamrock from green construction paper. From other shades of green paper, cut out squares and strips. Glue the squares and strips all over the shamrock. Place them close together and curl up the ends of the pieces so they stand out.

Color Collage. Using green and white construction paper, make a formless collage by cutting or tearing the paper into pieces and pasting them together randomly on background paper.

Glittery Shamrock. Cut out a shamrock shape from green construction paper. Cover it with glue and then sprinkle glitter over the glued area. Allow it to dry and shake off the excess glitter.

Green Finger Painting. Make a painting using green finger paint. Allow it to dry, then paste on green and white paper figures.

Green Vegetable Treat. Fix a special St. Patrick's Day snack using only green vegetables, such as lettuce, cabbage, cucumbers, avocados, bell peppers, and zucchini. Serve with a lime drink or a shamrock milk shake.

Heart Shamrock. Cut out three green hearts of equal size. Glue them point to point on a sheet of background paper to form a shamrock. Draw on a stem to complete.

Irish Jig. Celebrate St. Patrick's Day by dancing your own Irish jig! Hop on one foot, kicking the other foot out and across the hopping foot. Bring your kicking foot back and reverse your feet to repeat the step. Dance the jig to lively music.

McNamara's Band. You and your friends can create McNamara's Band using cardboard tube horns and juice can shakers decorated with green paper streamers. *(See Music section for creating additional homemade instruments.)*

Paper Plate Decoration.   Paint a paper plate green. When it dries, paste on a white doily. Then paste on some shamrock seals. Thread a green ribbon through the plate and hang it.

Potato Heads.   There is nothing more Irish than a potato! So why not celebrate St. Patrick's Day by making a potato head? To start, collect some buttons, beads, sequins, pins, ribbons, and scraps of felt, yarn, paper, and a potato.

Be sure to wash and dry the potato ahead of time. Then, make a face on the potato using the items you gathered. Display the finished potato head in a paper cup or on a ring cut from a cardboard tube.

Pot O' Gold.   Cut a paper plate in half to form two half circles. Paint one half circle black for a pot. Then paint some very small pebbles gold and glue them along the top of the pot to represent the gold in the pot.

For a rainbow, cut out the outer rim from the second half circle and paint it with rainbow colors. Glue one end of the rainbow to the top of the pot, then glue the whole assemblage on background paper.

Shamrock Face.   Cut a shamrock from green paper. For facial features, glue on pieces of paper, felt, and other materials. If you want, draw freckles and add a paper hat to the top.

Shamrock Headband.   Cut a paper strip to fit around your head. Then cut out a shamrock from green paper and glue it to the front of the headband. Wear it to be a member of McNamara's Band or simply to celebrate the holiday.

Shamrock Shakes.   With adult supervision, place 1 scoop of vanilla ice cream, 1 cup of milk, and 2 drops of green food coloring in a blender. Put on the lid and blend until smooth. Pour into a glass and serve. (You can add ¼ teaspoon of peppermint flavoring to make a mint shake.)

Stabiles

Clay Stabile.   Shape a ball from a chunk of clay or playdough. This will be the base for your stabile.

There are many things you can stick into the base—pipe cleaners, ice cream sticks, meat skewers, plastic utensils, and straws. Look for other things around the house to use. When you are ready to build, stick these items into the base. Then stick balls of clay on top of them, and build the construction upward by sticking other connecting pieces into these balls of clay. If you want, use bits of felt or paper to decorate the stabile.

Construction Stabile.   Stack different materials, using such things as foam rubber, wire,

Pot O' Gold

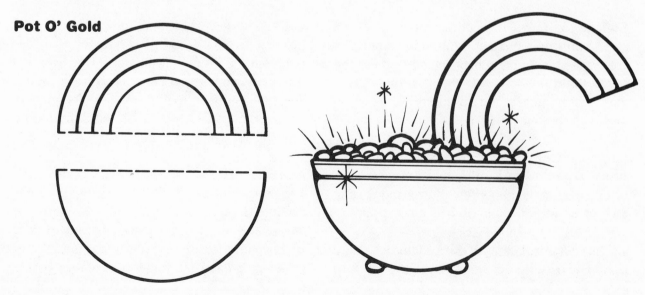

spools, pipe cleaners, cardboard tubes, candy papers, plastic vegetable baskets, straws, and pieces of cardboard. Use tape to hold the stabile parts together.

Plastic Foam Constructions. For this project, you need the stiff kind of plastic foam not the kind used for packaging. Cut the plastic foam into small squares and rectangles. Use pointed toothpicks to stick the plastic foam pieces together. Constructing in this manner, you can make silly animals, cars, buildings, or practically anything else.

When you are finished building, you can take apart the structures and save the pieces for another time.

Static Electricity (Science)

On a cold, dry day, walk across a rug, dragging your feet. Then touch someone. Did you get shocked? Next, hold a piece of paper in your hand while you shuffle across a rug. Hold the paper against a wall and let it go. It sticks to the wall!

These things are caused by static electricity. Following are some more interesting stunts and demonstrations you can do using the strange powers of static electricity!

Bending Water. Charge a plastic comb with static electricity by combing it through your hair briskly or rubbing the comb with a piece of wool. Hold the charged comb near some running tap water, and watch the water bend toward the comb!

Dancing Tissues. Cut a piece of tissue paper into about 15 tiny pieces. Put them in a metal pie pan. Cover the pie pan with a piece of glass. Rub as fast as you can over the glass with a silk or nylon cloth. By doing this, you are charging the glass with an electric field!

Now look at the pieces of tissue paper "dancing" around inside! They "dance" because they are being attracted by the electric field.

Magic Balloon. Inflate a balloon and then rub it against your clothing or hair. Touch the balloon to a wall and let it go. What happens?

Sparking Hair. Darken the room. Stand in front of a mirror and rapidly comb your hair to see the electric sparks.

Static Box. Look around the house for a small plastic box with a lid. Put a handful of puffed rice and some bits of tissue paper in the box. (If you want, you can cut the tissue bits into bug or doll shapes.) Put the lid on, then rapidly rub the lid with your hand or a piece of wool. Watch the objects in the box "dance" and cling to the lid!

Swinging Rice. Thead a single puffed rice on a silk thread. Suspend the thread from a small stick or rod and allow it to dangle.

Next, rub a plastic comb with a piece of wool or run it through your hair six or seven times to charge it. Hold the comb near the hanging rice, and watch the rice swing toward the comb!

Stunts

Beans on Your Head. Sit on the floor with a bowl of dry beans in front of you. Place a foil pie plate on your head and see how many beans you can spoon into the pie plate without knocking the plate off your head!

Book Balancing. Place a book on your head. See how far you can walk without dropping the book.

Helpless Hands. Lie down on the floor and cross your arms over your chest. Now, try getting up without using your hands, arms, or elbows!

Knotty Problem. Tie a knot using only one hand!

Mirror Magic. Place a piece of paper in front of a hand mirror. Then try writing your name or drawing a simple picture on the paper while looking only at the paper's reflection in the mirror!

Nosey Business.   Standing on one foot only, bend over and try to touch the floor with your nose!

Pencil Pick-up.   Pick up a pencil with the toes of one foot.

Pretzel Step.   Link your hands together in front of you. Now try to lift both feet through them one at a time while you keep the hands linked.

Pull the Pin.   Place a pin inside a glass. Hold a magnet to the outside bottom edge of the glass so it attracts the pin. Raise the magnet along the outside of the glass to see if you can pull up the pin along the inside without dropping it!

Talented Teeth.   Hold a pencil with your teeth and then write your name or draw a simple picture on a piece of paper.

Wacky Blindfold Drawing.   Place a pencil and a piece of paper in front of you. Ask someone to blindfold you. Try drawing a picture of a house, including windows, a door, and a chimney, while you are blindfolded. When finished, remove the blindfold. How wacky is your draw-

ing? Have your friends try this, also. Soon you will have quite a collection of crazy drawings!

Summer

Barefoot Texture Painting.   Lay a long piece of butcher paper or brown wrapping paper on the sidewalk outdoors. Set a rock on each corner to hold down the paper if necessary. At one end place a tray containing some liquid tempera paint. Then remove your shoes and socks.

Step barefooted in the paint, then step on some sand or dirt next to the paper. From there, step on the paper and tiptoe or walk all over it. This results in an unusual "textured" footprint painting! Be sure to wash off your feet before going indoors.

Barefoot Walk.   Go on a barefoot walk in an area free of sharp rocks, nails, or other harmful items! Feel the cool grass under your feet or the warmth of a smooth sidewalk. Walk on some sand, step into some mud, or walk through some crunchy leaves. What other fun sensations will your feet discover?

Cardboard Fan.   Cut out an 8-by-7-inch fan shape from a piece of thin cardboard. Then, if you want, shape it into a leaf, a flower, a circle, etc.

Pick out a magazine picture and glue it to one side of the fan. After the glue has dried, staple a tongue depressor to the fan so at least four inches extend over the edge—to make a handle.

Country Scene.   Finger-paint on a long sheet of glossy shelf paper, making a summertime country scene. Use blue paint for the sky and green paint for the mountains and the grass. Then, from colored paper, draw and cut out trees, animals, and other figures to paste on your finger painted background.

Duck Pond Visit.   Plan a trip to a local duck pond, and be sure to take along plenty of bread crumbs to feed the ducks! Remember that the ducks are your friends, so do not tease or frighten them. After your trip, read a book about ducks.

Iced Drink Stand.   You can make some money in the hot weather by setting up an iced drink stand. Find a small table or strong box and set it up outside your house or on a nearby street corner.

Ask an adult to help you prepare the drinks. You can serve lemonade, fruit punch, iced tea, or other drinks. Put the drink and some ice cubes into a large vacuum bottle to keep the drink cold.

Set the bottle and plastic foam or paper cups on your table. Make a sign advertising your prices and tape it to your table. Use an empty cardboard box for a trash can and place it under the table. Put a few pennies, nickels, and dimes in a small box so you can make change. Now you are ready for business!

Painting with Water.   On a hot summer day, obtain a large house-painting brush. Go outside with a bucket of water and "paint" with the water! You can paint your house, a fence, the garage, the sidewalk, and even your car! It is fun, and there is no mess afterward!

Paper Fan.   Fold a rectangle of colored construction paper accordion-style. When completely folded staple it at one end. Open the other end to form a fan that is ready to use!

Picnic.   With the help of an adult, plan a picnic for the park, the beach, or even your own backyard. Decide what kind of food to take, then pack it in a basket or bag. Take along a ball, a Frisbee, or a book so you can have fun before and after your picnic lunch.

Plastic Fan.   From a well-rinsed gallon-sized plastic bleach bottle, cut out a large fan. Flatten the fan by covering it with a towel and ironing the towel with a warm iron. While the plastic is still warm, set it under a heavy book so it will cool into a flattened shape. Then it is ready to use!

Cardboard Fan

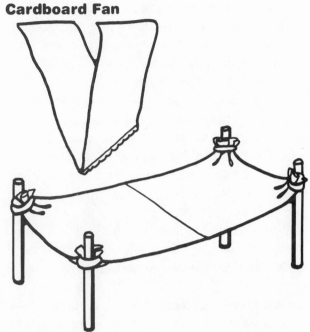

Plastic Shade Canopy.   Tear a large plastic trash can bag along the seams on each side. Then find four sticks of nearly equal lengths. Tie a stick to each corner of the plastic bag, and place the free end of each stick firmly into the ground. Now you have a shady place to rest for sunny summer days!

Sandy Tempera Painting.   Add a little sand to some liquid tempera paint. Then paint a scene of your favorite summertime activity. The finished picture will have a grainy texture.

Sidewalk Mural.   With colored chalk, draw a mural on the sidewalk outdoors. Make a sunny day scene, a seashore picture, or a vacation picture. If you want to make the mural a little different, wet the sidewalk before drawing with the chalk. *Another way to do it:* Use mud instead of chalk when drawing your mural!

Summer Snowballs.   For this you have to plan ahead and make your snowballs in the winter when it snows. Wrap the snowballs in plastic bags and save them in the freezer.

In the summer, surprise everyone and bring out the snowballs for an exciting summertime snowball target game!

Summer Thunderstorm. A summer thunderstorm offers you the chance to watch thunder, lightning, high winds, hail, and heavy rain. After all, this kind of weather is just as much a part of summertime as the sunshine!

You need not be afraid of thunderstorms. Simply stay in the safety of your front porch to observe them, or watch from inside your house.

Collect some hailstones that have fallen to the ground. Look at them closely and compare their sizes. Cut one open to see what it looks like inside. Read a book that explains thunderstorms and how hail is formed.

Notice how the rain washes off the streets and sidewalks and cleans and cools the air.

Summertime Collage. Make a summertime collage of summer subjects clipped from pictures in magazines, catalogs, posters, and travel brochures. Look for pictures showing water play, picnics, camping, vacation trips, boats, beaches, baseball and sunshine. Glue the pictures together into a collage on background paper.

Sun Picture. Draw a sky on paper with blue crayons. Then paste a gold seal on the picture to represent the sun.

Sunshine Picture. For this you need some white, orange, and yellow paint. Drop blobs of each color on a sheet of construction paper. With a brush, an old feather duster or a cotton swab, spread the colors around to form a painting of the sun.

Vacation Objects. Search through magazines for pictures of objects you might take with you on a vacation. Cut out the pictures and paste them on a sheet of paper. Talk to an adult or a friend about the objects and why you would take them along on a vacation.

Vacation Time Trip Pictures. Look through magazines and travel brochures for pictures of places you would like to visit on a vacation. Cut out the pictures and paste them into a spiral notebook to make a "wish book" of places you would like to visit.

Some travel magazines have ads in the back telling you where to write to get free travel brochures. Sometimes it is fun to send for these and have your own collection of travel brochures!

Watermelon Picture. Cut out a large circle from green construction paper. Then cut out a slightly smaller circle from red construction paper. Glue the red circle on the green one and then glue some dried watermelon seeds (saved from your last watermelon snack) on the red circle.

Swings

Gunny Sack Swing. Fill an old gunny sack with straw. Tie a piece of strong rope tightly around the top end of the gunny sack. Then hang the sack from a tree branch. (Ask an adult to help you.) Grasp the rope right above the gunny sack, wrap yourself around the sack, and swing away!

Rope Swing. Tie knots at various points near one end of a strong piece of rope. Hang the rope from a tree branch so the knotted parts are nearest the free end. (Have an adult help you.) Cling to the knots as you swing, swirl, and whirl on the rope!

Tire Swing. Tie a strong piece of rope around an old tire and hang it from a tree branch. (Have an adult help you.) Make sure the tire hangs close enough to the ground so you can climb onto it. Sit inside the tire and start swinging!

Telephones

Hose Telephone. Find an old garden hose to use in making this tube-type telephone. Tape over any holes or cuts in the hose. Then cut off the metal couplings at each end. (If necessary, have an adult help you.)

Stick a metal or plastic funnel into each end of the hose. Now you and a friend can talk and listen to each other through the hose telephone. (The tube does not have to be straight to work. You can bend it around corners as much as you want as long as you do not pinch the hose shut at any point.)

Tin Can Telephone. Obtain two equal-sized tin cans that are open at one end and closed at the other. Make sure they are clean and that any rough edges are smoothed down with sandpaper. (Ask an adult to help you.)

Drill or poke a small hole in the center of each bottom lid. Then obtain a length of twine about five or six feet long. Poke each end of the twine through the hole at the end of a can, going through from the outside to the inside. Tie a knot at each end, inside the can, so the cans are hooked onto the ends of the twine and cannot slide off.

Now, pick up one can and have a friend pick up the other can. Stretch the twine between the two cans so it becomes taut. You can talk and listen to each other through the cans. Your voice will vibrate along the twine as long as it is stretched tightly between the cans!

Televisions

"Changing Pictures" Television. Cut out pictures from magazines. Then find a large box and cut a hole shaped like a television picture in front. Next, find two round rods that are long enough to extend two inches beyond each side of the box.

Paste the pictures you cut out on a long roll of shelf paper. Use masking tape to fasten the ends of the roll of paper to the rods. Insert the paper roll through the slots cut on the sides of the box so you can roll the pictures behind the picture hole.

Furniture Box Television. Find a tall cardboard furniture box and cut a TV screen hole in the front. Cut the hole so that when you stand inside the box, your head and shoulders show through the screen hole.

Glue on some wooden knobs below the screen to represent the controls. Then cut away part of the side panel so you can step in and out of the television box.

Now you can step into the TV and playact a TV show behind the screen. To others who are watching it looks like you are on TV! Also, you can crouch down below the hole and hold up hand puppets behind the screen to act out stories and skits.

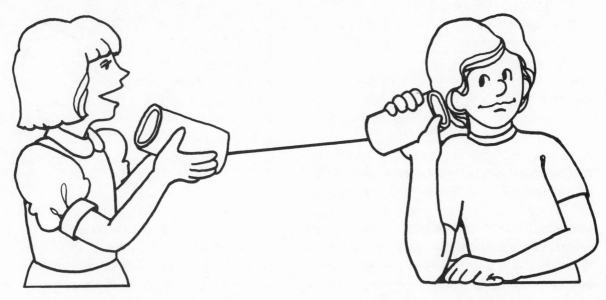

Milk Carton Television.   Cut off the top from a half-gallon milk carton. Turn it over so the bottom is on top.

Add some liquid detergent to paint, and paint the carton to look like a television. (The liquid detergent helps the paint stick to the waxy milk carton.)

When the paint has dried, cut a television screen hole in the front of the carton. Reach inside the carton and paste a picture to the inside of the screen so the picture shows through the screen hole. Paint dials and knobs on the front of the TV. Glue pipe cleaner antennae to the top.

Wiggly Picture Television.   Cut off the lid and top flaps from a light bulb box. Turn it over so the solid bottom is on top. Paint the box to look like a television.

After the paint has dried, cut out a small television screen hole on the front of the box. To the inside of the screen hole, glue a small wiggly picture (available from variety stores) so it shows through the screen hole like a television picture.

Now you have a miniature television with a "moving" picture!

Wrapping Paper Television.   On a large sheet of brown wrapping paper draw a large outline of a television screen. Also draw on the knobs and dials that would appear on the front of a TV. Then cut out the screen part.

Hang the paper from the edge of a table, fastening it to the top of the table with tape. Now you can sit under the table with your face showing through the screen hole and entertain your friends with your own television show!

Tents

Clothesline Tent.   Go outside and overlap two old blankets or sheets across the top of a clothesline. Fasten the blankets along the clothesline with clothespins or safety pins. Hold down the bottom edges of the tent blankets to the ground with rocks. Or tie the blanket corners to stakes pounded into the ground.

Clothesline Tent II.   Ask an adult to sew several old sheets or blankets together. Place the sheets over two parallel clotheslines to form the roof and sides of your tent.

Tree-Tie Tent.   An adult might have to help you with this project. Loop a length of rope around a tree and tie it above a low branch. With the free end of the rope, walk six paces away and fasten the rope to the ground. The best way to do that is by tying the rope to a peg that is stuck in the ground.

For the tent itself, use canvas if you can because it keeps out the rain. Otherwise, an old sheet will do. Fold the material into a triangle and lay it over the rope to make the tent. If needed, tie down the three corners with pegs.

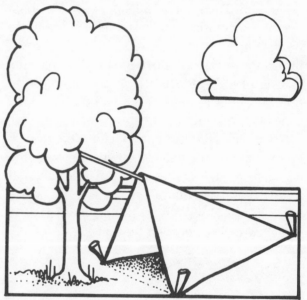

Umbrella Tent.   Open an old umbrella and stick the handle firmly into the ground so the umbrella stands up by itself. Drape an old sheet or blanket over the umbrella to form a small tent.

Terrariums

Jar Terrarium.   Make a terrarium for turtles, lizards, and snakes by laying a clear, gallon jar on its side. Remove the lid and insert a layer of charcoal. Then cover that with sand or soil. Plant some small succulents, ferns or moss inside.

Jar Terrarium

Prop up the jar slightly at the open end. Punch some air holes in the lid, and if you want, place a lizard, or a turtle, inside. Place the lid back on the jar.

Water the plants from time to time and feed your animals as required.

Miniature Terrarium. To make a miniature terrarium, use two disposable plastic drinking glasses that are short and wide. Put your terrarium contents into one of the glasses.

Go on a woodland walk to look for moss, lichen, tiny pebbles, twigs, acorns, and small low-growing plants to put in the terrarium. Carry a pail to collect these treasures and take them home.

Place a layer of pebbles in the bottom of the terrarium. Add a layer of charcoal. (Crush a piece from your fireplace or barbeque.) Then put down a layer of soil and arrange the items from your pail inside the terrarium. Moisten them with water.

To finish, turn the other drinking glass upside down, place it over the terrarium glass, and tape the two glasses together. Water the terrarium occasionally, and it will last a long time!

Thanksgiving

Activities and Art

Cut and Paste Fruit Basket. Draw and color a fruit basket on paper and then cut it out. Next, draw various fruits and vegetables and cut them out. Glue the basket on background paper and glue on the frui and vegetables so they appear to be in the basket.

Cut and Paste Scene. On separate pieces of paper, draw Pilgrims and Indians. Then cut them out. On mural paper, draw a woodlands scene including trees, grass, wild turkeys, etc. Then paste the Pilgrims and Indians in the scene.

Dinner Setting. Color or paint some paper plates in autumn colors. Then paste pictures of food on the plates (turkey, corn, potatoes, cranberries, etc.). Make placemats from the cardboard that comes with shirts from the store or laundry. Paste construction paper leaves on the mats for decoration.

"Happiness Is" Collage. Look through some old magazines for pictures of things that make you happy and for which you are thankful. Cut out the pictures and glue them together on background paper to make a collage.

Playacting. Act out your own Thanksgiving dramas, including such activities as a Thanksgiving feast, an Indian dance, the harvesting of some crops, pretending to be Pilgrim children and Indian braves, or wild turkeys.

Thankful Hands. Fold a piece of construction paper in half and set it in front of you. Place your hand over the paper so your wrist sticks over the folded edge. Then trace around your hand.

Remove your hand and poke a hole through the wrist area of the outline through both thicknesses of paper. Tie a piece of yarn through the holes, then cut out the hands. Now you have two thankful hands that are linked together!

Open the hands slightly and draw a picture of something you are thankful for on the inside of each hand.

Thank-You Book. Stack some 12-by-18-inch sheets of newsprint on top of each other, then fold them to form a book. Staple them together along the crease to hold the book together.

Then, flip through magazines to find pictures of things you are thankful for, such as food, a home, clothing, parents, etc. Cut out the pictures and paste them into your "thank-you book."

Woven-Look Placemats. Using brown paper or paper towels, draw parallel lines across the paper the long way using a variety of colors. (These lines represent the yarn used by the Pilgrims.) Next, turn the paper and draw parallel lines across the paper the short way, again using various colors to draw the lines. This will create a woven effect on the paper!

If you want, you can cut fringes around the edges of the placemat. Repeat the whole process to make as many placemats as you want.

Pilgrims
Construction Paper Pilgrims and Indians.
Paste together the ends of construction paper pieces to form cylinders. Stand each cylinder on end and paint a face on one side to represent a Pilgrim or an Indian. Add paper strips for hair or feathers, and make construction paper hats if you want.

Paper Bag Pilgrim Heads. Stuff a small sack with crumpled newspaper and tie it closed at the end. Turn it over so the tied end is on the bottom. Paint on eyes, a nose, and a mouth, and paint the bottom of the sack white to make a collar. Make a Pilgrim's hat with a black square and a long rectangle. Paste it above the forehead.

Paper Cone Pilgrim. Obtain a sheet of black construction paper, two pink paper circles (2 inches wide), and some scrap paper. On the black paper, draw a circle that is about eight inches across. Then cut the circle in half. Form each half circle into a cone for two Pilgrim bodies. Staple the cones to hold them in place.

Make a face on each pink circle. Glue the faces to the cones. Use the scrap paper to make features such as collars, belts, aprons, etc. Paste the features on the cones.

If the Pilgrim is supposed to be a boy, cut a small doughnut shape from black paper and slip it over the top of the cone for a hat. If the Pilgrim is supposed to be a girl, make the hat from white paper.

Pilgrim Collar. Using white butcher paper, cut out a Pilgrim's collar as illustrated. Wear it when playacting Thanksgiving stories.

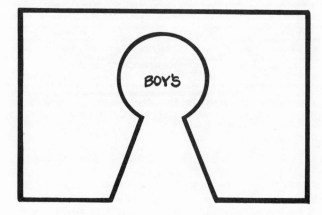

Pilgrim Hat (Boy's). From black construction paper, cut a doughnut-shaped brim to fit around your head. Then, from white construction paper, cut out a strip six to eight inches wide for a hatband that is also long enough to fit around your head.

Next, join the ends of a sheet of black construction paper to form a cylinder. Adjust the size of the cylinder so it fits around your head. Attach the brim piece to the bottom of the cylinder, and glue the white hatband around the cylinder, several inches up from the brim. From yellow paper, cut out a buckle and glue it on the front of the hat over the hatband. It is ready to wear!

Pilgrim Boy's Hat

Pilgrim Girl's Hat

Pilgrim Hat (Girl's). Cut an empty laundry detergent box in half across the middle. Keep the half with the solid end. Paint it white or cover it with pieces of white construction paper cut to fit.

Set the box in front of you with the solid end on top. Staple or tie a length of yarn from each side of the box, near the bottom, for ties. Place the hat on your head and tie the yarn under your chin so the hat will stay in place.

Turkeys

Circle Turkey. On a piece of brown construction paper, draw two circles. Make one circle about five inches across, and the other about three inches across. Cut out both circles. The small circle will be the front of the turkey's body and the large circle the back.

Next, accordion-pleat a short strip of brown paper. Glue one end of the pleated piece to the center of the large circle and the other end to the center of the small circle. Now the circles are

linked together by the pleates strip! Lay the whole piece in front of you so the small circle is above the large one.

From scrap paper, make the turkey's head and neck, and glue them on the front, smaller circle. Notice that the front circle jiggles when tapped!

Cut out colored paper feathers and glue them along the top edge of the back circle. Or attach clothespins to represent feathers.

Circle Turkey

Cut and Paste Circle Turkey. Cut out four circles from colored paper, each circle slightly larger than the other. Glue the circles together on top of each other, starting with the largest circle on the bottom and ending with the smallest circle on top. As you glue them above each other, place each circle off-center to the right of the circle below.

When all the circles are glued together, cut fringes along the outside edges of the bottom circle. The fringes represent feathers. If you want, curl the fringes for added effect.

From scrap paper, cut out eyes, a beak, and a wattle, and glue them on the small circle for a face. Paste the turkey on background paper and draw in legs underneath.

Handprint Turkey. Place your hand on a sheet of paper. Spread your fingers apart and trace around your hand, fingers, and thumb with a crayon. Now you have the outline of a turkey!

Turn the thumb part of the outline into a turkey head by drawing in an eye, a beak, and a wattle, Draw on the feet and draw feathers in the finger parts of the outline.

Paper Sack Turkey. Stuff the bottom of a small brown paper sack with crumpled newspaper. Tie the bag closed about halfway up. Shape the open end of the bag into a tail. Color in feather details. Use the bottom of the bag as the head end of the turkey. Glue or tape on a head cut out from paper.

Pinecone Turkey. Obtain a pinecone and three pipe cleaners. Form one pipe cleaner into a neck and head piece, and glue it to the narrow end of the pinecone. Bend the other two pipe cleaners into feet and attach them to the underside of the pinecone body. If you want, tape the feet to a coardboard base to help the turkey stand up.

Pleated Turkey. To make a front view of a turkey, cut out a large circle of brown paper for the body. To make the head, cut out a rectangle and round it off at one end. Glue the head piece to the body circle just above the center.

For feathers, cut out long rectangles. Pleat each rectangle accordion-style, and attach them around the top edges of the body circle. Glue the turkey onto background paper, and draw a pair of feet on the underside of the body.

Turkey Mosaic. Draw the outline of a turkey on a piece of paper. Fill in the outline by gluing in scraps of different-colored paper and kernels of Indian corn.

Turkey with Handprint Feathers. First, paint a large circle turkey on paper. Paint a few wavy lines within the body circle to represent feathers. Draw a circle head at one end of the body.

Next, outline your hand a number of times on a separate piece of paper, or make a number of handprints on the paper. Then cut out the hand shapes.

Paste all the handprints sticking out from one side of the turkey to represent tail feathers.

Turkey with Paper Strip Feathers. Draw a turkey on paper, leaving off the feathers. Cut out the turkey.

To make feathers, cut out some long paper strips. Paste the ends of each strip to each side of the tail end of the turkey, forming loop feathers.

Walnut Turkey. Gather three pipe cleaners, a paper baking cup, and a whole walnut. The walnut will be the body of your turkey.

Flatten the baking cup and cut it in half. Spread one of the baking cup halves into a fan (for tail feathers) and glue it to the tail end of the walnut body.

Make a head and feet from pipe cleaners, and glue them to the body. After the glue has dried, stand the turkey on a clay base.

Turkey with Paper Strip Feathers

Toys

Broomstick Hobbyhorse. Pull a sock over the end of a broomstick for the head of your hobbyhorse. Stuff the sock with pieces of material, then tie it tightly at the "neck." Attach buttons for the eyes and a strip of red fabric for a tongue. Ride away!

Cone Catcher. Roll a thick piece of paper into a cone and fasten it in place with tape or staples.

Next, crumple some sheets of thin paper into a tight, small ball and tie a piece of string around it. Then tie a length of string to the inside of the cone. The ball is now attached to the cone by the length of string!

Now, toss up the ball and see how often you can catch the ball in the cone!

Cup Catcher. Glue a plastic foam cup upright at one end of a paint paddle. Next crumple up a piece of paper and cover it completely with tape to form a ball. Tape a length of string about as long as your arm to the ball. Tape the free end of the string to the inside of the cup.

Toss the ball into the air and see if you can catch the ball in the cup!

Fantastic Fluid Bottle. Fill a small, clean, clear plastic bottle half full of water. Add a few drops of food coloring to color the water. Then fill up the bottle with vegetable oil. Screw on the lid tightly.

Turn the bottle to make interesting designs and patterns in the liquid.

Make the bottle into a toy for the baby in your family by putting some glue around the bottle top and bottle cap before screwing it on. Let it dry completely before giving it away as a toy.

To make the fluid even more interesting, add some small pieces of colored plastic to the liquid before sealing the bottle.

Goofy Wheel. Look around for two heavy paper plates that have strong rims. Glue a small rock to the inside edge of one plate. Allow the glue to dry. Then glue the two paper plates together face to face, and allow them to dry.

Later, set your paper plate "wheel" on its edge, and give it a push! Watch your goofy wheel roll along in a wobbly, crazy way!

Handkerchief Parachute. Use a handkerchief or a piece of cloth that is about 12 inches square. Cut four pieces of string that are each 12 inches long. Tie each string to one corner of the handkerchief. Then tie together the loose ends of the four strings at the bottom around a piece of cork.

Toss the parachute into the air and watch it float back to the ground. If a heavier weight is needed, use a small stone instead of a cork.

Marble Pinball Game. Place the lid from a shoe box upside down in front of you. Then obtain an oatmeal box lid. Turn it upside down and cut a two-inch section from the rim. Glue the oatmeal box lid upside down at one end of the shoe box lid, with the open side of the oatmeal box lid facing toward the opposite end of the shoe box lid. This forms the "goal" for the marble pinball game.

After the glue dries, put three marbles in the shoe box lid at the vacant end. By tilting the shoe box lid in different ways, try to get all three marbles into the oatmeal lid goal!

Nesting Cups. Save some clean, empty tin cans until you have four or five different sizes that will fit inside each other. Make sure the rims are sanded smooth. (Have an adult help you.) Remove the labels and play with the cans in the bathtub, sandbox, or wading pool.

Newspaper Ball. Crumple some sheets of newspaper into a ball. Wind some masking tape around and around the ball to make it sturdy enough for throwing.

Oatmeal Box Doll Cradle. To make a cradle, cut away a section from an oatmeal box as illustrated. Then paint the cradle or glue on paper and lace for decoration.

A folded scrap of cloth makes a mattress and a small piece of cloth makes a pillow. Another piece of material makes a blanket for your doll.

Panty Hose Snake. Cut off the leg from a pair of discarded panty hose. Crumple some newspaper sheets and stuff them into the stocking leg. Close the open end with a piece of yarn or string. Glue on eyes and a tongue cut from felt.

Paper Kite. From a large sheet of colored construction paper, cut out a diamond shape for a kite. Poke a hole a few inches from one end and attach a string for pulling the kite. Then make a tail from yarn or cloth or crepe paper streamers. Attach the tail to the other end of the kite.

If you want, decorate the kite with colorful patterns, designs, a picture, or a funny face. Then take it outside, hold onto the pull string, and make the kite fly behind you while you run with it.

Picture Story Box. Obtain an empty detergent or cereal box. Punch a hole about two inches from the top and two inches from the bottom on

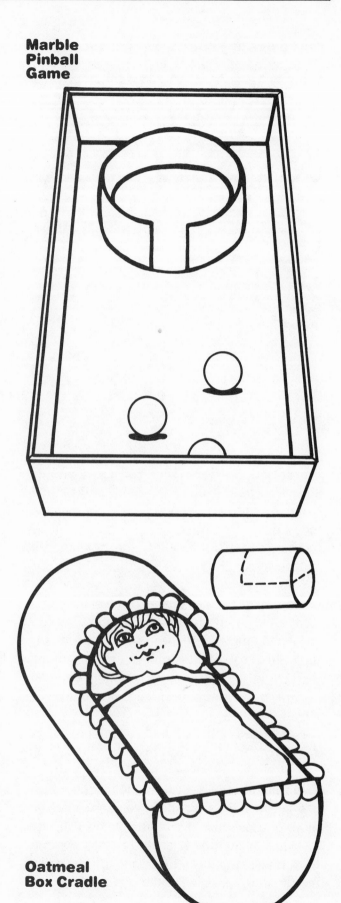

Marble Pinball Game

Oatmeal Box Cradle

the skinny sides. You should have four holes in all. Insert two dowels or sticks in the holes and out the other sides.

For the pictures, you will need a long, narrow piece of paper—adding machine paper or the back of a long grocery store cash register receipt, for example. Draw a picture strip that tells a story. Start the first picture at the top and finish with the last picture at the bottom of the paper.

In the center of the box, cut out a window the same size as the individual pictures on your story sheet. Tape the ends of the story sheets to the dowels so the paper can be rolled back and forth like a scroll. You will probably have to open the top and bottom flaps of the box to do this; tape them shut again.

Now you can turn the dowels and roll the story from beginning to end, watching it through the picture hole! If you want, make a series of story sheets for showing on your picture story box!

Pinwheels. Fold a seven-inch square of construction paper in half diagonally from one corner to another. Fold the paper in half again, bringing together the two opposite corners along the straight edge. Then unfold the paper completely.

Cut almost to the center of each fold mark. Glue every right-hand corner to the center of the paper, forming a pinwheel. Allow it to dry.

With a thumbtack poked through the center, fasten the pinwheel to the end of a stick or unsharpened pencil. Press the thumbtack only partway into the stick so the pinwheel has room to spin.

Now, blow on the pinwheel to make it spin, or run with it outdoors so it catches the wind and spins!

Tin Can Towns. Collect 20 or 30 clean, different-sized empty tin cans with the labels removed. Make sure all the rims are smooth. (Ask an adult for help.) Stack and arrange the cans in different ways to form cities, villages, forts, castles, and towers.

Twizzler. From a sturdy piece of cardboard, cut out a circle. (The center part of a paper plate works well.) Decorate it with bright colors or a pretty spiral pattern.

Make two holes near the center of the circle and thread a loop of string through them. Next, hold an end of the loop in each hand and swing the circle over and over toward you to wind it up. The twizzler will spin as you tighten and slacken the string!

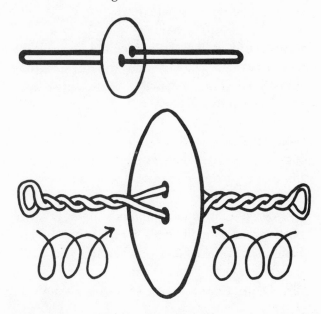

Wrestling Twin Pins. Obtain two old-fashioned, one-piece wooden clothespins. Decorate both exactly alike with paint or felt-tip markers so they look like twins!

Then hold the "pin people" side by side and bind them together with a rubber band. Twist the twins around and around each other until the rubber band is very tight. Place the twins on the floor and watch them wrestle each other!

Trains

Cardboard Box Train. Obtain three or four large cardboard boxes, ones that are large enough for you to sit inside. Paint the outside of each to look like a train car, such as an engine, a boxcar, a passenger car, and a caboose.

Punch a hole in the front and back of each car, as needed, so they can be hooked together. Cut some lengths of rope to use as connectors. Tie a small dowel section to each end of the ropes. Insert the dowel and rope ends through the holes in the cars, and turn the dowels on the inside so the ropes will not slip back out. Repeat in this way to link all the cars together. Now you and your friends can climb into the train cars and play!

Crate Train. Use large wooden crates to form a train you can play in. Each crate will be a separate car for the train.

Make train wheels by cutting out large circles from poster board. Make an engine by attaching a small barrel to a rectangular box. Use tin cans for train lights and whistles. Lay a ladder on the ground for a track.

When playing with the train, make paper hats for the engineer and the porter, and make tickets from construction paper for the passengers.

Crayon Box Miniature Train. Use crayon boxes or other small boxes to make a small train. Fasten small poster board wheels to the boxes with paper fasteners, and paint the boxes to look like different kinds of cars with poster paints.

Human Train. This is a group activity for you and your friends at parties or at school. Form a long train of people by standing behind each other in a single file. Join yourselves together by placing your hands on the shoulders or waists of the person in front of you.

Imitate a train by taking short, sliding steps and making whistle sounds. The person in front, who is the engine, can lead the train around the backyard or playground, as the rest of the train follows.

Two trains may be formed by two lines of players. One person can act as a signal light, guiding the two trains away from danger.

Milk Carton Miniature Train. Remove the lids from empty school-sized milk cartons. Paint them with tempera paints, to which you have added a little liquid detergent, to make the cartons look like different kinds of train cars.

When finished, hook the cars together with staples or paper clips. You can fill the cars with toy people and cargo.

Paper Cup Miniature Train. Use clothespins to fasten a series of small paper cups together at the rims, making a simple toy train. Place small dolls, paper dolls, or other toys in the train.

Picture Display. Display your own train pictures cut out from magazines and newspapers. Try to show as many kinds of trains as you can, including old trains as well as new ones.

Shoe Box Train. Paint some shoe boxes to look like train cars, or cover them with cut-out pieces of paper. Use colors to resemble real cars, such as black for an engine, silver for a passenger car, and red for a caboose.

Crate Train

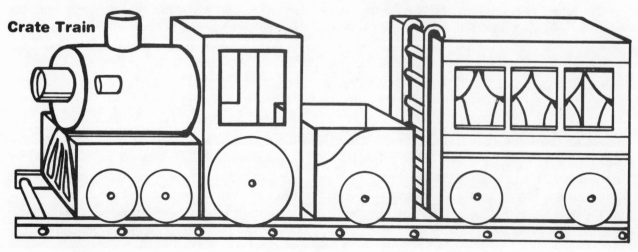

Draw the outside markings for each car with a felt-tip marker. If you want, glue on decals and stickers for added decoration.

To hook the cars together, punch a hole at each connecting end of the cars. Thread a short length of string between each car and fasten the strings on the inside with tape.

Train Tunnel. Cut a two-gallon ice cream container lengthwise so one piece will form a tunnel tall enough for your train to go through. Cover it with papier mâché, and allow it to dry. Then paint the tunnel to look like it is made of stone or is covered with earth and grass. You can also cover the tunnel with sand clay.

Transfers

Carbon Paper Transfer Drawing. Slip a piece of carbon paper between two sheets of paper. Fasten them together with paper clips, so the sheets will not move while you are drawing.

Draw on the top sheet with a pencil. Then lift the carbon paper to reveal your drawing duplicated on the sheet of paper underneath! *Another way to do it:* Slip the carbon paper upside down between the two sheets of paper. Make your drawing, then remove the carbon paper to see your drawing reversed on the back side of the top paper! (Look at the backward picture in a mirror, if you want, to see it straightened out again!)

Cartoon Transfer. Firmly rub a sheet of white paper with a white candle stub. Try to rub a lot of wax onto the paper.

Then cut out a colored cartoon from the funny papers. Turn the cartoon face down on the wax-covered paper. Rub the back of the cartoon with the bowl end of a spoon. Lift the cartoon up, and see the colored ink of the cartoon transferred to the paper!

Crayon Transfer Picture I. Make a crayon drawing on a piece of paper. Then set the drawing face down over a piece of cloth or a sheet.

With adult supervision, iron over the paper with a hot iron, and lift the paper to reveal the drawing transferred to the cloth!

Crayon Transfer Picture II. Fold a sheet of paper in half like a book. Completely fill in the inside left-hand page with crayon. Be sure to press hard when you color!

Shut the book. On the front "cover," draw a picture with a pencil. Then open the book and see your drawing transferred, in color, onto the inside right-hand page of the book!

Transportation

Freeway Mural. Make paper cutouts of houses and paste them onto a mural-length piece of paper. Make some of the houses larger, for closer houses, and others smaller, for houses farther away. Add freeways and roads, including off ramps, traffic signals and cloverleaf intersections, among the houses. Draw cars and trucks on separate pieces of paper and cut them out and paste them on the freeways.

Streets and Highways. Make your own streets and highways on a smooth-surfaced floor, using masking tape to outline the roads. Make street signs and traffic signals from index cards folded in half and propped up like A-frame cabins. Play on the roads with toy cars, trucks, and buses.

You can also use masking tape to outline much larger streets on the pavement outdoors, or use string for outlining roads on the dirt or grass. Drive on the "roads" outside with your tricycles or bikes.

Transportation Collage. From magazine clippings, paste together a collage showing all kinds of transportation vehicles, including cars, trucks, buses, ships, airplanes, helicopters, trains, rockets, bicycles, tricycles, and even roller skates!

Transportation Scrapbook. Make a scrapbook of magazine clippings and drawings showing examples of transportation methods, including cars, trucks, airplanes, boats, etc. You can make a separate scrapbook for each kind of transportation vehicle or make a single scrapbook showing all the different kinds.

Travel Activities

Automobile Ornament Watch. Study the cars you see on the road. How many do you see with ornaments on the hoods? Keep track of how many and what kinds of ornaments.

Clapping Tunes. Clap out the rhythm of a tune you know. See if anyone can guess it. The person who thinks he has guessed the tune must sing the answer!

Color Game. Pick one person to be the "leader." The leader calls out a color. The players quickly name things that are that color. When no one can think of any other things the same color, a new leader is chosen. The new leader picks a different color.

Cut-Out Art. Before you leave home, cut out many interesting pictures from magazines. Put them in your trip bag. Then, while traveling, use pieces of tape or a glue stick to fasten the cutouts to a blank piece of paper to make a new picture.

Do Not Say It! Pick out a word that no one must say. (A simple word such as "I" or "me" is good.) Next, start talking to each other. Everyone must try to trick everyone else into saying the forbidden word! But watch out! If you say the word, you lose a point! At the end of the game, the person with the least points is the winner.

Guess the Word! Think of a word and say, "I am thinking of a word—it rhymes with _____ ." (Say a word that rhymes with the word you are thinking of.) The others must guess what the word is within a time limit. The person who correctly guesses the word gets to think of the next word.

Guess What I See? Think of something you see inside or on your car. Have the others take turns guessing what you see. They can ask you questions, but you can only answer "yes" or "no." The person who guesses the object gets to be the next person to think of something he sees.

I Am Going on a Trip. Start the game by saying, "I am going on a trip. I am taking my suitcase and a _____ ." (Name something you would take on a trip.)

The next player repeats the sentences and adds something he would take on the trip, too. The game continues until one player misses by leaving something out or mixing up the order of the things being taken on the trip.

Initials Game. While traveling, have everyone watch for objects that begin with the same letter as their own names. The person who spots the most wins.

License Plate Watch. How many cars can you spot with out-of-state license plates? Can you name the capital cities of the out-of-state cars you see? How many different states have you seen? Do not count the same cars twice!

"Mirror" Game. This is a funny game you can play with one other person while you are traveling. First, you should face each other. One person is the "mirror" and must copy everything the other person does. The other person can make frowns, smiles, sad faces, funny faces, mad faces, ugly faces, or goofy faces. The mirror person must copy all those expressions!

After awhile, let the other person be the mirror.

Newspaper Games. If you have a newspaper in the car, you can play some word games. With a felt-tip marker, circle all the words that start with the same letter as your first name. Or on an advertising page, circle all the numbers that are the same as your age.

Pipe Cleaner Fun. Take along a pack of colored pipe cleaners. While traveling, you can simply twist them in different ways to make chains, animals, numbers, or anything else you can think of.

Scavenger Hunt. Have an adult make up a list of things for you to look for while you are traveling. Some things should be easy, such as a red car or a dog. Others should be a little harder, such as a motorcycle or a tractor. See how many things you can spot from the list!

Take-Turns Story. Start telling a story. After a while suddenly stop. The next person must then continue the story, making up his own parts as he goes along. Then he stops, and another person keeps the story going. The last person is the one who must finish the story, perhaps with a whopper of an ending!

Use your imagination when telling the story. The more ridiculous the story, the more fun it is!

Tape Fun. If your family has a battery-operated tape recorder, it is a fun thing to take along on a trip. Tape your own stories, and if you have any tape-and-story books, bring them with you. You can also record your conversations while traveling, and you can tape the sounds of things you hear along the way. Be sure the batteries are fresh before you leave!

Tom Thumb. "It" picks out an imaginary place in the car where Tom Thumb is hiding, such as under the seat, in the gas tank, or in the glove compartment. The other players ask questions that can only be answered by "yes" or "no," such as "Is he hiding in the ashtray?" or "Is he hiding behind the sun visor?"

The person who guesses the answer correctly is the next "It."

Trip Bag. Pack a supply of the things you can use on your trip. A good container for your things is a cake pan that has a slide-on lid. You can also use the lid as a firm drawing surface. A zip-lock food storage bag is also good for keeping things together.

Some basic things to put in your trip bag include crayons, felt-tip markers, pads or sheets of paper, cellophane tape, a glue stick, pipe cleaners, and a deck of cards. Add any other things you want to take on your trip

What Did I See? Start this game by spotting something out of the car window and saying, "What did I see?" You can give certain clues, such as size, shape, or color of the object you saw. The others must try guessing what was seen.

Set a time limit for guessing the answer. If no one guesses what you saw, take another turn. If someone does guess the answer, he is the next to say, "What did I see?"

Trees

Apple Blossom Tree. On a piece of brown paper, draw the outline of a tree trunk. Cut it out. Paste the tree trunk on a sheet of construction paper.

From pink and green tissue paper, cut out small squares. Crumple the squares and glue them close together over the tree branches to complete the apple blossom tree.

Bark Rubbing. With thumbtacks, pin a sheet of paper to the trunk of a tree. Softly rub over the paper with a pencil so the pattern of the bark appears.

Make similar rubbings from other kinds of tree

trunks. Put your bark rubbings together into a scrapbook. Label each sample with the name of the tree it was taken from.

Cherry Tree.   Draw a large tree on paper. Then, paint some pop bottle caps red. Allow the paint to dry. Then glue the bottle caps to the branches of the tree to complete your cherry tree.

Crayon Changes.   On separate sheets of paper, or on one sheet, draw four copies of the same tree. With crayons, color the first tree, showing what it looks like in the fall. Color the second tree to show what it looks like in the winter. Then color the third tree to show what it looks like in the spring, and the fourth tree to show what it would look like in the summer.

Handprint Tree I.   Outline your hand and arm on a sheet of drawing paper. Color it in with brown crayon to make it look like the trunk and branches of a tree. Color in the leaves with green crayon or paste on greenery cut from paper.

Handprint Tree II.   Outline your hand on a sheet of green paper. Then cut along the outline. Curl each finger of the cutout by rolling the fingers over a pencil. Then, from brown paper, cut out a tree trunk and paste it to the handprint greenery. If you want, you can make a whole forest of these trees, pasting them on background paper.

Handprint Tree III.   Paste a large brown cutout tree trunk with three large branches on a 12-by-18-inch sheet of construction paper. Next, dip a hand into green paint. Print your hand over and over on the tree branches, overlapping the prints to create the effect of tree leaves.

Marshmallow Tree.   Dip marshmallows into some diluted green food coloring. Then poke a toothpick into each marshmallow.

Cut away part of a plastic foam ball so it is flat on one edge and set it down for a base. (Or use a plastic foam cone for a base.) Poke the free ends of the toothpicks into the base to form a marshmallow tree!

Popcorn Peach Tree.   Place some popped popcorn in a paper bag with some powdered pink tempera paint. Shake the bag to color the popcorn. Then, draw or paint a tree trunk and branches on paper. Glue the pink-colored popcorn to the branches for peach blossoms. Do *not* eat this popcorn!

V

Valentine's Day

Bracelet o' Hearts.   Cut out small red felt hearts and glue them along a white felt strip cut to fit around your wrist. Tie the bracelet at the ends to hold it on your wrist.

Carrot-Print Hearts.   Cut a carrot in half crosswise. Cut away at the end of one of the pieces to leave a heart shape standing out from the surface. Dip the heart shape into red paint and print it on white paper.

Catsup-Painted Heart. Cut out a heart from pink or white construction paper. Finger paint the surface of the heart using catsup.

Cookie Cutter Heart Printing. Obtain a heart-shaped cookie cutter. Pour some red tempera paint into a shallow pan. Dip the cookie cutter into the paint and print heart designs on a white or pink piece of paper.

Cut and Paste Valentine Card. Form a card by folding over an 8½-by-11-inch sheet of construction paper. From red construction paper, cut out a heart and paste it on the front of the card. Use bits of aluminum foil, tissue paper, colored construction paper, lace, ribbons, paper doilies, etc., to decorate the heart and the rest of the card.

On the front of the card, write "Who Do I Love?" On the inside, write "You!"

Doily-Printed Cards. Use doilies as "printing presses" by gluing several unseparated paper doilies to the underside of a paper plate. To print, dip a brush in some paint and brush the paint across the bottom of the doily. Press the painted surface of the doily onto a piece of paper and rub lightly across the paper plate with your hand, making sure not to jiggle the plate. Lift the plate to reveal the printed pattern on the paper. (Three prints can usually be made from a single inking.) Use this doily-printing method to make valentine cards.

Doily Valentine Card. Glue a pretty heart cutout in the center of a doily. Then glue the doily on the front of a paper card. Write a message inside to finish.

Fold and Cut Heart. Fold a piece of paper in half, then draw a large "elephant ear" shape from the folded edge of the paper. Cut out the shape and unfold to reveal a heart.

Gelatin-Colored Creation. Dribble lines of glue on a sheet of paper in the outline of a heart,

a valentine picture, or a design. Spread glue around the areas inside the heart, picture, or design. Shake some dry red or pink gelatin or soft-drink mix over the glue-covered areas. Shake off the excess into a sink. Allow it to dry, then display.

Gelatin Hearts. Dissolve 4 envelopes of un-flavored gelatin and 9 ounces of cherry-flavored gelatin into 4 cups of boiling water. Pour the liquid into a shallow baking pan. Place in the refrigerator until it becomes chilled and firm.

Then remove it from the refrigerator and cut hearts from the gelatin with a heart-shaped cookie cutter. Eat them with your fingers!

Heart Basket. From red, pink, or white construction paper, cut out two large hearts of equal size. Then staple the two hearts together along the side and bottom edges. Bend a paper strip handle over and fasten the ends to each top side of the heart to complete the basket.

Fold and Cut Heart

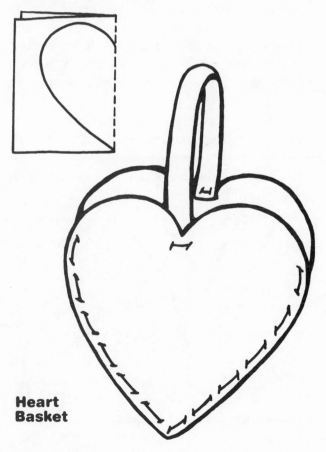

Heart Basket

Heart Collage.   Cut a large number of hearts in different sizes and colors from paper. Glue them on background paper to form objects, animals, and designs.

Heart Corsage.   From red paper, cut out a small heart. Poke a hole in the center of the heart. Insert a flower stem through the hole so the flower blossom rests on the outside of the corsage. Now it is ready to pin on!

Heart Headband.   Cut out a strip of red paper two inches wide and long enough to go around your head. Staple the ends together to form a headband. Cut out some heart shapes and glue them to the headband.

Lollipop Heart Flower.   Cut out two small hearts from red paper. Glue the hearts on each side of a lollipop to form a "heart flower." Cut several small leaf shapes from green paper, and poke them onto the lollipop stick to resemble leaves growing from a stem.

"Love Bug" Puppet.   Cut out a heart and draw a cute face on it with a felt-tip marker. Attach some accordion-pleated strips to the top of the heart for feelers. Glue a small heart to the top of each feeler.

Glue the heart head on the bottom of a paper lunch bag. Decorate the rest of the bag with heart-shaped "spots." Place your hand in the bag and work the fold near the bottom with your fingers and thumb to make the bug "talk."

Message Mobile.   Cut some hearts from red construction paper and write a cute message on each one. Make the messages similar to the ones you see on tiny heart candies, such as, "I Love You," "Cutie Pie," and "Sweet Kid." (Make up your own!) Hang the hearts close together with string to form a mobile.

Old-to-New Valentine Card.   Cut out the best parts from some old valentine cards and paste the cutouts together on a folded piece of paper to form your own, new valentine card.

Paper Doily.   Fold a square of white paper in half, then fold it in half once more. Cut triangles along the edges, with the triangle points aimed toward the middle. Open to reveal a pretty doily.

Paper Plate Valentine Card.   Paint a white paper plate red. When dried, glue a heart-shaped doily to the center. Write a message under the doily. *Another way to do it:* Glue a round, white doily to the center of the plate. Then stick a valentine seal at the center of the doily.

Paper Strip Heart Mobile.   Paste together the ends of paper strips to form heart shapes, as illustrated. Hang with yarn from a mobile hanger or a branch.

Pinprick Valentine Card.   Outline a heart on a red sheet of paper. Using a paper clip with the end bent out, poke little holes all over the surface of the heart. Cut out the heart and paste it to a

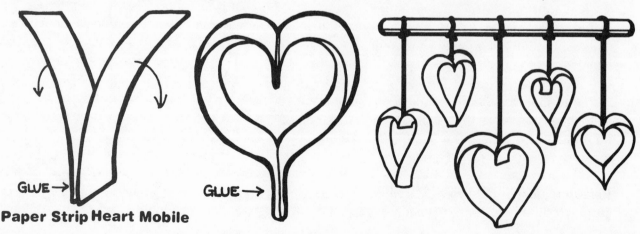

Paper Strip Heart Mobile

Valentine Animals

sheet of white background paper. Now it looks like a heart made with lace! Cut out the heart piece and paste it to the front of a valentine card.

Smiling Heart Button. From red or pink paper, cut out a small heart. With a felt-tip marker, draw a smiling face on the heart. Fasten the heart to your shirt or blouse with a straight pin or a piece of tape.

Sparkling Heart Painting. Cut out a large heart from a sheet of white paper. Paint the heart with red, white, and pink tempera. Before the paint dries, sprinkle some salt over the painting. The heart will sparkle when it dries!

Sponge-Painted Hearts. Cut any number of heart shapes from different size sponges. Dip them in shallow pans containing red, white, or pink paint. Press the painted sides of the hearts onto red, white, or pink paper to make heart prints.

Sweetstuff Salad. Combine 16 ounces of cherry pie filling, 13 ounces of drained pineapple bits, 1 cup of miniature marshmallows, and 2 sliced bananas. Serve in bowls.

Valentine Animals. Cut out a variety of different-sized hearts. Paste them together in unusual ways to make cute or funny valentine animals.

Valentine Bags. Obtain a white lunch bag. From red paper, cut out hearts and other decora-tions and glue them on the bag. A handle can be made by stapling a double-thick strip of paper to the top sides of the bag. Use the bag to hold the valentine cards you receive from friends and relatives.

Valentine Bookmark. Cut out three small hearts from red construction paper. Using a black felt-tip marker, print the word "I" on the first heart, "Love" on the second heart, and "You" on the third. Paste one above the other on a strip of paper with the "I" heart on top and the "You" heart on the bottom. Allow it to dry, then use as a bookmark.

Valentine Cake. Obtain a boxed cake mix and follow the directions on the box for mixing a cake. (Ask an adult for help if needed.) Pour part of the mix into an eight-inch square cake pan and the rest into a round eight-inch pan. Bake both and allow them to cool off.

When cooled, remove the cakes from their pans. Cut the round cake in half. Place the square cake in front of you so it looks like a diamond. Place the straight edge of each half circle cake along a top edge of your "diamond." Look—now you have a heart-shaped cake!

Spread white or pink frosting over the cake and use heart-shaped red-hot candies to deco-rate your Valentine Cake.

Valentine Card with Paper Ribbon. At the top front of a card, loop and glue the middle section of a narrow strip of white paper so the

Valentine Card with Paper Ribbon

ends of the strip hang free on both sides. Glue a cut-out heart to each end of the paper ribbon. Write a message inside.

Valentine Card with Rickrack.   Fold a card from a piece of white construction paper. Glue several pieces of rickrack from the inside front of the card so they come over the top of the card and hang down in front. Glue a small heart to the end of each piece of rickrack. Write a message inside.

Valentine Flowers I.   Cut out some hearts of equal size, then glue them on background paper in different ways to form flower blossoms. Add stems and heart-shaped leaves.

Valentine Flowers II.   Cover an empty frozen juice container with red paper. Then place a lump of modeling clay inside.

From squares of red, pink, and white paper, cut out hearts. Glue each heart to a pipe cleaner stem. When the glue has dried, make a flower arrangement by poking the stems into the clay inside the can.

Valentine Mosaic.   On white construction paper, lightly outline a heart with a pencil. Paint the area inside the heart with glue. Then sprinkle red aquarium gravel lightly over the glued area. The mosaic is complete when the glue has dried.

Valentine People.   From paper, cut out a heart for a head. Make arms and legs from a paper chain or accordion-folded strips. Paste smaller hearts at the ends of the chains for hands and feet. Finish by pasting small hearts on the head piece to make a face and fastening the arms and legs to the head piece.

Vegetable Art

Cucumber Centipede.   Use a cucumber for the body of a centipede! Stick many toothpicks along the sides for legs. Make eyes by sticking two thumbtacks into one end of the cucumber.

Growing Carrot Basket.   Cut off the end of a carrot and toss out the end piece. Hollow the

Growing Carrot Basket

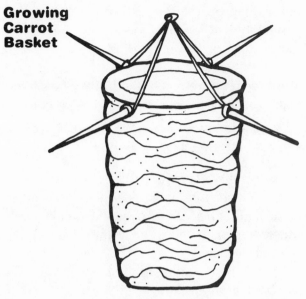

remaining piece of carrot. Make it into a basket by inserting four toothpicks around the top edge, equal distances apart, and attaching yarn to the toothpicks for hanging. Water the carrot basket from time to time and watch it grow!

Hairy Head Potato. Scoop out a hollow in the top of a large potato. Cut off the bottom so the potato stands up easily. Line the hollow area with cotton or blotting paper and set the potato upright in a small dish of water.

Sprinkle grass seeds into the hollow and keep it watered. After a few days, the potato will grow a fine head of green "hair!"

Make eyes, ears, and a nose with cloves or anything else that will stick into the potato.

Initialing Fruit. Try this activity on an apple or a pear while the fruit is still on the tree and before it begins to color. Cut out your initials on a small piece of black paper, then stick the cut-out initials on the apple or pear. Leave the initials there for about a month. After you pick the fruit, soak it in water and carefully lift off the initials.

Your initials will appear in a different color from the rest of the fruit!

Potato Octopus. Use a potato for the octopus body. Attach long string beans to the potato with toothpicks to form tentacles.

Vegetable Man. Make an interesting vegetable man by using squash for the body, endive for hair, ginger root for the feet, and string beans for the arms. Fasten the parts together with toothpicks.

Wall Hangings

Burlap Wall Hanging. Cut a piece of burlap about 9-by-12-inches in size. Staple a length of yarn to each side of one short end to make a hanger.

From a box of colored wooden toothpicks, choose the colors you want. Weave the toothpicks in and out of the burlap to make a design. *Another way to do it:* Glue paper, yarn, and cloth to a piece of burlap to make a design or picture, then hang it.

Cardboard Shadow Box. You can make a nifty shadow box using a small box with a see-through plastic lid! Note paper and greeting card boxes work quite well.

Things you can paste inside the box include paper cutouts, nature items, pictures clipped from magazines, collage materials, small toys, and other treasures. Glue the plastic lid on the box, fasten a ribbon or yarn loop to the back, then hand it from a tack on the wall.

Cardboard Wall-Hanging Plaque. Cut out a 5-by-8-inch cardboard rectangle. Cover the front with "woodgrain" contact paper. (The back does not need to be covered.) Staple the ends of a six-inch length of string or yarn to the back for a hanger.

On the front, over the "woodgrain" contact paper, glue shells, pebbles, beads, or paper cutouts into shapes or designs. Or you can glue a photograph to the front.

Coffee Lid Plaque. Use the plastic lid from a coffee can to make a small wall plaque. Make your own paper cutouts or drawings to glue to the inside of the lid, or glue pictures cut from greeting cards or magazines. If you want, you can paint a picture or design on the inside of the lid.

Punch a hole through the top edge of the lid and hang it with a piece of ribbon.

Handprint Plaque. Poke a hole into the back of a pie plate-type paper plate. Push a hairpin through the hole so the loop end hangs out the back. Twist the ends of the hairpin on the inside of the plate to keep it from falling out.

Next, pour some plaster of Paris into the paper plate. (Have an adult help you if needed.) Before the plaster hardens, press one of your hands into the plaster to make a print. Be sure to have a pail of water nearby so you can rinse the plaster off your hands. (Do not wash off any plaster in the sink. If you do, the pipes will clog when the plaster hardens.) Any leftover plaster should be dumped into newspapers and thrown away.

When the plaque hardens, paint it if you want, then hang it up for display.

Milk Carton Shadow Box. Cut off the bottoms of two milk cartons, leaving one-inch rims on the edges of each. Cover the sides with strips of colored construction paper cut to fit.

Glue the cartons together, as illustrated, forming a pair of shadow boxes. Draw and cut

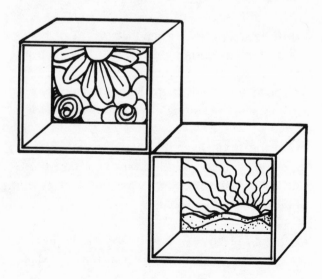

out a small picture for each of the boxes, and paste them inside the bottoms of the boxes. Mount them on a wall for display.

Mounted Picture. On the inside of a plastic foam meat tray or a paper plate, glue a picture or drawing you have made. Cover it with shellac if you want. Hang on the wall for display.

Paper Plate Wall Plaque. Use crayons to draw a design or picture on a paper plate. Be sure to press hard! Then wash over the picture with watercolor paint. Next spray the plate with a clear plastic spray.

Tape a loop of string to the back of the plate and hang it on the wall.

Tile Wall Hanging. Obtain a four-inch square metal or ceramic tile and a muffin pan for melting crayons. With the help of an adult, melt the crayons (with wrappers removed, of course) in the oven and then draw a self-portrait or other picture on the tile, using cotton swabs dipped in the melted crayon. Attach a hanger to the back and hang for display.

Wall Caddy. Cover a large, stiff square or rectangle of cardboard with colored paper. Poke a hole at each top corner and tie a piece of string through for hanging it later.

Next, obtain some small empty cardboard cartons and cut off their top flaps. Cover the cartons with colored paper matching the background piece. Glue the cartons to the background piece so they can be used for holding pencils, pens, papers, and other supplies. Decorate by gluing on tissue paper flowers.

Washington's Birthday

Cereal Tree. Outline a tree on paper. Paste cereal loops on the branches, using a paste made from water and powdered sugar.

Construction Paper Hatchet. After reading (or having an adult read) the story of George

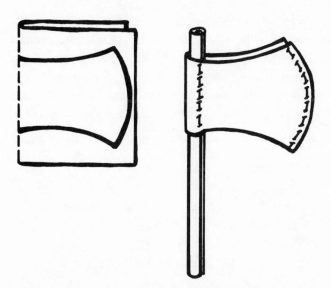

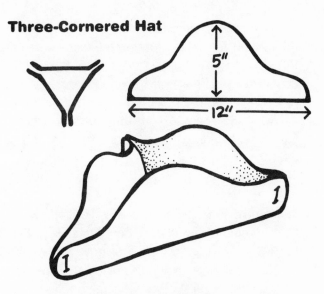

Three-Cornered Hat

5"

12"

1

1

Washington chopping down the cherry tree, get ready to make a paper hatchet! Make a handle by rolling a piece of brown construction paper around a pencil and taping it along the side to hold it together.

Fold a piece of black paper in half, then outline a blade, starting at the folded edge of the paper. Cut out the double blade and loop it around the top end of the handle. Staple it to the handle. Then staple the blade together at the outside edge.

Martha Washington Hat. Paste some paper doilies to the top of a paper plate. Attach a crepe paper tie to each side of the plate so you can tie it under your chin.

Popcorn Cherry Tree. Draw the outline of a cherry tree on paper. Then place some popped popcorn into a bag with some dry red tempera paint. Shake the bag so the powdered paint sticks to the popcorn. Glue the red popcorn all over the branches of the tree to make a cherry tree on paper. Do *not* eat this popcorn!

Three-Cornered Hat. Cut three pieces of blue construction paper into the shape illustrated. Staple them together at the ends to form a three-cornered hat. If you want, decorate the front point with red paper cherries and green paper leaves.

Water (Science)

Fresh Water from Salt Water. Pour some ocean water into a tea kettle. If you do not have ocean water, mix enough salt with fresh water so it tastes salty, then pour it into the kettle.

Bring the water to boiling. (Ask an adult for help if needed.) See the water vapor (steam) rising from the spout? Hold a small skillet above the spout, and place a pie pan underneath the skillet. Watch the steam condense into droplets on the skillet and drip down into the pie pan.

Taste the water you captured. Is it salty or fresh? Be sure to thoroughly rinse the tea kettle after the experiment.

Sink and Float Demonstration. Drop a variety of objects into a large, water-filled tub to see if they sink or float.

Start by comparing a stone with a piece of cork. Then add things such as nails, plastic foam, wood, feathers, screws, pencils, cups, etc. Notice that the objects with air inside them tend to float. Air often keeps things from sinking because it is lighter than water.

To demonstrate this, first place an empty baby food jar into the water without a lid. Tip it so the water fills the jar, and watch it sink. Pull the jar out of the water and empty it. Put the lid on tight and push the jar underwater. Watch it pop back to the surface!

Try another approach. Remove the lid from the jar and let the jar float on the water surface. Put some sand in the jar. Notice that the jar still floats. Keep adding sand in measured amounts until the jar finally sinks.

Empty the jar one more time and fill it completely with sand while it is out of the water. Put the lid on tightly and place the jar on the surface of the water. What happens this time? Why?

Suction in Water.   Some cities get their water by pumping it from underground water supplies. For a simple demonstration of how this works, place a drinking straw into some clean water and suck up the water. When you suck on the straw, the air inside is removed, causing the water to quickly take up the space of the drawn-out air. *Suction* draws the water up and out of your straw, just as it does in a water pump!

Water Has Pressure at Different Levels. Punch holes at various levels in an empty tin can. Place the can under running tap water. Keep it there and watch how the streams of water coming from the lower holes are stronger than those coming from the upper holes. The pressure at the bottom of the can is stronger than the pressure at the top.

Water Is in Our Air.   There are two things you can do to see that there is water in the air:

1. Blow on a mirror or window and see the moisture gather there.

2. Place some ice cubes in a covered jar and watch for water droplets forming on the outside of the jar. This is caused by the warm air in the room meeting the cold from the jar, making moisture in the air condense and form on the outside of the jar.

Water Sources.   Use a world globe or a map, study land areas, looking for sources of water such as lakes, streams, rivers, and reservoirs. Where else in the world are there large amounts of water?

Water Tension.   Tiny molecules hold water together. When they are close together, they create tension in the water. Tension can keep water from flowing away to a certain degree.

Fill a glass of water to the rim. Then, with an eyedropper, add drops of water. Watch how the water bulges up *over the rim,* but does not spill over the side! The tense, crowded molecules are holding the water in place!

Now place a piece of paper on the rim to release the water tension. Watch as the excess water spills over the rim!

Water Play

Beach Ball Rocket.   In a swimming pool, a lake, or the ocean, hold a small plastic beach ball under the water. Then suddenly let it go and watch the ball zoom to the surface and out of the water!

Container Water Play.   Place a plastic dishpan, baby bathtub, or large cooking pot in a spot where splashing is allowed. Fill the container with water. Next, collect some toys (see Water Toys) to play with in the water.

Inner Tube Floater.   Ask an adult to help you find an old inner tube. Fill it with air and make sure it does not leak. The next time you go to the beach or a swimming pool, lie, sit, or hold on to the tube in the water to float!

Mud Hole Fun.   Ask an adult if you can pick out a corner in the yard to make a mud hole. Soak the area with plenty of water, put on some old clothes, and go at it! Take pails, spoons, plastic containers, and shovels to the mud hole. Have fun digging, mixing, and pouring the mud. Try making some mud cakes and mud pies, too! Be sure to wash off the mud when you are finished.

Sprinkler Play.   If you cannot go to the beach or pool and it is hot outside, you can still get wet to cool off. Put on your swimming suit and go outside and turn on your water sprinkler! Have fun running through the sprinkler!

Tire Moat. See if you can obtain an old used tire from a gas station. A wide tire is best. Ask an adult to cut the tire in half lengthwise for you.

Lay one half of the tire on the ground so the inside part faces up. Fill the tire with water. Now you have a castle moat or a circular river for sailing your toy boats!

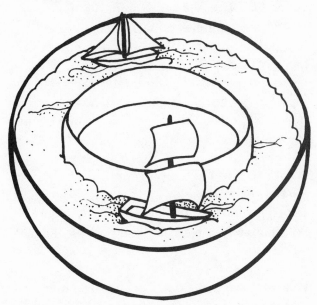

Water Fight. Save some old plastic detergent bottles until you have enough for you and your friends. Outdoors, fill the bottles with water. Also fill some buckets so you have plenty of refill ''ammunition'' on hand.

Use the water-filled bottles for water guns. Simply squeeze the sides of the bottles quickly to make the water squirt out! Pass out the bottles and get ready for a free-for-all!

Water Slide. Make your own water slide with an old plastic shower curtain! Lay it on the grass on a slope that is free of rocks. Weight down the corners of the curtain with jugs of water. Put a spray nozzle on your garden hose and lay the hose at the top end of the slide. Turn the water on in a fine spray.

As soon as the curtain gets wet, slide down the curtain in a sitting position. When you are finished, be sure to pick up the curtain so the grass will not be harmed.

Water Toys. Collect your own water toys for the pool, the bathtub, the beach, or for dishpan water play. Many household items make good water toys, including measuring cups, plastic pitchers, odd-sized plastic containers, funnels, plastic bottles, plastic condiment dispensers, plastic spray or sprinkler-top bottles, sponges, straws, plastic eyedroppers, toy boats, toy squirt guns, and so on. What other items can you find?

Caution: Do not play in the water with things made of glass! They could break and cut you!

Weather

Cardboard and Ribbon Thermometer. From heavy cardboard or poster board, construct a large-scale thermometer, as illustrated. Cut slits at the top and bottom, and insert a ribbon that is painted three quarters red. Move the ribbon up and down to match the temperature readings at the side.

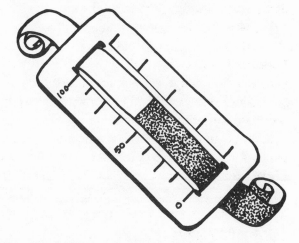

Flannel Board Weather Chart. From felt, cut out the shape of a person and some pieces of clothing to cover the person. Make different kinds of clothing to go with different kinds of weather. For instance, for warm weather make sandles, shorts, T-shirts, bathing suits, etc.; for rainy weather: a raincoat, rain hat, boots, an umbrella; for cold weather: a scarf, cap, overcoat, etc.

Each day, "dress" the felt person with the proper clothing to match the weather outside and place him on a flannel board.

Paper Plate Weather Clock. On a paper plate, draw or paste pictures of the sun, a cloud, a windblown kite, and an umbrella. Place the objects in a circle around the center of the plate to resemble numbers on a clock.

In the middle of the plate, fasten a large arrow, using a paper fastener. Move the arrow daily to point to the kind of weather you are having that day.

Seasonal Weather Chart. Make a different kind of seasonal weather chart by dressing paper dolls with the kinds of clothes that match the weather outside. Make a wall chart where you can pin the doll dressed in the appropriate clothes.

Seasons Tree. Attach a bare tree branch to a wooden base. Place it in a spot where you can easily reach it from time to time.

To decorate the seasons tree, make cut-out drawings to hang on the tree according to the season.

In the fall, hang cutouts of autumn leaves, pumpkins, turkeys, and other fall symbols. In the winter, hang cutouts of snowflakes, snowmen, and small animals storing winter foods. In the spring, hang cutouts of blossoms, green leaves, birds, and butterflies. In the summer, hang cutouts of the sun, beach toys, and picnic baskets.

What other things can you think of to hang on your seasons tree?

Storm Mobile. From construction paper, cut out shapes of clouds and lightning bolts. Hang the clouds from the ceiling and hang the lightning bolts under the clouds.

Umbrella Man. Draw and cut out the outline of an open umbrella from a piece of wallpaper or bright construction paper. Glue the cutout to a piece of background paper.

From a piece of black or brown paper, cut out a pair of boots. Glue the boots beneath the umbrella so it looks like a person is standing behind the umbrella.

Weather Mobile. From construction paper, cut out weather symbols, including an umbrella, raincoat, boots, snowflakes, mittens, lightning bolt, happy sun, etc., and hang with string as a mobile.

Weather Symbol Chart. With this chart, you can keep a day-by-day record of the weather! Draw and cut out some simple weather symbols, such as a sun, clouds, an umbrella, and a kite blowing in the wind.

Use a calendar that has a box for each day of the month as a chart for your weather symbols. Each day, paste the proper symbol on the calen-

Weather Mobile

dar box for that day. In this way, you will have a pictorial record of the daily weather for the full year!

Weather (Science)

Dew Observation. Early in the morning, go outside and feel the grass. Is it wet? If so, it is probably dew!

During the night, the cool air, which contains moisture, touches the warmer ground and makes the moisture in the air condense on the grass. Later, the warm sunshine will dry up the dew and the grass will feel dry again.

Frost on Rooftops. In the winter, watch for frost on the rooftops. Notice that the frost is on the side of the roof away from the sun! If any frost remains on the side facing the sun, it will evaporate before the frost on the other side will.

Compare the frost outdoors to the frost in your refrigerator. Put some of this frost in a jar, and watch how it melts the same way as snow!

Lightning Simulation. Lightning is actually electricity flashing in the sky between two clouds or between a cloud and the ground. You can make your own, completely safe lightning!

In a darkened room, rub two inflated balloons against your clothes or against a piece of fur. Then hold the balloons so close to each other that they *almost* touch. Watch the spark leap between the balloons! (This is *static electricity*.) Pretend that the balloons are clouds and that the spark is a lightning bolt!

Temperature Effects. Air temperature can have a strong effect on the moisture in the air or on the ground. Water, when the temperature is cold enough, will freeze into ice or snow. When it gets warm, the snow or ice will melt, turning back into water! To demonstrate this, fill a glass bowl with fresh snow or ice cubes. Keep it inside, where the temperature is warm. Watch the bowl as its contents become room temperature. What happens?

Thermometer Demonstration. Temperature can be measured with a thermometer. Dip a thermometer into some cold water and note how cold the water is. Then dip the thermometer into warm water and watch the mercury in the thermometer rise. That happens because the mercury is sensitive to temperature changes!

Next, go outside and place the thermometer in the direct sunlight and then in the shade. Note the differences in temperature.

Inside, first place the thermometer on the floor and then up high near the ceiling. How much temperature difference is there between the floor and ceiling?

By experimenting, you will find that the temperature changes a lot from one day to another and also within a single day. And at any time, you might find various temperatures at different places close to each other.

Thunder and Lightning. During a thunderstorm, watch the patterns made in the sky by lightning. (Watch from the safety of your home.) The lightning is actually a giant bolt of electricity jumping through the air.

Listen for the thunder. Thunder is made by the quick expansion of air when it is heated by the electricity. Notice that the lightning comes first, followed by the thunder! This happens because light travels much faster than sound, so we see the lightning before we hear the thunder. The farther away the lightning is, the longer it takes for the sound of thunder to reach us.

Thunder Simulation. Thunder is caused when lightning suddenly heats the air. The air expands and contracts quickly, causing a loud crashing sound. You can create the same thing by popping a paper bag. Blow some air into the bag and twist the top tightly closed so the air stays inside. Pop the bag between your hands. Like thunder, this noise happens when the air inside the bag expands and contracts quickly.

For another way to imitate the effects of thunder, place an inflated balloon over heat. The air inside will expand, causing the balloon to burst with a loud bang!

Who Am I?—Self-Concept Activities

Favorite Things Booklet. From magazines, cut out pictures or drawings of your favorite things. Or if you want, make your own drawings of your favorite things. You can also gather photographs showing some of your favorite things. Paste the pictures on the pages of a spiral-bound notebook to create a book of the things you like best.

You can also make drawings of your favorite experiences and put them into a "favorite experiences" booklet.

Footprints, Handprints, and Fingerprints. Gather a large cellulose sponge, a square cake pan, some blue tempera paint, and some sheets of white construction paper. Mix the tempera paint thin enough so it will be absorbed into the sponge. When this is done, place the sponge in the cake pan.

Now press the palm of your hand onto the sponge. Then lift your hand and press it onto the paper with your fingers slightly apart. Lift your hand carefully to reveal your handprint on the paper!

In a similar way, you can make prints of your feet. The best way to do that is to sit in a chair and place your foot onto the sponge pad. Be sure not to press very hard with your foot! Lift the foot and carefully step down onto a sheet of paper.

Fingerprints, too, can be made by simply pressing your fingers onto the pad and then pressing them on paper.

If your paint was mixed correctly, you should see skin lines in the prints from your hands, feet, and fingers.

Study the prints you made. Compare them to prints made by your family and friends. Each print is different, is it not? Your prints are different from anyone else's in the whole world. That is just one way to show that you are a very special person!

"How Old Am I" Paper Cake. On the bottom of a piece of paper, draw a rectangle to represent the side view of a cake. Cut some candles form colored paper and paste one candle for each year of your age on the cake. Then write your age below the cake or have an adult write it for you.

Matching Baby Pictures. The next time you have a party, ask your guests to each bring a picture of themselves when they were babies. Mix up the pictures and pin them to a bulletin board. Ask your friends to take turns guessing who the babies are!

Mirror Fun. Stand in front of a full-length mirror. Look at yourself closely. Examine your eyes, your tongue, and the way you smile or frown. Turn around and try to look over your shoulder to see your back side in the mirror.

Whatever you see in the mirror, remember that it is all part of you and different from anyone else in the world. That makes you kind of special, doesn't it!

Self-Outline. One really good way to "see yourself" is to make an outline of yourself! To do this, you will need a piece of butcher paper or brown wrapping paper that is just a little longer than you are. And, at first, you will need someone to help you.

Lie down on the paper and have your friend trace completely around you with a crayon. Then get up and start coloring in your clothing, face, and other features. When finished, hang the self-outline in your room for display.

If you want, in the space below your outline, write down a list of your favorite things, or have someone write them in for you as you tell about them.

Self-Outline Growth Measurement. Make a self-outline as directed above. When finished, store the outline for about six months. Then make a second outline and compare it with the first. How much have you grown?

Use this method to keep a record of how much you grow from year to year, making a new outline every six months.

Self-Silhouette. At the same height as your head, tape a 12-by-18-inch piece of newsprint to the wall. Dim the light in the room and stand before the paper with one shoulder facing the wall. Have someone shine a bright light toward you, so the shadow of your face is cast in profile on the paper. Be sure to hold very still while someone outlines your shadow on the paper with a crayon or felt-tip marker.

Next, remove the paper from the wall and cut out the outline. Set the outline on top of a piece of black construction paper. Using the outline as a pattern to guide you, cut along the edges of the outline through the black paper. When finished, you will have a cut-out silhouette of your own head!

Glue the black silhouette on a piece of white poster board and hang for display or give as a gift.

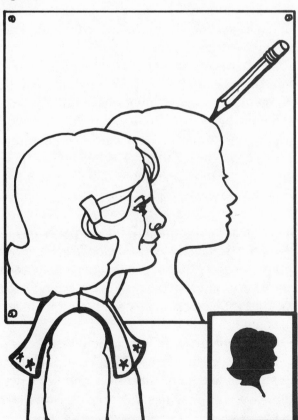

Tape Recordings. If you have a tape recorder at home, make tape recordings of yourself talking, laughing, singing, and playing. Later play back the tapes so you can listen to yourself. Sometimes you will discover you sound a little different than you thought!

If your recording includes voices of other people, try to identify the other people on the tape. See if you can pick out your own voice from the others on the tape!

Weight and Height Measurement. From time to time, measure how much you weigh and how tall you have grown. Write this information on a calendar or a chart so you can keep a record of your growth over a period of time.

An interesting way to keep track of your height is to tape a long length of blank adding machine tape vertically on a wall. Stand next to the tape and have someone mark the spot where the top of your head reaches the tape. Write the date next to the mark. Take a new measurement every four months, and mark how tall you are each time as well as the date. By looking at the marks, you can tell how much you have grown between each measurement!

Wind (Science)

Capture the Wind. On a windy day, obtain a large plastic trash can bag. Outside, open the bag into the wind. Perhaps a friend will hold the opposite side of the bag for you! Capture the wind in the bag, and watch the bag billow with the force of the wind. Do you feel the wind's power? Run with the bag to inflate it even more! *Caution:* Do not ever put the plastic bag over your head because it could cut off your air and cause suffocation!

Pinwheel Demonstration. Wind is often very helpful to us. It helps kites fly, blows sailboats across the water, and in some countries, helps windmills grind flour or pump water. It will also make a pinwheel spin!

Make a pinwheel, following the directions in the *Toys* section of this book. Then, hold the pinwheel up to the wind, and watch it as the power of the wind causes the pinwheel to spin!

Wind, Air, and Evaporation.   Wind is air that is in motion. Wind and heat together speed up the process of evaporation. To see this, wet two pieces of cloth of the same size. Leave one indoors and hang the other outside in the wind. Which one dries out first?

Wind and Smoke.   If possible, observe how smoke blows in the same direction as the wind. By looking at a column of smoke, you can tell which way the wind is blowing!

Wind Effects Observations.   Here are several easy experiments you can do to show how wind can sometimes affect things. First, on a windy day, place a strip of cloth through a window, allowing it to hang outside. Clamp it down by closing the window on the near end of the cloth. Watch how the wind blows the cloth! Repeat the experiment on a still, windless day.

Indoors, place some small paper scraps on a table or a desk. Blow on them, or make your own breeze by waving a folded newspaper at the scraps. What happens to them?

When the wind is blowing outside, watch the direction in which the leaves and small pieces of paper are blowing. Notice how they are lifted, whirled upward, and dropped down. This is caused by currents of air moving in an upward sweep and then slowing down slightly to allow the leaves and paper to fall.

Wind on Water.   Fill a wide basin or shallow pan halfway with water. Then blow hard on the water or fan it with a folded piece of newspaper. Notice how the water moves in reaction to the ''wind'' you have made! Also note how the water moves in the same direction as the wind. Does the water in a pond or lake move when the wind blows?

Wind Simulations.   Set up a large electric fan with a protective grill to duplicate the wind. Place different objects in front of the fan to see how the wind affects the objects.

Hold a paper streamer in front of the fan, a paper bag to catch the wind, a plastic bag, or anything else you can think of. Then place some heavy objects in front of the fan to see how these objects are *not* blown.

Stand in front of the fan so you can feel the wind in your face. Then turn off the fan to experience the calmness. If the fan has more than one speed, turn it on high, and then low, to feel the differences between high winds and a breeze.

Step outside to see what kind of wind is blowing.

Windmills

Milk Carton Windmill.   Fill an empty milk carton with sand and rocks to give it weight. Next, get a paper plate and cut into it from the edge up to the point where the lip starts to turn up. Make eight of these cuts around the plate, all equal distances apart.

Now, twist *each fringe* so it bends up on the left-hand side and down on the right-hand side. These are the blades of your windmill!

Stick a beaded pin through the middle of the paper plate, and then into the top of the front side of the milk carton. The blades are now attached to the windmill and will spin when placed in the wind!

Paper Cup Windmill.   Gather a paper cup, a four-inch square of construction paper, and a paper fastener. Cut into the square from each corner, to within half an inch of the center. Bend the alternating cuts to the center to form blades, making a pinwheel shape.

Use the paper fastener to attach the pinwheel to the side of the inverted paper cup. With a felt-tip marker, draw on doors and windows. Blow on the pinwheel to make the windmill blades spin.

**Milk Carton
Windmill**

**Paper Cup
Windmill**

Wallpaper Windmill. For this you need a 5-by-6-inch piece of bright wallpaper, a sheet of dark-colored construction paper, two matching 6-by-12-inch strips of paper for windmill blades, and a paper fastener. (Colored paper can be substituted for the wallpaper.)

Outline the shape of a windmill building on the wallpaper, then cut it out. Paste the windmill on the piece of construction paper. Attach the paper blades to the windmill with the paper fastener so the blades will move when you touch them.

Winter

Chalk Drawing. With white chalk, draw winter subjects such as snowmen, snowflakes, and snow scenes on light blue drawing paper.

Chalky Winter Scene. On a bright sheet of construction paper, color a winter scene with crayons. When the drawing is complete, draw over it completely with the side of a piece of white chalk.

Cotton Snowman on Paper. Glue three cotton balls to a sheet of paper, one above the other, to represent a snowman. Glue fabric and paper scrap cutouts over the snowman for clothing. Spatter-paint the rest of the picture with white paint to resemble snow.

Frosty Window Mural. Pick out a window to cover with glass wax. Allow the wax to dry. Then, using your fingers, draw a winter scene or a design through the wax on the window.

Icicle. Cut out a circle from foil paper. Starting at the edge, cut around and into the circle in a spiral pattern until you reach the center. Then hold onto the center end and let the rest of the design fall open. Hang for display.

Indoor "Snowball" Fight. If it is too cold to go outside, why not have a snowball fight indoors? Simply wad up some newspapers for snowballs and go to it!

Magic Winter Picture. Draw a winter scene on a sheet of colored construction paper with a crayon the same color as the paper. When the picture is finished, paint over it with white tempera paint thinned enough so it looks like cream. A crayon picture will appear "like magic" when the paint has dried!

Painted Winter Scene. On gray paper, paint with white, black, and blue tempera paint to make a wintry scene.

Paper Mittens. On construction paper, draw around each of your hands with your fingers together to make mitten shapes. Color the mittens with crayons, felt-tip markers, chalk, or water colors. Then cut out the mittens.

After cutting, fasten the mittens together below the thumbs with a piece of yarn. Use a stapler to hook the yarn to the mittens.

Paper Sled. Draw a simple sled on construction paper and cut it out. Fold the sides down for "runners," and punch a hole in the front end of the sled. Tie a pull string through the hole.

Pipe Cleaner Ski Scene. Collect some pipe cleaners in various lengths. Twist the pipe cleaners together in different ways to form the shape of a man. Glue the pipe cleaner man in a standing position to a pair of paper skis. Add a crepe paper scarf if you want.

Make several more skiers, then glue them upright on a sheet of blue construction paper. Glue on cotton tufts for snow.

"Signs of Winter" Drawing. Make your own drawing, showing the signs of winter. You might include such things as falling snow, bare-branched trees, snow on the ground, ice lakes, and icicles hanging from eaves.

Skier on Paper. Glue two Popsicle sticks parallel to each other on a piece of paper. These are skis. Now, with crayons, draw the skier on his skis, and also draw in background detail.

Pipe Cleaner Ski Scene

Snow Equipment Collage. Collect pictures of snow equipment, including skis, sleds, toboggans, snow shoes, a dog sled, a snow plow, ice skates, and even a sidewalk shovel! Paste them all on background paper to form a collage.

Winter Bear Cave. Tear away a section from the edge of a plastic foam cup, and turn the cup upside down to represent a bear cave. Paint the cup or add cave details with a felt-tip marker.

Glue a brown pompon or brown cotton ball to the inside back of the cup to represent a sleeping bear. (Make a cotton ball brown by shaking it in a bag with dry brown powdered tempera paint.)

Winter Soap Painting. Whip together a mixture of liquid starch and powdered laundry detergent. Using this mixture, paint a winter scene on blue paper.

Winter Sports Collage. From catalogs and magazines, cut out pictures showing winter sports, including skiing, ice skating, sledding, ice hockey, toboggan racing, and so on. Paste the pictures together into a collage on white background paper.

Woodworking
All of these activities require adult supervision.

Drilling. Ask an adult to show you how to use a hand drill. Clasp a piece of wood into a vise and try drilling into the wood. Do not turn the handle too quickly! Put just a small amount of pressure on the drill when working.

As you learn to use the drill, try drilling some holes through pieces of scrap wood and then stringing the pieces together with cord.

Filing. Obtain a file that has a fairly rough filing edge. Stick a piece of scrap wood into a vice or `C-clamp and then practice filing the wood. See if you can make your own sawdust!

Hammering. Look around for some soft scrap wood, some large nails with big heads, and a hammer. Next find a place where you can work, such as a work bench, an old table, or even a wooden crate. Set out your materials and leave yourself room to work.

Start by practicing how to hammer a nail into wood. Notice how a gentle ''tap-tap-tap'' will get the nail started! Once the nail is started, you can hammer harder to get the nail down. Watch your fingers!

Now you can hammer pieces of wood together in interesting ways to make toys and wood sculptures.

Key Hanger/Hotpad Hanger. Ask an adult to watch over you while you do this activity. Obtain a 5-by-10 or 6-by-9-inch piece of wood that is about three quarters inch thick. Stain or paint the piece of wood before you do anything else.

Next obtain six cuphooks that have screw threads at one end. Hammer some nail holes into the wood at the points where each of the cup-

hooks are to go. In the spaces between the holes, glue decorations such as stickers, photos, and decals.

Wipe over the wood with a damp cloth, then brush over it with varnish. Allow it to dry. Then screw the cuphooks into their holes, and attach several tape picture hangers to the back. Give as a gift for hanging keys or kitchen pot holders.

Nailboard Art. Find a piece of wood about 9-by-12-inches in size and three quarters inch thick. Paint or stain the board before you start the rest of the project.

When the board is ready, gather some nails with large heads, a hammer, and some colored rubber bands or colored yarn or wire. Hammer the nails partway into the board anywhere you want.

Now, using your rubber bands, yarn, or wire, twist them in and out among the nails to form designs. Notice that you can change your designs by removing the rubber bands and using them over again.

If you want the designs to be permanent, use only the colored wire and make sure it is wrapped tightly around the nails.

Sanding. Hunt for some scraps of wood and then obtain some sandpaper pieces in different grades of roughness.

Feel a piece of wood to see how rough it is. Then sand it with a rough grade of sandpaper. Feel the wood again. Then sand the wood some more with a finer grade of sandpaper. Does the wood feel different?

Experiment with other pieces of wood and different grades of sandpaper.

Sawing Practice. Ask an adult to show you how to clamp a piece of wood in a vise. If a vise is not available, try to obtain a C-clamp.

When the wood is firmly clamped, saw at the wood with a hacksaw. Practice a back-and-forth motion. You can even chant ''slow-and-easy, slow-and-easy'' as you saw to help you set the rhythm.

As you get used to sawing, try cutting pieces of wood in different shapes for hammering together later.

Screwdriving Exercise. Find a scrap block of wood and nail it down to your work bench. Now pound a nail deep enough into the block to make a starting hole for a screw. Remove the nail.

Hold the bottom part of thè screw with the fingers of one hand. Work the bottom point of the screw into the hole. Holding the screwdriver in your free hand, start to turn the screw down into the hole. Continue to guide the screw with the other hand.

After practicing a few more times, try screwing together some thin pieces of wood.

Wood Collage. Find a piece of wood about 10-by-12-inches in size and about three-quarters inch thick. Next, look for some wood scraps to use for nailing a wood collage together. Hunt for some interesting shapes. But do not use pieces that are *too* small because they might split when nailed.

Gather the wood scraps together. Smooth over any rough edges on the wood with sandpaper. Then, hammer the scraps to the 10-by-12 wooden base. Also hammer the pieces to each other in any way you want. If some pieces split, use glue to fasten them back in place.

When finished, you can paint your wood collage or decorate it with felt-tip markers.

Wood Puzzle. Obtain a piece of balsa wood about 6-by-7-inches in size and one inch thick. On the wood, mark with a felt-tip marker the lines along which you will cut the wood into puzzle pieces. You can make just a few simple wavy lines or try unusual shapes. Ask an adult to help you if needed.

Place the wood in a vise or C-clamp and use a hacksaw to cut the wood along the lines. When the wood is sawed into pieces, smooth the rough edges with sandpaper. If you want, color the pieces with paint or felt-tip markers. Now the puzzle is ready to put together!

Wood Puzzle

Wooden Boats. Using lumber scraps, nails of different sizes, wire pieces, and glue, construct any kind of boat you want. When the glue dries, play with the boat in a tub of water.

Wrapping Paper

Cookie Cutter Wrap. Ask an adult for some cookie cutters to use for decorating your wrapping paper. Dip the cutters into a shallow pan of paint and print the shape on a long piece of shelf paper. Do not use paper treated with insecticide.

During holiday seasons, you can use cookie cutters in the shapes of holiday symbols, such as angels, hearts, or shamrocks.

When finished, be sure to wash the paint off the cookie cutters!

Crayon Batik Wrap. Set out the paper you will be using to make wrapping paper. Color heavily all over the paper with bright crayons, using lots of yellow and white. Then, brush over the paper with a contrasting color of watercolor paint. The crayon will resist the watercolors to create a batik-like effect.

Cookie Cutter Wrap

Easel Paper Christmas Wrap. Color on easel paper with crayons. Then brush over with glue and add glitter.

Finger-Painted Wrap. Cover your wrapping paper with liquid starch. Add some powdered paint to the paper, making sure to keep the mixture from getting thick. Then, using your hands or objects such as a comb, bottle cap, or cookie cutter, create an overall design on the paper. Add glitter and allow it to dry.

Free-Art Wrap. On a long piece of white, dull-finished shelf paper, paint any designs or pictures you want. Colored stripes, pretty flowers, seasonal symbols, and wiggly lines are just a few ideas. Or you can paint a scene on the paper. Allow it to dry.

Newspaper Wrap. Paint on a sheet of newspaper, using different colors of tempera paint or watercolors. While the paint is still wet, add some glitter to the thicker areas of paint. Or let the paint dry and use glue to apply the glitter.

Printed Wrapping Paper. Use vegetables, household gadgets, sponges, or other unusual objects dipped in paint to print patterns, designs, and pictures onto a long piece of shelf paper. Allow it to dry before wrapping.

Seal and Sticker Wrap. Decorate a long piece of shelf paper with stickers, seals, or gummed stars. During holiday seasons, many special seals are available depicting the time of year. The paper is ready to use when you have applied enough stickers.

Stencil-Painted Wrap. Cut out stencil shapes to match the kind of paper you want, then lay the stencils on a long piece of shelf paper. To create designs, sponge paint over the stencils; spray paint over the stencils; or spatter paint over the stencils, using a toothbrush to scatter the paint.

Remove the stencils to reveal the patterns on the paper.

Subject Index